Homeschooling

Other Books in the Current Controversies Series

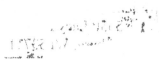

CONTROVERSIES

Homeschooling

Myra Immell, Book Editor

GREENHAVEN PRESS
A part of Gale, Cengage Learning

GALE
CENGAGE Learning

Detroit • New York • San Francisco • New Haven, Conn • Waterville, Maine • London

Christine Nasso, *Publisher*
Elizabeth Des Chenes, *Managing Editor*

© 2009 Greenhaven Press, a part of Gale, Cengage Learning

Gale and Greenhaven Press are registered trademarks used herein under license.

For more information, contact:
Greenhaven Press
27500 Drake Rd.
Farmington Hills, MI 48331-3535
Or you can visit our Internet site at gale.cengage.com

For product information and technology assistance, contact us at

Gale Customer Support, 1-800-877-4253
For permission to use material from this text or product, submit all requests online at www.cengage.com/permissions

Further permissions questions can be emailed to permissionrequest@cengage.com

Articles in Greenhaven Press anthologies are often edited for length to meet page requirements. In addition, original titles of these works are changed to clearly present the main thesis and to explicitly indicate the author's opinion. Every effort is made to ensure that Greenhaven Press accurately reflects the original intent of the authors. Every effort has been made to trace the owners of copyrighted material.

Cover image © Elena Elisseeva, 2008. Used under license from Shutterstock.com.

LIBRARY OF CONGRESS CATALOGING-IN-PUBLICATION DATA

Homeschooling / Myra Immell, book editor.
    p. cm. -- (Current controversies)
  Includes bibliographical references and index.
  ISBN-13: 978-0-7377-4140-7 (hardcover)
  ISBN-13: 978-0-7377-4141-4 (pbk.)
  1. Home schooling. I. Immell, Myra.
  LC40.H6673 2009
  371.04'2--dc22

                                        2008033984

Printed in the United States of America
2 3 4 5 6 7 12 11 10 09

Contents

Chapter 1: Why Do Parents Choose to Homeschool?

Chapter 2: Is Homeschooling a Good Option?

Yes: Homeschooling Is a Good Option

Chapter 3: Should Homeschooling Be Regulated?

Chapter 4: Should Homeschooled Children Have Access to Public School Resources?

Foreword

By definition, controversies are "discussions of questions in which opposing opinions clash" (Webster's Twentieth Century Dictionary Unabridged). Few would deny that controversies are a pervasive part of the human condition and exist on virtually every level of human enterprise. Controversies transpire between individuals and among groups, within nations and between nations. Controversies supply the grist necessary for progress by providing challenges and challengers to the status quo. They also create atmospheres where strife and warfare can flourish. A world without controversies would be a peaceful world; but it also would be, by and large, static and prosaic.

The Series' Purpose

The purpose of the *Current Controversies* series is to explore many of the social, political, and economic controversies dominating the national and international scenes today. Titles selected for inclusion in the series are highly focused and specific. For example, from the larger category of criminal justice, *Current Controversies* deals with specific topics such as police brutality, gun control, white collar crime, and others. The debates in *Current Controversies* also are presented in a useful, timeless fashion. Articles and book excerpts included in each title are selected if they contribute valuable, long-range ideas to the overall debate. And wherever possible, current information is enhanced with historical documents and other relevant materials. Thus, while individual titles are current in focus, every effort is made to ensure that they will not become quickly outdated. Books in the *Current Controversies* series will remain important resources for librarians, teachers, and students for many years.

In addition to keeping the titles focused and specific, great care is taken in the editorial format of each book in the series. Book introductions and chapter prefaces are offered to provide background material for readers. Chapters are organized around several key questions that are answered with diverse opinions representing all points on the political spectrum. Materials in each chapter include opinions in which authors clearly disagree as well as alternative opinions in which authors may agree on a broader issue but disagree on the possible solutions. In this way, the content of each volume in *Current Controversies* mirrors the mosaic of opinions encountered in society. Readers will quickly realize that there are many viable answers to these complex issues. By questioning each author's conclusions, students and casual readers can begin to develop the critical thinking skills so important to evaluating opinionated material.

Current Controversies is also ideal for controlled research. Each anthology in the series is composed of primary sources taken from a wide gamut of informational categories including periodicals, newspapers, books, U.S. and foreign government documents, and the publications of private and public organizations. Readers will find factual support for reports, debates, and research papers covering all areas of important issues. In addition, an annotated table of contents, an index, a book and periodical bibliography, and a list of organizations to contact are included in each book to expedite further research.

Perhaps more than ever before in history, people are confronted with diverse and contradictory information. During the Persian Gulf War, for example, the public was not only treated to minute-to-minute coverage of the war, it was also inundated with critiques of the coverage and countless analyses of the factors motivating U.S. involvement. Being able to sort through the plethora of opinions accompanying today's major issues, and to draw one's own conclusions, can be a complicated and frustrating struggle. It is the editors' hope that *Current Controversies* will help readers with this struggle.

Introduction

"*Unlike the diplomas received by most public—and private—school students, diplomas issued to homeschooled students are not always recognized by most states.*"

According to the National Center for Education Statistics, an estimated 1.1 million students in the United States are homeschooled. About 315,000 of these students are of high-school age. Like public school students, homeschoolers who have completed their high school course work graduate and receive some sort of diploma.

Unlike the diplomas received by most public—and private—school students, diplomas issued to homeschooled students are not always recognized by most states. Homeschoolers have a number of options for a diploma. Most, however, receive diplomas issued by their parents, who have homeschooled them in accordance with the graduation requirements they have set. To give the diploma more weight and, if necessary, provide proof that certain standards have been met, parents typically create and maintain a transcript that documents the student's academic record. Parent-issued diplomas are not accredited. They may be accepted by some employers and by some colleges and universities, but they are not recognized as valid in most states.

Even some state-issued diplomas for homeschooled students are not always recognized. Such was the case in Tennessee in 2008. Tennessee began recognizing homeschooling in 1985. The state offered several categories of diplomas, one of which is the category IV diploma issued to homeschooled students and church-related school students. These students did not need a public or accredited private school diploma to be hired for positions for which state law required a high school diploma. Their category IV diplomas were recognized in state institutions and for employment. A major controversy arose, however, in May 2008 when the Tennessee Department of Education declared it no longer would recognize Category IV diplomas. The basis for the decision was that the department had no way of telling what a homeschool diploma represented as it had no part in the selection of homeschool curriculum, teachers, or textbooks.

The ramifications of the department's decision were immediate and proved controversial. The category IV diplomas no longer were recognized by the Peace Officers Standards and Training Commission (POST), the Tennessee Police Training Organization, or the Department of Human Services, which sets policy for the hiring of day-care workers. These groups were required by statute to hire only individuals with recognized diplomas. Four day-care workers lost their jobs because their diplomas no longer were recognized. A police officer was told that if he wanted to keep his job he had to get his GED, commonly known as a General Equivalency Diploma. The officer had received his category IV diploma seven years earlier, had previously held various law-enforcement positions, had made perfect grades in graduating from a college law-enforcement certification class, and had an exemplary record. However, with his diploma no longer recognized, the POST declared he could not be certified as a police officer and could not hold his job. He was demoted to a desk job until he took and passed the GED—or until the Tennessee legislature passed a law making category IV diplomas acceptable for state-related kinds of employment.

Efforts put forth by Tennessee representative Mike Bell and others to have a bill passed that would make category IV diplomas valid and recognized by the state and its agencies proved unsuccessful. Critics of a bill proposed by Bell in 2008 argued that passage would give a legislative seal of approval to a homeschool or church-related school education when the state had no control over what was involved in that education. Others argued that passage would give special treatment to homeschool and church-related school students who were not required to take certain state-required proficiency exams, while public school students who had to take and subsequently failed the exams received a certificate of attendance instead of a regular diploma. Bell ultimately took his bill "off notice" and announced plans to bring a new bill to the House Education Committee in the near future.

The validity of homeschool diplomas is just one of a variety of homeschooling-related issues being debated nationwide today. The roots of homeschooling lie far back in history, long before universal public schooling was even a thought let alone a reality. The trend back to homeschooling that has become more prevalent in recent years continues to grow, and with it controversies surrounding even the most basic issues. In *Current Controversies: Homeschooling*, proponents of homeschooling and critics of homeschooling offer their differing viewpoints on several of those basic issues.

CHAPTER 1

Why Do Parents Choose to Homeschool?

Chapter Preface

If you ask parents who homeschool their children why they chose to do so you will get a variety of answers. The National Home Education Network (NHEN), an organization that advocates homeschooling, lists fifty-five reasons to homeschool. These range from "spend more time together as a family" to "children can learn to work for internal satisfaction rather than for external rewards" to "children's education can be more complete than what schools offer."

Some reasons, however, are more commonly voiced than others. Early on, for example, most parents homeschooled their children primarily for religious reasons. Later, in the mid-to-late 1990s, many parents still homeschooled primarily for religious reasons. But a good number also homeschooled to give their children a better education at home or because of what they considered "a poor learning environment at school."

Based on the National Center for Education Statistics (NCES) of the U.S. Department of Education Statistical Analysis Report "Homeschooling in the United States, 2003," issued in February 2006, those reasons still stand. Homeschooler parents who took part in the survey were given a set of reasons for homeschooling. First, the parents were asked which, if any of the reasons, applied to them. Concern about the environment of other schools, including safety, drugs, or negative peer pressure, was the reason for homeschooling cited most frequently as being applicable. Eighty-five percent of homeschooled students were being homeschooled, in part, because of that concern. The next two reasons most frequently cited were to provide religious or moral instruction (72 percent) and dissatisfaction with academic instruction at other schools (68 percent). A child's special needs was applicable for 28 percent of the parents; such other reasons as a child's choice, more control over what the child was learning, and flexibility were cited by 20 percent of the respondents; and a child's physical or mental health problem was named by 15 percent.

Next the parents were asked which one of the reasons was their most important for homeschooling. Thirty-one percent of homeschooled children had parents who cited concern about the environment of other schools, such as safety, drugs, or negative peer pressure, as the most important reason for homeschooling, and 30 percent had parents who said the most important reason was to provide religious or moral instruction. Another 16 percent of homeschooled students had parents who said dissatisfaction with the academic instruction available at other schools was their most important reason for homeschooling. Six percent cited a child's physical or mental health problem as the most important reason, and 7 percent cited a child's other special needs. Another 8 percent indicated other reasons, such as a child's choice, more control over what the child was learning, and flexibility, as most important.

One of the Frequently Asked Questions posted on the Web site of Homeschool Zone is "Why should I homeschool?" The response sums up the rationale for homeschooling of most homeschool parents and advocates: "I think the common denominator in many homeschoolers is that for whatever reason, homeschoolers feel that there is a better way for their children to learn or that the system has not addressed the needs of their children."

Homeschooling Helps Black Children Gain Educational Equality

Jennifer James

Jennifer James is the founding director of the National African-American Homeschoolers Alliance.

"**M**ommy, I finished my book. Do we still get to see the movie tomorrow?" my daughter Annlyel asked, triumphantly removing her bookmark from its place and closing her book.

"We sure do," I smiled. "You finished Harry Potter and, as promised, we're going to see the movie when it comes out tomorrow."

When my older daughter, then five, finished reading her first full-length novel—entirely on her own initiative—I knew at that moment that my husband, Michael, and I had made the right decision to homeschool our two children.

An Easy Decision

Opting to homeschool came quite easily for us, though we learned about it only by mere happenstance. Casually watching television one afternoon when Annlyel was still an infant, we watched as a homeschooled student competed quite well in the last rounds of the Scripps National Spelling Bee. We knew nothing about homeschooling, but just hearing the commentator speak the word homeschooled resonated deeply with us and instantly piqued our interest to the point of action.

The very next day, we set out on a fierce quest to learn as much about homeschooling as we could, and to gather the necessary information about how to begin homeschooling in

Jennifer James, "Homeschooling for Black Families," *Mothering*, January/February 2007, pp. 66–71. Reproduced by permission of the author.

our state, North Carolina. With the aid of a helpful local school administrator, we learned whom we needed to contact, then called our state's homeschooling organization.

"Surely we aren't the only black homeschoolers in America!" we often kidded aloud.

The rest is history. Before Annlyel could even sit up by herself, she had become a future homeschooled child. Just as quickly, we had become homeschooling parents. . . .

One reason Michael and I decided to homeschool was to ensure that our children received a sterling education. Based on what we learned about the steadily plummeting levels of achievement of large numbers of publicly schooled black children, we knew that that was not an option for our family. We also knew that private schools are extremely expensive. The prospect of homeschooling proved to be an excellent alternative for us—I was already a stay-at-home mother, and Michael and I are both excited about learning and are steadfastly focused on education. Homeschooling was perfect. We couldn't have been happier.

Unfulfilled promises prompt families such as ours to deem public education—in its present state—categorically unsuitable for black children.

Homeschooling Helps Achievement

What eventually dawned on us, however, was that we hadn't heard or read about, or run into, or known any black homeschoolers other than ourselves. "Surely we aren't the only black homeschoolers in America!" we often kidded aloud. But it felt that way. After noticing the absence of black homeschoolers in our area, and after a fruitless search of the Internet, I decided, in January 2003, to start the National African-

American Homeschoolers Alliance (NAAHA). Now four years old, NAAHA is the largest homeschooling organization for blacks in America, and provides the most comprehensive information and resources for black families on the Net. . . .

After speaking with hundreds of families across the country, I learned that blacks homeschool for the same reasons as other families, as well as for a unique set of reasons that do not apply to other races. For example, homeschooling is one way black children in America can gain true educational parity. Although many educational alternatives are becoming available, homeschooling parents are confident that they can educate their own children well enough that they will meet or exceed state and national standards and be ready for college. In so doing, these families reject the notion that their children cannot learn, or lack the capacity to learn. Most experts agree that in order for children to be well educated, parents must be actively involved in their education. This shift toward greater, if not primary, parental involvement will undoubtedly result in black children who achieve at levels that public schools cannot replicate, and who are subsequently better prepared for higher education. In fact, in one of the only studies to take a critical look at minority homeschoolers, Dr. Brian Ray of the National Home Education Research Institute found that minority and white homeschooled students both scored in the 87th percentile in reading; and in math, whites edged out minority homeschoolers by only five points—82nd and 77th percentiles, respectively.

One of the main sentiments echoed by black parents . . . is that they have to give their children a fighting chance in this world.

A Movement Away from Public Schooling

It is important to note that as the number of black homeschoolers increases, a noticeable divorce from public schooling—an educational option that blacks have, historically, been staunchly wedded to—is also taking place. In 2004, we all saw the celebrations, remembrances, symposiums, and conferences that marked the 50th anniversary of the Supreme Court's landmark *Brown v. Board of Education* ruling. Ever since this important decision, blacks have relied heavily, almost to a fault, on public education. After all, blacks fought hard to ensure that their children were afforded the same quality of education as everyone else. What they didn't count on was that the promises implied by *Brown v. Board of Education* would still be light-years away from fulfillment a half century later. Those unfulfilled promises prompt families such as ours to deem public education—in its present state—categorically unsuitable for black children.

If you look at the statistics of underachievement for black children, the ever-present achievement gap between black and white children, and the excessive dropout rates and generally unequal resources for black and inner-city schools, few can deny that public schools continue to fail the vast majority of black children. Even so, when black parents decide to homeschool, some educators consider this an act of disloyalty. Although some of that sentiment is beginning to wane, especially as reforms in the educational choices available to all parents become more widespread, there persists an overarching opinion that blacks, particularly those of us committed to education, should stay in and repair the public schools. While this may seem noble in many regards, black homeschoolers no longer want their children used as guinea pigs in educational experiments to see if their test scores will rise a percentage point or two. The expectation that black families should repair public education seems greater in black communities than in others. This is a distinct difference in how black homeschoolers are perceived, compared to others who opt for home education.

Another distinction: Blacks are homeschooling in growing numbers because they believe that is how they can better provide a high-quality, heritage-based education for their children. The many black homeschooling families I speak with across the country maintain that traditional education curricula neglect the full range of black history. The textbooks and curricula in traditional schools tend to focus on slavery, the Civil Rights Movement, and such obligatory historic figures as Harriet Tubman, Frederick Douglass, and Martin Luther King, Jr.—but little beyond that. Black families want their children to have a well-rounded education from a variety of standpoints and perspectives. Above all, they want their children to know that blacks have played important roles not only in US history, but in the history of the world. Parents believe that the time is ripe for their children to learn black and multicultural history on their own terms. Without a doubt, homeschooling lends itself to this end.

Not long ago, there was a general misconception that homeschooling was an option only for white middle- and upper-class families.

Education Is Vital

One of the main sentiments echoed by black parents from coast to coast, no matter where they live and no matter their socioeconomic status or family dynamic, is that they have to give their children a fighting chance in this world. They believe, as Michael and I do, that homeschooling is the best way to do that.

I often speak with parents who have three or four children, the older ones already having gone through the public education system but not achieving at levels acceptable to colleges. These parents are now determined to make a difference in the lives of their younger children. They often mention a subtle racism that begins in the early grades and say they wish they had taken control when those issues might still have been addressed and resolved. Parents cite instances where their children were inaccurately labeled "slow" and placed in remedial classes for the duration of their public school careers. They cite the absence of advanced-placement and honors courses in their children's schools, a lack of equal resources and technology, and constant finger-pointing among parents, teachers, and administrators, all of whom blame each other for the achievement gap. Although these parents attribute their children's lack of success to these variables, they are also quick to acknowledge the apathy about and lack of interest in education among some black students and their parents. By homeschooling, conscientious black families are countering these negative attitudes about learning and the peer-led disdain for education held by some blacks. They are, in effect, creating a movement of black families for whom education is vital to their children's success and the betterment of their communities. No longer accepting that their children must go to public school, they are instead standing up for home education, touting its advantages and praising its results.

I have spoken with many families who say that the potential rewards of homeschooling far outweigh any personal sacrifices they might have to make.

The Diversity of Black Homeschoolers

Not long ago, there was a general misconception that homeschooling was an option only for white middle- and upper-class families. Surprisingly, I regularly get calls and e-mails from black parents who are amazed that homeschooling is an option for them as well. Now that homeschooling stereotypes are being replaced by more accurate notions of who actually homeschools, increasing numbers of black families are joining the movement, setting up classrooms in their homes, and educating their children—to the tune of 103,000 black homeschooled children in the US.

As more blacks homeschool, it becomes increasingly apparent that black homeschooling families are as diverse as any other homeschooling group. Although there are no definitive statistics that reveal the specific demographics of black homeschoolers, I have learned through my work with the NAAHA that there are black single-parent homeschoolers, as well as homes in which the mother takes over the educational duties because she stays at home. There are black dual-income homeschooling families in which one parent homeschools during the day, the other during the evening. I have met several families in which grandparents homeschool their grandchildren. They may be retired, and teach their grandkids while the parents are at work, or they may be their grandkids' sole guardians and have the time and resources to teach them at home. There are sizable numbers of families such as our own, whose children are young and, barring unforeseen circumstances, will be homeschooled until they go to college. Other families are pulling their children out of school midstream in order to educate them themselves.

Some argue that homeschooling will never be an option for most blacks because of factors inherent in the black community, such as the large numbers of single-parent and dual-income homes. While statistics do not verify this, I have spoken with many families who say that the potential rewards of homeschooling far outweigh any personal sacrifices they might have to make. . . .

Black families practice a variety of homeschooling philosophies. Some are strict traditionalists because they want to ensure that their children will not fare worse educationally than they would in public schools. Others are more relaxed about their children's education, and are happy to let them learn from everyday living. These families believe that this will result not only in good learning, but in confident children who are excited about education. . . .

A Role for Support Groups

Local support groups are popping up all over the country. Like me, mothers and fathers are starting these groups because they want their children to see and socialize with other black homeschooled children. It is important that a child not feel isolated in a community in which he or she is the only black homeschooled student, or one of only a few. These parents also want to be available to address the specific needs of black families who have decided to homeschool or are considering it. While home education is gathering more supporters in the black community, the option is still not fully understood and is often met with strong resistance. These support groups provide much-needed educational and emotional support to black families who have taken the step to educate their children at home. . . .

Though we don't believe that public education is wrong for all black children, we know from our own experience, and from the experiences of other black families, that there are other ways of learning. Many black families across the nation are finding this to be true, and I'm sure others will as well. Now, as our daughters grow and learn every day, Michael and I are even more convinced that we have made the right choice for our family and for our daughters' educational futures. We have equipped them with a true and unwavering love for learning that has been made possible by homeschooling.

Homeschooling Enables a Rightly Ordered Life

Sally Thomas

Sally Thomas is a poet and a contributor to the monthly journal
First Things: A Journal of Religion, Culture, and Public Life.

W e had gone to dinner with old friends, and in the course
of the evening the conversation turned to our homeschooling. Our hosts didn't want to argue with the decision
my husband and I had made to homeschool; in truth, people
do that a lot less often than we had steeled ourselves to expect
early on. I suppose they didn't ask how we expected our children to be "socialized" because there the children were, in
front of everyone, doing their best impersonations of socialized people. The nine-year-old talked to the grownups about
Star Wars, the four-year-old helped to carry dishes to the
table, the three-year-old played nicely on the floor with our
friends' baby granddaughter. The twelve-year-old, away at a
ballet rehearsal, proclaimed her socialization by her absence.

In fact, our friends' questions had nothing to do with the
welfare of our children, because they could see for themselves
that the children were fine. But they were curious, and what
they wanted to know was simply this: *What do you do all day
long?*

Efficiency and Effectiveness

That's never an easy question to answer. When people think of
school, typically they think of a day dominated by a roster of
discrete subjects. In English, you do reading, writing, spelling,
and grammar. In math, you do numbers. In history, you do
what's been done before.

In our homeschool, though we cover all these necessary subjects, the delineations between subjects are often far from clear. For example, this fall my math-tutor brother gave us a book entitled *Famous Mathematicians*, a series of little biographies beginning with Euclid and ending with Norbert Wiener in the twentieth century. The nine-year-old asked if he could read it, so twice a week, during our math time, instead of doing regular computational math, I let him read. When he finished the book, he chose one famous mathematician to profile and wrote a little report. As I was describing this exercise for our friends, I kept thinking that we had either done an awful lot of math and given English the short end of the stick, or else had done a lot of English and shafted math. But then I realized that in fact we had done it all. He had learned math concepts, he had learned history, he had practiced reading and writing and spelling and editing—all by reading one book and writing about it.

At home we can do what's nearly impossible in a school setting.

In recent years, as homeschooling has moved closer to the mainstream, much has been said about the successes of homeschooled children, especially regarding their statistically superior performance on standardized tests and the attractiveness of their transcripts and portfolios to college-admissions boards. Less, I think, has been said about how and why these successes happen. The fact is that homeschooling is an efficient way to teach and learn. It's time-effective, in that a homeschooled child, working independently or one-on-one with a parent or an older sibling, can get through more work or master a concept more quickly than a child who's one of twenty-five in a classroom. It's effort-effective, in that a child doesn't spend needless hours over a concept already mastered simply because others haven't mastered it yet. Conversely, a child doesn't spend years in school quietly not learning a subject, under the teacher's radar, only to face the massive and depressing task of remediation when the deficiency is finally caught.

Interweaving Learning and Life

To my mind, however, homeschooling's greatest efficiency lies in its capacity for a rightly ordered life. A child in school almost inevitably has a separate existence, a "school life," that too easily weakens parental authority and values and that also encourages an artificial boundary between *learning* and *everything else*. Children come home exhausted from a day at school—and for a child with working parents, that day can be twelve hours long—and the last thing they want is to pick up a book or have a conversation. Television and video games demand relatively little, and they seem a blessed departure from what the children have been doing all day. "You know I don't read all that stuff you read," a neighbor child scornfully told my eldest some years ago during one of those archetypal childhood arguments about what to play. Our daughter wanted to play *Treasure-Seekers* or *Betsy-Tacy* and *Tib* [based on characters from books]; her friend insisted on playing the Disney cartoon character Kim Possible. Book-talk was for school, and she wasn't at school just then, thank you.

Our days are saturated with what school merely strives to replicate: real, substantial, active, useful, and moral learning.

At home we can do what's nearly impossible in a school setting: We can weave learning into the fabric of our family life, so that the lines between "learning" and "everything else" have largely ceased to exist. The older children do a daily schedule of what I call sit-down work: math lessons, English and foreign-language exercises, and readings for history and science. The nine-year-old does roughly two hours of sit-down work a day, while the twelve-year-old spends three to four hours. But those hours hardly constitute the sum total of their education.

We spend some time formally learning Latin, for example, but we also say our table blessing in Latin and sing Latin hymns during prayers. Both older children sing in our parish treble choir: still more Latin, which is not a dead language to them but a living, singing one. The twelve-year-old is working her way through an English-grammar-and-composition text, but she is also, on her own, writing a play, which our local children's theater will produce in the spring. The nine-year-old has his own subscription to *National Geographic* and fills us in at dinner on the events of the D-Day invasion or the habits of the basking shark. He practices handwriting, with which he struggles, by writing letters to friends in England, where we lived when he was small. Last November, the older children and a friend adopted a project for sending care packages to soldiers in Iraq; they wrote letters, knitted hats, made Christmas cards, and one Saturday went door-to-door around the neighborhood collecting funds to cover postage and to buy school supplies for the soldiers to hand out to Iraqi children. This undertaking by itself was something of a mini-curriculum, involving reading, handwriting, composition, art, math, community service, and even public relations. At their best, our days are saturated with what school merely strives to replicate: real, substantial, active, useful and moral learning.

Faith and Learning Integrated

Most important for us in the ordering of our life is that our homeschooling day unfolds from habits of prayer. We begin the day with the rosary and a saint's life; we say the Angelus at lunchtime; we do a lesson from the catechism or a reading in apologetics and say the evening office [prayers usually only said by professional religious] before bed. Our children have internalized this rhythm and, to my intense gratification, the older children marshal the younger children to prayers even when their father and I are absent. The day is shaped and organized by times of turning to God.

A lot of unscheduled learning seems to happen during these times. In saying the rosary, for example, we exercise our skills in memorization and recitation, as well as in contemplation. The little children practice sitting still; they also practice counting. In remembering our daily intentions together, we practice the discipline of inclining our hearts and minds toward the needs of others. Often, too, during devotions we find ourselves plunged into discussions about current events, ethics, and questions about God and life that have been simmering unasked in some child's mind until just that moment. The saints, whose dates we record in our family timeline book, provide us not only with examples of holiness but also with insight into the historical eras in which they lived. We have even found ourselves doing geography during prayers. . . .

What looks like not that much on the daily surface of things proves in the living to be something greater than the schedule on the page suggests, a life in which English and math and science and history, contemplation and discussion and action, faith and learning, are not compartmentalized entities but elements in an integrated whole from which, we hope and pray, our children will emerge one day so firmly formed that nothing in this world can unbend them.

Homeschooling Allows Parents to Teach Their Religious Convictions

Mark Field and Christine Field

Mark Field is a former lieutenant in United States Naval Intelligence and the Wheaton, Illinois, chief of police. Christine Field is senior correspondent and Resource Room columnist for The Old Schoolhouse Magazine *and the author of several books, including* Homeschooling the Challenging Child. *Together the Fields authored* Homeschooling 101: The Essential Handbook.

If we hadn't chosen homeschooling, we don't think our marriage would be as strong as it is, with the range and depth of experiences we have had. Without the calling to homeschool, we would not have the shared commitment to the ultimate home improvement project—homeschooling. While other couples may only get to share decorating projects and vacation decisions, we struggle together through everything from salvation to phonics to algebra. . . .

If we hadn't chosen homeschooling, we probably wouldn't have as many children, Christine practiced law until our first child was two years old and our second child was six months old. The siren call of an engaging career was strong and might have won out. If not for the happy arrival of two children seventeen months apart in age and the opportunity for a dream job in a distant city for Mark, we might not have abandoned our status as dual-income parents. Christine's time at home was supposed to be short lived. "The plan" was to be home for a few years, then reenter the courtroom arena. However God had another plan—to adopt two more children, bringing the total to four. The move from a prestigious comfort zone to home was the values clarifying experience that we both needed. . . .

Educating a Family Is Challenging

If we hadn't chosen homeschooling, we would know the hollowness of having more "things" but never know the richness of having all of each other. Many times we are tempted to lament our lifestyle of relative simplicity. We need only look at the many upwardly mobile families we know who are blessed materially, but bankrupt spiritually. . . .

If we hadn't chosen homeschooling, we might not have experienced our own much needed time on God's threshing floor. The challenges of raising and educating a family have been met on our knees, which was exactly where the Lord wanted us. Any vestige of pride or self-sufficiency that lurked in our desperately wicked hearts has been exposed by the rigors of this life. . . .

If we hadn't chosen homeschooling, we doubt our children would be as close as they are. As different as night and day, they are capable of shining moments of closeness and bonding. The tenderness (and sometimes the terror!) they bestow on one another causes our parent-hearts to leap. Capable of relating to a wide array of people, they often (not always!) choose to relate most profoundly to those they live with.

Freedom and Space to Explore and Nurture

If we hadn't chosen homeschooling, a foray into teenage rebellion might not have ended so graciously. When one of our brood sought out her birthmother, we prayed for a happy ending, not knowing what to expect. She made contact but got no response, causing our daughter many months of depression, doubt, and distrust. In her pain, she lashed out at us. We loved her through it, and she is now a happy young lady. We shudder to think of the course this incident might have taken if she had been exposed to the sea of adolescent angst and its remedies practiced in the schools. The pain relief she sought might have been found in self-destructive ways. . . .

If we hadn't chosen homeschooling, our children might not have had the time, freedom, and space to explore and nurture personal interests and talents. A passion for swimming, a flair for acting, an untapped talent for watercolor, and much more have all been nurtured in the greenhouse of our home. Schoolwork can be done efficiently, leaving time for other pursuits, or lingered over at our leisure. Nothing fosters self-discovery like freedom.

If we hadn't chosen homeschooling, our daughter with learning issues might not be the strong, wise, compassionate young lady that she is becoming. She could have been beaten down by a system that had no time to explore or appreciate her considerable strengths. Instead, we had the time to learn how to help her learn, and she is flourishing.

If we hadn't chosen homeschooling, our irrepressible son would certainly have been repressed and labeled. He is a busy, busy boy, and we have learned that he is extremely capable. It so happens that he does not learn well with his behind glued to a chair. With our freedom to tailor-make "school" to meet the needs of each child, he is learning while jumping, walking, fiddling, and bouncing. . . .

Christians . . . point to their religious faith as a strong factor in their decision to teach their children at home.

The Factor of Religious Faith

And we haven't even touched on the academic advantages.

The goal of our homeschooling is to prepare our children for a life dedicated to God—seeking his will, seeking to glorify him. This is in contrast to a culture drowning in secular humanism that says to glorify ourselves.

In schools, children are statistical entities to justify funding. In the homeschool, they are precious sacred trusts. The world doesn't need more geniuses or star athletes or beauty queens. It needs more committed, passionate Christians.

Statistics show that the overwhelming majority of American homeschoolers are Christians who point to their religious faith as a strong factor in their decision to teach their children at home. Somewhere along the line, each of these families first heard a calling, and hearing that calling set the stage for how their homeschooling would unfurl. Only fully understanding that calling will lead to peace and confidence. . . .

Knowing and Shaping Children's Hearts

If loving God and teaching our children about him is to be our first priority, we must first shape our children's hearts, not their minds. What does this mean? Allow me to employ a time-honored methodology cherished by ministers and teachers the world over: the acrostic—HEART.

As homeschoolers we have the distinct advantage of one-on-one interaction with our students.

H Is for Hearts. We must know our children's hearts and do all we can to ensure they are inclined heavenward. This is of far greater worth to us than a prestigious prep school or a perfect SAT score. Unless we have their hearts, their trust, and their obedience, we cannot teach them anything. But if we have their hearts, and if they will listen to God's rebuke, he will pour out his heart to us and make his thoughts known to them. . . . That, friend, is true education: the pouring of God's heart (and our hearts) into our children.

E Is for Eternity. We believe homeschooling is the best education for our children because it is education with an eye on eternity. We had a discussion about public school versus homeschooling with a Christian brother a while back. At the time he was the principal of a respected suburban high school. He noted that the facilities of our humble homeschool could not hold a candle to the high-powered microscopes that allowed his students to see the internal workings of a human cell. True, I said, we don't have the bells and whistles you find at a well-funded public school, but we are able to meet the individual needs of each of our students. We can teach them the way that they best learn, and we can instill in them a vision for eternity. . . .

The homeschool environment is simply more conducive than public school for helping our children pursue right relationships and a well-rounded social life.

A Is for Attitude and Abilities. As homeschoolers we have the distinct advantage of one-on-one interaction with our students. This allows us to recognize and work on bad attitudes and to encourage a child's unique abilities. In a large classroom setting a child can fly under the radar for years without anyone ever knowing he has a poor attitude toward learning, toward life, toward people. In the homeschool environment, such attitudes will be readily apparent and can be dealt with on a daily basis. Meanwhile, the child is not continually exposed to the dishonoring attitudes so prevalent in the public schools, where basic manners seem to have gone the way of the horse and buggy.

In addition to shaping attitude, we can foster a child's unique abilities. Homeschooling affords us the precious freedom to craft courses to the child's interests and to pursue activities outside of school that meet his or her needs.

R Is for Right Relationships. The homeschool environment is simply more conducive than public school for helping our children pursue right relationships and a well-rounded social life. For example, our days do not consist merely of academic pursuits in the home. The children interact with people of all ages, from all walks of life, whether through group activities with other homeschoolers, specialized lessons outside the home, or volunteer opportunities. Regular exposure to all age groups develops in a child the ability to communicate with anyone and to relate to everyone. In addition, we can keep our fingers on the pulse of family dynamics, friendships, and boy-girl relationships. A good deal of socializing is done in our home where we can observe interactions and talk about them, on the spot or later in private. An environment that allows for this type of life coaching is priceless.

T Is for Today and Tomorrow. We cherish today and relish the thought of tomorrow. We have precious few todays left until our children leave the nest, so we want to "suck out all the marrow of life" while we are still together. Meanwhile, homeschooling allows us to look to that tomorrow with joyous hope. We pray the normal prayers of parents—spiritual health, life purpose, a godly mate, college, career, children—but we rest in the knowledge that we have made wise investments of our resources, time, and talents as parents and that God holds our children's future in the palm of his hands.

Homeschooling Provides the Best Education

W.A. Pannapacker

W.A. Pannapacker is an associate professor of English at Hope College in Holland, Michigan.

I'm an English professor, and my spouse used to work in academic administration. We have three daughters, ages 6, 4, and 2. And we have been home schooling them for two years now. If all goes well, we plan to continue teaching them at home at least until they are old enough for high school.

We always planned that one of us would stay home while our children were young, but the idea of home schooling only developed recently in the context of our present circumstances.

A Natural Method of Education

Teaching our daughters to read and write, beginning around the age of 4, seemed like a natural thing for us to do. Along with potty training, it was just part of the ordinary business of being a parent. Being avid readers ourselves, we have about 4,000 books in our house, which now includes a children's library. I suppose it was inevitable that we would spend a lot of time reading to our children, and they would have an early desire to learn to read for themselves and for each other.

We live surrounded by woods and farmland, so our daughters are constantly asking us to look up plants and insects in the Audubon field guides. We have a reasonably well-supplied children's science lab and art studio. And, in the course of routine travel and shopping, it's easy to cultivate our daughters' curiosity about the world by visiting museums,

W.A. Pannapacker, "Children, the Case for Homeschooling," *Chronicle of Higher Education*, December 16, 2005. This article may not be published, reposted, or redistributed without express permission from The Chronicle.

zoos, libraries, schools, factories, and farms. These are things that most parents do, though they may not regard their activities as part of some kind of curriculum.

We want the best education for our children, and, on the whole, home schooling seems like the best option.

In a typical day, our 6-year-old daughter will study phonics, spelling, writing, history, geography, and math. She may perform some elementary science experiments, or she may work on an art project in emulation of [artists George Pierre] Seurat or [Jackson] Pollock. On some days other children—not necessarily other home schoolers—will come to our house to play. Sometimes they'll open our costume chest and dramatize something they've been reading, such as *The Hobbit*. Other times they'll go outside and play hide-and-seek or go on an "expedition" to find specimens for the family museum. Even though our younger daughters have not yet started their formal schooling, they are eager to imitate their oldest sister, and the pace of learning seems to accelerate with each new child. On good days, home schooling seems like the most natural method of elementary education one could imagine.

Home schooling . . . becomes a logical choice when the costs of private education and day care become greater than one parent's income.

We are not ideologically committed to home schooling any more than we are opposed to public education. And we are aware of the limitations of home under some circumstances, just as we are aware of the difficulties faced by many public schools, even in relatively well-financed school districts. Ultimately, we want the best education for our children, and, on the whole, home schooling seems like the best option. It is also one that our daughters seem to desire, and, if any of them wanted to go to the nearby public school, we would certainly consider it. . . .

Private Education Is Not the Answer

I have had many discussions with other professors who home school, primarily at my home institution but also with a number of faculty members in other parts of the country. From those conversations I have noticed a number of common motives, circumstances, and beliefs among faculty members who educate their children at home.

They are rarely religious or political extremists. Many professors observe that it is difficult to achieve consistent moral training in public education. They sometimes state that private education in religious schools is too doctrinal or resistant to modernity, particularly in the sciences. Some lament that public and religious education seem to have become battlefields for activists for whom the "vital center" has been abandoned, along with a spirit of civic responsibility.

They want the best education for their children, but they are not wealthy. Professors are usually well informed about what constitutes a good education in terms of methods and resources. The experience of small classes and one-on-one tutoring inevitably convinces teachers of the effectiveness of methods that can easily be replicated in the home, though they are prohibitive for all but exclusive private schools that are usually beyond the reach of academics with more than one child. Home schooling therefore, becomes a logical choice when the costs of private education and day care become greater than one parent's income.

They enjoy learning. For nearly all professors, the chance to review and expand their own youthful education in a variety of fields is a treat that almost transcends the educational needs of their children. Mathematicians, for example, relish the chance to reread the literature they half-missed when they were mastering geometry, and English professors, like me, enjoy the chance to relearn the astronomy they once loved before [failing to grasp] calculus crushed their hopes for a scientific career. They often see themselves as learning with their children rather than simply teaching them.

Confidence and Flexibility Are Key

They are confident in their ability to teach. Professors often see teaching their own children as part of a continuum of pleasurable obligations to the next generation; they seek to integrate the values of their profession with the values they live at home. Since professors often teach the teachers, they tend to believe—perhaps with some hubris—in their ability to teach effectively at all grade levels. But more often, they recognize their limitations and seek collaboration with other parents—often professors themselves—with different areas of expertise.

Home-schooled students are not always perfect, but they seem more respectful, attentive, mature, and academically prepared than their peers.

They benefit from flexible schedules. Academics tend to work about 50 hours per week during the academic year, but they also have control over their schedules and long periods of relative autonomy. Most professors have a co-parenting ideal, but in practice one partner—usually the mother—becomes the primary home educator, while the father assumes a secondary role with some seasonal variation. Some express discomfort with this circumstance because they recognize the sacrifices that each partner requires of the other.

They value unstructured learning. Professors know how much time is lost by learning in an institutional setting. A large portion of the time spent in school is devoted to moving students around, dealing with disruptions, health problems, different amounts of preparation, and unequal rates of learning. Without all the crowd control and level seeking, the formal requirements of education can be completed in only a few hours a day, leaving lots of time for self-directed learning and play. As a result, home schooled children generally learn faster and with less boredom and less justified resentment.

School sometimes teaches otherwise happy and intelligent children to become sullen and secretive and contemptuous of learning.

Negative Side of Public Education

They see the results of public education. Every professor seems to complain that most high-school graduates are not really prepared for college, either academically or emotionally. More and more, our energies are devoted to remedial teaching and therapeutic counseling. Most believe that something is wrong in public education, or the larger culture, that can only be dealt with, in part, by selective withdrawal. Home schooled students are not always perfect, but they seem more respectful, attentive, mature, and academically prepared than their peers. And they do not automatically perceive teachers as "the enemy" out of peer solidarity.

They privilege the family over peer groups. Professors often celebrate diversity as a value in education, and, among those who home school, many mention the value for their children of cross-generational experiences instead of identifying only with a peer group. In large families, children also benefit from teaching their younger siblings, who are generally eager to keep up. Home schooled students are less likely to become alienated from their families as a result of antisocial, anti-intellectual peer conformity. They develop a set of values that enables them to resist the negative socialization that outweighs, by far, the benefits of segregation by age.

They have negative memories of their own education. Although it takes some probing, nearly every professor with home schooled children mentions traumatic childhood experiences in school. Professors, as a group, tend to have been sensitive, intelligent children who were picked on and ostracized. They foresee the same treatment for their own children, and they want to do everything they can to prevent the children from experiencing the traumas they experienced. Professors recognize how many of our most brilliant students have been emotionally or physically terrorized for a dozen years before they arrive at college. School sometimes teaches otherwise happy and intelligent children to become, sullen and secretive and contemptuous of learning.

Worth the Sacrifices

It is hard to overemphasize this last point as a motive for home schoolers. In my own memory, the difficulty of school was never the work; it was surviving the day without being victimized by students whose violence was beyond the capacity or desire of adults to control. My spouse remembers the cruelty of girls in cliques, who can be even more cunning at the infliction of pain and permanent emotional scarring than any of the boys who sometimes sent me home with torn clothes and a bloody nose.

No doubt, my spouse and I have had to forgo some career options for our present way of life. Home schooling our children means we have to live on an assistant professor's salary. It also means living in a small town in the Midwest instead of an expensive city on one of the coasts. It means living in an old farmhouse that I am, more or less, renovating by myself. It means not eating out or going on vacations very often. It means driving older American cars instead of shiny new Volvos. But the big reward is the time we get to spend with our children.

I suppose, on some level, my spouse and I are rebelling against an academic culture that tells us we should both be working at demanding professional jobs while our children are raised by someone else. But we value this time with our children more than career advancement for its own sake. We don't regard ourselves as conservatives. We feel like we're swimming against the mainstream of a culture that has sacrificed the family for economic productivity and personal ambition. We don't think home schooling is right for everyone, but it works for us, for now. Of course we will make some mistakes, but on the whole, we think home schooling our children may be the most important thing we will ever do.

Homeschooled Children Learn Life Lessons

Christina Rosales

Christina Rosales is a reporter for the Laredo Morning Times *in Laredo, Texas.*

Hannah sits at her school desk in the brightly colored classroom, her legs swinging from her perch on the chair, her feet teasing the floor she can't reach yet.

As the first-grader reads her story from her book, "Mouse Soup," her voice and eyebrows express the differences between the character dialogue and the narrator.

"Sound it out, Hannah," said Toni Migura, her mother and schoolteacher. "Remember what the phonogram for A–I is. This word (mountain) breaks the rule." "M-ow-n-tAN," Hannah reads.

"Very good, baby girl," Migura said.

Incorporating Life Lessons

As ... students embark on the new school year—some worrying about mandatory uniforms, class schedules and test scores—homeschool students like Hannah and her brother, Matthew, head back to their familiar, homey classrooms.

"I love homeschool," said Matthew Migura, a fourth-grader. "The thing I like best is that my mom is my teacher, and that my dog can come into my classroom when I call him." Toni Migura said she, as well as several other homeschool parents, choose to homeschool their kids to teach life lessons and character.

"No matter what we're doing, we put life lessons into what they're learning," she said. "We're always teaching about patience and manners. You're able to teach a lot about character." Aside from instructing their children in virtues, the Miguras choose to homeschool their children to incorporate a Christian education.

"We want them to be educated," Migura said. "But above all, we want them to grow up to be godly men and women." Dominic and Nicole Vallone, parents who homeschool their three children, begin the school day with Bible study. Their three children, Duncan, 8, Nolan, 6 and Asher, 4 are all taught about their faith as Christians.

A Focus on Firm Education

"My mom and dad homeschool us because other schools don't have God in them," said Duncan Vallone, a fourth-grader. "They don't want us to go off and become non-believers in the end." Both Toni Migura and Nicole Vallone encourage their children to question their faith and why they believe.

We want them to have a very firm foundation and know how to learn and have a love of learning.

For example, Vallone said, the Christian curriculum used does not teach evolution as fact.

"I do teach them evolution in an apologetic way, but we're creationists," she said. "I want them to be able to defend their faith when they get to college and people ask them questions and debate those types of issues." The primary goal of homeschooling for the Vallones and Miguras is not for their children to get ahead, they said.

"We're not trying to make them into geniuses," Nicole Vallone said. "I do want them to be well-rounded, but that's not my first desire."

Dominic Vallone and Toni Migura said [that] with the children getting the attention they need, learning is easier for the students. "When you have them one-on-one, you can cater to their strengths and talents," Dominic Vallone said. "Their academic success is really a product of that." Toni Migura's focus when homeschooling Hannah and Matthew is to give them a firm foundation in their education.

Socialization Is an Everyday Happening

"It's not so they're ahead of the game," she said. "We want them to have a very firm foundation and know how to learn and have a love of learning. Once they have that, they can apply it to anything they want to do." While some people believe that homeschooled children may not be properly socialized, the Migura and Vallone children are very much in tune with their peers.

Hannah and Matthew take karate and piano lessons, and keep busy with their friends from church and the neighborhood, Migura said.

"They (Duncan, Nolan and Asher) have many friends," Nicole Vallone said. "There are always friends here at the house, and as they get older, we'll have them do golf camps and other things." In addition to their after-school activities, the Vallones and the Miguras are members of the Providence Homeschool Association, a Christian support group for homeschool families.

The group consists of about 50 families, said Dominic Vallone, one of the leaders of the group. Providence organizes monthly field trips for homeschool students, as well as annual science and history fairs.

That's what homeschool is about—accepting that sometimes plans and schedules don't work out.

Flexibility Is the Key

Homeschool isn't for everyone, Dominic Vallone said.

"There are a lot of different ways to educate kids," he said. "For us, homeschool is the best way to instill goals and character in our children." Duncan and Nolan Vallone said their friends, most of whom will go back to school on Monday, consider the boys lucky.

"I like that I don't have to sit in class all day," Duncan said. "I could take breaks." The Miguras, depending on the kind of day it is outside, sometimes take the whole day off.

"Sometimes we have those nice spring days and I'll say 'No school today,'" Migura said. "We'll spend the day outside or go to the library. It teaches you to appreciate the day. That's what homeschool is about—accepting that sometimes plans and schedules don't work out." Most homeschool families follow a curriculum purchased through different publishers.

The Importance of Teaching Character and Faith

Unlike the public school system, classes for the Vallones don't end until the curriculum is done Nicole said; the classes could extend into the first few weeks of summer.

Asked if he would rather go to school with his friends, Nolan, a first grader said he would rather be homeschooled.

"Not even my mom and dad have to stop me," he said.

People often ask what the motivation is for these families who have never sent their children to a school, Migura said.

"People sometimes think we're crazy," she said. "But the goal of all of this is to teach more than the curriculum ... [including] character and faith. It's more than getting through the textbook."

Homeschooling Benefits Special Needs Children

Meg Grooms

Meg Grooms is the homeschooling editor for BellaOnline, a women's Web site.

Every single child in this world is different and has different educational needs. Parents who have children with special education needs face unique challenges. I happen to have two special needs children who are homeschooled. The good news is that homeschooling your special needs child is often the best situation for the child, and your child doesn't have to give up school-funded therapies in order to homeschool, and it doesn't have to hurt your wallet. The hard work of homeschooling a special needs child is twice as rewarding.

Eligible for Outside Help

Most states allow children to be evaluated for special programs at the public school, including students who do the bulk of their learning outside of a traditional school. Homeschooled children in most states are eligible to receive free speech therapy, autism support, occupational therapy, gifted education and other programs through their locally zoned public school. Your child will attend school for these programs only; they do not need to be enrolled full-time. Using this option is generally the least expensive and most convenient for a family; however family participation isn't always encouraged and you may find yourself fighting to stay informed of your child's status. You may also feel pressure from the school to enroll your child full-time. If this happens remember that they are speaking from a numbers and funding standpoint; schools garner three times as much funding for

Meg Grooms, "Special Needs Homeschooling," *bellaonline.com*, 2008. Reproduced by permission.

special education students as they do "normal" students. Your local school district will have all of the information you need to have your child evaluated, and you generally do not have to have a prior evaluation or referral from a doctor. The school has a legal obligation to provide these services to your child regardless of where your child is educated. If you find the program just isn't working out you are free to remove your child at any time to seek services elsewhere.

Many private and church schools have programs for special needs children at a reduced cost, including autism support programs several days a week.

Most states also offer early interventions programs for children identified before the age of 5 as having special needs. In some states these programs work hand-in-hand with the local schools, but since all are publicly funded they are open to *all* children who qualify.

Evaluations, programs and therapies will be provided at no cost, and many can be performed in your home. A quick call to your state's Department of Health should gain you all the information you need to get your child evaluated.

Private Insurance Offers Alternatives

Parents who have private medical insurance might be surprised at what they will pay for. Many top-tier insurance plans now cover speech therapy, hearing aids, physical therapy, psychological care, occupational therapy and many other therapies and programs your child can benefit from. There are hoops that you will have to jump through, and you will most likely need the referral of a physician. This is a wonderful alternative for those who are unable to take their children to a school for these services or who want to try to keep everything in-house and under the radar. While this option is not free, it is desirable for those in the position to pay for therapy and who want the government school system involved as little as possible. If your family participates in a state-funded insurance program you are eligible for these services through your state Department of Health at no cost in most cases. When your child reaches compulsory school attendance age you will be referred to the local school district for most services. If you do not have insurance most hospitals that offer these services have a sliding scale, some have limited amounts of state funding to cover the costs of low income and uninsured children.

There are alternative service locations available if you know where to look. In many communities tutoring for all ages is offered for free or low cost at senior centers, community centers, churches and church schools, the YMCA and other community clubs, community colleges and universities. Many private and church schools have programs for special needs children at a reduced cost, including autism support programs several days a week.

Special Needs Children Benefit from Homeschooling

While homeschooling a special needs child takes more effort than homeschooling a child who doesn't need these services, you are your child's best advocate and you have the ultimate choice of where and how their education will take place.

- Your child doesn't need to go to school in order to receive the services they need.

- It is your job as parent to ensure your children get the best possible education, and for most special needs students traditional school isn't the best option, and it is certainly not the only option.

- Arm yourself with information and surround yourself with people who care and can support you. Locate a support group geared for parents of special education children who are homeschooled, research the Internet, talk to professionals and make a sound decision based on your information and child.

CHAPTER 2

Is Homeschooling a Good Option?

Chapter Preface

Most experts agree that homeschooling has become the fastest growing option for parents thinking about alternative education and school choice for their children. Yet, despite this, many people remain undecided as to whether or not homeschool is the best choice for today's youth.

One of the strongest critics of homeschooling is the National Education Association (NEA), which has taken the position that "home schooling programs based on parental choice cannot provide the student with a comprehensive education experience." Others point out that some parents are not qualified to teach; in other words, they are not knowledgeable enough or have not been trained sufficiently to do the job. Anyone, argued one member of the Illinois Education Association, can buy a social studies, science, or math book, but that does not mean that person knows how to instruct someone else about the subject matter contained in that book. Homeschool critics and skeptics also contend that most parents cannot create a full learning experience because they do not have easy access to the wide variety of resources readily available to classroom teachers.

On a par with concern about teacher certification or accreditation is concern about whether children who are homeschooled are subject to a lack of socialization. At one time or another, almost every homeschool parent has been asked, "What about socialization?" Socialization is an important component of getting along in life, goes the argument. You cannot teach it.

The NEA believes that children should have the opportunity to interact with their peers and others in order to develop physically and mentally, expand social skills, and acclimate to new people and surroundings. In the view of the NEA and of others who do not favor homeschooling or are uncertain about its merits, this interaction is what happens when children attend an academic institution. In a school environment, they say, children not only learn how to communicate with their peers, but also to respect those different from themselves and to work as a team to accomplish goals.

Some homeschoolers and homeschooling advocates refer to socialization as the "dreaded S word" and to the issue as the "Socialization Myth." They agree with homeschooling critics that socialization is extremely important. They do not agree, however, that children who are homeschooled are isolated, confined, or lacking in social skills. Homeschoolers, they explain, are involved in numerous extracurricular activities that enable them to spend time and interact with people of all ages and types.

Writing for About.com, Jennie von Eggers, author and co-owner of Trigger Memory Systems, a publishing company that focuses on creative learning, responded this way to assertions that homeschoolers could not integrate well into society because they lacked opportunities to learn and practice social skills:

"How would my children be able to integrate into society, without first learning the valuable "social skills" that only a public school experience could provide? After all, the socialization part of a typical day-in-the-life of a home schooled child, looks nothing like the government school experience. Many homeschoolers spend their day doing things such as: helping out with family business, running errands, going on field trips, visiting relatives and friends, doing odd jobs for neighbors and partaking in family responsibilities. As the "socially challenged" homeschool kids are out and about, partaking and interacting in real life situations, the government students are "socializing" under a controlled environment, behind four walls with a controlled group of people (also known as their peer group)."

Another parent, this time speaking to those who home-school, makes it clear that homeschoolers will indeed be socialized and able to function in society: "Your homeschooled kids will have as many friends and activities as they want and you allow (and likely more time than their PS [public school] peers to enjoy them). They will be socialized by their parents and other caring people who will help them learn appropriate behavior in different situations—at home, in public, in informal and formal activities."

Homeschool advocates believe strongly that children do not have to go to public school to be truly socialized. Some experts agree. One of these is Terry Osborn, professor and chair of the Division of Curriculum and Teaching at Fordham University's Graduate School of Education, who is quoted in the following excerpt from a January 21, 2008, posting on MySA.com titled "Home-Schooling Doesn't Stunt Kids' Socialization:"

"The idea of a homogenous grouping of 25 to 30 children who sit at their desks all day long and do activities—to call that socialization is tortured. You and I don't live and function in that kind of environment." Socialization involves interacting with people from various backgrounds in various contexts, and most home-schooled kids do that, he says. "Interacting with adults in the grocery store is a form of socialization," he adds. Many home-schooled kids have siblings of different ages, and that affords cross-generational socializing, which students don't get at school. As long as parents make an effort to expand the child's circle beyond the home, home-schooled kids do fine, he says. "Socialization isn't rocket science, after all," Osborn says. "When you go off to college you learn pretty fast when to speak and when not to speak."

Homeschooling Works Better than Traditional Public Education

Kate McReynolds

Kate McReynolds is a child clinical psychologist and the associate editor of Encounter *magazine.*

Across the nation, public schools are cutting back or eliminating recess, art, music, physical education, and drama. Excessive homework and test-prep are encroaching on children's free time and family time, making it difficult for them to engage in activities that are important for their full development. Competitive college entrance requirements push young people to take Advanced Placement courses and SAT-prep courses, adding to their already heavy homework loads. The school work itself, driven by high-stakes tests, is typically dull and lifeless, consisting of little besides the memorization of disembodied facts and concepts. Children seem to dislike school more than ever.

We are told that all this is necessary to prepare our children for the future. But is it? Is there an alternative way to educate our children that will respect their happiness and individuality, and will foster their natural love of learning? Growing numbers of parents are turning to homeschooling.

By its very nature, homeschooling cannot be easily described. There is no unified homeschool "movement," no standardized curriculum or centralized source of information on academic achievement. Parents have many different reasons for homeschooling their children. For some the motivation is not the repressive and dreary nature of the public school cur-

Kate McReynolds, "Homeschooling," *Encounter*, vol. 20, Summer 2007, pp. 36–41. Reprinted with permission from Encounter: Education for Meaning and Social Justice. https://great-ideas.org/enc.htm.

riculum, but the need to teach a religious-based education. Other parents fear violence in the schools. Still others want to spend more time with their children.

Homeschoolers attend college at higher rates than public school students.

Some homeschooled children follow a traditional curriculum and a set schedule, some are "deschooled," a style of homeschooling that permits children to follow their own interests at their own pace. Some homeschoolers engage in "distance learning," i.e., Internet-based instruction, and purchase books and ready-made curricula. Many make or find their own materials, join learning cooperatives, and make use of community-based learning opportunities, such as public lectures, community theater, and continuing education classes. Increasingly, homeschoolers are joining together to share resources and even to form partnerships with traditional schools. But regardless of the form it takes, homeschooling is a growing trend, increasing annually by 15 to 20 percent.

Evaluating the Outcomes

Academic achievement among U.S. homeschoolers is difficult to assess. There is no uniform curriculum; standardized tests are voluntary in many states; and federal systems of "accountability" are absent. Nevertheless, a variety of studies suggest that by traditional standards, homeschoolers do pretty well. They tend to score higher than public school children on standardized achievement tests, advanced placement exams, the SAT and the ACT. Homeschoolers attend college at higher rates than public school students.

About three-quarters of the nation's colleges have policies regarding homeschool applicants and many, including Harvard, actively recruit homeschoolers. In 2001 Stanford University admitted 27% of its homeschooled applicants, nearly twice the acceptance rate of traditionally schooled applicants. Once in college homeschoolers tend to have higher grade point averages than their traditionally schooled peers.

I knew something was wrong on the first day of school.

Despite its apparent academic success, a prevalent mainstream concern is that homeschooling deprives children of the social and emotional development necessary to make it in the "real" world. The socialization question, as it is often called, represents a number of concerns. If children don't attend traditional schools will they be able to cope with college? Will they be able to get and keep a job? Will homeschooled children know how to get along with others? Will they tolerate people's differences? Will they know how to behave as society expects? I decided to talk with homeschoolers to get a better idea of their day-to-day life.

From Apathy to Enthusiasm

Ellen, who lives in Brooklyn, New York, homeschools her five children. She was originally somewhat opposed to homeschooling, put off by her impression that homeschoolers were trying to shield themselves from the world, but all that changed when she sent Aidan, her first child, to kindergarten. "I knew something was wrong on the first day of school. I asked the teacher if I could meet with her and she seemed shocked. She agreed, but during our meeting her attitude seemed to be, 'What are you doing here?'" Although the school, which Ellen had researched and carefully selected, had an open door policy, Aidan's teacher didn't value parent cooperation. There were 37 children in Aidan's class and they were expected to sit in desks and do academic worksheets; there was very little playtime. Aidan, who already knew how to read, was bored and restless. Ellen was surprised to get reports that her well-behaved son was acting up in school. She discovered that the punishment was losing recess, which struck her as counterproductive. At home, her young son talked about teachers yelling at students, about students yelling, and about his feeling that his teacher was always watching him. Ellen suspected he had been pegged as a troublemaker. Six weeks into the school year a family emergency required Ellen's attention. She left town for two weeks, taking Aidan with her. When they returned, Aidan did not go back to school.

Ellen is a proponent of Waldorf education, developed by Rudolph Steiner, a holistic developmental approach that discourages introducing academics too early. Aidan spent his first year of homeschool primarily playing with friends, going to the library, doing art, and going on outings with his mother. Now, with five homeschoolers ranging in age from 3 to 13, some of the work is more academic, some of the time more structured. The children learn with books and workbooks, with friends, from programs at the Brooklyn Botanical Gardens, the Museum of Natural History, and other community resources. But each one has a unique developmental path that homeschooling is fostering. . . .

Ellen has been "methodical" about math but, in keeping with her philosophy, does not introduce it too soon.

> I observe my children very carefully to see how things are affecting them, not to cater to their every whim, but to make sure of healthy growth in every aspect of their lives, not just academics. It takes a lot of attention.

It seems to be working. When Ellen's daughter, Justine, who is sunny, artistic, and loving, was six, she spent the entire year drawing pictures. It was all she wanted to do and she was very focused and content. Now 8 years old, her interest is turning to academic subjects and she recently asked for a math workbook. When her mother gave her one shortly before bed-time, Justine took it to bed with her and began working out problems. She enthusiastically told her mother, "Don't be surprised if you see me here in the morning still working."

Ellen believes that by allowing children the freedom to develop their own interests and learn material when they are ready we are protecting their natural enthusiasm and preparing them in the best possible way for the future.

> Their enthusiasm for the things they are interested in is so untainted by competition and external expectations that it's retained. Their enthusiasm for what's coming in the future is preserved. If we expose them to academics too early we're stunting their ability to use their knowledge creatively and in their own way. If it's too early they won't know what to do with what they know, but if we pay attention to the unique way that each child learns and grows, they will be free to accomplish what they want in life.

We are out in the world everyday interacting with people.

The Nonissue of Socialization

Ellen is very familiar with the socialization question. She's puzzled that people think of public school as the "real" world. "It's silly," says Ellen. "This is the world; we all live in it." Ellen believes there are many aspects of traditional schooling that work against healthy socialization, such as age segregation, competition, and the near exclusive focus on academic subjects.

> My children, and other homeschoolers I know, interact with people of all ages. In my family we have to adjust to each individual on a daily basis. There is an awareness of differences, a give and take. The older children help the younger ones and this develops compassion and understanding. Multi-age socializing is a very natural, real world practice that children in traditional schools don't experience. Homeschoolers have more time to socialize too. We are out in the world everyday interacting with people. And the children have time to play with their friends because they're not burdened with afterschool programs and homework.

Ellen goes on to say that cooperation, which she defines as working together for the common good, is not fostered in traditional schools. "How does putting children in a very competitive environment, where the emphasis is on individual achievement, promote social harmony? What are we teaching children when we socialize them in this way?" But Ellen believes that one of the biggest advantages of homeschooling for socializing children is the cultural opportunities it can provide. "The things that we share in our culture, like art and music, are the things that socialize us. This is where we come together as a society. And this is what's being eliminated from public schools."

Ellen's son, Aidan, has decided to start public high school next fall. She's not worried about how he will cope. "This is what *he* wants. He's motivated to be a part of this experience and he's a creative problem solver. He has the skills to overcome whatever challenges he meets."

I'm doing things that really interest me, and that's the cardinal difference.

Fulfillment and Happiness

Elisa is a lively, articulate 15-year-old girl who has been homeschooled for the past year. She is a veteran of the Popcorn School, a parent cooperative pre-K and kindergarten, a public school, and a private school. When the homework started piling up in middle school, Elisa's mother suggested homeschooling. Elisa resisted, fearing she'd become a social outcast. By 8th grade, then in private school, Elisa was doing six hours of homework a night. She was overwhelmed, sleep-deprived, and wanted a break. Desperate, her worries about being a social outcast faded. "I didn't care if I ever saw my friends again." But it took meeting a group of homeschooled children for Elisa to get excited about what she was about to begin. Describing her reaction to a dramatic production that she attended staged by homeschooled children, Elisa said, "These are homeschooled kids and they are happy and they are doing this incredible production. I never looked back." . . .

Elisa told me that she has wanted to write a novel ever since she could say the word "novel." She's writing one now, and studying herbs and medicine. "I'm doing things that really interest me, and that's the cardinal difference. I'm getting to do things that I wouldn't have been able to do in school, things that will help me in my career path and in my life." Elisa also studies French, geography, mathematics, and English. She has two voice teachers and a dance teacher. Elisa and her mother have written a play, a parody of regular school that is currently in production. "It's the most surreal thing about homeschooling. You don't expect to be able to write a play and see actors voicing the words you wrote. It's unbelievably heart-warming and jaw-dropping at the same time."

Did her fears about her social status prove true? Elisa laughs.

> "There are so many misconceptions about homeschoolers, that they're nerds, they're isolated. If you take any class, you'll meet people. But when you choose the classes you take you meet people who are mutually interested, and you come together in a way that you can't in school because in school it's forced down your throat. The people I've met in these classes are friendships I've kept."

Elisa expresses her belief that holistic education is the natural way to learn and that experiential learning is its essence. "Actually getting to touch and feel what you are learning is what's missing in the public schools." She is so wonderfully alive and enthusiastic that I asked Elisa to say more about happiness. She replied:

> This might sound odd, but once when I was little I was at the grocery store with my Dad, I saw this organic milk and on the carton it said, "From happy cows, on happy farms." I

begged my Dad to buy that milk, and I could taste the difference. In schools kids are not naturally grown; they don't develop naturally. They can't tell happy from sad; they are fed emotions. It was a nightmare that I couldn't wake up from. Now I feel real. I feel this is what life should be like. I have never been more fulfilled and genuinely happy. . . .

The World as a Classroom

The stereotype of the isolated, misfit homeschooler is giving way as, in growing numbers, homeschoolers make the world their classroom. It appears that homeschoolers spend more time in their communities and have meaningful interactions with a wider variety of people than traditionally schooled children typically do. Perhaps this accounts, at least in part, for the empirical findings that suggest that parents who educate their children at home are doing a good job socializing them. In one study, Brian Ray of the National Home Education Research Institute surveyed over 7,300 adults who had been homeschooled, most for at least seven years. Ray found that homeschool graduates were significantly more involved in community and civic affairs, such as volunteering and working for political candidates, than were traditionally schooled adults. They also voted and attended public meetings at higher rates. Over 74% of the young adults surveyed had taken college classes compared to 46% of the traditionally schooled population. The overwhelming majority was gainfully employed or attending college. 98% of the homeschool graduates had read at least one book in the six months prior to the study, compared to 69% of the comparison group. Ray's study demonstrated that adult homeschoolers are happier and find life more exciting than their traditionally schooled peers. Other studies have concluded that homeschooled children are not socially isolated, that their self-concept, a barometer of socialization, tends to be better than traditionally schooled children, and that homeschooling fosters leadership skills at least as well as traditional schooling.

The British pediatrician and psychoanalyst D.W. Winnicott cautioned that there is a price to pay for education that neglects children's emotional and imaginative capacities. We can measure it, he said, "in terms of the loss of the opportunity for creative learning, as opposed to being taught." Creative learning is connected to Winnicott's concept of creative living, which he considers the foundation of health and happiness. He says, "In creative living you or I find that everything we do strengthens the feeling that we are alive, that we are ourselves." When children learn creatively, they retain a personal, self-directed sense of purpose that is unmistakably their own. And this can be measured in enthusiasm and vitality. The homeschoolers that I met are learning and living creatively.... Homeschooling represents a real alternative to traditional public education, as well as to the ideology of consumerism, conformity, and competition that permeates our increasingly standardized educational institutions.

Homeschooling Is a Widely Misunderstood Movement

Rachel Gathercole

Rachel Gathercole is a homeschooling advocate, teacher, speaker, and author whose book The Well-Adjusted Child: The Social Benefits of Homeschooling *was released in 2007.*

We're all familiar with the popular images of homeschoolers in America: Extreme fundamentalist families shutting out all other points of view. Tired mothers teaching in front of a blackboard after late nights of preparing lesson plans, or perhaps stumbling recklessly through unfamiliar subject matter they are not qualified to teach. Lonely, friendless children sitting at home, wistfully dreaming of an exciting, lively social life at school. Or worse, isolated little misfits tragically unaware that an outside world even exists.

These stereotypes are touted freely by the popular media and conventional schooling experts alike. We have probably all imagined them ourselves at one time or another. But they have little to do with the realities of homeschooling for most families today, and are rarely backed by factual data.

But even when we ignore these stereotypes and look to the news media for answers, it is hard to sort out what homeschooling is. The things we are told about it and the images portrayed are often contradictory and/or downright sensationalized. The mass media tell us on one hand that homeschoolers excel, and on the other hand that they are underregulated. One minute we hear that it is hard for homeschoolers to get into college, and the next minute that they are going to Harvard. We are told that homeschooling is

Rachel Gathercole, "Homeschooling's True Colors: Examining the Myths and the Facts About America's Fastest-Growing Educational Movement," *Mothering*, July/August 2005, Reproduced by permission of the author.

difficult and requires an incredible degree of sacrifice by parents, yet the number of parents choosing to homeschool is skyrocketing.

Just what is the truth about homeschooling? The hard facts might surprise you.

Homeschooling Is Prevalent

Below are some common myths about homeschooling, and the simple facts behind this widely misunderstood movement.

Myth:

Homeschooling is a fringe movement, less prevalent than advocates suggest.

Fact:

The US Census Bureau reports that in 2001, more than 2 million children were being homeschooled in the US alone, and the number is rising at the astounding rate of 15 to 20 percent per year.[1]

Patricia M. Lines, the foremost homeschooling expert in the US Department of Education, further notes (in 1999) that since some families homeschool for only part of their children's school years, the number of children with some homeschooling experience, by age 18, would be around 6 to 12 percent of the population.[2] The percentage would be greater today.

Demographically speaking, the homeschooling population comprises families of all socioeconomic groups, religions, sizes, political affiliations, family structures, and ethnicities.[3-6] Statistically, homeschooling families tend to be large, conservative, white, two-parent families, and the average homeschooling parent has a moderate to high level of income and education.[7-10] However, according to the US Census Bureau, differences between homeschooling families and conventional-schooling families are not very large, and the demographic gap appears to be narrowing.[11]

Religion Is Only One Reason

Myth:

Homeschooling is a primarily religious phenomenon.

Fact:

According to the US Census Bureau and other sources, in 2000 only 33 percent of homeschooling parents cited religion as a reason for homeschooling (and many of these parents cited other reasons as well). On the other hand, 50.8 percent cited a belief that their children could get a better education through homeschooling, while 29.8 percent stated that school offers a poor learning environment, and 11.5 percent said that their children were not being challenged in school.[12]

According to the US Census Bureau ... only 33 percent of homeschooling parents cited religion as a reason for homeschooling.

Statistics that correctly state that the majority of home-schoolers in America identify themselves as Christian should not be mistaken for evidence that homeschooling is a religiously based phenomenon. The vast majority of Americans in general identify themselves as Christians—85 percent in 2003, according to a Gallup poll—so it is no surprise that the majority of both homeschoolers and conventional schoolers also identify themselves as Christian.[13–16] Some families choose homeschool, private school, or public school for religious reasons, and some homeschooling families are religious fundamentalists, just as some non-homeschooling families are. Like the general population, the homeschooling population comprises families of all religions, as well as many families who would classify themselves as agnostic, atheist, or unaffiliated with any established religion.[17]

Homeschoolers Excel Academically

Myth:

Homeschooled children are undereducated.

Fact:

Numerous studies of homeschoolers' achievement show that homeschoolers score exceptionally well on standardized tests, with the average/median homeschool students outperforming at least 70 to 80 percent of their conventionally schooled peers in all subjects and at all grade levels.[18,19] Studies also show that the longer a student is homeschooled, the higher his or her test scores become.[20] In addition, homeschoolers have been described as "dominating" national contests, such as the national spelling and geography bees, and are now sought by many colleges.[21−26]

Numerous studies of homeschoolers' achievement show that homeschoolers score exceptionally well on standardized tests.

Teaching Methods Vary

Myth:

Most homeschoolers learn through a formal curriculum, taught to them by their parents (for example, at the kitchen table).

Fact:

Homeschoolers learn through a variety of methods, which may include some teaching by the parent, as well as self-directed projects, real-life activities (such as gardening, cooking, sports, volunteer activities, etc.), free play, independent reading, group classes with other homeschoolers, cooperative learning experiences with other families, field trips and outings as a family or with a homeschooling group, and social activities and gatherings.[27−31] The majority of homeschooling families do not purchase prepackaged curriculums but instead use some individually created combination of the above methods determined by the parent and/or child to suit the child's individual needs and learning style.[32]

Homeschoolers also employ a wide range of overall approaches and philosophies, from "school-at-home" approaches that match the popular image, to (perhaps most common) an eclectic approach in which the family selects materials and activities according to the children's needs at the time, to unschooling—"delight-driven" or "child-led" learning in which the child learns all necessary material through pursuing his or her own interests in a real-world setting, with a parent available to help, answer questions, and direct the child to resources.[33–36] Those who engage in formal lessons do so to varying degrees: one family might purchase and adhere to a full curriculum, while another might devise a complete or partial curriculum of their own using alternative methods and focus; still another might reserve formal lessons for a particular subject area, such as math.[37–40]

As new and varied as these methods may sound, all are effective methods for home educating. Dr. Lawrence M. Rudner, in an independent study of more than 20,000 homeschoolers, found that though homeschoolers tend not to use prepackaged curriculum programs, they nevertheless score "exceptionally high" on standardized tests, ranking typically in the 70th to 80th percentile (compared to the national average of the 50th percentile). "It is readily apparent . . . that the median scores for home school students are well above their public/private school counterparts in every subject and in every grade," regardless of the presence or absence of formal curriculum use,[41] says Rudner. Homeschooled students, regardless of teaching method, have gone on to attend Ivy League universities. According to an article in *Stanford Magazine*, "among homeschoolers who end up at Stanford, 'self-teaching' is a common thread."[42,43]

The Socialization Issue

Myth:

Homeschoolers are "stuck at home."

Fact:

Per week, the average homeschooled child participates in at least five outside activities, such as sports teams, scouts, clubs, classes in the community, volunteer activities, etc.[44] Some (about 18 percent) participate in public school part-time.[45] Many homeschooling parents are also very involved in their communities—volunteering, attending or teaching classes, pursuing part-time or full-time careers, operating family businesses, and/or developing close friendships with other homeschooling families.[46,47] Homeschooling parents and children, free of externally imposed school schedules, are in charge of their time and are free to come and go as they please. Homeschooling enables family members to be very involved in outside activities without sacrificing their time together to do so.

Homeschooling enables family members to be very involved in outside activities without sacrificing their time together to do so.

Myth:

Homeschooling deprives children of proper socialization.

Fact:

Homeschooling affords children plenty of time and opportunity for social interaction and friendships, as well as time to learn appropriate social behaviors from their parents. The available research shows that homeschoolers tend to be very well adjusted. In 1986, even before the rapid growth in the homeschooling movement that we are seeing today, social researcher John Wesley Taylor V found that the self-concept of homeschooled children was significantly higher than that of their traditionally schooled peers when tested using the widely accepted Piers-Harris Children's Self-Concept Scale. Among his conclusions was the statement that "it would appear that few home-schooling children are socially deprived. Critics of the home school should not urge self-concept and socialization rationales. These factors apparently favor homeschoolers over the conventionally schooled population."[48]

More recently, psychotherapist Dr. Larry Shyers, in a study involving "blind" observation of the behavior of homeschooled and conventionally schooled children, found that home-schooled children exhibited significantly fewer "problem behaviors" than their conventionally sohooled peers and had no significant difference in levels of self-esteem.[49] Thomas Smedley, studying communication skills, socialization, and daily living skills through the Vineland Adaptive Behavior Scales, concluded that homeschooled kids in his study were more mature and better socialized than the conventionally schooled.[50] And finally, in a survey of adults who had been homeschooled for at least seven years, Dr. Brian D. Ray found that 59 percent said they were "very happy" with life, while only 27.6 percent of the general population said they were "very happy" with life.[51]

Homeschooled children exhibited significantly fewer "problem behaviors" . . . and had no significant difference in level of self-esteem.

Due to the excellent teacher-student ratio that home-schoolers enjoy and the lack of time-consuming administrative tasks such as attendance taking, busywork, etc., the academic aspects of homeschooling require only a fraction of the time necessary for the same tasks in a conventional school setting, leaving lots of extra time for social activities. Not limited by strict "school hours" and brief interactions in the hall, homeschooled children are often found instead spending long days at the park with friends, gathering with other kids for group activities, sleeping over at each other's houses on week-nights or weekends, and enjoying long conversations with their parents and siblings.[52,53] Homeschooled children also tend to have both homeschooled and conventionally schooled friends, and, like conventionally schooled children, they can and do play with neighborhood children and participate in scouts, 4H, church groups, community bands, orchestras, and sports groups, as well as outside classes such as dance and martial arts.[54–56] Many homeschooling parents consider their children's social learning to be as integral a part of their education as academic subjects, and they are careful to provide their children with both social skills and opportunities to use them.

Myth:

Homeschoolers are insulated from the real world, democracy, and diversity.

Fact:

Homeschooling families live and learn in the real world (see methods outlined above), typically interacting with real people of various ages and backgrounds on a real-world basis rather than just with peers in a classroom. They have time and proximity to observe firsthand the social and political activities of their parents, who, according to Patricia M. Lines's report in the *ERIC Digest*, "are more likely to vote, contribute money to political causes, contact elected officials about their views, attend public meetings or rallies, or join community and volunteer associations" than are the parents of conventionally schooled children.[57] "This holds true even when researchers compare only families with similar characteristics, including education, age, race, family structure, geographic region, and number of hours worked per week."[58] Moreover, homeschoolers are a diverse population (see above) and often have lots of freedom to travel to diverse locations for both educational and social purposes.

Achievement Is an Outcome

Myth:

Homeschoolers have a hard time applying for, getting into, and adjusting to college.

Fact:

College admissions officers now seek out homeschoolers due to their excellent preparation for academic success at college. An article in *Stanford Magazine* indicates that Stanford has a "special interest" in homeschoolers, and is "eager to embrace them" despite their lack of formal credentials. "The distinguishing factor is intellectual vitality," says Dr. Jonathan Reider, a former senior associate director of undergraduate admissions at Stanford and a national expert on college-bound homeschoolers. "These kids have it, and everything they do is responding to it."[59] David and Micki Colfax, authors of the well-known book *Homeschooling for Excellence*, homeschooled four sons, three of whom attended Harvard.[60] These are just a few examples; Karl M. Bundaya's well-known website (www.learninfreedom.org) lists more than 1,000 colleges and universities, including Ivy League schools and many other very selective and prestigious schools, that have readily admitted homeschoolers.[61]

Myth:

Parents without teaching certificates, college degrees, and so on are not qualified to teach their children.

Fact:

Rudner's large study (mentioned earlier) found that there is "no significant difference" in homeschoolers' achievement according to whether or not a parent is certified to teach. "For those who would argue that only certified teachers should be allowed to teach their children at home, these findings suggest that such a requirement would not meaningfully affect student achievement."[62] Another study, by Dr. Brian Ray, similarly found that while homeschooled students scored on average in the 76th percentile or higher in reading, language, and math, children of certified teachers had no advantage over children whose parents were not certified teachers.[63]

The Issue of Regulation

Myth:

Greater government regulation is needed to make homeschooling a more viable or valid option.

Fact:

There is plenty of evidence that increased regulation is unnecessary for homeschoolers. In addition to the studies cited above showing that teacher certification and use of a formal curriculum are not relevant factors in homeschoolers' achievement, a study of more than 5,000 students from 1,657 families found that homeschoolers score very high on standardized tests, even when their state does not highly regulate.[64]

Keeping in mind that the average homeschooled student appears to exceed the achievement of her or his average conventionally schooled peer, it is illogical to impose curriculum or other requirements aimed at making homeschooling more school-like or requiring homeschools to adhere to the standards of public or conventional schools. Such regulations would be superfluous and could potentially lower the level of achievement by removing the freedom and flexibility that make homeschooling so effective.

Myth:

Homeschooling is associated with neglect and abuse.

Fact:

There is no evidence that homeschoolers are at higher risk for neglect or abuse than publicly or privately schooled children.[65] In fact, there is reason to believe that neglect and abuse are actually less common in homeschool situations.[66,67] Moreover, 85 percent of child fatalities occur in children younger than six years of age, before children begin their formal schooling in any form.[68]

Effect on Public Schools

Myth:

Homeschooling is a threat to the public schools. Home-schoolers abandon or "suck the life out of" public schools in their choice to homeschool.

Fact:

Homeschoolers and public schools are, in many ways, boons to one another. By removing their children from public schools, homeschoolers inadvertently help the schools by relieving overcrowding and freeing up resources for other students while still paying the taxes that fund public education. In this way, homeschoolers actually save taxpayers millions of dollars per year.[69] To put it another way, every child who is homeschooled opens up a free seat in a classroom for another child. In this sense, every time 3 to 10 new taxpaying families (or about 20 new homeschooled kids) choose to homeschool, it is as if a new teacher has been hired for the public schools at no cost to taxpayers. Thus the growth of homeschooling is the equivalent of a host of new, high-achieving schools being built to relieve overcrowding and reduce class size at no expense to taxpayers.

Moreover, it is private schools, not public schools, that appear to bear the true brunt of reduced enrollment. While enrollment in public schools and home schools continues to grow with the population, enrollment in private schools remains stagnant.[70] In other words, it appears statistically that the majority of homeschooling parents would otherwise be sending their children to private school, not public school. Finally, it has been noted that educators in conventional schooling situations stand to learn much from homeschoolers, who are conducting field research on education that can never be conducted in a school setting, even as they educate their kids very successfully. As the late educator John Holt commented: "It is a research project done at no cost, of a kind for which neither the public schools nor the government could afford to pay."[71] He also wrote: "From these people and their work, all serious schools and teachers, many of them now severely limited and handicapped by the conditions under which they have to work, stand to learn a great deal."[72]

Whatever images pass through the media and popular culture, the facts of homeschooling ultimately speak for themselves. As more and more homeschoolers grow up and become adult citizens, perceptions of homeschoolers will gradually change, but the facts will remain the same. Although it is understandable that perceptions and fears exist, there is a reason that homeschooling is growing at the rate it is. There is a reason that so many educated parents are choosing it despite popular stereotypes and assumptions. The reason is simple: In the face of fact, those muddled images are cleanly washed away by homeschooling's true colors.

Flying colors.

Homeschooling's True Colors: Notes

Issue 131

1. Kurt J. Bauman, "Home Schooling in the United States: Trends and Characteristics," Working Paper Series 51 (Washington, DC: US Census Bureau Population Division, 2001): 2.

2. Patricia M. Lines, "Homeschoolers: Estimating Numbers and Growth," National Institute on Student Achievement, Curriculum, and Assessment, Office of Educational Research and Improvement, US Department of Education, Web Edition (Spring 1999; previously released as a paper in Spring 1998): www.ed.gov/offices/OERI/SAI/homeschool/index.html

3. Personal interviews.

4. Lawrence M. Rudner, "Scholastic Achievement and Demographic Characteristics of Home School Students in

1998," HSLDA (1999): www.hslda.org/docs/study/
rudner1999/FullText.asp www.hslda.org/docs/study/
rudner1999/Rudner2.asp www.hslda.org/docs/study/
rudner1999/Rudner2.asp

5. Stacey Bielick et al., "Homeschooling in the United
   States: 1999," NCES Technical Report (Washington,
   DC: US Department of Education, National Center for
   Education Statistics, 2001): 2001–2033; http://nces.ed
   .gov/programs/quarterly/vol_3/3_3/q3-2.asp

6. See Note 1: 6–13

7. See Note 5.

8. Robin R. Henke et al., "Issues Related to Estimating the
   Home Schooled Population in the United States,"
   NCES Technical Report (Washington, DC: US Department of Education, National Center for Education Statistics, 2000): 2001–2311; http://nces.ed.gov/pubsearch/
   pubsinfo.asp?pubid=2000311

9. See Note 4.

10. See Note 6.

11. See Note 1: 10.

12. See Note 1: 8–13.

13. Lydia Saad, "Religion Is Very Important to Majority of
    Americans," Gallup News Service, World Wide Reli-
    gious News (5 December 2003): http://209.157.64.200/
    focus/f-news/1034289/posts

14. Egon Mayer et al., "American Religious Identification
    Survey" (New York: Graduate Center of the City Uni-
    versity of New York, 2001): www.gc.cuny.edu/studies/
    aris_index.htm

15. "Religious Beliefs of Americans" (2004): www
    .religioustolerance.org/chr_poll3.htm

16. "Beliefs: General Religious" (2005): www.barna.org/
    FlexPage.aspx?Page=Topic&TopicID=2

17. Patricia M. Lines, "Homeschooling," ERIC Digest (Oregon: Clearinghouse on Educational Management, College of Education, University of Oregon, September 2001): 2.

18. See Note 4.

19. Brian D. Ray, Home Schooling on the Threshold: A Survey of Research at the Dawn of the New Millennium (Salem, OR: National Home Education Research Institute, 1999).

20. Brian D. Ray, Strengths of their Own: Home Schoolers Across America (Salem, OR: NHERI, 1997).

21. Vaishali Honawar, "National 'Bees' Buzz with Home Schoolers," The Washington Times (21 May 2002).

22. Dean Reynolds, "Home Schoolers Strong Competitors in Spelling Bee," www.abcnews.com (29 May 2003): 1–2.

23. Rich Jefferson, "Home Schoolers Win First, Second, and Third at National Spelling Bee" (2001): 1–2; www.hslda.org/docs/news/hslda/200006010.asp

24. Jennifer Vernon, "Washington State Eighth Grader Wins National Geographic Bee," National Geographic News (21 May 2003): 1–4.

25. Jennifer Vernon, "Ten Students Advance to Geographic Bee Finals," National Geographic News (20 May 2003): 1–6.

26. Stentor Danielson, "Geographic Bee Champ: Michigan Ten-Year-Old," National Geographic News (22 May 2002): 1–5.

27. See Note 3.

28. Christine Foster, "In a Class by Themselves,"Stanford Magazine (November/December 2000): 1–11.

29. Grace Llewellyn, The Teenage Liberation Handbook: How to Quit School and Get a Real Life and Education (Eugene, OR: Lowry House Publishers, 1998).

30. David Guterson, Family Matters: Why Homeschooling Makes Sense (New York: Harcourt, Brace, Jovanovich, 1992): 11–36.

31. David and Micki Colfax, Homeschooling for Excellence (New York: Warner Books, 1988).

32. See Note 4.

33. See Note 29.

34. John Holt, Teach Your Own: A Hopeful Path for Education (New York: Bantam/Doubleday/Dell, 1981): 125–146, 208–232.

35. See Note 28: 7.

36. See Note 3.

37. See Note 29.

38. See Note 34.

39. See Note 28: 7.

40. See Note 3.

41. See Note 4.

42. See Note 31.

43. See Note 28: 7.

44. See Note 19.

45. See Note 5.

46. See Note 3.

47. See Note 17: 3.

48. John Wesley Taylor V, Self Concept in Home-Schooling Children, doctoral dissertation (Michigan: Andrews University, 1986); summarized in Home School Researcher 2, no. 2 (1986): 2–8.

49. Larry E. Shyers, Comparison of Social Adjustment Between Home and Traditionally Schooled Students, doctoral dissertation (Gainesville: University of Florida, 1992): 306–311.

50. Thomas C. Smedley, "The Socialization of Homeschool Children," master's thesis (Radford, VA: Radford University, 1992); summarized in Home School Researcher 8, no. 3 (1992): 9–16.

51. See Note 19.

52. See Note 3.

53. See Note 29: 138–149.

54. See Note 3.

55. See Note 19.

56. See Note 5.

57. See Note 17.

58. See Note 17.

59. See Note 28: 2–11.

60. See Note 31.

61. Karl M. Bunday, Learn in Freedom! (2000): http://learninfreedom.org/colleges_4_hmsc.html

62. See Note 4

63. See Note 19.

64. See Note 20.

65. National Home Education Network, "Thoughts on Protecting Children in Homeschooling Families: The NHEN Response to Questions Posed by the North Carolina Task Force of Child Fatalities" (2002): www.nhen.org/LegInfo/default.asp?id=420

66. National Clearinghouse on Child Abuse and Neglect Information, "Child Maltreatment 2001: Summary of Key Findings" (2001): http://nrcys.ou.edu/pdfs/publications/cmsummary.pdf and http://nccanch.acf.hhs.gov/pubs/factsheets/canstats.pdf

67. J. Michael Smith, "CBS Scare Stories Miss the Mark Badly"The Washington Times (3 November 2003).

Posted as "The Dark Side of CBS"at www.hslda.org/docs/news/washingtontimes/200311040.asp

68. See Note 66.

69. Ray, Brian D. National Home Education Research Institute, "Facts on Homeschooling" (8 January 2003): www.nheri.org/modules.php?name=Content&pa=show page&pid=21, 1.

70. Patricia M. Lines, "Homeschooling Comes of Age," The Public Interest, Discovery Institute (1 July 2000): 2, www.discovery.org/scripts/viewDB/index.php?program =Misc&command=view&id=277

71. John Holt, "Schools and Homeschoolers: A Fruitful Partnership," Phi Delta Kappan (February 1983): 393.

72. See Note 34: 330–331.

Homeschoolers Are Excelling

Andrea Neal

Andrea Neal is an eighth-grade English and history teacher at St. Richard's School in Indianapolis, Indiana, and an adjunct scholar with the Indiana Policy Review, a nonprofit education foundation focused on state and municipal issues.

Excelling in and out of the home, home-schooled kids are thriving across the country. Students demonstrating exceptional academic honors are capturing the top slots at national competitions.

Recognized for Achievement

It wasn't so long ago that home-schoolers like Johanna Schilling, Jonathan Gainer and Eli Owens were oddballs in the education landscape. Not anymore.

You name the contest—National Spelling Bee, National Geographic Bee, National Merit Scholarship—and chances are good that home-school kids have participated, performed with distinction, and won. These days, headlines of academic achievement are as likely to feature home-schooled children as their peers from traditional public and private school settings. Perhaps just as noteworthy, nobody's jaw drops when it happens.

[In 2006], four home-schooled students were named semifinalists in the Presidential Scholars competition, which recognizes the nation's most distinguished high-school graduates. The honor served notice of two important trends: one, home-schoolers have entered the mainstream of academic achievement; two, they're being recognized for it.

Home-Schoolers Win Prestigious Awards

Stories abound of home-schoolers' success:

At 17, Johanna was recognized as the first home-school winner of a $40,000 Ruth DeYoung Kohler Scholarship for Artistic Merit in her home state of Wisconsin. She will use the money to pursue her studies at the Houghton College school of music in New York.

> *It's not surprising that a home-schooler gets much better academic results. There's just no way around the structure.*

Eli, 19, a home-school graduate who attends West Virginia University, was named a 2006–2007 Goldwater Scholar. He was one of 323 college students nationally to receive the award, established by Congress to encourage advanced studies by select sophomores and juniors who excel in math, science and engineering.

Jonathan, 14, was the first home-schooler picked for the Kelley Junior Executive Institute, a summer program at Indiana University that identifies 50 high-achieving, primarily minority high-school students interested in studying business. Note that he's the age of a typical eighth grader, yet he's already completed Algebra II.

These stories are just the tip of the iceberg. In 2005, a home-schooler won the National Geographic Bee. Home-schoolers swept the first three spots in the 2000 National Spelling Bee. In 2003, the latest year for which figures are available, a record 129 home-schoolers were named National Merit Scholars, an increase of more than 600 percent over 1995. The estimated 1.8 million home-schoolers—out of 54 million children in kindergarten through high school—seem to be achieving honors disproportionate to their numbers.

Structure Makes a Difference

"It's not surprising that a home-schooler gets much better academic results. There's just no way around the structure," says Ian Slatter, director of media relations for the Home School Legal Defense Association in Virginia.

Yes, structure matters. Although it varies by family, the typical home-school consists of one parent teaching one or more children in the home. But not just in the home. Home-schoolers take field trips and visit museums and libraries. They network with other home-school families. They use books and curricula that reflect their own academic and religious values, yet align closely enough to state academic standards that students are prepared for standardized tests, which some states require. In a home-school, the teacher-student ratio for any given lesson is 1:1 or 1:2. Not even an elite private school, where class size is capped at 6 or 18, can rival that.

The structure works especially well in the elementary years as students are mastering math and reading skills that will be the foundation for later learning. When course work grows more complex, many home-school families contract with experts to teach their children more advanced subjects, sometimes pooling resources to create small classrooms not too different from a traditional school.

Because of structure and flexibility, the typical home-school student can complete graduation requirements by age 16.

Flexibility Is Key to Success

It's the flexibility that so many home-schooling families lift up as the key ingredient. In home-school, parents can quickly identify a student's areas of strength and weakness, offering enrichment opportunities for the former and focused attention on the latter.

Those with a gift for music can take instrument lessons or catch a symphony matinee when their traditional classmates are in school. Johanna, for example, spent up to three hours a day practicing piano for 10 years. Computer whizzes can seek out apprenticeships with nearby businesses; those who love sports can finish their workout in the morning before the YMCA gets crowded.

Because of structure and flexibility, the typical home-school student can complete graduation requirements by age 16. As a result, some go to college early; many enroll in local community colleges until their parents deem them ready to live on a campus with older students. . . .

Growth of Home-Schooling as an Option

Although evangelical Christians remain the single biggest group in the home-schooling movement, they are by no means the only ones. In her book *Homeschoolers' Success Stories*, Linda Dobson notes that "families from every conceivable religious, economic, political, and philosophical background in the United States" have realized the benefits to home-schooling.

"This wave has been impelled by home-schooling's greater visibility as an educational option; local, state, and national home-schooling support groups; easy networking and information sharing via the Internet and e-mail; and continuing government-school problems, such as dumbed-down curriculum, violence, drugs, bullying, and more," she writes. . . .

What has changed is public understanding and acceptance of the home-school phenomenon. The percentage of those feeling that home-schooling is a "bad thing" dropped from 73 percent in 1985 to 57 percent in 1997, according to a Phi Delta Kappa (PDK)/Gallup poll. In a 1999 poll, PDK asked if public schools should make services available to children who are schooled at home, and a surprising number of respondents said yes. The numbers ranged from a high of 92 percent for special education courses for disabled or handicapped children to a low of 53 percent for transportation services.

There are critics, to be sure, including members of the National Education Association, the powerful teachers' union. . . .

Data Supports Home-Schoolers

The data, however, are on the home-schoolers' side.

In the most significant study to date, "Scholastic Achievement and Demographic Characteristics of Home School Students in 1998," researcher Lawrence M. Rudner made the following findings:

- Almost 25 percent of home-school students are enrolled one or more grades above their age-level peers in public and private schools.

- Home-school student achievement test scores are exceptionally high. The median scores for every subtest at every grade (typically in the 70th to 80th percentile) are well above those of public and Catholic/private school students.

- On average, home-school students in grades one to four perform one grade level above their age-level public or private school peers on achievement tests.

- The achievement test score gap between home-school students and public or private school students starts to widen in grade five.

- Students who have been home-schooled their entire academic life have higher scholastic-achievement test scores than students who have also attended other educational programs.

Smaller studies have affirmed the findings, and Slatter says his organization hopes to do an updated achievement study in the near future. . . .

Yes, home-schools have entered the mainstream of America's educational system, and their students intend to compete with the best and brightest in the country.

Homeschooling Is Not for Everyone

Carole Moore

Carole Moore is a former law enforcement officer and writer based in Jacksonville, North Carolina.

I became interested in homeschooling a few years ago when a friend told me how much she loved it. A former cop turned writer, I approached the editor at the newspaper where I worked and convinced him to let me write a series on the topic. I interviewed dozens of homeschooling parents and students. All told, including the work on the series plus my own follow-up research, I spent over a year studying the possibility and debating whether learning at home would be best for my kids—a daughter, then age 10, and a son, age 8.

I learned that many families homeschooled because they didn't like the secular curriculum. Others complained that classes were dumbed down, which caused boredom and restlessness in bright students. A lot chose to remove their kids from what they perceived as an unhealthy social atmosphere. All were convinced they'd done the right thing.

They explained the differences in the types of homeschooling to me: Some followed rigorous religious-based curricula, while others used the same materials as their public schools. A few, called unschoolers, followed nothing but their hearts and let the kids themselves pick what they wanted to study. Many bartered with other parents on subjects requiring special expertise, such as trading French instruction for piano lessons.

The kids' education seemed balanced and academically sound, but most appealing was the bond they shared with their parents. My own daughter, anxious to grow up, nibbled at her ties to me, with her younger brother fast on her heels. I wondered if homeschooling could bring us closer.

Some of the most troubled kids I dealt with came from homes where they'd been very sheltered.

Still, as I spoke with homeschooling families from one coast to the other, certain troubling questions bubbled to the surface—many of them familiar to me from my days in law enforcement.

Our community is nowhere near a major city. Still my children went to elementary school with a girl whose father committed suicide in her presence, kids with both parents in prison, and youngsters who couldn't read, yet knew all the words to filthy rap songs. As a police officer, I often dealt with adolescent drug dealers, pregnant teens, and runaways—kids whose lives were out of control. Certainly the largest majority of them were enrolled in public schools, but not all. Some of the most troubled kids I dealt with came from homes where they'd been very sheltered.

I remember one teenager in particular. After years of alternately being homeschooled and attending a very strict, small, church-based school, she moved to a public school—where she spiraled out of control. She drank. She took drugs. And she had sex. Her parents were appalled; that was not how they'd raised their daughter.

Some would blame the influence of the public school system. They'd say she made friends with bad kids. And they'd be right. But that wasn't the only reason she got into so much trouble. In my opinion, her problem went much deeper: she didn't know how to handle the sudden combination of freedom and exposure to a side of life she'd never personally confronted. Her parents had talked about these things. She'd heard about them in church. But talk alone isn't a substitute for reality, and the forbidden often looms sweet and tantalizing by virtue of its mystery.

Academics form only part of the equation when it comes to teaching life skills. Kids need to know how to write a persuasive essay, but they also should learn about real life and, in the process, develop the skills they need to cope with it.

We can't raise our children in carefully controlled environments and expect them to instinctively know how to handle evil.

My daughter, who now attends a public high school, has made good choices in both her academic and social lives so far. We've talked about sex, but nothing I've ever said to her has provided as strong a deterrent to casual, early sex as the girl in her class with the ever-expanding belly. Nothing makes my daughter more aware of the effects of drugs than seeing burnt-out kids. And nothing brings home the consequences of drinking and driving than the empty seat of a boy who did just that.

They're tough lessons, but ones she will never forget. Seeing the aftermath of negative behavior with her own eyes impresses her much more than simple words or even our own good examples.

Do I like that my children are exposed to life's underbelly? Of course not. I'd much prefer to bring them up in an atmosphere of innocence and trust. But we can't raise our children in carefully controlled environments and expect them to instinctively know how to handle evil. Pretending that it doesn't exist won't make it go away.

Homeschooling would have built a wall around my kids and kept them safe—for a little while. Ultimately, they would have had to go out into the real world. Public school has exposed them to bad influences as well as good ones. I believe they're stronger for having had to make tough choices. And going through it together has strengthened our relationship, making it easier for me to start letting go of their hands.

CHAPTER 3

Should Homeschooling Be Regulated?

Chapter Preface

In February 2008, a California appellate court ruled that parents in that state must have a teaching credential to homeschool their children. After declaring that homeschooling was not a constitutional right, the judge went on to warn that instructors teaching without credentials would be subject to criminal action. Uncredentialed parents who did not provide a credentialed tutor or send their children to a public or private school that requires daily attendance could be prosecuted for truancy, as well as lose custody. The ruling, one of the most controversial in recent years, made most homeschooling in the state illegal and shocked and angered the homeschooling community nationwide. Many supporters of homeschooling viewed the ruling as an outright attack on the very idea of homeschooling.

At the time of the ruling, California was considered a state with low regulation for homeschooling. It offered four legal homeschooling options: (1) qualifying as a private school, (2) using a private tutor, (3) enrolling in a private school satellite program, or (4) enrolling in an independent study program offered through a public school. Only those parents who declared their homeschooling program a private school had to provide official notice to the state, and only those parents who chose to teach as a private tutor had to be certified.

The California episode is just one of a number over the years in the ongoing battle over whether homeschools should be subject to government legislation or regulation. Some homeschooling parents are not totally opposed to a small or moderate degree of oversight. Others believe it is their fundamental right to decide what is best for their children and are opposed to any and all homeschooling legislation or regulation. They resist any involvement at the federal, state, or local level and view legislative and regulatory actions as a means for anti-homeschooling supporters to weaken homeschooling or get rid of it entirely.

The National Education Association (NEA), on the other hand, sanctions the idea that parents who teach their own children should be licensed by the state, use a state-approved curriculum, and pay all their own expenses. While not all opponents of homeschooling agree in full with the NEA, most believe strongly that some regulation is necessary to ensure accountability and that homeschooled children should master certain levels before they "graduate."

The issue is a complex one. The general requirements regarding education are laid out at the federal level. But for the most part, the responsibility for public education falls to state and local government, and no two states treat homeschooling in exactly the same way. Homeschooling regulation is a result of compulsory school attendance laws, which vary from state to state. As a result, even though currently about two-thirds of all states have specific laws authorizing and regulating homeschooling, each has different homeschooling regulations. According to the Home School Legal Defense Association (HSLDA), there are four categories of legal options for homeschooling: states requiring no notice, states with low regulation, states with moderate regulation, and states with high regulation.

In the ten states that have no requirements for homeschooling, parents do not even have to notify the state that they are homeschooling their children. This is not to say that these states all have the same regulations beyond no notice. Texas, for example, is a no-notice state. In Texas, a homeschooling family must establish and operate its homeschool as a private school, and the parents must teach grammar, reading, spelling, good citizenship, and math. Indiana is another no-notice state. Indiana does not have any requirements for curricula or formats for math, science, or social studies. It does have a statute that requires home educators to provide an equal program of learning, but there is no enforcement.

In the fourteen states with low regulation, all that parents have to do is notify the state that they are homeschooling their children. In the fifteen states with moderate regulation, parents not only must notify the state of their intent to home-school but also must submit test scores and/or professional evaluation of their children's academic progress. In the eleven states with high regulation, in addition to notifying the state that they are homeschooling their children, parents must sub-mit achievement test scores and/or professional evaluations and fulfill other requirements such as use of state-approved curricula or teacher-certification of parents. In some cases, they must permit home visits by state officials.

States Must Maintain Control and Oversight of Education

Louis A. Greenfield

Louis A. Greenfield is an attorney currently practicing law in New York and New Jersey.

Home-schooling and religious beliefs are a familiar combination. While religious beliefs are not the only reason for home-schooling, it appears that religion plays a significant role in home-schooling programs. At the very least, the topic of home-schooling for religious reasons receives a lot of attention. A primary focus for home-schooled children is religious values. Parents of home-schooled children more and more are challenging the monitoring of their programs by the government, claiming that their religious values are being compromised. . . .

Resisting Government Intrusion

This debate regarding what regulations over home-schooling should be in place, if any, has viewpoints located at two completely opposite ends of the spectrum. At one end, there are those who view education as a compelling interest of the state; perhaps its most compelling interest and primary function. Those with this view would most likely favor more government regulation of home-schooling. On the other end of the spectrum are those who see education as inherently religious in nature. This end of the spectrum would likely, in part, consist of those who home-school their children for religious purposes and object to government monitoring of their home-schooling programs. . . .

As home-schooling became accepted by the courts as a legitimate means of education, home-schooling parents shifted

Louis A. Greenfield, "Religious Home-Schools: That's Not A Monkey On Your Back, It's a Compelling State Interest," *Rutgers Journal of Law and Religion*, vol. 9, Fall 2007, pp. 1–28. Reproduced by permission.

their attention to challenging regulations that monitor these home-schooling programs. Some were successful and some were not. While it is evident that many of these home-schooling parents want the government completely out of the education of their children, I believe that they will most likely not get their way since the state has a duty to enforce a compelling interest in ensuring their citizens are adequately educated. . . .

Some parents believe that it is a God-given right to home-school their children.

It appears that religious reasons [for home-schooling] provoke higher standards of scrutiny. While this trend tends to make the restrictions for religious home-schools more lax than non-secular home-schools, religious home-schools will still be exposed to some regulation and monitoring due to the state's compelling interest in the education of its citizens. These methods of monitoring include standardized testing, teacher certification requirements, and the submission of portfolios used to monitor the progress of the home-schooled children. . . .

Religious Motivation

According to a 1999 survey that asked why parents home-school their children, the top three reasons provided were the following: (1) a better education could be offered at home, (2) religious reasons, and (3) there was a poor learning environment at public school. While, according to this study, the leading reason why parents home-school their children is because the parents believe that they can do a better job than the public system, and often do, a more controversial discussion (and one more relevant to this paper) arises when one explores the religious reasons why children are home-schooled and the issues that arise from such home-schooling programs.

Some parents believe that it is a God-given right to home-school their children. These families tend to live and die by the word of the Bible and try to use this theory as a means of casting out state monitoring from their home-school program. At most, this theory can show that one's religious beliefs are genuine; on its own, it cannot stymie government monitoring. . . .

More extreme religious reasons also motivate parents to home-school their children. Christian Fundamentalists tend to use these more extreme religious reasons for home-schooling. "The main reason these Fundamentalist Christian parents opt out of public schools is their perception that [according to Neal Devins in the 1992 *George Washington Law Review*] the 'secularization of public schools . . . denies their right to oversee the upbringing of their children as they see fit.'" . . . These fundamentalists are, by and large, those who are objecting to state monitoring home-schooling programs. . . .

A parent merely has to receive church backing to begin instruction with little interference from the state.

Regulation Varies by State

So, what reasons do the states provide to justify the monitoring of home educational programs? [As Eric A. DeGroff writes in the 2003 *BYU Journal of Education and Law*,] "States have a substantial interest in ensuring that all children receive an adequate education." As a result of this substantial interest, the states must ensure that [as De Groff writes,] "schools perform their basic educational function and . . . meet certain minimum standards." In the private school context, the state justifies their mandated approval or accreditation to [De Groff continues,] "ensure compliance with its educational standards."

Religious vs. Secular Home-Schooling

In a study on education statutes in Alabama, the regulation of home-schooling in the United States is categorized into a number of distinct approaches. One of these approaches [comments William L. Campbell Jr. in the Winter 2001 *Alabama Law Review*,] "involves states enacting statutes that expressly allow for home-schooling but also provide for some form of state approval or notification by the parents to the local school board." The strictest of these approaches requires home-school teacher certification and permission from the state to home-school. . . .

The question of which approach is used depends on the type of home-schooling program. If the home-schooling program is a "church school," it will receive a more lenient degree of state regulation than if the program is not backed by a church. As a result of this dichotomy, a parent merely has to receive church backing to begin instruction with little interference from the state.

One of the most hotly contested methods of state monitoring of non-public schools programs (including home-school programs) are teacher certification requirements.

However, while the specific challenges to home-schooling statutes often vary depending on whether or not the home-schooling program is religious based, their respective outcomes may turn out to be the same. . . .

Certification Requirements

One of the most hotly contested methods of state monitoring of non-public schools programs (including home-school programs) are teacher certification requirements. Religious schools, almost always oppose mandatory certification for a variety of reasons. In order for a court to allow any sort of teaching certification requirement, the government must show that such a requirement [according to Campbell] "is rationally related to a legitimate state interest."

Statutes mandating teacher certification are not illegal, per se. While the teacher certification statutes have been over-turned in some states, mainly because they were viewed as un-reasonable, other state and federal courts have found such a requirement reasonable. Although teacher certification re-quirements are not illegal, per se, there is a strong objection to them. . . .

Courts have treated the enforcement of teaching certifica-tion requirements for home-school instructors differently, de-pending on whether the home-school was backed by a church (religious reasons) or was non-religious based. For example, in Alabama, all teachers are required to receive state certifica-tion except those teaching at church schools. This difference in teaching certification requirements indicates a disparate treatment of home-schooling programs. . . .

A home-school monitoring program should, at bare-minimum, require . . . each home-schooled child to take an annual standardized achievement test.

Teacher Certification Necessary

I believe that a teacher certification requirement should be necessary regardless of the reason for home-schooling. How-ever, the acquisition of such a certification should require a minimum burden on the parents. Therefore, the educator should have, at minimum, a high school education (or an equivalent) and the parent's proficiency of this level should be proven by a standardized test. I also believe that each home-schooling parent must be made aware of any standards that their children would be required to meet, including test scores, subjects they would be required to teach, and hours of study. The parents awareness should be memorialized by a signed form.

Perhaps the most common method of state monitoring is achieved through standardized testing requirements. Typically, home-schooled children are required to take a standardized achievement test annually as a means of measuring their progress. The reason this method of monitoring is so common may be due to its lack of intrusiveness on both the home-schooled child and the family. . . .

A home-school monitoring program should, at bare-minimum, require . . . each home-schooled child to take an annual standardized achievement test. . . .

Mandated Monitoring Program

This country places the freedom of religion as one of the most important values. We see this freedom everywhere in our society, from special tax treatment for religious groups to religious garb in public. However, this freedom is not unlimited. As has been shown, there is an ongoing struggle between home-schooling parents (both secular and non-secular) and the government as to how much regulation and monitoring of home-schooling programs should be allowed.

There are many religious-based home-schooling parents that would like nothing better than to be left completely alone in the education of their children. However, this will not happen. The government has a compelling interest in the education of their citizens and must ensure that this education takes place using the least restrictive means available. This least restrictive requirement sets the government's limitation on home-school regulation. With these parameters in mind, the state should mandate a home-schooling monitoring program for religious and non-religious based programs as follows. Note that I group both religious and non-religious based programs together because these requirements will not restrict what can be taught or practiced at home. These requirements will ensure minimum standards for home-schooling programs in the least burdensome way. While I do not necessarily agree with this disparate treatment, it is the prevailing law and I will work within its parameters.

First and foremost, each home-schooled child should be required to take a monitored annual standardized achievement test. The Arkansas home-schooling statute provides an excellent example on how this requirement should be administered. A parent gets to choose the exact test to be administered from a pre-approved list. If a child does not meet the minimum scores for their age level, they must be placed into a public, private, or parochial school.

Essential Monitoring Components

Second, and probably most controversial, there should be a certification requirement for home-schooling teachers. Many states require that a parent hold at least a GED [General Education Development certificate], as they should. In addition to this GED requirement, I propose that home-schooling teachers be required to take a standardized test similar to the Praxis 1 exam that substitute teachers in New Jersey are required to pass. No extra classes and no exorbitant degrees; just pass a test. Anyone with a high school education should be qualified to pass such an exam. Due to the minimum knowledge requirement, this would place a small, but necessary, burden on home-schooling parents in order to ensure their qualifications.

Finally, each home-schooled child should be required to submit a portfolio at the beginning and middle of each academic year based on a state pre-approved list of the minimum educational requirements for a child of that age. The list would be available to every home-schooling parent before submitting the portfolio. The first portfolio should show what the parent intends to teach the child for the first half of the year. The second portfolio should include samples of the child's work showing what he or she has accomplished during the first half of the year and what the parent plans to teach during the second half of the year. The child's work in the second portfolio will serve as evidence that the child is being taught what was outlined in the first portfolio. Each portfolio would need to be approved by administrators and its approval would be based on whether it meets the list of pre-approved requirements. No portfolio would be needed at the end of the academic year due to the standardized achievement test.

Educational Welfare Must Be Monitored

Meg Jalsevac

Meg Jalsevac writes for LifeSiteNews.com, a nonprofit Internet service dedicated to issues of culture, life, and family.

Honorable Thomas Zampino of the Family Division of the New Jersey Superior Court has penalized a home-schooling mother of seven. According to a report by Matt Bowman on the website constitutionallycorrect.com, the mother's supposed infraction is home-schooling her children without supervision from the local school board—a right explicitly upheld in New Jersey law.

According to the court's opinion, Tara Hamilton is the defendant in a suit brought against her by her recently estranged husband, Stephen Hamilton. Stephen brought the suit in an attempt to force Tara to enroll their school-age children, aged 12 to 4 years, in parochial school because he believes that they are not receiving an adequate education while being home-schooled. All seven children currently reside with Tara.

Not in Children's Best Interest

According to the court document, Stephen claims that "continued home schooling is not in the children's best interest, they lack socialization skills and that it is too difficult for the mother to teach the children at five different grade levels. The father argues that the children are not receiving an education equivalent to a public or parochial school."

Prior to the marital discord that led to this suit, the Hamiltons had similarly home-schooled all of their school-age children.

Meg Jalsevac, "New Jersey Judge Scolds Mom for Home-Schooling, Throws Judicial Temper Tantrum," *LifeSiteNews.com*, March 7, 2007. Reproduced by permission.

In an effort to implement "certain basic requirements and safeguards," the Judge ordered Tara to submit her home-schooling children to standardized tests supplied by the local school district despite NJ law which says, "A child educated elsewhere than at school is not required to sit for a state or district standardized test."

The judge also ordered the local school board to file a suit against Tara in order to be able to "evaluate the instruction in the home," a requirement only permissible if the local school board determines that there is credible evidence that the home education is below the standards of the public school.

The judge . . . lamented the fact that [the law] upholds the rights of parents to home-school their children without interference from the government.

Laws Protect Home-Schoolers

Because of NJ's explicit laws protecting the parental right to educate their children at home, the judge had only limited options when it came to personally implementing his philosophies of "monitoring" and "registering" home-schoolers. The judge cautioned that, should the school board refuse to comply with his "suggestions", the court would "consider, by formal opinion, a request to join those parties to action."

The New Jersey Department of Education website states, "The provision, 'to receive equivalent instruction elsewhere than at school,' in N.J.S.A. 18A:38–25 permits parent(s)/guardian(s) to educate the child at home." According to New Jersey law, parents desiring to home-school their children are not required to submit any type of communication of intent to a local school board. Parents are also not required to have their home-school curricula approved by a school board.

An NJ school board may only act against a home-schooling parent "If there is credible evidence that the parent, guardian or other person having custody and control of a school-age child is not causing the child either to attend school (public or nonpublic) or to receive equivalent instruction elsewhere than at school . . ." Under those circumstances, the school board is permitted to request the parents/guardians of a school age child provide proof, such as a letter of intent, that the child is receiving "equivalent instruction."

Home-Schoolers Must Be Monitored

The judge criticized the NJ law and lamented the fact that it upholds the rights of parents to home-school their children without interference from the government. Implying that children being educated by their parents are unsupervised, the judge stated, "This is shocking to the court. In this day and age where we seek to protect children from harm and sexual predators, so many children are left unsupervised."

The judge continued, "In today's threatening world, where we seek to protect children from abuse, not just physical, but also educational abuse, how can we not monitor the educational welfare of all our children?" He then gave the case of a recently found starving child locked "in a putrid bedroom" as an example of what happens when home-schooled children are not "registered and supervised."

In what Bowman refers to as a "judicial temper tantrum" the judge opines, "This is not an attack against home schooling, but rather a statement that it is necessary to register those children for whom this alternative is chosen and to monitor that their educational needs are being adequately nurtured. Judicial interpretation of the statute requires such steps to measure 'equivalent instruction' when the alternative 'elsewhere than at school' is chosen by parents."

More Regulation or Oversight of Education Is Not Needed

Anne Basso

Anne Basso is a nurse and homeschooling mother.

Homeschooling debates come up from time to time on the message board that I belong to, and certain themes seem to repeat themselves. It's frustrating, at times, to have to defend something that I believe is a basic right that I have as a parent and something that I believe has been so good for our family and our children. Especially when I feel that the objections are well intentioned, but not especially well thought out. I thought I'd take a blog post and share a few.

Belief: Homeschoolers need more regulation because children could be abused.

Answer: Children are abused every day, all over this country, and the vast majority of them are in public schools. Many children have gone through public schools without their abuse being caught. So, obviously, if seeing a child *every day* is not a guarantee that they will not be abused, it seems unlikely that more paperwork or even occasional meetings with homeschooling families is unlikely to prevent or catch ongoing abuse.

Children spend 5 years in the care of their parents before going to school. It seems that to really get the government involved in stopping abuse, mandatory checks would be required for all children in all homes. Otherwise, homeschooling parents are being unfairly targeted.

Spotting child abuse is the work of an entire community. Not just teachers, but doctors, nurses, dentists, neighbors, and all sorts of people. Thinking that it's the school's responsibility

Anne Basso, "Regulating Homeschooling," *Our Homeschool.com (wordpress blog)*, August 29, 2007. Reproduced by permission.

to catch child abuse is not fair to the schools, and could allow the rest of us to think that it's not our responsibility when it is.

I see no proof that parents are having difficulty finding a curriculum or teaching it.

Belief: Parents haven't been trained. Oversight is needed to make sure that parents are getting the right curriculum and teaching it appropriately.

Answer: I believe that when discussing the need for more government intrusion into my life and that of my family, those proposing it have an obligation to prove that it is necessary. Now, I'll admit, as a Conservative, I'm likely going to bristle at the idea of more government to fix things. But even more so when it comes to my family. And I see no proof that parents are having difficulty finding a curriculum or teaching it. And if they are, there are a ton of resources within the homeschooling community with which to supplement or find something that works better. If the child is in public school and is being failed by the curriculum, they can't change it.

I don't believe that more government is going to help. I have too many public school teacher friends who are frustrated and annoyed by the "No Child Left Behind" laws which, though well intentioned, have gotten in the way of teachers actually teaching the students. Instead they have to teach to the test. That's what our increased regulations have given us in Public Schools. Not what I want in my home, thanks!

I already have to jump through more hoops than other parents because I don't have a college degree. Now, you can have a college degree in anything, not necessarily education, and it cuts down on what is required of you. And what's required of me that is different is that I provide grades (which I could just make up) and that I have my child tested yearly, though I don't have to share the results with the school district. So what's the point? I have four kids, a job, and I work hard to homeschool. I'm busy enough without having to jump through more hoops to prove myself to the school district.

There are quite a few oversights and regulations on public schools and yet children still fall through the cracks.

Belief: Homeschoolers need more oversight so that we can prevent students from falling through the educational cracks.

Answer: The truly awful homeschooling parent (whom I believe is rare but will concede exists) is not going to be deterred by such things as more regulation. They will simply move around and find new ways to avoid the regulations. Those punished will be homeschoolers like myself who are trying desperately to do everything right.

I don't think you can prevent some students from falling through the educational cracks. My father used to get students who, in High School, couldn't read. There are quite a few oversights and regulations on public schools and yet children still fall through the cracks. It's sad, and I don't like it, but I don't think more regulations for homeschoolers is the answer. Yet again, I think it must be proven that this is a problem within the homeschooling community and warrants such intrusion by the state and that such intrusion will make a difference. Less than 2% of America's students are homeschooled at all, so I can't see as there's a big epidemic.

Belief: It is our duty and obligation as a Democracy, and as a community to ensure that all children are educated, and that means making sure that homeschooled children meet certain expectations as well as public schooled children.

Answer: Our Founding Fathers believed that, for a Democracy, an educated populace was essential. However, they trusted the *parents* to provide that education as they saw fit. None of the Founding Fathers attended public schools, nor were they common in the United States until almost a century later. I will provide an education to my children, and I expect the *freedom* to do so as I see fit. Freedom being another idea that the Founding Fathers held dear.

I don't believe that it is the job of the community to raise my children. And if you're proposing greater demands or restrictions on me, I think you have to prove that it's necessary. But the research that I've read says that homeschooled children are more involved in the community, statistically speaking, than their [public] schooled counterparts:

> *Dr. Gary Knowles, of the University of Michigan, explored adults who were home educated. None were unemployed and none were on welfare, 94% said home education prepared them to be an independent person, 79% said it helped them interact with individuals from different levels of society, and they strongly supported the home education method....*

Belief: If teachers have to jump through so many hoops, so should homeschoolers.

Answer: I am not asking to be paid government money to teach other people's children. I am actually paying taxes and spending my own money on top of that while educating my own children. I don't see how the two can be compared.

In the end, people are going to form their own opinions and have their own ideas about homeschooling, and I believe that those who advocate greater restrictions, oversights, or demands have the *best* of intentions. They really just want to make sure that kids are getting the education that they deserve. But, in my experience, the parents I've met *are* very concerned about their children's educations, and devoted to their learning. The community is vast, resourceful, and encouraging to one another. I don't think there's anything to be fixed with homeschooling, because I don't see any proof that it's broken.

I will never object to the state making resources available for those homeschoolers who wish to take advantage of them.

I will always object to their resources being forced upon me, or more government regulation and intrusion being the first resort for a problem that hasn't even been shown to exist.

Homeschooling Freedoms Must Be Maintained

Larry Kaseman and Susan Kaseman

Larry Kaseman and Susan Kaseman are executive directors of the Wisconsin Parents Association, a statewide grassroots organization dedicated to ensuring legislation does not limit homeschoolers' freedoms. The Kasemans also are columnists for Home Education Magazine.

Would you like to

- ensure that your family can make as many decisions as possible about the approach to homeschooling you will choose, the curriculum you will use, what you will do each day, and what principles and beliefs you will share with your children;

- make an important contribution to homeschooling both now and in the future; and

- learn more about taking responsibility for your own life and activities, lessons you can apply to other areas of your life?

You can do all this and more by following a few simple principles for maintaining homeschooling freedom. . . .

Homeschooling is complicated enough when we just focus on our own families. It takes time, energy, and experience to organize our lives around the fact that we are homeschooling, choose an approach that has a reasonable chance of working for each child, gather materials we need, defend our sanity when questioned by friends and relatives, and keep our own

Larry and Susan Kaseman, "Eight Principles for New and Experienced Homeschoolers, Taking Charge," *Home Education Magazine*, September/October 2005. Copyright © 2005 Larry and Susan Kaseman. Reproduced by permission.

doubts under control. Add to this the mid-course corrections that need to be made because we discover a better approach or our children outgrow what we've been doing and are ready for something new. It sometimes seems like focusing on our own family is all we have time or energy to do.

Working to Maintain Freedoms

But we make a big mistake if we don't put some time and energy into working to maintain our homeschooling freedoms. Unless we work to ensure that state regulation of homeschooling is not increased, critics and opponents of homeschooling (such as some school officials, social workers, legislators, teachers unions, etc.) are likely to increase it. If this were to happen, our own homeschooling would be much more difficult. We'd be more limited in what we could do. For example, state requirements that we submit our curriculum for review end approval, have our children take standardized tests, or send periodic reports to public school officials tend to undermine our confidence in our ability to choose an approach to homeschooling that will work for our family and follow it. We become handicapped and may have to spend more time complying with state requirements and figuring out ways to homeschool according to our principles and beliefs despite the requirements. To be sure, many families homeschool successfully in states that have such requirements, but it is more difficult. Homeschoolers who have to work with public school standards (by adopting a curriculum that public school officials approve, or reporting to public school officials, or taking tests based on conventional school curriculum, etc.) often have a more difficult time discovering and creating approaches to homeschooling that will allow their children to interact with the real world and prepare for adult life than they would have if they were free of such regulations and could simply concentrate on their children's educations. It's much better to include plans to work to maintain our homeschooling freedoms with our other activities as homeschoolers. When conventional schools are beginning a new academic year is a good time to review what we are doing to maintain our freedoms or to begin working to maintain our freedoms if we're new to homeschooling or to this idea.

But, you may be thinking, isn't maintaining our freedoms dull, onerous, difficult, sometimes hopeless work? Not at all! Most of the time, all that we have to do is to be alert and make sensible choices as we go about homeschooling our own families. The few specific steps we need to take, outlined below, are relatively quick and easy, provide great learning opportunities, increase our confidence, and help us learn to take responsibility for ourselves, something we can use throughout our lives. The work is especially manageable if every homeschooler does their part. The only major time- end energy-consuming work is dealing with a crisis, like countering legislation that undermines our freedom. Fortunately, such crises do not occur often and are much less likely to occur if we (and other homeschoolers) have followed the basic points outlined below.

Any action that exceeds statutes or regulations sets a precedent.

Here Are Eight Essential Principles

1. Know what is required of homeschoolers in your state. Have a copy of the homeschooling statutes and/or regulations available for reference in case you need it. You may be able to get a copy from a statewide homeschooling organization, a local support group, or an experienced homeschooler in your state. In addition, be sure to ask experienced homeschoolers how the statutes or regulations are enforced. Enforcement may not follow the letter of the law, and it's important to know what your choices and risks are. Don't ask school officials or

the state department of education for information about statutes, regulations, or what is required. They often do not know, have been misinformed, or misunderstand what the statutes or regulations say. Be careful about information from books or web sites that cover the laws in all 50 states. They sometimes provide only the text of the statutes without crucial information about how they are interpreted or enforced. The best source of information is knowledgeable, experienced homeschoolers who live in the state you're interested in.

2. Do only the minimum required by statute or regulation. If a school official asks or tells you to do more than is required, politely refuse and explain what is required. If they persist, ask them to show the statute or regulation that gives them the authority to make such a request. Occasionally, it may be tempting to exceed the minimum requirements of the law by showing school officials our curriculums, samples of our children's accomplishments, test scores, etc. even though these are not required by statute in our state [Wisconsin]. Perhaps we are proud of our children's accomplishments or want to educate officials about homeschooling or show them how well it works. It is very important to resist such temptation. Any action that exceeds statutes or regulations sets a precedent. It's likely to increase demands officials make of us and other homeschoolers in the future. It also may increase the questions, doubts, concerns, and criticisms that officials have about our homeschooling. Requirements vary greatly from state to state. Be careful not to do more than the minimum required in your state.

3. Don't ignore violations of your rights even if they seem too small to matter. Major freedoms are sometimes lost one small step at a time. Our failure to respond also encourages those who are limiting our freedoms to con-

tinue the process. For example, suppose a school district requires that homeschoolers submit their test scores, even though the statutes in the state do not give districts the authority to require them. If homeschoolers do not object, in a while the district may ask for copies of homeschoolers' curriculums in addition to their test scores. On the other hand, if homeschoolers object strongly the first time the district exceeds its authority (either by mistake or in a deliberate attempt to increase its power and authority over homeschoolers), school officials will probably be more reluctant to take on homeschoolers in the future. Responding to small infringements of our freedoms not only prevents loss of freedom in the specific situation in question. It also prevents future, perhaps more serious, such challenges. People who think that homeschoolers shouldn't complain as long as no one declares homeschooling illegal greatly misunderstand the importance of choosing an approach to education and a curriculum, allowing children to pursue their interest and learn at their own pace, and offering our children an education consistent with our principles and beliefs rather than those of the public school system.

4. Do not seek or accept any benefits from the government, including direct funding, tax deductions, or tax credits. Work to prevent the government from offering money or favors to any homeschoolers. There is no such thing as a free lunch. Such benefits are likely to be followed by increased regulation, especially since the government is accountable for how tax dollars are spent. Even benefits that seem quite safe, like allowing homeschoolers to play on public school sports teams, open the door for increased regulation of homeschooling. Such regulation would apply to all homeschoolers; families could not refuse the benefit and avoid the increased

regulation. It is important to remember that there are people and organizations (for example, some school official, social workers, legislators, teachers unions, etc.) who are looking for opportunities to increase state regulation of homeschooling.

5. Do not push for new homeschooling legislation except in very unusual situations. Small minorities generally have difficulty getting legislation passed, especially if they don't have large sums of money to hire lobbyists. In addition, once a bill has been introduced, it is very difficult to control. It can be changed so much through amendments that it actually ends up the opposite of what it started out to be. Some of the best homeschooling laws in the country have resulted from legislation introduced by opponents of homeschooling being changed through amendment. It is easier for a small minority like homeschoolers to gain support from non-homeschoolers when we are a beleaguered minority being put upon by a large interest group like a teachers union than to find support for legislation we initiated ourselves.

6. Stay out of court if at all possible. It is almost always better for homeschoolers to try to reach settlements through negotiation or arbitration than to take cases to court. Rulings in court cases generally uphold the status quo and support the dominant culture. This means that rulings concerning small minorities such as homeschoolers tend to be biased in favor of conventional education rather than alternatives. We are much better off without any court rulings than with rulings that go against us. Evidence to support this idea can be found in a 1990 report written by Jane Henkel of the Wisconsin Legislative Council titled "Recent Court Cases Examining the Constitutionality of Other States' Laws Regulating Home Schools." Her report showed that court cases tend to

uphold the constitutionality of state regulation of home-schooling. The report states, "Special care was taken to attempt to find reported cases striking down state regulations. With the limited exception of cases which found regulations to be unconstitutionally vague, that effort was unsuccessful, which tends to indicate that there are few, if any, such cases." The report is available at http://www.homeedmag.com/HEM/185/henkel/info_memo90-23.html or from the Wisconsin Legislative Council, One East Main Street, Suite 401, Madison, WI 53703, (608) 266–1304.

7. Understand and apply the distinction between compulsory school attendance and compulsory education. Basically, remember and remind school officials and others that the law requires that young people attend school, but it does not require that they receive an education while doing so. Therefore, it is discriminatory for school officials, judges, court commissioners, and others to insist that homeschoolers demonstrate that their children are receiving an education that is equivalent to the education that children supposedly receive in public schools or that they are at grade level or penalize them for failing to achieve specific educational goals. For more information, see the recent Taking Charge column, "Don't Let Compulsory Attendance Turn into Compulsory Education," available at http://www.homeedmag.com/HEM/224/jatch.html. . . .

8. Work with other homeschoolers. Some of homeschooling's greatest strengths stem from the fact that it is a grassroots movement. It becomes even stronger as we communicate with each other, share information and experiences, support each other, and work together to maintain our freedoms.

If your state has a statewide inclusive grassroots home-schooling organization, consider supporting it. Such organizations have contributed enormously to the work that has been done to maintain homeschooling freedoms. Become a member, make a donation, purchase materials, and attend their conferences. It is very important to be organized and prepared before challenges to our freedoms arise. Such organizations are also a very good way to connect with other homeschoolers.

Also consider joining a local homeschooling support group. If none exists in your area, start one yourself. It can be as simple as getting together with one or two other families for whatever activities you choose.

Conclusion

There's no doubt about it: the choices we can make about how we will homeschool each day are influenced by what our state requires of homeschoolers. As homeschoolers, we need to take responsibility for preventing an increase in state regulation and an accompanying loss of homeschooling freedom. No one else will maintain our freedoms for us; in fact, a number of individuals and groups are continually looking for ways to increase state regulation of homeschooling. Fortunately, working to maintain our freedom is not difficult or time-consuming, especially if each of us does our part. It does require understanding some fundamental principles, including those discussed [above], and keeping them in mind as we go about our homeschooling. Don't let the rest of us down. Do your part. Make a significant contribution to the present and future of homeschooling.

Parents Can Legally Instruct Their Children

Deborah Stevenson

Deborah Stevenson, mother of two grown children, Samantha and Cassandra, realized that homeschooling is what all parents do from the time children are born, and that it was a natural thing to continue to do so. So she did. Deborah became involved in legal work as a result of homeschooling her children. She became involved in protecting her right to homeschool as a parent before she began attending law school. She homeschooled, as well as drove her children to college, where they took courses during the day, and went to law school at night. She currently practices education law and appellate law privately in addition to working as executive director of National Home Education Legal Defense (NHELD), LLC. Ms. Stevenson formed Connecticut Citizens to Uphold the Right to Educate (C.U.R.E.) in 1989 in order to assist all parents in the state to retain their right to instruct their children at home without government interference. Because she believed in the Tenth Amendment's provision that all powers not specifically granted to the federal government belong to the states and to the people, C.U.R.E. remained a state organization protecting the rights of citizens in the state. It was not until 2003, when Deborah realized that there was a continuing effort by another organization to actively promote the adoption of federal regulation of homeschooling, that she decided to form NHELD. A national organization was necessary in order to inform and assist parents in all states in halting federal regulation and retaining authority in the states to instruct their children in freedom. Ms. Stevenson has an extensive background as a public speaker. She spent ten years as a reporter interviewing all sorts of interesting people from parents to presidents. She also hosted many radio programs on a variety of topics throughout her ten

Deborah Stevenson, "One Parent's Demand for the Truth About the Legality of Homeschooling," *Family Times*, May/June 2006. Reproduced by permission.

year career. She has conducted many workshops on homeschooling and the law. You can find articles that Ms. Stevenson has published in Home Education Magazine, Home Educator's Family Times, *and on NHELD's Web site, www.nheld.com, to name a few.*

Nothing makes me angrier than a lie, except when a lie is repeated so often that people believe it to be truth. I'm sick of lies, distorted truth, spin, and revisionist history. Can we just get back to reality? Can we just hold people accountable for their purposeful distortions?

Can we just set the record straight?

Homeschooling Is an Age-Old Custom

The lie that makes me the angriest is the lie that "It's legal to homeschool 'now'." The implication in that statement is the lie. The implication is that it wasn't legal to homeschool before, or that homeschooling only became legal in the past 20 years or so. Nothing could be farther from the truth.

At no time during the growth of the public school system . . . did state governments declare the instruction of children by their parents to be illegal.

What is "homeschooling?" It is the act of parents undertaking their responsibility to instruct their own children. This is the most basic, the most natural, the most instinctive undertaking of the human race. Since the beginning of the human race, whether you accept the scientific view that man lived as early as seven million years ago or whether you accept the religious view that God created man four or five thousand years ago, the inescapable fact is that parents have instructed their children from the moment of birth to adulthood since the inception of the human race whenever that was. It wasn't illegal to do so in the beginning, and it's not illegal to do so now.

What is "new" is the public school system. The first public school in America was established by Puritan settlers in Boston in 1635. It was established by the Reverend John Cotton who wanted to create a school modeled after the Free Grammar School in England, in which Latin and Greek were taught. The truth is, though, that the opening of that first public school did not automatically mean that the instruction of children by their parents somehow automatically became illegal. Quite the opposite is true.

In the early days in New England, in fact, parents were expected to instruct their children. If parents didn't instruct their children such that the children became "unruly", the selectmen of the town could take the child from the parent and place the child, not with government officials, but with another surrogate parent of sorts called a master. It then became the master's responsibility to instruct the child.

It is important to note that the compulsory attendance laws were aimed at those children who were not being educated by other means.

A Compulsory Attendance Law Adopted

Over time, small public schools were opened, many of which were operated and overseen by ecclesiastical societies. Oversight slowly gave way to oversight by towns and, later, to what we now know as boards of education. At no time during the growth of the public school system, however, did state governments declare the instruction of children by their parents to be illegal.

The popularity of the public school system increased dramatically during the nineteenth century, thanks in large part to [educator] Horace Mann. He persuaded the Massachusetts legislature, in fact, to set up a six-month minimum school year and led a movement to set up teacher institutions throughout the state. Even while Mann was tending to this task, the Massachusetts legislature at no time declared the instruction of children by their parents to be illegal.

As the public school system grew, legislatures adopted more laws about the system. The law that most people are familiar with that state legislatures adopted is the "compulsory attendance" law. This law has many permutations depending on the state in which it was adopted. Its basic thrust is to tell parents that their children "must attend" public school. Massachusetts was the first state to enact such a law in 1852.

It required children between the ages of eight and fourteen to attend school for at least three months each year.

Instructing Your Children Is Not Illegal

The compulsory attendance laws, for the most part, initially were adopted during the height of the industrial revolution in the nineteenth century. This was a time when the growth of industry opened new sources of income for families. It was a time when parents allowed their children to work in the factories, instead of on the family farms of yesteryear. For a multitude of reasons, those in power deemed it inherently injurious to the children to work in the factories, and, instead deemed it eminently more important for them to attend public school. By 1918 all states followed suit. It is important to note that the compulsory attendance laws were aimed at those children who were not being educated by other means. In fact, there were many exemptions to these laws. Most importantly, these laws simply did not apply to those children who were being educated by other means. In other words, the legislatures did not declare education of children by their parents, or by private schools or tutors for that matter, to be illegal.

Today, most states still have "compulsory attendance laws". *But that does not necessarily mean that it was ever illegal for parents to instruct their own children. The truth is, it was never* "*illegal*" for parents to instruct their own *children*. Can we please stop perpetuating the lie that it was illegal?

It is the development of this "new" public school system that, in part, has fueled the lie. The public school system has become so huge and so powerful that it dominates the public's thinking. It is also the agenda of some to perpetuate the lie. The lie benefits different groups such as the established public school system or established organizations purporting to "assist" parents fearful of the public school system taking their rights away.

Government Has Limited Authority

What is true is that many states did, and still do, impose government regulations on how and when parents instruct their children. It is unfortunate that the government imposes any regulations on parents who instruct their own children. It is my belief, however, that one of the reasons why the government has been successful in adopting regulations affecting the right of parents to instruct their children is because the lie that it was illegal for parents to homeschool in the first place has been perpetuated for so long. From this lie flows a host of issues. For example, if you believe the lie that it was illegal for parents to instruct their children, it follows that parents would have to seek "permission" from the government in order to do so. If you believe the lie, it follows that parents would be fearful that they would not receive that "permission." If you believe the lie, it follows that parents would be grateful when the government magnanimously grants that "permission." If you believe the lie, it follows that parents are more apt to see "regulation" of parental instruction by the government as a matter of course. After all, if the government has the "authority" to grant "permission" to parents to instruct, certainly the government has the "authority" to impose "regulation" of parents' ability to instruct, and it is reasonable for the government to do so.

Armed with the facts, armed with the truth, however, parents can begin to realize that, in reality, the government never did have the "authority" to declare the right of parents to instruct their children as illegal, and it's a safe bet that the government in your state never did declare the right of parents to instruct their children as illegal.

CHAPTER 4

Should Homeschooled Children Have Access to Public School Resources?

Chapter Preface

The great majority of homeschooled children are very happy with their educational lifestyle and do not feel they are missing anything by not attending public or private schools. Some, however, want to enjoy both worlds. They would like to continue to be home-educated but at the same time be able to attend certain public school classes, play on public school athletic teams, or play an instrument in a school band. This is especially true of high school-age students.

In recent years an increasing number of states have been more amenable to allowing more participation. In 2007, the High School Legal Defense Association (HSLDA) reported that eighteen states—Arizona, Colorado, Florida, Idaho, Iowa, Maine, Michigan, Minnesota, New Hampshire, New Mexico, Nebraska, North Dakota, Oregon, Pennsylvania, Utah, Vermont, Washington, and Wyoming—had statutes that authorized some form of public school access by homeschooled students. Arizona and Oregon required school districts to allow access to interscholastic activities only.

In those states without such statutes, it generally falls to school districts or local school boards to set a policy. Local boards often turn for input to state athletic associations, which tend not to want to allow homeschoolers equal access to public school athletics. Very few state high school athletic associations have adopted by-laws that allow homeschoolers to play on public school sports teams.

Even in those states that do have laws allowing homeschoolers to participate in public school programs, certain requirements must be met. These vary from one state to another but typically mandate that the homeschooler must be in compliance with the state homeschool law, meet the same eligibility requirements as public school students, and provide test scores or academic reports that prove he or she is passing his or her core subjects.

Even though a growing number of states are permitting homeschoolers to take part in at least some public school extracurricular activities, the issue of equal access remains problematic from a number of perspectives. It continues to be a subject of debate among homeschoolers themselves. Many oppose equal access because they believe pushing for access laws will lead to more government regulation of homeschoolers. Some homeschooling parents take another position, choosing often reluctantly to allow an athletically talented child to enroll in public high school so he or she can play on the school team where there is sufficient competition to showcase his or her talent—and hopefully win an athletic scholarship to college. Other homeschoolers and their advocates across the nation have reacted to the issue by choosing to start homeschooler athletic associations, leagues, and teams, whose numbers continue to grow. Homeschoolers can derive satisfaction from the fact that their efforts, the growth and success of their teams, and the talents of their athletes have not gone unnoticed. According to a 2008 article in the *New York Times*, "Only a decade ago, home-school athletics was considered little more than organized recess for children without traditional classrooms. Now, home-school players are tracked by scouts, and dozens of them have accepted scholarships to colleges as small as Blue Mountain in Mississippi and as well known as Iowa State."

Participation of Homeschoolers in Public School Extracurricular Activities Should Be Allowed

State of Pennsylvania

The following is a news release posted on the state of Pennsylvania's official Web site, http://PA.gov, which provides news and information related to the state of Pennsylvania.

Governor Edward G. Rendell [on November 2005] signed Senate Bill 361, sponsored by Sen. Bob Regola (R-Westmoreland), into law to help the state's 25,000 children who are taught at home participate in extracurricular activities in their local school districts.

"While I have long been an advocate of public education and the need to ensure a world-class public education system in our state, I think the commitment to education demonstrated by homeschool parents has too long been undervalued," said Governor Rendell in his signing letter to the legislature.

"As Senate Bill 361 worked its way through the Legislature, I asked my staff to review such critical questions as the financial implications of the bill, whether it imposes any new financial burdens and whether such burdens could be met with current resources. I also asked that we consider the appropriateness of state legislation given the local control structure of Pennsylvania's school system. This thorough review process gave me an opportunity to understand the personal circumstances and the goals of homeschool parents and their children."

"Governor Rendell Says Home-Schooled Children Can Participate in School District Extracurricular Activities," in State of Pennsylvania's Governor's Office, November 2005.

"I read of Barry Clay's desire for his children to participate with their friends in extracurricular activities in the Carlisle Area School District, of Carol Loys' hope that her children could do the same with their friends in the West Shore School District, and of Beverly Wiezorek's efforts to convince the Pittsburgh School District to let her son, Wesley, play football. These were just a few examples that illustrated the pleas of parents, asking that their children be able to enjoy the benefit of extracurricular sports, the opportunity to compete for college sports scholarships and the ability to participate in and contribute to their communities."

> [Homeschool] parents deserve our respect and their children are entitled to be included in the activities of their school district.

Inclusion Is Appropriate

"I found it disheartening that 221 of our school districts do not permit homeschool children to engage in school sports, plays, clubs or other programs that promote good social values, integrate our communities and clearly contribute to the positive social development of our children. I agree with these dedicated parents that they have every right to be frustrated. As any good parent would, they are looking out for the interests of their children. And not only are they involved in their child's education, they share in their local school's cost by paying property taxes. It seems disingenuous to suggest that permitting these students to take part in school-based extracurricular activities would be unjust or a burden on public school budgets since their parents are paying property taxes."

"It's clear that parents who homeschool their children do not make this decision lightly. Some do so because they want their child's education to be integrated with their faith and do not have access to a private school that reflects their religious beliefs. Others choose homeschooling in an effort to offer more challenging coursework to children who have advanced beyond the available curricula offered locally. Others may have a child with special needs and opt for homeschooling as a way to provide individualized attention that may be unavailable or impractical for their school district. These parents make tough choices, rearranging their lives entirely around the needs of their children. These parents deserve our respect and their children are entitled to be included in the activities of their school district."

Senate Bill 361 amends the Public School Code of 1949. As of Jan. 1, 2006, a school district of residence must permit a child enrolled in a home education program to participate in any extracurricular activities provided by that local district. The child must meet both eligibility and the activities' try-out requirements. The child will also have to comply with the rules of the club or organization he or she chooses to join.

Interscholastic athletics and activities, which occur between schools within the district or between schools outside of the district, are also included this amendment. If the activity requires a physical exam or medical test, the district must post the information on their web site and circulate it in an area publication.

The bill passed the Senate 34-16 and the House, with amendments, 197-2. The Senate concurred, with additional amendments, 33-17. The House agreed 195-3. The bill is effective immediately.

Homeschoolers Deserve Equal Access to Extracurricular Activities

Alabama EqualAccess

Alabama EqualAccess is a group of concerned Alabama citizens who united to lobby for the passage of a bill to allow home-schoolers equal access to interscholastic sports and other extra-curricular activities.

W e offer the following Q&A topics but none of the answers make any difference, regardless of how true the facts may be, if the reader is biased against homeschoolers to begin with. The reader must first ask themselves if they believe that all student-athletes of our state deserve an equal opportunity to participate in extracurricular activities. That is the bottom line. Let us keep in mind as a state that a student is a student—regardless of where they receive their education. Each child is already a part of our society. Turning out the best equipped individuals should be the goal of us all. Some states, such as Florida, wisely offer an almost complete *cafeteria-style* approach for home-schoolers where the parents get to choose not only public school extracurricular activities but also academic subjects such as science, music, math, or other classes that their child needs. As frightening as that prospect may seem for many entrenched public educators, the reality is that it works out very well. Studies also prove that states which allow equal access, like Minnesota, who is ranked number one academically according to the ALEC [American Legislative Exchange Council] study, are consistently ranked in the top academic performance states.

Regardless, the system should not get in the way of what is best for the student. School administrators and coaches are some of the hardest working and most conscientious people in our state. They have constant demands on them from all sides whether it be teachers, other employees, the state education system, the Federal government, unions, parents, and last but not least the students. They are to be commended for their diligence. They need to realize though that equal access is not a problem waiting to happen to them but rather a wonderful opportunity to add a few great students and parents to the *team*. Not just the school sports team but the overall school team, the community *team*. All the negative thoughts that come to mind for an administrator simply have not materialized in the 23 other states that permit equal access. We encourage administrators not to be so caught up in the past or in the demands of the present that they forget what our schools are supposed to be about. . . .

We are all citizens . . . with hopefully the same goal in mind and that is to provide the best for our children.

Cost Should Not Be a Factor

- *What is the cost?*

Most school teams will not add extra positions for a sport or band to accommodate homeschoolers so the cost is nil in this case. Some schools may choose to add extra positions on a team or individual sport. However, typically it is the booster clubs that raise the lion's share of the athletic money spent. It is likely that homeschool parents would be some of the most enthusiastic supporters of a booster club!

The answer to the cost issue also depends on if the schools decide to count a *partial* student. What is not pointed out by the opposition is that Alabama spends on average about $6,300 per student per year. The state's 25,000 or more homeschoolers save the taxpayers approximately $157,500,000 *each* year in state and Federal funds by not requiring public school services! Below is a fitting quote from a letter from a dedicated homeschool mom, Marcia Guyse, who holds a masters degree and is a certified teacher who taught for years in the Alabama and Texas school systems:

A homeschooled student is a student . . . just the same as a public or private schooled student and therefore deserves equal and fair treatment.

"If we as educators truly want what is best for the student, then we will include all students, including home-schooled students. A new day is dawning for education. In states like Minnesota, whose educational program is ranked number one in the nation, parents can choose the best path for the education of their children, whether it be public schools, private schools, charter schools, or home schools. The state does not penalize them for this choice by excluding them from any services, but state funds actually follow the child to the school that is chosen. Presently, those 25,000 home schoolers in the State of Alabama are saving the state a $6,300 per student expenditure. [Alabama Education Association executive secretary] Dr. Paul Hubbert is worried about the "cost" of passing this legislation. Couldn't just a little of that money follow those students to a school's sports or music program? It's time for educators [and teacher's unions] to quit worrying about economic and political costs of education and start thinking of the cost of not offering the best educational opportunities to all students in Alabama." . . .

Homeschoolers Deserve Equal Treatment

- *What does "extracurricular activities" encompass?*

This has been addressed in the rewritten [Tim Tebow] bill. The bill includes only sports and band. As homeschoolers already participate at some local public schools in certain extra-curricular activities such as music, it seems that individual local schools have already decided that allowing certain students to participate in certain areas already produces a win-win situation. This bill does not seek to limit that opportunity for homeschool students that live in a district that *already* permits such activity. The bill would even-out the opportunity and make it more fair as it would apply to all students regardless of school zone. . . .

- *"If our sports are good enough for you then why not our academics"?*

This is an old argument with inherent bias against home-schoolers. First of all there is no "you" nor "our" to this issue. We are all citizens of this state with hopefully the same goal in mind and that is to provide the best for our children. This is about what is *best* for the student—not what is merely *good enough*. A homeschooled student is a student in this state just the same as a public or private schooled student and therefore deserves equal and fair treatment—especially by the state-sponsored educational establishment. This should apply to athletics as well as academics. A child can freely walk into any school in this state in the district where they legally reside and obtain educational services. This should not exclude extracurricular activities that are offered by that school. Many who exhibit this attitude often have the misconceived notion that homeschoolers think they are "better" than others. While this notion may be the case in some instances, the same could be said of public-schoolers. So it simply points out a bias or resentment towards homeschoolers. Again it has nothing to do with the intelligent debate that many on both sides of this issue are trying to conduct. Those who choose to continue to hold this attitude should realize at least that this *is* an instance where homeschoolers are offering an olive branch and trying to reach out to the public school system.

- *Illegal Immigrants and Exchange Students have more rights than homeschoolers in this regard!*

On a side note, it is blatantly unfair to many citizens that illegal immigrants to our great country and state can enroll their children, technically, the day they move into a district and receive all benefits offered to any other student. This participation includes the right to participate in extracurricular activities. This applies to foreign exchange students as well. Even they have more rights than our state's very own homeschoolers. Homeschool families, many of whom have been upstanding, legal, tax-paying citizens of this state for decades, are excluded. Is this fair?. . .

Participation in a comprehensive extracurricular and academic program contributes to student development of the social and intellectual skills necessary to become a well-rounded adult.

Children's Best Interest

- *Is this going to allow the government to interfere with the rights of homeschoolers?*

This is a voluntary opportunity only for homeschoolers who fill out a form and request to be involved in the program. It will have no effect on other homeschoolers who wish not to be bothered.

We homeschoolers are indeed an independent bunch! We homeschoolers who support this legislation understand the battle that had to be fought nationwide to be able to exercise the God-given responsibility and the right to educate our children at home if we deemed it best for the student. But frankly that is a past battle; it will not be fought again. We won! Homeschooling is well accepted as part of the educational options for many citizens. While it will take the educational "system" a while to accept this, it is occurring. I'm afraid that in our zeal for homeschooling, we often forget that it is not about the right to do this or do that but *it is about what is best for each child* that is important. . . .

Interscholastic extracurricular activities are an important complement to the academic curriculum. Participation in a comprehensive extracurricular and academic program contributes to student development of the social and intellectual skills necessary to become a well-rounded adult.

Many extracurricular activities can be provided to students on an individual basis, such as tennis, golf, piano lessons or art. However, some sports or activities require groups of students and cannot be achieved on an individual basis.

Options Afforded by Public Education

Children have different gifts. Not all can or want to play football or baseball, but each deserves to have the opportunity to develop his or her talents.

Most of us have been involved in homeschool teams and have seen many other great examples of valiant efforts by great homeschoolers to field teams of excellence. But let's be honest, short of Bill Gates joining the movement, do we think we could ever fund sports programs to the level necessary to bring them up to the caliber of most of the public and private school teams? While we know full well that there is more to athletics than funding and visibility, it is nonetheless an important part. And what about continuity of the program and coaches? Homeschoolers don't have the options afforded by public schools in this regard. . . .

Again, this option is available at some level in over 20 states already and we have not found one state that experienced adverse effects or instances where the freedom or rights of homeschoolers have been harmed. In 2006 when a local Pennsylvania school tried to "retest" a homeschooled athlete they were quick to drop the requirement when confronted by facts from the HSLDA [Homeschool Legal Defense Association].

HSLDA also states, in the states where equal access laws have been passed, there has not been one case where additional laws have been passed that affect the homeschool population of that state. . . .

Public schools do not "own" competitive athletics; they belong to the students, their families, and the residents of Alabama.

Discrimination Against Homeschoolers

- *Religious Discrimination imposed by a "State Actor" - A very real argument with a Supreme Court precedent:*

Just as the Alabama legislature has decided that public schools do not hold a monopoly on education, so the AHSAA [Alabama High School Athletic Association] should not hold a monopoly on competitive athletics.

The AHSAA is a private organization which governs all middle and high school competitive athletics in Alabama and discriminates against certain classes of students based on their educational choice.

It is time for the State Legislature to require the AHSAA to stop discriminating against students because of an educational choice. Students taught at home under a church school covering or by a private tutor cannot participate in athletics because a private organization, acting on behalf of the State, prohibits their participation.

The SUPREME COURT OF THE UNITED STATES in the *BRENTWOOD ACADEMY v. TENNESSEE SECONDARY SCHOOL ATHLETIC ASSOCIATION et al.* stated in the opinion of February 20, 2001, "Save for the Sixth Circuit, every Court of Appeals to consider a statewide athletic association like this one has found it to be a *state actor*".

Whether the AHSAA is a statutory agency of the State is immaterial because the AHSAA fulfills a certain function on behalf of the State for public schools. Just as public schools and governments are not allowed by federal law to discriminate against students based on race, sex, religion, the AHSAA as a "State Actor" cannot discriminate either. Therefore, the State of Alabama has given parents the right to teach their children under a church school covering and must allow these students based on their religious choice of schooling to participate in competitive athletics.

Children Should Not Be Penalized

Public schools do not "own" competitive athletics; they belong to the students, their families, and the residents of Alabama. It is just as much in the interest of the State of Alabama to help students in private and church schools to develop to their full potential as students in the public schools. The Legislature should not allow such a discriminatory practice to take place. The AHSAA is, in essence, a private exclusive club, which permits only certain students in Alabama to enjoy the privilege of group activities because of the schools they attend.

At least 23 other states recognize the importance of extracurricular activities in the development of a child. Alabama needs to do what is in the best interest of all children. All parents pay taxes to support the free public education system, but their children are penalized because they chose a different path to education. Education is a requirement for Alabama children. Extracurricular activities is a privilege and should be an opportunity for all children, not just those who attend a public school.

Homeschoolers Have the Right to Participate in After-School Activities

Provo Daily Herald

The Provo Daily Herald *is a daily newspaper in Provo, Utah.*

Do home-schoolers have as much right as any other kid to take part in a school district's after-school activities? Of course.

This has been a topic of growing interest since Florida quarterback Tim Tebow, who was home-schooled, won the Heisman Trophy.

Sen. Mark Madsen, R-Eagle Mountain, [Utah,] has introduced bills to clarify the right of charter, online and home-schooled students to take part in extracurricular activities at public schools, tailoring the language to address criticisms. He would restrict students to extracurricular activities at schools they otherwise would have attended, or schools they attended in the past. Madsen has also crafted a fair funding formula.

The proposal should be passed. The parents of home-schoolers pay taxes to support the schools, even as their kids impose no expense burden whatsoever on classrooms, labs or anywhere else. The programs we're talking about fall outside the regular curriculum—they're not necessary for graduation. They're extras, as the term *extracurricular* implies.

It's only fair that these families get something for their tax money.

Backers of ballroom dance, athletics, the performing arts and other extracurricular activities rightfully trumpet the value of such programs, which enrich lives, build character,

"In Our View: Let Home-School Kids Participate," *Daily Herald*, January 27, 2008. Reproduced by permission.

promote teamwork and keep kids out of trouble. Those attributes are exactly why the programs should be available to everybody.

If a kid is not a top performer academically, but a gifted athlete, why should he be prevented from developing that gift which he does possess?

Grades Should Not Be an Issue

A legislative committee has held up Madsen's proposal so that its backers can add requirements that home-schoolers' academic progress be monitored by third parties.

Opponents have conjured up a nightmare—unrealistic, in our view—that some parents will claim home-school status so that their budding superstars won't be barred from a team on account of poor grades. We suppose this could happen in theory, but it is no reason to block Madsen's proposal. The question should not turn on the rarest of exceptions.

Besides, it's fair to ask: If a kid is not a top performer academically, but a gifted athlete, why should he be prevented from developing that gift which he does possess? This question should be answered one of these days.

Madsen bridles at the suggestion that parents would resort to fraud. "Somehow every parent is suspect, and a closet perjurer ready to abandon their honor so that their kids can participate in extracurricular activities," he said.

It's not even a matter of honor. Utah parents generally want their kids in public school. End of story.

Third-Party Verification

If amendments are needed to Madsen's bills, they should be modest. Lawmakers should not erect major barriers to solve minor theoretical flaws. Athletes are simply not going to leave the hallowed halls of local high schools en masse to be home-schooled.

As for qualifying grades, the Legislature should move equally gently. So long as home-school is recognized as a valid, legal option for education in the State of Utah, it follows that measurement of whether a student is academically qualified to participate in extracurricular activity should flow from the home school, just as it flows from the public school for a public school student.

As a rule, parents who choose home-schooling for their kids are highly motivated; and home-schooled students tend to perform at high levels. Thus, requiring third-party verification of a home-schooled kid's academic standing is pretty much a waste of effort. Worse, it's an intrusion on the prerogatives of home-school educators (the parents) who are operating within the bounds of state law.

The "grade check" strikes us as a political nod to the public education establishment, which thrives on bureaucracy. But paperwork should not be confused with actual outcomes. After all, even graduation from a public high school is no guarantee of intelligence or future success. Home-school actually delivers better odds.

Cost Issues

As for costs associated with the inclusion of home-schooled students in extracurricular activities, the main costs are already sunk in stadiums, training equipment, pools, basketball courts and more. Coaches have been hired. A few extra kids trying out for a team or choir will have negligible—if not zero—impact on finances. Most extracurricular programs also require the payment of fees for participation.

But let's go back to Tim Tebow. As a high school quarterback, he had 95 passing touchdowns and scored 62 running. Let's imagine the next Tim Tebow is being home-schooled in Utah County right now. Why shouldn't he be allowed to play?

There is simply no link between any extracurricular program and the style of academic instruction a kid is getting in other parts of the school day.

And again, home-schoolers are taxpayers. Their tax dollars have purchased the right for their children to participate.

Allowing Access to Public School Resources May Harm Homeschooling

Valerie Delp

Valerie Delp is a senior blogger for families.com, a blog network for family topics.

One heated issue in homeschooling is whether or not homeschoolers should be allowed equal access to public school's "extras." Should a homeschooled student get to use the local school's computer lab, or library? Should they have the right to text books or AP [advanced placement] classes if they choose to use them? Many schools and districts allow this sharing of materials with homeschoolers, even if there are no state laws that mandate them to do so. However, the debate heats up when people start talking about extracurricular activities. Should homeschooled students be allowed to play sports on school teams or what about join the debate team or chess club?

Proponents of Equal Access Legislation point out that homeschooling families pay taxes to support public schools. Many families feel that their children miss out on opportunities, particularly in the area of athletics, because they don't have a chance to play. This would apply to students who are gifted athletes for example, that can't get "scouted" by a college because they're not playing.

Eligibility Guidelines Vary

I am likely in a minority as a homeschooling parent but I am not generally in favor of allowing homeschooled students access to public school resources. Homeschooling, like private school, is a choice. Every schooling choice comes with pros and cons and I feel like homeschoolers need to find other ways to get what they need rather than turning to the public school. Using public school resources comes with strings attached that can affect the entire homeschooling community. There are enough resources out there now that homeschoolers can have access to necessary materials without going through the public school for them.

Something that many homeschooling families do not realize is that the decision to play on a sports team (or other interscholastic team) is not as much a school or district decision as it is a league decision. Every team that plays in a league has guidelines that it must adhere to, otherwise it can't play in the league. Some guidelines include eligibility for four years (so if there is a 5th year senior, he generally cannot play), certain GPA [grade point average], etc. Athletic leagues keep these rules so that the competitions stay fair, and for the safety of all students involved.

Homeschooling families should also remember that if they were allowed to play on a public school team, they must meet eligibility requirements, which would likely include additional testing or others means to determine grade level work . . . where it otherwise would not be required.

Homeschoolers Should Be Denied Access to Public School Resources

Sherry F. Colb

Sherry F. Colb is a professor at Rutgers Law School in Newark, New Jersey, and a columnist for the FindLaw legal website.

A growing number of parents in the United States are home-schooling their children, as an alternative to sending them to public or private schools. For a variety of reasons, these parents believe that they can provide an equal or superior educational experience at home.

Yet even parents who home-school their children (whom I will call "home-schoolers") have begun to recognize the benefits of group after-school activities. And increasingly, they have become interested in taking advantage of extracurricular activities offered to children enrolled at public schools.

States, and individual districts within states, are split on the question of whether to admit home-schooled children into activities, such as sports teams, at schools that they do not attend. Some places give home-schooled children this option, while others do not.

The debate on the subject of access raises important questions about the meaning of a public school education, for those who opt in as well as for those who do not.

State and Local Taxes as Public School "Tuition"

One argument that home-schoolers make in favor of access to extracurricular offerings is simple: They, too, pay the taxes that finance the public school enterprise. Therefore, they claim, they are entitled to take advantage of the school's offerings to the extent that they and their children are interested in doing so.

Paying taxes is not the equivalent of paying tuition for public school.

They say, further, that their decision to educate their children at home saves public schools money. Paying to support the public schools, they explain, provides a free benefit to the enrolled students—funds for education without the expense of having to teach an additional student.

To admit the home-schooler's child into extracurricular activities is, on this reasoning, to provide one small part of the complete benefit package to which such outside students are really entitled, based on the "tuition" payments their parents make by paying state and local taxes.

This argument may sound persuasive, but it is based on a faulty premise about a taxpayer's entitlements. Paying taxes is *not* the equivalent of paying tuition for public school. If it were, then people who have no children, or whose children are grown, would not have any obligation or reason to pay. Yet we *all* pay taxes, regardless of whether we have children and of how many we have.

A Flawed Analogy

The reason that governments (and thus taxpayers) fund public schools is that every person living in our society benefits from an educated and well-socialized next generation. The people currently in public school are part of the general population that will be voting and running this country down the road.

Thus, though the children themselves undoubtedly benefit from going to school, the role of public school in the community's life goes well beyond the provision of benefits to individual students and their families.

By analogy, consider the government funding that goes to pay police officers' salaries. Such money subsidizes a service that we all wish to enjoy—the reduction of crime and the protection of our communities from destructive and violent behavior. As taxpayers, then, we can legitimately complain when police are not well trained, just as we can all complain when children are not properly educated.

But neither children who attend private (or home) schools nor private people who hire armed security guards are entitled to negotiate alternative packages for their own education or protection from the government. There is no direct correspondence, in other words, between payment and services, when it comes to taxes.

Public School as a Consumer Package

That being said, however, public schools *do* provide a benefit to school-age children and the parents who send them there: They educate those children and thus prepare them for careers, without charging a fee.

There is a flawed underlying assumption at work: that public school is an assortment of products that families and their children consume.

Home-schoolers who wish to enroll their offspring in extracurricular activities accordingly argue that even if they do not have *special* rights as taxpayers, they do have the more *general* right to send their children to public school, like everyone else in the community. This claim is a fair one.

If so, home-schoolers ask, why can't they send their children to some *limited* component of public school and not the entire program? As the home-schoolers suggest, the family that consumes only one portion of what the school has to offer, instead of the complete package, does seem to save the public schools money. It may thus seem unfair to permit only all-or-nothing consumption of the public school's benefits.

To provide an analogy, public libraries provide borrowing privileges to all members (and membership is free). Theoretically, then, one person could borrow a large number of books from the library. But that does not preclude another person's borrowing a very small number of books.

Benefits and Burdens

Doesn't the greater right to attend public school include the lesser right to participate only in extracurricular activities—as home-schoolers contend?

No. Once again, there is a flawed underlying assumption at work: that public school is assortment of products that families and their children consume, like a meal offered at a shelter. On this assumption, some children can consume the meal in part, rather than in whole. One should not have to eat broccoli in order to eat corn.

It is the reciprocity component of public school education that gets lost when families opt in for only some of what is offered.

This picture of education as a consumption item, however, is a bit like the picture of taxes as tuition. The opportunity to go to public school carries with it both benefits and burdens—and the burdens shouldered may ultimately yield general benefits to the larger society.

The benefits can include access to teachers, lessons, and classrooms. The burdens might encompass the responsibility to attend, to study the mandatory subjects, to complete the assignments, to demonstrate respect for teachers and for other students, and, more generally, to become a productive and valuable member of the school community. It is these burdens that become difficult to fulfill when a child does not attend school.

Partial Home-Schooling as an Option

A school might legitimately argue that a family should not be able to pick and choose benefits and burdens. Say that Sally Student is interested in mathematics and science, but not in reading or writing. She should not be allowed to exempt herself from the classes in which she has no interest. This is true, moreover, even if her parents agree to teach her reading and writing at home, so that she can achieve the same level of proficiency as the other children. Her presence in the various classes, in other words, is not just a privilege but an obligation as well.

Though home-schooling is permissible, then, *partial* home-schooling need not be. A school can rightly view as disruptive the menu approach to public school. One of the lessons that children learn at school is that each person has obligations to the group that do not depend on her own personal desires (or those of her parents). To be able to opt in or opt out would undermine the seriousness of the overall endeavor.

All of the mandatory curricular offerings are accordingly both *available to* and *required of* the attending students. It is the reciprocity component of public school education that gets lost when families opt in for only some of what is offered.

Extracurriculars as a Distinct Endeavor

Home-schoolers have a response to this argument, though. They protest that extracurricular activities are really not an inseparable part of public school education, in the way that reading classes are. After-school programs are simply an opportunity that children have for developing athletic and other skills.

On this view, there is coherence to the inclusion of home-schoolers in athletics and other extracurricular activities. A child can legitimately participate in one of two *independent* programs without participating in the other.

This argument may be the strongest home-schoolers can offer, but it, too, is not entirely convincing.

The argument at first seems plausible because extracurriculars are in fact categorically distinct from other subjects in the curriculum (hence the prefix "extra" in their name). They are not mandatory, and the students therefore gravitate toward the activities that interest them the most. Some students do not participate in any of them (and thus select the reverse of what home-schoolers want). The activities are primarily recreational, and grades are not ordinarily assigned.

A school can, for example, place conditions—both positive and negative—on participation in extracurricular activities.

The Eligibility Link

If Paul Pupil receives his schooling at home but shows up at P.S. 1 for basketball practice, home-schoolers can argue, he does not therefore generate the message that he lacks respect for the school. Such activities are logically severable from the "schoolday" curriculum.

The home-schooled student . . . is not part of the community in which her academics . . . and . . . interactive conduct will be in evidence to the authorities that run the school.

The U.S. Supreme Court has implied its concurrence with this view in *Board of Education of Pottawatomie v. Earls* a decision upholding against a Fourth Amendment challenge the drug-testing of all students who participate in extracurricular activities, precisely because such activities are optional and stand outside of the regular curriculum.

The separation, however, is not quite as clear as it might seem. A school can, for example, place conditions—both positive and negative—on participation in extracurricular activities. A student might have to maintain a minimum grade point average to join an athletic team, for example. Or she might need to avoid getting into trouble during the day in order to be eligible for particular (or all) after-school activities.

In either case, the school has drawn a direct link between one's performance, behavior and attitude regarding the regular curriculum, on the one hand, and one's eligibility for extra-curriculars, on the other.

The home-schooled student, however, is not well positioned to be judged along these dimensions, because she is not part of the community in which her academics, classroom contributions, and other interactive conduct will be in evidence to the authorities that run the school.

A Message of Disrespect for the Public School

To understand further how home-schooled children who participate in extracurricular activities might detract from the atmosphere of a school, consider the reasons people keep their children out of public schools in the first place.

One major motivation seems to be the perception (or even the reality) that the public school in one's area does not have high quality teachers and/or students. Another may be the view that the values embraced by the school (and/or by families that enroll their children there) are misguided (or even evil).

If these beliefs motivate home-schooling, then the presence of home-schooled children after school—and their "in your face" commitment to avoiding the faculty and students during the day—can seriously undermine the morale of the children who attend public school. Sending one's children to extracurricular activities alone is a way of saying, "we don't think your school or you have much to offer us, in terms of intelligence or morality, but we like your basketball team, so here we are."

It is not obvious that teachers and students should have to contend with this disrespectful message, implicit in such after-school limited joining. Disrespect uncoupled from any real investment in the place can make life depressing for those on the inside.

The Option to Participate

As I noted above, though, there are states and districts in which home-schooled children do have the option of participating in extracurricular activities at public schools. In such places, public schools may choose to create a clearer separation between in-school and after-school activities. They may also limit the curricular or behavioral conditions attached to joining extracurriculars and thus create a laissez-faire extracurricular world.

In such a world, participants must observe the rules of the game, compete for competitive positions, and otherwise conduct themselves in the way they might do in a publicly funded program that has nothing to do with the public school system.

This is perhaps the vision that home-schoolers have of extracurriculars everywhere. For schools that take a different and more holistic approach to education, though, this may represent an unwelcome state of affairs. And it is one that neither taxpayers nor a reciprocity-based public educational system should have to embrace.

Sports Are an Extension of the Classroom and Should Thus Exclude Homeschoolers

Preston Williams

Preston Williams writes a weekly column about high school sports in the Washington, D.C., area for The Washington Post.

As Aesop's fables for the cynical age, "Seinfeld" can provide insight into just about any life situation, even the ongoing debate about whether home-schooled students should be allowed to play on public high school sports teams.

There's an episode in which a floundering George Costanza is trying to figure out what career to pursue after quitting his real estate job. He hits upon sports broadcaster.

"Well," skeptical pal Jerry says, "they tend to give those jobs to ex-ballplayers and people that are, you know, in broadcasting."

"Well, that's really not fair," George replies.

The joke is, of course it's fair. Just as it's fair for state high school athletic associations to prohibit home-schooled students from competing on public high school teams because they're not, you know, public high school students.

Parents who choose to home-school do so for a variety of reasons: because their child is ahead or behind academically, religious beliefs, family considerations or dissatisfaction with local schools. Whatever the reason, they have chosen to bypass the extracurricular activities that the local public school offers, including sports.

Public high school uniforms don't have the names of neighborhoods or school districts on them. They have the names of schools. Being an area resident doesn't make you a representative of the school. Going to that school makes you a representative.

If you're ineligible to walk across the stage in your cap and gown, then you should be ineligible to walk on the field with your cap and glove.

Turns out, though, that more of the country is taking a Costanza view when it comes to home-schoolers suiting up for sports. According to the . . . Home School Legal Defense Association, 15 states allow home-schoolers to compete on public high school teams, with a steady trickle of states opening their programs in recent years, said Chris Klicka, senior counsel for the organization. Some other states allow local school divisions to set policies.

Maryland, the District [of Columbia] and Virginia have resisted accepting home-schooled students on their teams, but a bill came up in the Virginia General Assembly that would have forced the Virginia High School League [VHSL] to allow home-schoolers to participate in sports at public high schools. The bill died in the House Education Committee.

The VHSL was concerned enough in the preceding days, however, to distribute an e-mail with information on how to contact state representatives. After House Bill 375 failed to gain traction, the VHSL sent out another e-mail saying, "We appreciate the efforts of all who contacted their personal delegate and senator to express their opinions and support of VHSL athletics and activities."

You can't stiff-arm the public school's curriculum, administration and teachers and then expect to roll into the parking lot at 3:15 every day for practice.

So, the issue is on the minds of the public high school brass, and some area counties allow home-schoolers to take up to two classes or join school clubs. Sports could be next.

The cause has a high-profile public face: University of Florida quarterback Tim Tebow, the 2007 Heisman Trophy winner and the first sophomore to win the award. Tebow was home-schooled in Florida but played for his local public school team, Nease High in Ponte Vedra, where he was a Parade all-American. Miami Dolphins defensive end Jason Taylor also was home-schooled when he played for a public school team in Pennsylvania.

The Tim Tebow Act, similar to the failed measure in Virginia, was proposed in Alabama [in 2007]. It, too, failed to make it out of committee, but it was to be reintroduced at the legislative session that began [in early 2008].

High school sports are supposed to be an extension of the classroom. You can't stiff-arm the public school's curriculum, administration and teachers and then expect to roll into the parking lot at 3:15 every day for practice like you're going to Gold's Gym for a workout. That's playing time or a roster spot that belongs to a regular student.

If public school parents are discouraged from transferring their children for athletic reasons, then students who aren't even in the school system shouldn't show up just for athletics. For many sports, the home-schooled student has other options, including home-school teams or leagues, rec leagues and church leagues. Some private schools allow home-schoolers to play.

Public high school athletes have to meet standards in regard to attendance, grades and behavior. If your punishment is being sent to your room and not to the principal's office, then a coach or school cannot monitor whether a player should be eligible. And, as Alabama school officials pointed out, a rogue coach could cajole his academically challenged star player into being home-schooled just to preserve his eligibility.

The main argument cited by those in favor of allowing home-schoolers to compete for public school teams is that the home-school parents are taxpayers, too. Continuing in that vein, the parents might be saving the school division money by not sending their kids to public schools.

Fine. But there are plenty of residents without kids. They're paying taxes, too, but they can't expect to walk in off the street and have access to the school facilities. Residents pay taxes for parks, libraries, roads and hospitals that they might never use, but their community is better off for having those services.

The Home School Legal Defense Association does not take a stand on the issue of home-schoolers playing in public schools, Klicka said, because there's no consensus in the home-school community.

Granting home-schoolers greater access to public schools would result in more governmental meddling into home schools, which most home-schooling parents do not want.

If we think long enough, we probably could come up with a "Seinfeld" analogy for that, too.

Organizations to Contact

The editors have compiled the following list of organizations concerned with the issues debated in this book. The descriptions are derived from materials provided by the organizations. All have publications or information available for interested readers. The list was compiled on the date of publication of the present volume; the information provided here may change. Readers need to remember that many organizations take several weeks or longer to respond to inquiries.

American Association of School Administrators (AASA)
801 N. Quincy St., Suite 700, Arlington, VA   22203-1730
(703) 528-0700 • fax: (703) 841-1543
Web site: www.aasa.org

AASA is the professional organization for more than thirteen thousand educational leaders across the United States. Its mission is to support and develop effective school system leaders dedicated to the highest quality public education for all children. AASA members advance the goals of public education, champion children's causes in their districts and nationwide, help shape policy and oversee its implementation, and represent school districts to the public at large. The organization's publications include *School Administrator* magazine, as well as numerous journals, e-newsletters, books, and toolkits.

American Homeschool Association (AHA)
PO Box 3142, Palmer, AK   99645
(800) 236-3278
e-mail: aha@americanhomeschoolassociation.org
Web site: www.americanhomeschoolassociation.org

AHA is a service organization created to network homeschoolers on a national level. It is sponsored in part by the publishers of *Home Education Magazine*. Current AHA services include an online news and discussion list that provides news, information, and resources for homeschooling families.

Education Law Association (ELA)
University of Dayton, Dayton, OH   45469
(937) 229-3589 • fax (937) 229-3845
e-mail: ela@educationlaw.org
Web site: www.educationlaw.org

ELA is a nonprofit, nonadvocacy organization open to anyone interested in education law. The association, which is affiliated with the University of Dayton's School of Education and Allied Professions, has been providing unbiased information about current legal issues affecting education in schools, colleges, and universities since it was founded in 1954.

Home School Legal Defense Association (HSLDA)
PO Box 3000, Purcellville, VA   20134-9000
(540) 338-5600 • fax: (540) 338-2733
e-mail: info@hslda.org
Web site: www.hslda.org

HSLDA is a national membership Christian organization of families who homeschool their children. Its goal is to defend and advance the constitutional right of all parents to direct the education of their children and to protect family freedoms. The organization supports homeschooling families by negotiating with local officials, serving as an advocate in court proceedings, monitoring federal legislation, and fighting any proposed laws perceived as harmful to homeschooling.

National African-American Homeschooling Alliance (NAAHA)
e-mail: info@naaha.com
Web site: www.naaha.com

NAAHA is a nonsectarian organization and national online resource dedicated to providing timely and reliable resources for African American homeschoolers and anyone homeschooling African American children. Formed in 2003 to unite African American homeschoolers nationally, it is the largest homeschooling organization for blacks in America.

National Black Home Educators (NBHE)
13434 Plank Rd., PMB 110, Baker, LA   70714
e-mail: contact@nbhe.net
Web site: www.nbhe.net

NBHE is an online resource network founded in 2000 to encourage, support, and offer fellowship to families exploring the benefits of home education. The organization provides information about getting started in homeschooling, connects experienced families with new families, and recommends resources such as books, music, films, conferences, and curriculum.

National Center for Education Statistics (NCES)
1990 K St. NW, Washington, DC   20006
(202) 502-7300 • fax: (202) 502-7466
Web site: www.nces.ed.gov

NCES is part of the U.S. Department of Education and the Institute of Education Sciences and serves as the primary federal entity for collecting and analyzing data related to education in the United States and elsewhere. The center organizes training seminars, holds conferences, and publishes its findings in reports and publications, including the *Education Statistics Quarterly* and the *Digest of Education Statistics*.

National Education Association
1201 Sixteenth St. NW, Washington, DC   20036-3290
(202) 833-4000 • fax: (202) 822-7974
Web site: www.nea.org

NEA is a volunteer-based organization whose goal is to advance the cause of public education. The association lobbies legislators for school resources, campaigns for higher standards for the teaching profession, and files legal actions to protect academic freedom. At the local level, the association conducts professional workshops and negotiates contracts for school district employees.

National Home Education Network (NHEN)
PO Box 1652, Hobe Sound, FL   33475-1652
fax: (413) 581-1463
e-mail: info@nhen.org
Web site: www.nhen.org

NHEN is a volunteer organization that encourages and facilitates the grassroots work of state and local homeschooling organizations and individuals by providing information, fostering networking, and promoting public relations on a national level.

National Home Education Research Institute (NHERI)
PO Box 13939, Salem, OR   97309
(503) 364-1490 • fax: (503) 364-2827
e-mail: mail@nheri.org
Web site: www.nheri.org

NHERI is a nonprofit research organization that collects, tracks, and analyzes research on home-based education. A clearinghouse of research for the public, researchers, homeschoolers, the media, and policy makers, the organization strives to educate the public about homeschool research through speaking engagements, research reports, books, videos, and the journal *Home School Researcher*.

National School Boards Association (NSBA)
1680 Duke St., Alexandria, VA   22314
(703) 838-6722 • fax: (703) 683-7590
e-mail: info@nsba.org
Web site: www.nsba.org

NSBA serves the national and federal needs of local school boards. The association seeks to raise awareness of school board issues, assists school boards and educators in the uses of technology, reports the results of research on education issues, and lobbies Congress. NSBA publishes a variety of books and reports on school governance and other education topics, plus the magazine *American School Board Journal* and the newspaper *School Board News*.

United States Department of Education
400 Maryland Ave. SW, Washington, DC   20202-0498
800-872-5327
e-mail: customerservice@inet.ed.gov
Web site: www.ed.gov

The United States Department of Education works to ensure equal access to education and to foster educational excellence. The department establishes policies on federal financial aid for education and provides grants to primary, secondary, and postsecondary education institutes; financial aid to students for postsecondary education; and underwrites education research. It produces hundreds of publications annually, including *Community Update*, which informs readers about available resources, services, and publications.

Bibliography

Books

David H. Albert
Have Fun. Learn Stuff. Grow. Home-schooling and the Curriculum of Love. Monroe, ME: Common Courage, 2006.

Mimi Davis
So—Why Do You Homeschool? Longwood, FL: Xulon, 2005.

David d'Escoto and Kim d'Escoto
The Little Book of BIG Reasons to Homeschool. Nashville: B&H, 2007.

Milton Gaither
Homeschool: An American History. New York: Palgrave Macmillan, 2008.

Rachel Gathercole
The Well-Adjusted Child: The Social Benefits of Homeschooling. Denver: Mapletree, 2007.

Christopher J. Klicka
Home School Heroes: The Struggle and Triumph of Home Schooling. Nashville: B&H, 2006.

Martine Millman and Gregory Millman
Homeschooling: A Family's Journey. New York: Penguin, 2008.

Tamra B. Orr
Asking Questions, Finding Answers: A Parent's Journey Through Homeschooling. Tonasket, WA: HEM, 2008.

| Brian D. Ray | *Worldwide Guide to Homeschooling: Facts and Stats on the Benefits of Homeschool.* New York: Palgrave Macmillan, 2008. |

| Lisa Rivero | *The Homeschooling Option: How to Decide When It's Right for Your Family.* New York: Palgrave Macmillan, 2008. |

| Bonnie Kerrigan Snyder and Mark Robert Snyder | *Public School Parent's Guide to Success: How to Beat Private School and Homeschooling.* Lincoln, NE: iUniverse, 2007. |

| Jack F. Troy | *School's Out: The Case for Abandoning Failing Public Schools and the Rebirth of American Education at Home.* Lincoln, NE: iUniverse, 2007. |

| Amy Schechter Vahid and Frank Vahid | *Homeschooling: A Path Rediscovered for Socialization, Education, and Family.* Lulu.com, 2007. |

| Gary Wyatt | *Family Ties: Relationships, Socialization, and Homeschooling.* Lanham, MD: University Press of America, 2008. |

Periodicals

| Michelle Conlin | "Meet My Teachers: Mom and Dad," *Business Week*, February 20, 2006. |

| Bruce S. Cooper and John Sureau | "The Politics of Homeschooling— New Developments, New Challenges," *Educational Policy*, January–March 2007. |

Christa L. Green and Kathleen V. Hoover-Dempsey — "Why Do Parents Homeschool?" *Education & Urban Society*, February 2007.

Chloé A. Hilliard — "The New Home Room," *Village Voice*, April 9, 2008.

William G. Howell, Martin R. West, and Paul E. Peterson — "What Americans Think About Their Schools," *Education Next*, Fall 2007.

Eric J. Isenberg — "What Have We Learned About Homeschooling?" *Peabody Journal of Education*, Issue 2/3, 2007.

Christina Sim Keddie — "Homeschoolers and Public School Facilities: Proposals for Providing Fairer Access," *NYU Journal of Legislation and Public Policy*, Spring 2007.

Virginia Kelley — "Home Schooling: Beneficial, or Not?" University of Mississippi *Daily Mississippian*, May 29, 2008.

Dan Lips and Evan Feinberg — "Homeschooling: A Growing Option in American Education," *Heritage Foundation Backgrounder*, April 3, 2008.

Sandra Tsing Loh — "Tales Out of School," *Atlantic Monthly*, March 2008.

Neil MacFarquhar — "Resolute or Fearful, Many Muslims Turn to Home Schooling," *New York Times*, March 26, 2008.

Gregory J. Millman — "Home Is Where the School Is," *Washington Post*, March 23, 2008.

Brian D. Ray	"The Evidence Is So Positive: What Current Research Tells Us About Homeschooling," *Old Schoolhouse Magazine*, Winter 2006–2007.
Michael H. Romanowski	"Revisiting the Common Myths About Homeschooling," *Clearing House*, January/February 2006.
Robert Sanborn, Adolfo Santos, Alexandra L. Montgomery, and James B. Caruthers	"Four Scenarios for the Future of Education," *Futurist*, January/February 2005.
Michael Smith	"Acceptance Grows but Myths Persist," *Washington Times*, May 19, 2008.
Paula Wasley	"Home-Schooled Students Rise in Supply and Demand," *Chronicle of Higher Education*, October 12, 2007.
Kimberly A. Yuracko	"Education Off the Grid: Constitutional Constraints on Home Schooling," *California Law Review*, February 2008.
Mary Ann Zehr	"U.S. Home Schoolers Push Movement Around the World," *Education Week*, January 4, 2006.

Index

THE
CHAIRMAN

STEPHEN FREY

THE CHAIRMAN

A NOVEL

BALLANTINE BOOKS · NEW YORK

Published in the United States by Ballantine Books, an imprint of The Random House Publishing Group, a division of Random House, Inc., New York.

Ballantine and colophon are registered trademarks of Random House, Inc.

Library of Congress Cataloging-in-Publication Data
Frey, Stephen W.
    The chairman : a novel / Stephen Frey.—1st ed.
        p.   cm.
    ISBN 0-345-45760-9
        1. Capitalists and financiers—Fiction. 2. Investment
    bankers—Fiction. 3. Corporate culture—Fiction. 4. New
    York (N.Y.)—Fiction. 5. Wall Street—Fiction. I. Title.
PS3556.R4477C47 2005
813'.54—dc22   2004046210

Printed in the United States of America

Ballantine Books website address: www.ballantinebooks.com

9 8 7 6 5 4 3 2 1

First Edition

Book design by Julie Schroeder

For Diana.
I love you so much. You are incredible.

ACKNOWLEDGMENTS

A special acknowledgment to my editor, Mark Tavani, who did a tremendous job on this book.

My daughters, Christina and Ashley, I love you dearly.

And the people who have constantly been so helpful:
Cynthia Manson, Gina Centrello, Kevin Big Sky Erdman, Stephen Watson, Matt, Kristin and Aidan Malone, Jack Wallace, Bart and Allison Begley, Bob and Allison Wieczorek, Scott Andrews, John Piazza, Marvin Bush, Gordon Eadon, Jane Barrett, Andy and Chris Brusman, Jeff Faville, Chris Tesoriero, Walter Frey, Gerry Barton, John Grigg, Jim and Anmarie Galowski, Tony Brazely, Dr. Teo Dagi, Arthur Manson, Alex Fisher, Chris Andrews, Barbara Fertig, Mike Pocalyko, Baron Stewart, Pat and Terry Lynch, Rick Slocum.

THE CHAIRMAN

1

The Chairman. *The chairman of a large private equity firm is the ultimate decision maker. Which companies to buy. How many billions to pay. Who to hire as CEO. How many millions to pay.*

If his judgment is flawed, the chairman loses everything. Maybe even his freedom. But if he negotiates the lies, lawsuits, and vendettas that haunt his world, he becomes one of the richest and most powerful men on earth.

CHRISTIAN GILLETTE GAZED OUT FROM the pulpit at a grim-faced congregation, then down on an open coffin—and Bill Donovan's face. Until two days ago, Donovan had been the chairman.

Gillette was just thirty-six, but suddenly that enormous responsibility had been thrust upon him, the decision to promote him made by a razor-thin majority of Everest Capital investors late yesterday at the climax of an emotionally charged meeting held in a conference room overlooking Wall Street. The controversial vote had come within three days of Donovan's death—as stipulated in the partnership's operating agreement.

"The world has lost a great man," Gillette declared, ending his brief eulogy. Donovan wouldn't have wanted something long and drawn out. He'd been obsessive about efficiency—and the lesson had been learned.

As Gillette stepped down from the pulpit, he heard the muffled sobs of family, the stony silence of enemies. Donovan had touched many lives for better *and* worse. It was the inevitable consequence of being chairman.

"I'm sorry for your loss, Ann," Gillette said quietly, getting down on one knee before the veiled widow in the front pew. "We all admired Bill very much."

"Thank you," she whispered.

Gillette rose and moved deliberately up the cathedral's center aisle, pausing to acknowledge high-profile guests: George Stockman, U.S. senator from New York; Richard Harris, CEO of U.S. Petroleum; Jeremy Cole, quarterback of the New York Giants; Miles Whitman, chief investment officer of North America Guaranty & Life; Thomas Warfield, president of J.P. Morgan Chase. Each one standing up well before Gillette reached him. Pledging their loyalty and assistance in low voices after taking one of his hands in both of theirs. Each with a different agenda, but all focused on one thing: Gillette's sudden control of billions.

Gillette gave them a subtle nod in return, studying their expressions with his piercing gray eyes. Gauging their sincerity. For the first time truly experiencing the power he now wielded. The three men who until yesterday had been his equals—Troy Mason, Ben Cohen, and Nigel Faraday—trailing him at a respectful distance as he worked his way up the maroon carpet. Not until Gillette had made it to the back of the church did the congregation begin filing out.

Dark clouds hung low over New York City and raw November gusts whipped trash and newspapers down Park Avenue as Gillette moved through the church's arched double doorway. It had been a warm autumn—until the day of Donovan's death.

Gillette paused at the top of the marble steps leading to the sidewalk, taking in the scents of wood smoke and caramel wafting from a street vendor's cart. Taking in the moment. He'd dedicated the last ten years of his life to Everest—the powerful Manhattan-based private equity firm Donovan had founded two decades ago with just $25 million of limited partner commitments. Typically logging eighty hours a week for the firm. Rarely taking a vacation day. Suddenly, that sacrifice had paid the ultimate dividend.

A pretty blond woman walking past the church flashed Gillette a coy smile. He watched her move down the sidewalk, looking away when she glanced at him again over her shoulder. He'd been seriously involved with just two women during the last ten years, both of whom had left after only a few months when they realized they'd always come in second to Everest. The lack of companionship only made his desire that much stronger.

As the woman neared the limousine waiting to take him to the cemetery, Gillette allowed himself a final glimpse.

"Come on, Chris," Cohen urged, clasping Gillette's elbow and pulling him down the stairs. "You don't have time for eye candy right now. We've got to get you to the cemetery."

Until yesterday, Cohen and Gillette had been equals. Together with Mason and Faraday, they'd formed the managing partner team supporting Donovan. But now he'd risen above them. Now he had absolute power. There would be jealousy, maybe worse.

"Take your hand off me," Gillette ordered. "And, Ben, from now on call me *Christian*." He watched Cohen's demeanor chill, but he didn't care. He was going to establish dominance quickly. "Understand?"

"Is that a *sine qua non?*" Cohen asked solemnly.

Gillette's right hand contracted slowly into a fist. He hated Cohen's habit of using Latin. "Dead languages don't impress me." He'd been waiting a long time to say that.

Cohen's lower lip quivered ever so slightly. "So it starts already?"

"Do you understand?"

"Yes." Cohen hesitated. "Christian."

As they reached the bottom step, a heavyset chauffeur emerged from the limousine and lumbered toward the back. The instant the chauffeur lifted the passenger door handle, the limousine exploded in a brilliant flash of white and yellow light, killing him and the blond woman walking past. The massive concussion spewed jagged metal fragments hundreds of feet in all directions.

Gillette brought his arms to his face but he was a fraction of a second too late.

2

Private Equity. *High-risk investment dollars committed by large institutions and wealthy families to a few financial gunslingers who operate from behind a shroud of secrecy.*

*The gunslingers' mandate: Deliver **huge** returns. Fifty, 75, 100 percent a year—consistently. Much more than investors earn on money market accounts, bonds, or publicly traded stocks. And don't tell anyone outside the circle how you do it. Confidentiality at all costs.*

If they get it right, the gunslingers make their investors—and themselves— incredible amounts of money. Billions and billions. If they get it wrong, and the extent of the risks taken comes to light, they scatter for places where English is rarely spoken.

GILLETTE GLANCED PAST THE DRIVER into the rearview mirror of the hastily ordered Lincoln Town Car. The wound on his forehead had finally stopped bleeding at the cemetery, but there were several red stains on his starched white shirt, blood on his handkerchief, and he had a thin maroon cut at his hairline. Stark reminders of how close he had come to quickly following Bill Donovan into the ground.

"You okay, Christian?" Cohen sat beside Gillette in the backseat. A wisp of a man with thinning, curly black hair, Cohen remembered every number he had ever calculated. He took off his glasses and cleaned the lenses with a tissue. He was only thirty-seven, but he already needed bifocals—the price of staring at a computer screen day after day. "You've got to be worried about what happened."

"I'm fine," Gillette answered firmly. Cohen was the one who looked like he'd seen a ghost right after the explosion. And he hadn't been hit.

"Maybe you should skip the reception," Cohen suggested gently.

"No."

"Looks like you might need a couple of stitches."

"I'm fine."

"You don't always have to be so tough."

"Enough, Ben."

"We'll figure out who was responsible," Cohen vowed angrily. "We'll use the McGuire brothers. I'll call Tom tomorrow."

McGuire & Company offered security services—surveillance, background checks, investigations, and executive protection. It was a worldwide operation with offices stretching from New York to London to Hong Kong. Tom and Vince McGuire, brothers and ex–FBI agents, ran the firm for Everest Capital, which owned the company through its sixth private equity fund.

"It won't take long to nail whoever did this," Cohen added.

Gillette peered out the rear window. Faraday and Mason were in the limousine behind them. Escorting the widow from the cemetery to Donovan's thousand-acre Connecticut estate for the reception. "Don't waste the time or the money, Ben."

"What?"

"I mean it."

"There has to be a *quid pro quo*," Cohen insisted. "People have to understand that we'll come after them if they do something like this."

"You'll never figure out who blew up the limousine," Gillette said. "No one will. Not even Tom McGuire. The same way no one will ever figure out what really happened to Bill Donovan in that stream."

Donovan's body had been found Wednesday morning, facedown in a trout stream that snaked through a remote part of his heavily wooded property.

Cohen squinted. The way he always did when he was startled or confused. "What do you mean, '*What really happened to Bill*'?"

"Don't be naïve, Ben."

"Bill drowned."

"Did he?"

"Christian, the police are sure he—"

"I walked that stream with Bill a few years ago. It isn't very wide and it doesn't get deeper than a few feet. It's hard for me to believe anyone could drown in it accidentally. Bill was murdered," Gillette said bluntly.

"My God," Cohen said, his voice hushed. "I never even thought about that."

"What about the limousine exploding? Doesn't that tell you something?"

Cohen hesitated. "That's a good point. I guess I—"

"There's something I want you to do," Gillette interrupted him.

"What?"

"Find out about the woman."

"The woman?"

"The woman who was walking past the limousine when it exploded. If she had children, I want Everest to take care of them. And do it *anonymously*," Gillette emphasized. "No money trail, understand? I don't want some ambulance chaser turning generosity into opportunity."

"I'll see to it," Cohen promised, slipping his black-frame glasses back onto the bridge of his nose.

They were silent for a few minutes while the Town Car headed deeper into the Connecticut forest.

"Mason's angry," Gillette spoke up as the driver slowed down ahead of a sharp curve.

"Why do you say that?"

"He thought he'd be chairman."

"He would have if Bill hadn't died so suddenly," Cohen agreed. "Troy was Bill's favorite. Everybody knew that. But I don't think Troy's angry. Just sad."

"Troy wanted what I now have more than anything in the world. The same way Faraday did." Gillette looked over at Cohen as the car came out of the curve. "The same way you did, Ben."

Cohen's pale cheeks flushed instantly. "You need to understand something, Christian. My wife and daughters are much more important to me than my career."

"I know how devoted you are to your family," Gillette acknowledged brusquely. He'd worked with Cohen for a decade and heard about the girls constantly. "I also know you wanted to be chairman. Don't lie to me."

Cohen pursed his lips, unable to hide his irritation at Gillette's comfort with candor. "I would have done a good job," he muttered under his breath.

"Do you think Troy will resign?" Gillette asked.

"How can he? Most of his net worth is tied up in Everest. If he re-signs, he forfeits his stake in the firm. That's the deal we all signed up for."

"What do you think his stake is worth?"

"Sixty million. Same as yours and Faraday's. Same as mine."

Donovan had been careful to make each of the managing partners equal minority owners of Everest Capital.

"What if I fire Troy?" Gillette asked, aware that Cohen knew the ins and outs of Everest's legal documents better than anyone.

Cohen had always been focused on details. Which was why he hadn't been elected chairman yesterday, Gillette realized. Not even really con-sidered. The chairman of a big private equity firm had to think strategi-cally, and Cohen was constantly off in the weeds, chasing minutiae. He'd received only one vote—his own.

Gillette knew how many votes each of them had gotten after check-ing the minutes of the meeting just before the funeral. As chairman, he was the only one inside Everest—other than Donovan's widow—who had access to them. He'd beaten Mason by a single vote. It had been that close.

"What happens then?" Gillette pushed when Cohen didn't answer. "If I fire Troy."

"We get an investment bank to do a formal appraisal of his stake," Cohen answered. "To confirm the $60 million figure. Then we pay it to Troy in equal monthly installments over five years. But he doesn't share in the upside if his stake turns out to be worth more than sixty later on. You, Faraday, and I keep that."

"What if he's terminated for cause?"

"You mean if he's convicted of a felony?"

"Right."

"He forfeits his stake immediately, and, again, the three of us get it." Cohen shook his head. "There's no chance of that, though, Christian. Troy's a lot of things, but he's no criminal."

"Isn't there a broader definition of cause in the partnership agree-ment?" Gillette saw a curious expression spread across the other man's face. As if Cohen was surprised anyone else might know the complexities of the agreement as intimately as he did. "Something less black and white than being convicted of a felony?"

"Yes."

"Something about committing acts that could harm Everest's reputation or be detrimental to its business prospects. *Our* business prospects."

"If you fired Troy using that clause, he'd sue us," Cohen said confidently, "and probably win. Like our lawyers always tell us about the employment contracts of the CEOs at our portfolio companies, it's very hard to rely on that clause if you want to fire them. You've got to have something more."

"But it's there," Gillette prompted. "Right?"

"Yes." Cohen hesitated. "Are you really thinking about firing Troy?"

Gillette glanced at the railroad tracks paralleling the road. He'd been fascinated by trains for a long time. Ever since that summer—years ago, a lifetime ago—when he'd been forced to depend on them. "What about Donovan's stake in Everest?" he asked, avoiding Cohen's question. "What happens to it now that he's dead?"

"There's a special exemption in the partnership's operating agreement for Bill," Cohen explained. "Because he was the founder, his widow stays in and shares the upside as we sell companies. She doesn't get paid out right away in one lump sum like Mason would if he resigned. And thank God," Cohen added quickly. "The widow's share of Everest is worth more than four billion at this point."

"But she has no authority," Gillette spoke up. "She can't tell me how to run Everest."

"No, she can't. As chairman, you now have total control." Cohen paused. "Unless a significant number of the partners get together and vote to remove you."

"Tell me about that."

Cohen shrugged. "It's pretty simple. If 60 percent of the partners decide to remove you, they can. Someone calls a meeting and they vote. But that vote can only be called once a calendar year. The only other way you can be canned is if you're convicted of a felony. Then it's automatic."

"I thought I saw something in one of the ancillary documents to the partnership agreement that covered the widow's voting rights," Gillette said. "Does she have something different from everyone else?"

"Definitely. And it's big."

"Oh?"

"Yeah. No matter how many limited partners there are in the funds, she gets 25 percent of the vote. It's a provision Donovan always insisted on. As I understand it, he had a tough time getting the limited partners to buy in to that early on, before we got here. But when his track record got good, when he started making all that money for the limiteds, they stopped caring about it."

Donovan hadn't advertised that. "What if we raise another fund?" Gillette asked, watching the train tracks veer away from the road and disappear into the forest. "Would she share in the upside of that one, too?"

"No. She keeps Bill's stake in all of our existing funds, but she doesn't automatically get a piece of any new ones we raise. She might come in as an investor in the next fund if we asked her to, but she wouldn't get a piece of Everest's upside share of that fund. She'd be a limited partner in that one like everybody else."

Investors in Everest Capital's private equity funds were known as limited partners, "limited" because they had no management authority over the fund. Gillette, Cohen, Mason, and Faraday were the managers. Responsible for identifying companies to buy; finding executives to operate them; and deciding when to sell. With Gillette now being the ultimate decision maker on all major issues.

The investors had limited financial liability as well. They couldn't lose more than they put in. Which had never been an issue for any of Everest's seven funds. Going back twenty years, each Everest fund had returned *at least* three dollars for every dollar invested.

Everest Capital earned an annual fee from the limited partners to cover expenses—for things like the salaries of Everest's thirty-three employees and the lease expense for its Park Avenue offices. The aggregate fee—a percentage of the total dollars Everest managed—was a hundred million. Big money. But the real sizzle for Gillette, Cohen, Faraday, and Mason was the opportunity to share in the profits, or "ups," from the sale of portfolio companies out of the funds.

Typically, Everest acquired ten to twenty companies with each fund, running the companies for three to five years after buying them. Significantly increasing profits before taking them public or selling them to bigger companies. In most cases cashing out for much more than they paid. Distributing the sale proceeds back to the limited partners after the transaction.

The kicker for Gillette and the others came after the limited partners had gotten back their original investment. Once that happened,
Everest kept 20 percent of the profits. So, if the original investment by
the limited partners was ten dollars and Everest turned that into forty
over the life of the fund, Everest kept six—20 percent of the thirty-
dollar gain. Of course, if the original size of the fund was ten *billion* and
that ten billion turned into forty billion, the "ups" were six billion. Six
billion split just four ways—now that Donovan was dead.

The last private equity fund Everest had raised—Everest Capital
Partners VII—was 6.5 billion. It was the seventh fund Everest had
raised, and was one of the largest of its kind. Donovan and Nigel Faraday
had led the money-raise, completing it eighteen months ago. A little
over half of the 6.5 billion was invested in seven companies.

Already, Gillette was planning a new fund—Everest Capital Partners VIII—which would be ten billion dollars. Along with the five billion
Everest still managed in funds I through VI—and the 6.5 in VII—the
firm would control more than twenty billion dollars of private equity
capital. Once VIII was raised, Everest would become the most powerful
private equity firm in the world.

"The four of us keep all the Everest upside in the next fund," Cohen
continued. "And, as chairman, you decide how that's divided."

Gillette's eyes narrowed. Twenty billion dollars. A tremendous
amount of money. Easily enough to convince whoever had just tried to
kill him to try again. "You said the widow wouldn't share in the upside of
the next fund."

"That's true," Cohen confirmed.

"I assume she wouldn't get that 25 percent voting block either."

"No, she wouldn't."

"How does that work?" Gillette asked. "When does she lose that
right?"

"As soon as we raise another fund that's the same size or bigger than
the last one. Once that happens, she's just like everybody else. Her vote
is equal to her pro rata piece of the current fund. Her dollar commitment
divided by the size of the fund."

There were implications to that—good and bad—Gillette would
have to sort through. But it would take at least a year to raise VIII, so it
would be a while before he'd have to deal with them. "Ben, we're going
to start raising the eighth fund next week," he announced. "The target

for Everest VIII is going to be ten billion dollars." It was the first time he'd mentioned this to Cohen.

Cohen squinted and his mouth fell slowly open. "Ten billion?"

"Yes."

"But we're only a little over halfway through the seventh fund."

"The partnership agreement states that I can start raising the next fund after we've invested 50 percent of the current one." He'd checked that clause this morning, too.

"Sure, sure, but Bill always waited until we'd invested at least 75 percent," Cohen countered. "He thought it was better that way. So the limited partners would feel like we were more focused on generating returns and not just raising more money so we could collect bigger management fees. We didn't start raising VII until we were 80 percent of the way through VI."

"Ten billion is a lot of money. We'll need extra time."

"Will the insurance companies and the pension funds commit that much?" Cohen asked skeptically. "Is there enough money in the market to do this?"

"There's always enough money."

"I don't know."

"Don't worry."

"It's what I do best." Cohen sighed, adjusting his glasses. "Christian, there's something you should know."

Gillette glanced over. "What?"

"Both Kyle and Marcie have been approached by other private equity firms. They've been offered very nice packages. Big salaries, guaranteed bonuses, and big pieces of the ups."

Kyle Lefors and Marcie Reed were managing directors at Everest Capital. One rung below Cohen, Faraday, and Mason on the Everest organization chart. There were several other managing directors at the firm, but Lefors and Reed were the most talented.

"I knew about Lefors," Gillette said.

"How?"

"Tom McGuire."

"Of course."

"But I didn't know about Marcie." Gillette took a deep breath. "I don't want to lose either of them."

"What are you going to do?"

Gillette heard the concern in Cohen's voice, and the reason was obvious. There was really only one way to deal with the problem. Promote Lefors and Reed to managing partner and give them a piece of the ups in VIII. Of course, Cohen, Faraday, and Mason wouldn't want that because it would mean less for them. Cohen and Mason might argue against the promotions calmly, but Faraday would go ballistic. He had a terrible temper.

"I don't know yet. I need to think about it some more."

"Just don't—"

"Did I see Faith Cassidy at the funeral?" asked Gillette, switching subjects as he pulled out his Blackberry—a cordless, handheld e-mail and cell phone device—and began rifling through his messages.

Faith Cassidy had exploded on to the pop music scene last year with a debut album that sold millions. Her second album had come out recently. Through the sixth fund—the same one that owned McGuire & Company—Everest owned the entertainment company that controlled Faith's music label.

"Yes, she was at the church," Cohen confirmed.

"She's an attractive young woman."

"I suppose," Cohen agreed indifferently, watching the trees flash past.

"Who invited her?"

Cohen stayed silent.

"Ben?"

"All right, I did," Cohen admitted. "Bill liked her a lot. I thought it would be a nice gesture. You have a problem with that?"

When the Town Car had climbed the long, steep driveway and eased to a stop in front of Donovan's mansion, Gillette stepped out and waited for Troy Mason to escort the widow up to him.

"Thank you again for delivering the eulogy," she murmured from behind the black lace, still clasping Mason's arm. "I know Bill appreciated your kind words."

Gillette glanced at Mason's bitter expression. Mason was tall, blond, and handsome. A man who would have been playing football on Sundays instead of buying and running companies if he hadn't destroyed his left knee in the Rose Bowl his senior year at Stanford. He still walked with a slight limp.

Gillette and Mason hadn't spoken since the decision of the partners had been announced yesterday afternoon. Normally they talked five to ten times a day.

"It was an honor, Ann," Gillette assured her, turning his attention back to the widow. Trying to see behind the veil.

"People will be here soon," she whispered.

Gillette nodded. "We should get you inside." There was a gust of wind and the veil fluttered. For a moment he caught sight of her pale face and drawn lips. "May I use your husband's study this afternoon?"

The widow slid her arm from Mason's and moved beside Gillette. "You know people will want your time, don't you?"

"No doubt."

"Even if all they can get is a few seconds," she murmured. "Because of all that money."

Now that she was close, he could see through the lace. "Yes."

"We chose wisely the other day," she whispered, her back to Mason. "Bill would have voted for Troy. He loved Troy like a son." She hesitated, gazing off into the distance.

Like the one she could never give him, Gillette thought to himself.

"Offer me your arm, Christian."

Gillette glanced over the widow's shoulder into Mason's burning eyes before turning to escort her down the stone path. "Thank you for your vote at the meeting," he said. "Without it, I wouldn't be chairman."

"You should thank Miles Whitman. I was going to vote for Troy until Miles called and told me you were the best person for the job. I'm glad he did."

Miles Whitman was Everest's largest investor. "So am I," Gillette agreed.

The widow clasped his arm tightly. "Take care of my money, young man."

"Like it was my own."

They were quiet until they were almost to the mansion.

"Always make people come to you, Christian," she advised him as they reached the stone terrace in front of the main entrance. "Always make people see you on your terms. When *you're* prepared. Never before." She turned to face him. "I learned a lot over the last twenty years. Even as *just* the wife."

3

Negotiations. *The purchase of a company—price, cash or paper, representations, warranties. Details of a senior executive's pay package—salary, bonus, stock options, perks. Terms of a critical financing—interest rate, repayment schedule, covenants. Issues that the private equity professionals deal with constantly because the CEO of a company owned by a private equity firm can't make a move without his chairman's approval.*

And, in a world dominated by constant negotiation, there is one hard and fast rule. It isn't the one who wants something less who has the advantage. It's the one who appears *to want it less.*

EVERYTHING ABOUT DONOVAN'S STUDY WAS imposing. The huge stone fireplace. Big desk. Dark wood walls. Expensive furniture. Oil paintings. Photographs of him with famous people—politicians, sports figures, entertainers—cluttering the credenza and floor-to-ceiling bookcases. All of it designed to intimidate the visitor.

Gillette took a deep breath. The scents of leather and wood smoke. It reminded him of his father's study.

The wooden chair behind the wide desk creaked as Gillette eased into it. Through the dim light he gazed at himself in a gold-framed oval mirror hanging on the far wall. Black hair parted on one side, combed back behind his ears. Sharp facial features—a thin nose, strong jaw, prominent chin, and high, defined cheekbones. And intense gray eyes that people naturally locked on to. At six two and a fit 190 pounds, he was an imposing figure on the other side of the negotiating table—which always helped.

The image in the mirror blurred as the exploding limousine flashed through his mind once more. He grimaced. Two people dead. A few more paces and he would have been—

A knock on the office door broke the stillness.

"Christian."

He recognized the heavy English accent immediately. "Come in."

The door opened and closed quickly, and Nigel Faraday appeared out of the gloom. Faraday was pale, round-faced, and rarely without a drink in his hand if he wasn't at the office. This afternoon was no exception.

"Bloody hell."

"What's wrong, Nigel?" Gillette asked, watching the Brit swirl the ice in his glass with his finger.

Faraday was Ben Cohen's alter ego. Faraday hated details and had no desire to be tied down by a family. Thriving instead on Manhattan's nightlife. Entertaining Everest investors three or four evenings a week, often until two or three in the morning. An expert at raising cash, he had that knack for knowing the exact moment to ask for big money—and getting it.

"Our plan was a bust," Faraday muttered, throwing back a healthy swallow of scotch. "Fucking Cohen."

"Not even going to try to deny the conspiracy?" Gillette asked, touching his forehead to make certain it wasn't bleeding again. They weren't particularly close, but he'd always liked Faraday. His sarcasm was entertaining, and, if you weren't careful, the accent could be hypnotic.

"Cohen was supposed to get you down those steps faster, then tell you he'd forgotten something in the church and get away from the limo. But all that little fucker can do is run numbers. And babble Latin," Faraday added, smiling. "Mason and I should have remembered that."

Gillette almost smiled back—three days ago he would have—but he controlled his expression. Things were different. He had to maintain his distance now that he was chairman. "Next time you'll do a better job of preparing."

"You're fucking right we will."

Gillette shook his head. Faraday dropped the f-bomb constantly.

"Chris, I—"

"Christian," Gillette interrupted.

Faraday chuckled, then coughed and wiped the smile away with the back of his hand when he realized Gillette was serious. "Well, look, I just wanted to make sure you were all right. I was worried about you there for a few minutes, what with all that blood. I'm not going to lie and tell you I wasn't disappointed that I didn't get the nod from the limited partners yesterday. I thought I had more than a few of them in my pocket. After all, I raised a lot of their dough." Faraday paused. "But I'm glad you're all right."

Of the ninety-three investors in the Everest funds, Faraday had won only three votes. Translation: The limited partners enjoyed the entertainment, and they committed dollars to Everest when Faraday asked, but they had no confidence in his ability to actually manage the money. To acquire healthy companies and make savvy operating decisions once Everest owned them.

"Thank you," Gillette said quietly.

"I also came to let you know that Senator Stockman fucking wants to see you."

Gillette glanced up from a manila folder lying on one corner of Donovan's desk. "Looking for handouts, is he?" It hadn't taken long for the parade to start.

"I'm sure he'd refer to it as 'support.'"

"Aren't you *fucking* sure?" Gillette shot back, spotting a razor cut on Faraday's cheek. Faraday was swarthy and always nicking himself.

Faraday's round face slowly broke into another grin. "Yeah. I'm fucking sure."

Gillette nodded. "I'll see him. But tell him it'll be a few minutes."

"Should I come back in with him?"

"No, send Cohen." Faraday's grin evaporated and anger flashed across his face, but Gillette motioned toward the door before the other man could complain. "Go."

When Faraday was gone, Gillette glanced back into the mirror. Urgency and efficiency. Make the most of every second. Bill Donovan's mantra. Over the last ten years Gillette had become a disciple.

. . . .

Faraday worked his way through the crowd toward Cohen. A thousand people had been invited to the reception and all of them seemed to have accepted.

He tapped Cohen on the shoulder. "Hey, Moses." His nickname for the little man.

Cohen excused himself from his conversation with Faith Cassidy. "What is it, Nigel?" he snapped, irritated at being interrupted.

The Brit grinned smugly. "Where's your wife?"

"Why?"

"She's usually smarter about monitoring your fucking pecker."

Cohen pursed his lips. "Why do you like hassling me so much?"

"Because it's so fucking easy." Faraday gestured with his glass. "Our new leader has summoned you to the study. By the way, he's calling himself 'Christian' now."

Cohen rolled his eyes. "Yeah, I know."

"Sit down, Ben." Gillette motioned toward the two chairs in front of the desk.

Cohen chose the one farthest from the door.

"I need your help."

"I want to help in any way I can, Christian. Especially right now when you're just taking over."

Gillette studied Cohen's expression, trying to determine whether the signs of submission were sincere. "Senator Stockman wants to meet with me, and I need someone else in here while we talk." Gillette watched Cohen relax. He understood that a new order had just been established, and that he was now second in command. "Just so there's no misunderstanding later about what was said."

"Thanks," said Cohen, looking down. "I appreciate your including me."

Gillette waited for Cohen's eyes to come back up to his. "Did you talk to Mason?"

"Yes."

"And?"

"And you were right, Christian. One drink and Troy wouldn't shut up. He's definitely bitter. Apparently, Donovan was planning to step down at the end of the year and turn everything over to Troy."

Gillette nodded. It was exactly as he'd thought. "How about Miss Cassidy? Did you talk to her?"

Before Cohen could answer, the door opened and Senator Stockman walked into the study. He was tall and distinguished, with silver hair and a healthy tint to his skin. He strode purposefully to the desk and extended his hand without glancing at Cohen.

"Look at you, Mr. Gillette," Stockman said as they shook. "Suddenly you're a powerful young man."

Gillette motioned for Stockman to sit in the chair beside Cohen's. He'd met the senator several times over the last few years but always in Donovan's presence. Before today, Stockman never seemed to remember his name.

"It's such a terrible thing about Bill," Stockman observed, crossing his legs at the knee as he sat down. "But one man's loss is another's gain. Isn't that true, Mr. Gillette?"

"It's a zero-sum world," Gillette agreed quickly, gesturing toward Cohen. "Senator, meet Ben Cohen."

Stockman tilted his head slightly without looking over. "What do you think happened to your boss, Mr. Gillette? Was it an accident like the police are saying? Or did Bill have help filling his lungs with water?"

"Why would I think Bill was murdered?"

"Because if you'd come out of the church thirty seconds earlier, we wouldn't be having this conversation."

The office went deathly still for a few moments.

"Why did you want to see me?" Gillette finally asked.

"I thought it made sense for us to get together as soon as possible." The senator smiled. "To talk about ways we can work together."

Stockman and Donovan had never gotten along. They'd always made a point of being good at public palm-pressing, but they were at opposite ends of the political spectrum, and that had ultimately turned into an intense personal dislike. There was no chance that they would have ever helped each other. But maybe there was an opportunity here.

Gillette opened one hand and gestured. "I'm interested."

"I'd like to ask a few questions about Everest first."

"Go ahead."

"How many companies do you control?"

"Twenty-seven."

"And how much do those companies have in combined sales?"

"Wait a minute," Cohen objected. "That information is highly confidential."

"It's fine, Ben," Gillette said smoothly. "Senator Stockman would never disclose anything confidential about us to anyone. Would you, Senator?"

Stockman smiled thinly. "Of course not."

"Answer the question, Ben."

Cohen took an irritated breath. "The twenty-seven companies have combined sales of over eighty billion dollars."

"How many employees is that?"

Cohen shot Gillette a quick look.

"Tell him."

"Almost a million."

"A *million* employees," the senator said wistfully. "That's a lot of votes. How many of those companies are you chairman of, Christian?"

"Seven," Cohen answered for Gillette. "But with Bill's death, as the new chairman of Everest Capital, Christian will automatically take those chair positions as well. That's another thirteen."

"Jesus. Chairman of twenty companies. *And* chairman of Everest." Stockman chuckled. "I hope they can clone you, Christian. Otherwise, you won't have time to take a crap let alone—"

"What do you want, Senator?"

Stockman folded his hands in his lap. "In a few days I'm going to announce my candidacy for president," he explained, his voice low. "I want Everest Capital's support, specifically those million votes. Employees listen to their chairman."

Over the last few weeks, Gillette had heard rumors about a Stockman campaign for the White House.

"As you know," Stockman continued, "I'm a Democrat. As you *also* know, Bill Donovan was a conservative. A senior member of the Republican National Committee, in fact. It never made sense to ask him for help. I would have had better luck with a brick wall. But I hear you're different. I hear that even though you grew up in Beverly Hills, you relate to the common man. To the blue-collar set, especially minorities. Those people are a significant piece of my constituency. So, I want your support, Christian. I want you to tell all those Everest employees to vote for me, and I want you to be active behind the scenes. Calling on people who matter and getting them to support me." Stockman glanced at Cohen for the first time. "We're not talking about a one-way street here." He ran the fingertips of his hand over the lapel of his suit jacket. "As I'm sure you both know, I have friends in high places. At the Securities and Exchange Commission, for instance." He paused. "Over the years Everest Capital has made billions selling companies it controls to the public. True, Mr. Cohen?"

"True."

"In fact, one of my aides told me you still own big pieces of several of those companies. In addition to those twenty-seven companies you own outright. Is my information accurate?"

Cohen nodded.

"With all the scrutiny on corporate accounting and control these days, public offerings can easily get bogged down by SEC bullshit. Even shelved sometimes."

Cohen flashed Gillette an angry look, anticipating what was coming.

"Obviously, that's not something you want," Stockman pointed out, following Cohen's glance. "I can help you there." He raised his eyebrows. "Or not."

"Hold on," Cohen snapped. "We've taken fifteen companies public over the last ten years. We know plenty of people who can—"

"Have someone in your office call my assistant," Gillette instructed Stockman, cutting off the conversation. There was no need for this to escalate. Not right now, anyway. "Her name is Debbie." He rose and moved out from behind the desk. "Have them arrange a lunch for us next week," he continued, taking Stockman's hand, helping him up out of the chair and guiding him to the door. "We'll go to the Racquet Club. Would you like that?"

"That's a nice place, Christian. I haven't been there in a while. Yes, I would like that."

Gillette opened the door. "I look forward to hearing more about your campaign, Senator."

"Thank you."

"What a prick," Cohen muttered when Stockman was gone. "Threatening us like that with his SEC contacts. Like we're babes in the woods when it comes to IPOs. And telling us he's so damn sensitive about minorities. I've checked his track record, Christian. He's big business all the way. He's just got a great PR machine behind him."

"Have Tom McGuire put together a report on him," Gillette instructed, sitting back down. "Tell him to get me everything on the guy. I want it by tomorrow afternoon."

"You'll have it," Cohen promised.

"And, Ben, I don't want to have to show someone out of a room like that again. You'll do those things from now on. Got it?"

"Uh-huh," Cohen agreed hesitantly. As though he wasn't sure he wanted to be anyone's butler.

There was a soft tap on the door, and Gillette's eyes flicked to Cohen's.

Cohen rose and moved to the door. "Now Richard Harris wants time," he called.

"Fine."

Cohen gave the okay to Harris's messenger.

"Do you think Mason is having affairs with women who work at his portfolio companies?" Gillette asked. Mason was chairman of the other seven Everest-controlled companies, and there were always rumors that he used his position to manipulate women into bed. But nothing had ever been proven.

"I . . . I don't know."

"I didn't ask if you *knew*, Ben. Just what you *thought*."

"I don't want to speculate. Troy's my business partner. And my friend."

"*Damn it, Ben,* tell me what you think."

Cohen squinted and adjusted his glasses. "I'd guess it's possible."

"Really going out on a limb, aren't you?"

"Huh?"

"Nothing."

Another reason the investors hadn't given any consideration to his being chairman of Everest, Gillette realized. And why Donovan had never made Cohen chairman of any of Everest's portfolio companies. Cohen could calculate numbers better than any quant jock on Wall Street, but he couldn't be tough. If there was one thing a top private equity professional had to be, it was tough. Sometimes even with friends.

"The guy is a walking sexual harassment suit," Gillette said flatly.

"Oh, I don't know. I think a lot of that stuff is overblown."

"It's a lock he's banged women who work at his companies."

Cohen didn't respond.

"A big, well-publicized sexual harassment suit could negatively impact our reputation and our business prospects. Wouldn't you say, Ben?"

"Maybe."

Gillette stared hard at Cohen for a few moments, irritated by his indifference. "When you speak to Tom McGuire about Senator Stockman, have him find out if Troy's doing anything stupid when he goes to board meetings."

"I'm not comfortable doing that. It's not right."

"I don't care if you're comfortable, Ben. Just do it. Understand?"

There was another knock at the door.

This time Cohen was up immediately. A moment later, Richard Harris followed him into the office.

After shaking hands with Gillette, Harris sat in the same chair Stockman had used. "Congratulations, young man," he offered warmly. As chief executive officer of U.S. Petroleum, the country's largest industrial company, he was one of the most influential men in corporate America. "Your promotion was well deserved, Christian."

"Thank you." Gillette gave Cohen a quick nod of approval. Harris had always called him "Chris." Obviously, Cohen had given Harris the message at the door. "What do you want?"

Harris blinked several times. "Well, I can see why the limited partners chose you to take over the firm. It's like I'm speaking to Bill. Never a wasted second."

Gillette glanced at his watch.

"You own a Canadian production company that's got some very nice oil and gas reserves," Harris continued quickly, catching Gillette's impatience. "Laurel Energy."

So, that was the reason for the meeting. Harris wanted Laurel. Which could be a tremendous opportunity to solidify his position in the minds of the Everest limited partners right away, Gillette realized. To negotiate a sweetheart deal to sell one of the portfolio companies at a high price immediately after being elected chairman. Early wins were so important.

"I want it," Harris continued.

"A lot of people do," Gillette countered.

"I'll pay you whatever amount gives Everest Capital a 50 percent annual return. That's damned good. Your limited partners will be very happy. It'll be a nice announcement to make so soon after taking control."

"What did we pay for Laurel Energy, Ben?" Gillette wanted to know, irritated that Harris had anticipated his desire to have a big win right after becoming chairman. That wouldn't help his negotiating position.

"Two billion," Cohen answered. "We used three hundred million of equity out of Fund Six, and we put together a $1.7 billion loan from Citibank to close the transaction."

"When did we buy it?"

"Almost three years ago."

"How much of the billion seven debt is still out?"

"Around a billion two, but—"

"So I'll pay you a billion in cash for your equity," Harris offered. "That's seven hundred million more than the three hundred million you invested. *And* U.S. Petroleum will take over that Citibank loan. You'll be free and clear of that."

Gillette glanced at Cohen. He seemed nervous. Like he was calculating his share of the $700 million profit, and he was worried the deal might not go down. "What do you think, Ben?"

Cohen shrugged.

"It's not enough," Gillette said, shaking his head, frustrated with Cohen again.

"It's *more* than enough," Harris retorted.

"I've got a suggestion. A way to bridge the gap."

Harris looked warily at Gillette. "Oh?"

"U.S. Petroleum owns an oil field service business based in New Orleans. You picked it up a few years ago when you bought out that exploration company up in Alaska. It's not a core asset."

Harris smoothed his tie. "No, it's not," he admitted.

"I'm told that the company does a billion a year in revenue and a hundred million in net income."

"That's about right. So what?"

"So I'll pay you four hundred million for it."

Harris's face turned red. "*Four hundred million? Four times net income?* You might as well steal it from me, Christian. You could turn around and sell it the next day for at least a billion and a half. My public shareholders would crucify me."

"Don't tell them," Gillette suggested bluntly. "We won't say anything about the deal. It'll be quick and clean. No publicity."

Harris shook his head. "It wouldn't work. Our accountants would make me put the transaction in the footnotes to the year-end financial statements. That's when the shareholders would find out."

"No way. U.S. Petroleum is huge. Two hundred billion a year in revenues. Your accountants shouldn't make you mention it. It's immaterial to the overall size of the company. But, hey, if the green eyeshade guys start yammering about sticking it in there anyway, let them know you'll move the accounting engagement to another firm." Gillette pointed at Harris. "What do your accountants make a year off U.S. Petroleum? Twenty, thirty million?"

"More like forty," Harris muttered.

"Then it's an easy decision for the lead partner. It'll be like our transaction never happened."

"I don't know."

Gillette let the suggestion sink in for a moment. "Well, that's my offer, Richard. You sell me the oil field service company for four hundred million, and I sell you Laurel Energy with all those sweet oil and gas reserves for a billion dollars plus the Citibank debt." He hesitated, tapping the desk. "Look, I know why you really want Laurel," he said flatly. "It's got exploration options on several large tracts of land up there in Canada that may contain a huge new field. We haven't shot our seismic tests yet, and it'll be a while until we do and we get the results back. But if all that oil and gas is there, it'll make a billion dollars plus debt look like pocket change. At that point, my investors will be crucifying me. Let's not dance without music. It's a waste of time. Now, do you want to do the deal or not?"

Harris fumed for a few seconds, then nodded. "Yeah, I do."

"Good. Get your attorneys started on the documents right away. I want both transactions closed no later than January tenth."

"I'll see you to the door, Mr. Harris," Cohen spoke up, catching Gillette's subtle indication that this meeting was over.

"What do you think?" Gillette asked when Harris was gone.

"I think a billion dollars plus debt is a lot to pay for Laurel Energy if the engineers don't find any major reserves on the option properties."

"I agree, but Harris probably had his people do some preliminary work on the area. He's making a bet. If he loses, he overpaid, but not by that much. If he wins, he looks like a superstar." Gillette raised one eyebrow. "What he doesn't know is that we'll be finished with the seismic tests before January tenth so we'll know what the deal is up there before we ink to sell. If we strike black gold, we'll renegotiate. Right?"

Cohen shrugged. "Hey, *caveat emptor.*"

Gillette counted silently to five, then spoke. "Next time you want to say 'buyer beware,' just say it. Understand?"

"Come on," Mason said quietly, running his finger down the woman's arm. They were standing in a corner of the mansion's great room, at the edge of the crowd. Mostly hidden from view. "Follow me."

"You're terrible, Troy," she said, an anxious smile playing across her lips. "No, I couldn't."

"This isn't a request, honey, it's an *order*. Just like when I tell you to get me coffee." He slid his hand down the back of her dress and squeezed one of her buttocks. "Now, get to the basement."

"*Troy!*" she hissed, slapping his hand away.

"I'm just playing," he whispered, leaning down and kissing her on the cheek, but not before first making certain no one was watching. "You know how much I care about you."

"Where's your wife?" she asked.

"At home. Back in Manhattan."

"How did you manage that?"

"The baby's sick," Mason explained. "Besides, my wife isn't big on funerals."

"Oh."

"Meet me downstairs in five minutes," he instructed. "There's a guest room down the hall past the pool tables." He'd stayed at the mansion before and knew his way around. "The stairs to the basement are on the way to the kitchen."

"Forget it. I'm not going to—"

"And take off your panties before you come," he interrupted.

"Troy, you're terrible. I'm not going to . . ." Her voice trailed off. He was already heading through the crowd.

. . .

"Thanks for stopping by." Gillette shook Miles Whitman's hand as they stood by the office door. Whitman was the chief investment officer of North America Guaranty & Life. "I appreciate it."

"Glad you won." Whitman glanced at Cohen, then back at Gillette. "I won't take any more of your time, Christian. I'm sure lots of people are trying to get in to see you today." He turned to go, then stopped. "Nine o'clock Tuesday morning, right?"

Gillette had requested a meeting with Whitman to discuss the new fund. "Right, nine o'clock."

When Whitman was gone, Gillette headed back to Donovan's desk. As he was sitting down, Cohen called from the doorway. "Now Tom Warfield wants to see you." Warfield was the president of J. P. Morgan Chase & Co., one of the world's biggest banks.

Gillette shook his head. "Warfield's going to beg me to replace Citibank with J. P. Morgan as our house bank. He was always on Donovan's ass to do that. I'm not going to deal with him now. Tell him to call Debbie to arrange a meeting. But no lunch," Gillette added quickly, rubbing his eyes. His contacts were starting to burn. "Warfield tells too many stories. He bores me to death."

Cohen relayed the message to the Morgan vice president waiting outside the office, then called to Gillette again. "How about Jeremy Cole? Got time for him?"

Gillette had met the Giants' quarterback several times. The first this past September outside the team's locker room after the season opener. "Yeah, five minutes."

Cohen turned to head back to his chair.

"Ben."

Cohen stopped in the middle of the room. "Yes?"

"Go find Roger Nolan for me." Nolan was CEO of Blalock Industries, a power-tool manufacturer that Everest owned. "He's here, isn't he?"

"Yeah. Why do you want him?"

"Just get him, will you? Tell him to wait outside until I'm finished with Jeremy."

Cohen turned and headed for the door.

A few minutes later Jeremy Cole limped into the office.

"What happened?" Gillette asked, pointing at the leg.

"Ah, I got hit in practice yesterday," Cole explained in his heavy Alabama accent, wincing as he sat down.

Cole was big, like Troy Mason. He'd led the Giants to the play-offs as a no-name rookie and quickly become a star in Manhattan.

"We're going half speed, just running through a couple of plays out at the Meadowlands, you know, and one of the defensive vets with a rookie grudge spears me way after the whistle blows." Cole laughed harshly. "They cut him this morning at eight o'clock."

"But, what about the Packers next weekend. You going to be ready?"

"I'll be okay. If I'm not, one of the doctors'll shoot me up with something good."

"*One* of them?"

"Yeah, it's like they're everywhere. Sometimes I think we've got more medical people on payroll than players."

"Well, as a season ticket holder, I'm glad to hear the Giants are focused on maintenance. Always keep the assets well oiled."

The two men shared a quick laugh.

"Did you want to see me about something specific?" Gillette asked. "Or is this just social?"

Cole took a deep breath. "I hate to bother you, but people tell me you might be my best bet."

Gillette anticipated the request, already considering what he'd get in return. "You want me to convince the Giants to renegotiate your contract, even though you inked a five-year deal back in July."

The young quarterback gazed at Gillette, astonished. "How did you know?"

"I hear things, Jeremy." Gillette was friends with the oldest son of the Giants' majority owner. They'd gone to college together at Princeton and had stayed in touch over the years. "Tell me about the contract."

"I was an idiot. I agreed to five hundred thousand per." Cole banged the chair with his fist. "I should be making five *million* next year, but I was a sixth-round pick, Chris. I had to take what I could get."

Gillette considered correcting Cole for calling him Chris, but didn't. Cohen would take care of that later. "And, even though you've had a great year, they won't give you more money."

"They told my agent to pound salt. They told him they wouldn't renegotiate anything for at least two years. Which is crap. Professional football is a brutal sport. My career could be over every time out. I deserve better than—"

"I get the point," Gillette said, raising his hand.

Cole fell silent.

"I'm willing to help, Jeremy. But if I get somewhere, I may ask you for a favor in return."

Mason grabbed the young woman's wrist and pulled her into the guest room, then shut the door and pushed her back against the wall beside the bed. Reaching beneath her dress, he slipped two fingers deep inside her. As instructed, she'd removed her panties before coming downstairs.

"This is crazy," she moaned, her hands fumbling with his belt buckle, then the button. Unzipping his pants carefully. "We shouldn't be doing this here."

"Why not?"

"Someone might find us," she gasped, leaning back against the wall as his lips came to her neck and his fingers moved in and out. "Jesus, I work for you, Troy."

"Don't worry. No one will find us down here."

"You better be sure."

"Relax. I know what I'm doing."

The office door opened and Marcie Reed appeared. She was tall and blond with long legs she constantly accented by wearing short dresses—even at funeral receptions. Roger Nolan followed her through the door.

"Hello, Christian," she said.

Gillette glanced up from a file he was studying. "Hi."

"Ben said you wanted to see Roger." Marcie was on the board of Blalock and responsible for it on a day-to-day basis, reporting major issues to Donovan as necessary. "I'm assuming that you'll take over as chairman for Bill, but that you'll want me to stay on the board?"

"Probably."

"So, I thought it made sense for me to be here."

Gillette shook his head. "This is going to be one-on-one."

"Oh." She'd been about to sit down.

"But thanks for bringing Roger back here."

"Sure," she sniffed, irritated.

Gillette nodded at Nolan, then gestured toward the chairs in front of the desk as Marcie turned and stalked out of the room.

"Hello, Christian." Nolan sat down without shaking hands. He was heavyset, bald, and had dark, thick eyebrows that gave him a naturally serious expression. "Why do you want to see me?" He was tapping his thigh impatiently.

"What's the matter, you double-parked?"

"Huh?" Nolan gave Gillette a confused look.

Gillette pointed at the other man's fingers. They were still tapping.

"Oh . . . no." Nolan crossed his arms tightly over his chest. "I've got all the time in the world for you, Christian," he muttered.

"Having a nice time today?" Gillette asked politely.

"As nice as possible under the circumstances."

"Good." Nolan and Donovan had been close. Too close as far as Gillette was concerned. Everest had owned Blalock Industries for three years, and, as CEO, Nolan had never made budget. It was one of those rare instances in which Donovan allowed personal feelings to influence his business judgment. Gillette leaned forward. "Remind me, Roger. What's your salary?"

Nolan's eyes flashed to Gillette's. "What?"

"What's your salary?"

"I only answer to the chairman as far as those kinds of questions go."

Nolan must not have heard Marcie, Gillette thought to himself. "That would be me, Roger. Now that I'm chairman of Everest, I automatically take all of Bill's chair positions at the portfolio companies as well."

Nolan's defiance drained away quickly. "Oh."

"What's your salary?" Gillette demanded again.

"Two million."

"And what did Bill give you as a bonus last year?"

"Five."

"Christ," Gillette hissed under his breath. "How much did Blalock do in revenue last year?"

"Three billion."

"What was net income?"

Nolan hesitated.

"Answer me, Roger."

"Twenty-one million."

"*Damn it,*" Gillette said loudly, pounding the desk. "Your salary and bonus were almost 25 percent of the company's earnings. That's ridiculous."

"Hey, we did pretty well."

"*Pretty well?* You make $20 million on $3 billion in revenues and you tell me you did pretty well? If that had been the Allies' attitude during World War Two, we'd all be goose-stepping and eating bratwursts. Look, you've never hit your budgets and, given the preliminary reports I saw yesterday, you aren't going to this year either."

Nolan shrugged. "Foreign competition is tough. You gotta accept that."

"I don't *gotta* accept anything. My investors don't. They want results, and so do I. One way or the other, I'm going to get them." Gillette pointed at the older man. "Roger, you're fired."

Nolan recoiled in the chair, grabbing the arms so tightly his knuckles turned white. "You prick," he seethed, gritting his teeth. "You can't do that."

"I just did."

"Who's going to run the company? *You?*"

"I can't do any worse than you." Gillette shook his head in disgust. "Your office at HQ in Philadelphia is being packed as we speak. Your personal items will be delivered to your house tomorrow. Under no circumstances are you to go back to the office."

Nolan took a deep breath. "You still have to pay me two million a year for the next three years," he retorted, trying to find a silver lining. "That's how my contract reads. You gotta pay me no matter what." He forced a smile to his lips. "I'll enjoy playing my daily round of golf knowing I've made fifty-five hundred bucks on you."

"Fifty-five hundred bucks a day," Gillette repeated. "Two million a year divided by three-sixty-five, huh?"

"Yes," Nolan said hesitantly.

As though he hadn't expected the calculation to be understood so quickly, Gillette thought to himself, easing back in his chair. Taking his time to deliver the smart bomb. "I understand your son just had a nasty little run-in with the law."

Nolan's eyes flashed to Gillette's again. "What the—"

"Cocaine, right? Tough rap for a college kid."

"You son-of-a—"

"The cops caught him with a bag when they pulled him over for speeding," Gillette kept going. "Given your personal net worth and, therefore, your ability to hire legal talent, you ought to be able to get him off without too much damage. And I'm impressed with your ability to keep it out of the newspapers. You pay off an editor up there?" Nolan's mouth was falling slowly open as Gillette spoke. "But here's the thing, Roger. Your son's dealing." Having McGuire & Company at his beck and call was like having the world's best bloodhound on the hunt. Tom McGuire seemed to be able to find anything on anyone. "We have video. We know who his regular clients are. Believe me, the cops up there would love to find out about him. He's a big campus supplier."

"My God," Nolan whispered.

This was the dirty part of business, but Nolan had brought it on himself. He was playing golf at least three times a week. Mostly at Pine Valley, where you couldn't talk business even if you wanted to—club rules. He'd totally neglected the company, and now he was going to pay. And he wasn't going to earn six million dollars for the next three years just to play golf. "There's no need for this to get nasty, Roger. I'm willing to be reasonable."

"What does that mean?" Nolan asked, his voice barely audible.

"A hundred thousand dollars a year for the next three years, and you keep your medical and dental benefits. You agree to that, and your son gets off free and clear. You won't even have to hire an attorney."

"How can you do that?" Nolan whispered.

"I have friends in Portland who can help. I've already spoken to them."

Nolan's breathing was labored. "How about two-fifty?"

Gillette shook his head. "No. It's the deal as offered, or—"

"All right, all right." Nolan held up his hands. "I'll take it."

There was a sharp rap on the door.

"Who is it?" Gillette called loudly, annoyed that Cohen hadn't gotten back yet to perform his gatekeeper duties.

"Kyle," Lefors called back. "It's important."

"Come in." Gillette pointed at Nolan. "We're done."

Lefors moved to the desk, waiting until Nolan was gone before he said anything. Lefors was tall and dark; physically, he resembled Gillette. "You're going to love this," he said, grinning.

. . .

Mason kissed the woman deeply for a few moments, addicted to that feeling of her fingers wrapped around him. Then he pulled her dress over her head and tossed it on the floor. He smiled to himself as she sank to her knees without being told to, taking him in her mouth. After three months she knew him so well.

As her tongue flicked up and down, he reached between her breasts and unhooked her bra, watching approvingly as she dropped her arms to her sides to let the lacy garment fall from her shoulders onto the floor next to the wall behind her. Now she was naked, except for those black suede high heels which wouldn't be coming off. He loved the look of a woman in nothing but heels. Of the five women he was involved with, he enjoyed her the most. She was gorgeous and uninhibited. Willing to do anything.

Mason peeled off his shirt as she helped him step out of his pants. Then he pulled her to her feet and picked her up, carrying her to the bed and laying her down gently on the mattress. Kneeling in between her legs and kissing her again.

"I love you," she whispered as she spread her legs wide and reached for him.

"Me, too," he moaned, entering her. Moving gently at first, then harder.

"Yeah, sweetheart," she urged, her voice turning gravelly. "That's what I like, Troy. Hard. Real hard."

"I know, I know." Mason groaned, pulling her legs up over his shoulders. He interrupted his motion for a moment when he saw the strange look in her eyes. As he followed her gaze toward the door, she let out a shriek and scrambled away. "Oh, Christ," he muttered.

Gillette stood at the end of the bed, glancing back and forth between the woman's face and a piece of paper. Then he locked onto Mason's eyes.

Cohen was by the door, arms folded across his chest, staring down at the floor. Kicking at something on the carpet with the toe of his black shoe.

Mason gazed back into Gillette's icy expression, the dark features blurring before him as the blood pounded in his brain. Finally, he looked away, too embarrassed to meet Gillette's stare any longer. "Chris, I—"

"Put your clothes on, Troy," Gillette ordered, handing the piece of paper to Cohen as he headed for the door. "I'll be outside."

Gillette took Faith Cassidy's hand and smiled. Moments ago he'd fired Troy Mason, his closest competitor in the race for the chairmanship of Everest Capital. Giving Mason a million dollars in severance. Informing Mason that he would never be allowed inside Everest again, and that he would forfeit his equity stake in the firm, a stake Cohen had estimated at sixty million dollars. Sex with a woman who reported to him had cost him fifty-nine million dollars. It was a hell of a price to pay for getting laid, Gillette thought to himself.

"I've always wanted to meet you, Miss Cassidy," Gillette began, subtly motioning for Cohen to move off. "You're very talented."

"Thank you," she said, stepping closer and putting her hand on his arm. "Please call me Faith."

Gillette nodded, recognizing in her expression that she understood who he was. That, as instructed, Cohen had explained it all before Gillette joined the conversation. While he was axing Mason downstairs.

As Faith smiled up at him, he allowed himself a brief moment to drink in his victory—and revel in his power.

"Christian."

Gillette's gaze snapped left, and he peered into the darkness. It was late and the light from the mansion didn't reach out here. He'd been about to get into the back of the Town Car. "Who's there?"

Mason appeared out of the darkness. "Can I talk to you for a minute, Christian? Please."

Gillette let out a quick breath. He needed to be more careful now, he realized, scanning the area as his eyes became accustomed to the dark. In fact, he probably needed a full-time bodyguard. He'd speak to Tom McGuire about that in the morning. "Go on."

"Thanks. Look, I'm sorry about what happened in the basement," Mason apologized, running one hand through his tousled hair. "It was a one-time thing. It'll never happen again. I swear."

"You expect me to believe that was really a one-time thing?"

"Huh?"

Gillette stepped toward Mason until they were close. "Have you had sex with other women at the companies you chair for us?"

"No."

"You're a terrible liar, Troy." Gillette didn't know if Mason was lying, but it didn't matter. One indiscretion was enough. All it would take for a vindictive woman to drag Everest into a nightmare of a lawsuit.

Lefors had given Gillette the tip about Mason being in a basement guest room with the young woman, but Gillette had been careful about using the information. Going on the Internet to confirm—on the company's website—that a woman with the name Lefors had mentioned really did work in the marketing department there. Then he'd pulled the woman's picture down off her bio and printed it out. Standing at the foot of the bed, he'd compared the face in the picture with the face of the woman beneath Mason before either of them knew he was there. Deciding, as the woman scrambled away, that she was, in fact, the one in the picture.

"You're a liar, Troy," Gillette said coldly. "I won't have a partner who's a liar."

"I'm not a liar. I'm telling you the truth."

Gillette shook his head in disgust and turned back toward the waiting car.

"Christian!" Mason trotted to the car as Gillette got in, prying the door open when Gillette reached for the handle. "Don't do this to me," he begged. "I've worked my ass off to get to this point. We've been partners for ten years. Don't leave me with nothing because of one stupid mistake."

"I told you, Troy. You'll get a million bucks as severance. Cohen will make the arrangements next week."

"When my wife finds out I've lost my stake in the firm, she'll divorce me and take every penny the IRS doesn't."

"Sounds like she wouldn't believe tonight was an isolated incident either."

"I'm begging you," Mason pleaded desperately, sinking to his knees beside the Town Car. "Don't do this to me."

"You should have thought this through before."

"I'll be lucky to get a job washing cars."

"At least in New York," Gillette agreed.

"Christian." Mason was beginning to hyperventilate "Come on. What do I have to do?"

"There's nothing you can do."

Gillette slammed the door shut, the car lurched forward, and Mason tumbled to the asphalt.

"Here you are, Ms. Hays, 250 thousand dollars." The man placed the leather briefcase on the table in front of her. "The 25-thousand-dollar monthly payments will start once you get to the destination. Which shouldn't take long. We'll be monitoring you. You'll receive the monthly payments in cash, as agreed."

Kathy Hays gazed at the briefcase. Two hundred fifty thousand up-front, plus twenty-five thousand a month. *And* their promise not to tell her family what had happened five years ago. A horrible chapter in her life she thought was closed forever. One she thought she'd hidden from everyone. But they'd found it—and so much more.

But they'd promised they wouldn't tell anyone what they'd found— as long as she stayed quiet about setting up Troy Mason.

4

Conflict. *Nation vs. nation. Neighbor vs. neighbor. And the most destructive conflict of all—self vs. self. The fuse of all evil.*

MARIA WAS THE BABY OF the family. But at five years of age, she already had more personality than most adults.

Gillette grinned at the little girl sitting on his lap. Admiring her jet black hair and the fire dancing in her mahogany eyes while she studied him with her serious look, tiny brows furrowed. Maria would have made something of herself even without his help. He'd come to recognize that fire in the eyes of all successful people.

She giggled, wrapped her small arms tightly around his neck, and kissed his cheek hard. "Te amo, Chreeees."

"I love you, too, Maria." Gillette liked coming here because he could completely relax. "I'm thinking of a number between one and ten," he said loudly so that Selma, Maria's mother, could hear, too. She was standing in front of the stove stirring a pot of stew. "You go first, Selma."

Selma stopped stirring for a moment and thought. "Um, three."

Gillette looked down at the little girl and raised one eyebrow.

"Four," Maria piped up.

"Very good," Gillette said approvingly. He had taught her how to play the game last time, and she'd learned fast. Always play the odds. A much better chance of the number being greater than three. "The number's seven."

Selma groaned. "I always lose at this."

"You go first this time, Maria," Gillette said.

"Six," the little girl answered quickly.

"I'll say four," Selma called as she began stirring again.

"Seven, again," announced Gillette.

"I'm not playing anymore." Selma laughed. "It's too hard on my ego."

"Why did you say six?" Gillette asked Maria, making sure of her strategy.

"If I go first, I should say five or six," she answered, looking toward the ceiling and putting a finger to her lips, remembering what he'd taught her. "That gives me the best chance. You used a big number the first time, and I thought you'd use a big one again."

Gillette broke into a huge grin. "Very, very good."

"I'll take her," Selma said, picking Maria up off Gillette's lap and setting the little girl on her wide hip. Selma had been slim as a younger woman, but having seven children had taken its toll. "How have you been, Chris?"

Gillette loved Selma. When she asked how you were, she meant it. She really wanted to know. It wasn't just some throwaway question as it was for most people. "I've been good, Selma." Bad grammar. "Well" would have been correct, but he wanted her to think he was a regular person.

She wagged her finger. "That's what you always say. You've done so many nice things for me and my family. I want to know more about you. Like what's going on in your life."

"It would take too long to tell you. Besides, my life is pretty boring."

"Oh, I bet."

"Could I get some water?" he asked, starting to stand up.

"Sit, sit," she ordered, moving quickly to the cabinet for a glass, then to the sink.

As she put the glass down in front of Gillette, eight-year-old Jose Jr. burst into the kitchen clutching a toy truck, his younger brother, Ruben, in hot pursuit. They raced around the table several times, shouting at each other in Spanish, then darted back into the living room.

"I don't know how you do it," Gillette muttered, taking a drink.

"I don't even hear them anymore." Selma shot him a sly look. "Someday soon you'll be doing it."

"Oh no, I won't."

"Oh yes, you will. Some young thing will melt your heart and you'll give in."

"Selma, I'll be a bachelor until the day I—"

"*Buenas noches, Señor Gillette.*"

Gillette felt a hand on his shoulder and glanced up. Jose Medilla stood beside the chair, smiling down from beneath a bushy black mustache. Jose was short and wiry with leathery brown skin and a wide face. He was first generation Puerto Rican American. His grandparents still lived in a shack on the outskirts of San Juan.

"*Buenas noches, Señor Medilla.*"

"Can you stay for dinner?"

"Thanks. I'd like that."

The spread at the funeral reception had been exceptional—long rows of sterling silver trays full of everything imaginable, catered by several five-star Manhattan restaurants—but Gillette hadn't had the time to sample any. Tom Warfield had wedged his way into Gillette's conversation with Faith and suddenly there were four more people involved. So Gillette had returned to Donovan's office to regain control.

"I'd never pass on Selma's stew." Gillette knew it was important for Jose to feel like he was giving something back. Even if it was just a meal. "Not even for a steak at Sparks."

"Selma's cooking is better than any Manhattan steak house's," Jose said proudly. He motioned toward a pair of French doors that opened onto a deck spanning the back of the four-bedroom home. "Can I show you the house?"

"Sure."

They moved out into the chill of the central New Jersey night. Princeton University, where Gillette had gone to school, lay only a few miles to the west.

"That's the one." Jose pointed across the back of his one-acre lot toward the brightly burning lights of another home. "The husband is a professor."

"When did it go on the market?"

"Yesterday."

"What are they asking?"

"Four hundred and seventy thousand."

"Offer five hundred Monday morning," Gillette instructed. "Let him see what he gets tomorrow, then move. Understand?"

"*Sí.*"

"Your brother is in the Bronx?"

"*Sí.*"

"How many children does he have?"

"Three."

"Will this house be enough?"

"This house will be like a castle for him, Christian. Alex lives in a two-bedroom apartment on top of a bodega and with many *cucurachas.*"

"Call him tonight. Tell him we've agreed. And tell him to leave everything he has at that apartment. We'll get him what he needs down here. Furniture and clothes. The same way we did for you."

"Good. *Cucurachas* have a bad habit of hitchhiking."

"What about the neighbors?" Gillette asked, scanning the rooftops looming in the darkness. "How are they treating you?"

"They tolerate us."

Gillette grunted. "Pricks."

"You can't expect people here to accept us with open arms, Christian. They're all professionals. All *gringos.* When they bought in this neighborhood, I don't think they expected a Puerto Rican factory worker with seven children to move in." Jose pointed across the yard. "It'll be interesting to see what happens when my brother comes."

"If anything does," Gillette said, "let me know."

"I can take care of myself."

Gillette glanced at Jose. "Yeah, I'm sure you can."

"That's why nothing's happened so far. People are afraid of how *well* I can take care of myself. Of how far someone like me would go." Jose twirled a finger beside his ear. "*Loco,* you know?"

Gillette leaned against the deck railing. "Did you really kill a man?"

"*Sí.*"

"How?"

"I slit his throat."

"Why?"

"He was trying to slit mine. He wanted to be the father of Selma's children, too."

"How old were you?"

"Seventeen."

"Jesus," Gillette muttered. At seventeen he'd been surfing off Santa Monica and hanging out on Rodeo Drive.

"Christian?"

"Yes?"

"Why do you do all this for me and my family?"

Gillette took a deep breath and glanced at the house he was about to buy for Jose's brother. Conflict. Always conflict.

Mason held his head in his hands. A week ago he was sure he was going to be the next chairman. Donovan had promised him. Now he was barred from Everest for life, and fifty-nine million dollars poorer.

"I'm screwed," he murmured, tears filling his eyes as he sat in the darkness of his Manhattan penthouse.

He swallowed hard and reached for a .38-caliber pistol lying on the coffee table. His career, his money, his future. Gillette had taken them all.

Mason cocked the gun, pressed the barrel to his temple, and slipped his finger behind the trigger.

Gillette stepped back into the kitchen from outside just as Jose Jr. and Ruben ran a lap around the table again. He grinned, watching them disappear into the living room. Then his smile faded, and for a moment he simply stared. The young woman the two boys had darted past was gorgeous. One of the most beautiful creatures he'd ever seen.

Selma bit her lower lip, trying to hide a smile.

Gillette caught Selma's smile, realizing in that instant that this had been neatly choreographed. But he didn't care. The young woman was too beautiful for him to care.

"Chris, this is Isabelle, my youngest sister. She's visiting from San Juan."

The man shivered inside his triple-layered, goose-down parka as he moved carefully across the frozen ground toward the ghostly outline of his specially outfitted Ford Explorer. You had to move carefully up here, no matter how much you wanted to reach the warmth of your truck. If you fell and something snapped in the bitter cold, you were a dead man. Survival time out here was measured in minutes, not days.

He brought his hands to his ski mask as a brutal gust of wind whipped snow past him. People thought they understood the meaning of "remote." They watched specials about places like this on the Discovery Channel, so they thought they knew. But they had no idea. Images on a television screen couldn't convey the isolation that dominated this barren area of Canada eight hundred miles north of Montana.

His breath iced up the window of the idling truck when he reached it, but he didn't stop to admire the geometric patterns. He yanked the door open and hopped inside. He was one of the few people in the world who did understand this place. Who understood how weeks of little or no human contact spent almost entirely in darkness could play on your mind. How watching the aurora borealis shimmer across a star-laden sky could send shivers up your spine, no matter how many times you'd seen it. How you questioned your sanity ten times a day for being up here.

Once inside the truck, he removed his thick gloves, picked up a clipboard, and scrawled notes on a pad. They'd plant the last of the dynamite near this spot tomorrow and run the test. Then he was going to get the hell out of here and go someplace warm.

Gillette stopped in front of the pool hall and watched the Town Car's taillights disappear down the Brooklyn street. He'd sent the driver off, telling him he'd get a cab back to Manhattan. The guy hadn't hesitated a second. Just taken off like a bat out of hell the moment Gillette closed the door, happy to get out of the rough neighborhood as fast as possible.

It was late, almost one in the morning, but Gillette wasn't tired. He didn't need much sleep. Never had. Just a few hours a night and he was fine.

He was still dressed in the neatly pressed charcoal suit he'd worn to the funeral. Tie stuffed in his pants pocket, white shirt open a couple of buttons at the neck. He reached for the inside pocket of his suit jacket and his wallet. Before leaving home this morning for the funeral, he'd taken everything out of it except the cash and his driver's license.

He took out what was left of the cash—two hundred dollars—and put the bills into the shirt pocket of a man lying on the ground in front of the pool hall cradling a wine bottle in both arms. The guy never moved, never even said thank you. But this wasn't about charity. It was about going in unarmed.

The place was loud, smoky, and crowded. Rap music blared, and there was the constant crack of the cue ball. Every table had onlookers. People keeping an eye on the quarters they'd put down to reserve the next game. People there to root for the players—girlfriends, boyfriends. People just interested in seeing a good game. And sharks waiting for the best time to slip into the flow without seeming too enthusiastic.

Gillette was keenly aware of the looks he was getting. It wasn't hard to catch them. He was the only white guy in the place—and the only guy wearing a suit.

He'd never been here before. He'd heard about it from a couple of guys in Queens. There were supposed to be some very good players, guys who could have made it on the circuit, and he liked the pressure their games would give him. He used it to test himself. He could beat anyone in here on a quiet, neutral table. He knew that. But in front of the home-town crew, without a dime in his pocket, it might be a different story.

He watched for a while, getting the lay of the land. It was clear to him after a short time that the back four tables were reserved for the best players. No smiles, no conversation, no alcohol. Just hard looks, crisp shots, the sounds of the game, and the dance of the two players around the table.

And one guy managing the gate for each table. The guy who held the money.

"How long's the list?" Gillette asked loudly.

The gate glanced up, casing Gillette. Toothpick moving to the left side of his mouth as he took one more look at the expensive suit. "Just one ahead."

"What's the bet?"

"Five grand."

"Put me down." Gillette nodded at the gate's scratch in his notepad.

"Money first."

"I'm good for it," Gillette said evenly. "I'm sure you understand why I don't want to let go of my cash."

The gate shook his head. " 'Fraid not. You got to give it to me now."

Gillette smiled confidently. "You really think I'd walk in here without the money?"

The gate looked Gillette up and down again. "You better be good for it. You tell me you don't have the money when you lose, and you won't make it out of here alive."

An hour later, Gillette leaned over the green felt, curled his left forefinger around the cue, and lined up the shot. Other than the cue ball, the eight was the only one left on the table. It was an easy scratch, and, if he didn't make the shot *and* didn't scratch, the other guy would definitely drop the eight on his next attempt—and win. He'd owe five grand to a man whose biceps were as big around as his thighs. With no way to pay. And an IOU wasn't going to cut it.

Gillette closed his eyes for a moment, tuning out the crowd. More and more people had circled around the table as the match—best of five—had unfolded. There were probably fifty people watching at this point. Some screaming at him. Not wanting him to beat the neighborhood hero.

The cue ball rolled smoothly toward the eight, smacking it exactly where Gillette had aimed. No doubt the eight would drop, but the problem now was the cue. If it dropped, too, he'd scratch and the human mountain who was his opponent would win five thousand without having to take another shot.

In his peripheral vision, Gillette was aware of the eight ball dropping into the far corner pocket. But he was watching the cue as it rolled back the length of the green table toward him and the near corner. It was headed straight for the pocket, moving more and more slowly. The crowd screamed as it rolled and his opponent watched bug-eyed. Finally, it stopped, a quarter of the ball hanging over the pocket. The crowd groaned loudly and man mountain broke his cue in half over his knee.

Gillette handed his cue to someone in the crowd and moved to where the gate sat. The gate handed Gillette a wad of bills, which he slipped into his pocket with the tie.

"Hey, boy," the gate asked as Gillette turned to go.

Gillette turned back. "What?"

"Did you have it?"

"Have what?"

"You know."

Gillette moved back to where the gate sat, reached into his jacket pocket, and removed his wallet. Then he opened it up just enough that the gate—but no one else—could see that it was empty.

The gate smiled broadly. "Cool, man, but I'll remember next time."

"There won't be a next time."

"What? You think you're too good for us now?"

"Got nothing to do with it," Gillette answered, looking around. "I like this place, but I just beat the best in the house, so I'll never get a money game in here again. And I never play for fun."

5

The Male Curse. *The relentless urge to hunt. The ruthless drive to conquer. The insatiable need to amass.*

FAITH CASSIDY SCRIBBLED ANOTHER AUTOGRAPH, this time on the label of a champagne bottle. As she handed the pen back to the nervous young man who had approached her, she gave him the smile that had sold millions of CDs. It was the third time in the last ten minutes she'd been asked to sign something.

"You ever get tired of that?" Gillette asked when the guy was gone.

Faith picked up her glass of Chardonnay. "Tired of what?"

"People constantly wanting something from you."

"No. Not fans, anyway." She took a sip. "Do you ever get tired of managing all that money?"

Gillette ran the tip of his forefinger across his bottom lip. "No."

"You aren't telling me the truth."

He looked at her curiously. "Why do you say that?"

"You hesitated when you answered."

He shook his head. "You shouldn't read anything into that. I give every question due consideration."

She groaned. "*Due consideration?* Are you really that boring, Christian? If you are, I'm leaving. I want someone who talks to me like a real person, not somebody who sounds like the lawyers micromanaging my career."

"I'm thirty-six. I can't change who I am."

"Can't or *won't*?"

Gillette gazed at Faith over the flame of a single candle. She was blond with large green eyes and a voluptuous figure he knew had been surgically enhanced. She wasn't classically beautiful—not like Isabelle was. Faith overpowered you with her curves and enticed you with those bedroom eyes.

Still, it was Faith's personality Gillette found most intriguing. She was confident but not arrogant. And she had a charisma and a passion about her that was contagious. She seemed to say whatever was on her mind—a luxury he didn't have. What he said, he said with candor. But he didn't say everything. He couldn't.

"How about when your limousine explodes?" she pushed when he didn't answer. "Do you get tired of managing billions then?"

He smiled for the first time. "No. I call the dealer and order a new one."

She laughed. "You have a wonderful smile, but you don't show it enough."

"Always leave people wanting more. You know that. You're an entertainer."

"Are you really that calculating?"

He pushed his spoon around the tablecloth. "Are you really that direct?"

"I heard *you* were. I thought you'd appreciate it."

"How exactly did you hear I was?"

"Mutual friends."

"I doubt we have any mutual—"

"Okay, I guessed," Faith admitted. "But it seems logical. One of my assistants researched you on the Web. A man who's chairman of so many companies, of the company that owns my record label," she reminded him, "a man like that would *have* to be direct. He'd have so many demands on his time, he'd have no choice." She paused. "But maybe a man like that doesn't appreciate having the tables turned on him."

"Maybe not," Gillette agreed coolly.

"And maybe I'm risking my next contract."

"Not as long as your CDs keep selling."

"Oh, I see how it is."

"Business is business." Gillette folded his hands in his lap. "Remind me again, Faith. How many albums have you done?"

"Two."

"When did the first one come out?"

"A little over a year ago."

"How many copies did it sell?"

"Over five million."

No wonder so many people were begging for her autograph. "And the second one? When was it released?"

"A few weeks ago."

"How's it doing?"

She glanced down. "Fine."

"Better than the first one?"

"It's early, you know," she murmured. "Still early."

Clearly there was a problem. "Is it as good as the first one?"

"Better," she said firmly, her expression turning steely. *"Much* better."

"Then what's the matter?"

Faith shrugged. "I don't know."

"Is the music label giving you the dollar support?" Gillette thought for a second, trying to remember if he'd seen or heard any plugs for her new album. "I'm probably not a very good measuring stick, but I don't remember seeing or hearing anything. I'd think they'd be flogging TV and radio at this point."

"I don't get into all that," she said quietly. "I just sing."

"Uh-huh." Definitely something wrong. "I'll make a few calls and see what's going on."

"Thanks," she said softly.

Their eyes met again and he caught appreciation in her expression. Then, what he thought was sadness.

"So, how *did* you feel when your limousine exploded?" Faith asked.

"The same way you felt when you got that letter a few weeks ago."

McGuire & Company handled Faith's personal security. Yesterday morning, after going through the file he'd put together on Senator Stockman, Tom McGuire had given Gillette the *Reader's Digest* version of Faith Cassidy's life. Including a quick mention of her bra cup size going from a "B" to a full "C" after surgery six months ago.

"What letter?" she demanded, her tone turning apprehensive.

"The one from the wacko who's been stalking you since your Chicago concert."

"How do you know about—"

"I just do, Faith." She had no idea that Everest Capital owned McGuire & Company. It was the only portfolio company not mentioned on the Everest website. For good reason. It didn't make sense to advertise to the outside world that Everest spied on people. "I have access to a lot of information."

"Obviously." She nodded at his unused wineglass. "Is it what you do that keeps you from having a glass of wine? Do you always have to be in complete control of everything? Including yourself?"

"No." A lie.

"What is it, then?"

His first instinct was to say nothing, but he understood the power of pulling the curtain back on a fragment of his life. People felt like you were allowing them inside. Even if it was just for a few minutes, they appreciated it. Sometimes to the point where they felt like they owed you something.

His gaze moved slowly down over her breasts—barely covered by a sheer midriff top—to a diamond dangling from a gold belly ring.

"My mother was an alcoholic," he finally said, glancing away. "She drank too many martinis one day and dove into the pool. My father found her on the bottom that night when he got home."

Faith brought her hands to her mouth. "She hit her head when she dove in, didn't she?"

"It's more complicated than that. You see, she couldn't swim. She hated the water. Before that day she'd never been in the pool, not even up to her ankles." Gillette picked up his glass of water and took a sip. "The coroner put the time of death at three that afternoon, but she'd turned on the pool light beneath the diving board."

"Why?"

"So my father would see her as soon as he got home. It was suicide."

Faith shook her head. "I'm sorry. I shouldn't have pressed."

"That's why I don't drink, Faith. I can't risk outside influences like that clouding my judgment." Gillette hesitated. "You were right. I do have to be in control of myself. I have too many decisions to make all the time. Sometimes it seems like I have to make one every minute."

"Does the pressure ever get to you?"

"No," he answered firmly. "I can't allow that."

"What *exactly* do you do?" she asked. "Your messenger tried explaining it to me at the reception, but all I picked up was that you control a lot of money and you're chairman of quite a few companies. Including Everest, now."

"Was it that obvious I sent Ben Cohen?"

"Yes, but he wasn't the first front man to come up to me. Senator Stockman sent his guy, and so did that football player. What's his name? Jeremy something."

Gillette glanced over the flame again. "Jeremy Cole?"

"Yeah, that's it. I'm supposed to see him later this week."

Gillette felt his pulse jump. A competitive combustion fueled by some basic instinct deep inside.

"Does that bother you?" Faith asked, grinning.

"Does what bother me?"

"That I'm going to see Jeremy Cole."

"Of course not."

"Sure," she said sarcastically, leaning back in her chair and smoothing the napkin in her lap. "So, tell me what you do."

"We buy companies," he explained, glancing at the diamond belly-button ring sparkling in the candlelight. "After we buy them, we grow them. A few years later we sell them. And we usually sell them for more than what we paid."

"You must be very rich."

"I don't worry about making the monthly mortgage payment."

"You probably don't even *have* a mortgage." She hesitated. "Have you always been rich?"

"Meaning?"

"Is your father wealthy?"

"My father died when I was twenty-two. The summer after I graduated from college."

Gillette had been motorcycling cross-country when he'd gotten the news about his father. Killed in a private plane crash at the Orange County airport. On takeoff. It had been a clear day with no wind and, after fourteen years, Gillette still didn't buy the official "pilot error" explanation. There were rumors about what had really happened, but everything he'd ever investigated had led to a dead end. Even Tom McGuire had come up empty-handed.

Faith put her elbows on the table and held her head in her hands. "I keep asking the wrong question, don't I?"

"It's not your fault."

"I'm still sorry."

"Thanks." Gillette cleared his throat. "I was very proud of my father. He was a hell of a man. He started a Los Angeles investment bank in his early thirties, and sold it ten years later to one of the big New York firms for a hundred million. Then he went into politics. He was a United States senator when he was killed in a plane crash."

"Wow. I guess I should have known all that, but I'm not really into politics."

"And you're from the East," he pointed out. "Probably more relevant, you were twelve years old at the time."

Faith raised both eyebrows. "You certainly know a lot about me."

"Having information is the key to success in my business. The key to success in anything, really. Without it you're like every other jerk out there who's just hoping for good luck." He thought about Tom McGuire for a moment. How McGuire gave him that advantage. "Fortunately, I have people working for me who are good at getting information."

"Is it hard having a father who was so successful?"

"What do you mean?"

"Do you feel like you have to live up to what he accomplished?"

Gillette thought about the question. He'd never had anything but support from his father. He'd never felt envy or jealousy, never been pressured. "No." He would have put the question right back to her, but, thanks to McGuire, he knew she'd grown up poor in rural Kentucky. She was completely self-made.

"So, you've always had money," Faith said wistfully. "That must be nice."

He stared at her hard. He'd pulled the curtain back enough. There was no reason to let her in on what it was like to be cut off at the knees by someone who owed him so much.

"What do you do with it all?" she asked.

He gave her a curious look. People he dealt with either understood what he did with his money or were afraid to ask. "I invest."

"If you already have so much, why work so hard to make more? Why be chairman of all those companies and have to deal with a mountain of stress?"

She didn't understand that everything he had—his net worth was more than $70 million—he'd made on his own. That he was constantly driven to make more because you never knew what could happen. You never knew who was going to try to screw you and take what you had. But he wasn't going to tell her all that because then he'd have to explain why he was such a hard man. "It's what I do," he answered quietly.

"But for what *purpose?*" she pushed.

"Purpose?"

"What's the point? I mean, do you work that hard so you can buy houses and planes and cars and boats that you'll never use? Or is there more to it than that? Something deeper."

"I give a lot to charities, if that's where you're headed with this."

"Do you give to those charities just for appearance, or for real?"

"I don't understand."

"Do you give to those charities because you think *The New York Times* might call you out if you didn't? Because it would be an embarrassment to Everest Capital if its chairman wasn't socially responsible," Faith continued, making quotation marks with her fingers. "Because your investors and your competitors might figure Everest wasn't doing well if the chairman of the firm didn't give to charities. Or do you do it without an agenda? Is it purely a selfless act without any expectation of a benefit to you? Without any of that calculation you seem to be so good at?"

"There's no such thing as a selfless act."

She groaned. "Oh, God."

"Look, there's always a benefit. Nothing's pure. Maybe the act just makes the person who does it feel good, but that's a benefit. Think about it."

"I have."

"And?"

"And I believe there are definitely people who give and don't ask for or get anything in return."

Gillette shook his head. "This is like arguing about the sex of angels."

"What's that supposed to mean?"

"It means there isn't a right answer."

She laughed. "Maybe they're both sexes. Angels, I mean."

Gillette rolled his eyes. "Look, the bottom line is you have your view, I have mine, and neither one of us is going to change the other's mind."

"Normally, I'd agree with you. But I might make an exception. At least, temporarily."

"Why?"

"You're very attractive, and not just physically. You're . . . precocious. I like that in a man."

"Precocious. That's a big word."

"Hey, I may not write all the lines, but I don't sing a syllable until I know what every word means."

It was Gillette's turn to smile.

"I know one thing," she continued. "*You* could be an angel."

"Yeah, right."

"I'm serious. You put up this tough veneer, but underneath you're a very caring person."

"You don't know that."

"Yes, I do," she replied firmly, leaning across the table and entwining her fingers in his. "I have good instincts that way."

He looked down at her hand, aroused by the softness of her skin.

"Don't just give money, Christian. Get down in the trenches. Get involved at the grassroots level. You're so charismatic. You could make such a difference."

Gillette stared at her over the flame, tempted to tell her about Jose and Alex. Then he spotted another young man headed toward the table clutching a napkin and a pen. He gestured to a bodyguard standing against the wall a few feet away, who quickly intercepted the fan. When the young man had been escorted away, he turned back to her. "Tell me about yourself, Faith. Where did you grow up?"

"If you know about that stalker letter," she said, pulling her hand from his, "I'm sure you know where I grew up."

So, she was smart, too. Which was good. He far preferred a challenge than a pushover. "Fair enough. So, tell me something I don't know."

She finished what was left in her glass. "I'm a twenty-six-year-old pop singer."

"I'd know that by—"

"And, since I was a teenager, I've been too busy with my career to ever have a real romance." Faith gazed into his eyes. "But I think I might finally be ready." She gave him a determined look. "Now it's your turn. Tell me something about you."

"Like what?"

"Like what do you do for fun?"

Typically, he would have sidestepped the question, but he was tempted to answer. Maybe because she was one of those creative types he rarely got to spend any time with but found so compelling, or because he wanted her to be interested in him. At least, tonight. "The other night I won five grand shooting pool out in Bed-Stuy."

Faith giggled and waved. "*Sure* you did."

"Seriously. I'm not too bad."

"Uh-huh. Where do you play?"

"Places in the Bronx and Brooklyn where there's real talent."

"Do you take a posse for protection?"

"No. I go by myself."

Faith shook her head. "Do you really expect me to believe that?"

"Believe what you want."

"Give me a break, Christian. Win or lose, you wouldn't make it out of those places alive. Come on, tell me something else. Something I can believe."

"Something else," he repeated. "Like—"

"Like, do you have any brothers or sisters?"

He hesitated, glancing away after a few moments.

"Christian."

"No, I'm an only child."

"Oh. Well, how about this? Tell me something you believe in."

"Something I *believe* in?"

"Yeah. Something that guides your life. A principle."

Gillette thought for a few seconds. "Okay, I don't really trust anyone."

She looked up, the smile on her face disappearing. "Why?"

"Because sooner or later, everyone will let you down."

Jose and Alex stood on the deck of Jose's home, gazing through the gloom at the house that would be Alex's.

As instructed, Jose had walked across the lawns separating the homes at nine o'clock this morning and bid $500 thousand dollars— thirty thousand more than the listed price. The professor had laughed callously at the offer, assuming Jose had no way of paying for another house in the neighborhood. So Jose had turned around and walked back home.

Ten minutes later the man was on Jose's doorstep, out of breath. Apologizing profusely for his insolence. He'd called the bank officer Jose had given as a reference and found out that Jose could pay cash.

Alex's chin fell slowly to his chest, and he rubbed his eyes to wipe away the moisture. "I'm going to be able to give my children a nice home, *hermano*," he whispered. "I'm going to be able to give them a real chance at life."

Jose put an arm around his brother's shoulder. "I know, Al. I say the same thing to myself every day."

"This is beautiful, Christian." Faith stood beside Gillette on the balcony of his duplex apartment overlooking Central Park. The lights of the West Side shone brightly in the distance. "Really."

"Thanks."

She turned so she was facing him. "I had a wonderful time tonight."

"Good."

"I want to get to know you better," she said quietly. She kissed him deeply, then stepped back, slipped off her top, and tossed it over the railing. Allowing him a few seconds to see her breasts in the moonlight, nipples erect in the chilly November night, before putting her arms around his neck and kissing him again. "I don't want to go home yet."

"And I don't want you to see Jeremy Cole," Gillette said firmly.

She moved back again, stepped out of her jeans, and stood before him naked, arms at her sides. "Okay."

"Ready, Alpha?" The voice came crackling through the walkie-talkie.

The man hesitated, making certain the sensors were online, making certain the laptops were picking up everything. He checked each screen to make absolutely sure that all of the sensors were transmitting data. He didn't want to have to do this again. For some reason he had a bad feeling about being up here this time.

"Affirmative. Alpha instructs you to blow the load."

Moments later, the Explorer shuddered as the dynamite detonated.

6

Allies. *As vital in business as in war. Because business is war.*

"GOOD MORNING, CHRISTIAN."

Gillette rose from his chair at the head of the long conference table. He'd been waiting ten minutes. Typically, he would have walked out after five. But not with this man. "Hello, Miles," he said, nodding respectfully.

Miles Whitman was chief investment officer of North America Guaranty & Life. With more than three trillion in assets, it was the country's largest insurance company. Whitman had sole authority over a trillion of that, making him one of the most influential people in the financial world. He could make and break Wall Street careers with his decisions, because an investment banker was nothing without a dependable flow of cash—and Whitman controlled the biggest river of all.

For the most part, Whitman invested in liquid securities: bank deposits, federal and state debt obligations, and the stocks and bonds of highly rated public corporations. But, like most insurance companies and other big investors, North America Guaranty—known as "NAG" in financial circles—allocated a percentage of its portfolio to private equity firms like Everest Capital. To the gunslingers like Christian Gillette who were generating huge returns. Whitman and his staff didn't have the expertise to buy and manage companies themselves, but, like everyone else, they salivated at the profits.

"I see you've adjusted quickly to your new position," Whitman observed drily, sitting down.

"What do you mean?"

"You're at the head of *my* table."

"Donovan training," Gillette replied unapologetically. "Always take the head of the table. *Especially* when it isn't yours. Gives me an immediate edge. People assume I'm running the meeting, even when I'm not."

Whitman chuckled, running his manicured fingernails along the razor-sharp part in his snow-white hair. "That's why we elected you chairman last week, Christian. Right here in this room." He made a sweeping gesture toward the far end of the table. "Because you take control," he said, adjusting his trademark bow tie. "I should be more specific," he said, holding up a finger. *"Those of us who know what we're doing elected you."*

"Thanks for hosting the meeting, Miles."

"Glad to. Hopefully, the speech I made right before the vote about backing you and not Troy helped sway one or two of the limited partners who were on the fence."

"Apparently you swayed *just* enough."

"Checked the results, did you?"

Gillette watched the other man stretch, fingers straight out as he reached for the ceiling. Whitman was sixty-two but still very active. He played squash three times a week at the Harvard Club against men half his age—and won—and cross-country biked at least twenty miles each weekend through the Connecticut state forest adjacent to his Greenwich property. "Of course I did."

"Good for you. Always understand who's with you." Whitman finished stretching. "And, more important, who's *against* you."

"I appreciate your talking to Ann Donovan, too. Without her 25 percent voting bloc, I would have lost."

"How did you find out about that?" asked Whitman curiously.

"Ann told me at the funeral reception. She said she was going to vote for Troy but that you convinced her that wouldn't be a good idea."

"I'm glad she took my advice. I felt strongly about that." Whitman turned his head to the side and grinned. "You okay? You look a little tired this morning."

"I'm fine."

"Already feeling the stress of running the second largest private equity firm in the world?"

After peeling off her clothes on his balcony at midnight, Faith had led Gillette to his bedroom and kept him up most of the night making love to him over and over until he'd finally ushered her down to the lobby and into a taxi at six this morning. He'd given her one of his shirts to replace the top she'd tossed over his railing, and he'd been relieved when they hadn't been met by a mob of paparazzi. Faith was a popular target.

"I'm not feeling any stress at all, Miles. I'm saddened by Bill's death, but I'm ready to carry on the Everest legacy."

"Very good," Whitman said approvingly. "Just the right amount of deference to the fallen leader, combined with energy for the future. Did you talk to a consultant or are you just a natural?"

"My father was a senator," Gillette reminded Whitman. "I know what to say and when to say it."

"Oh, that's right." Whitman's expression turned serious. "How are the troops at Everest doing?"

"What do you mean?"

"Well, the general just died. You'll have to be careful you don't lose lieutenants. Especially the good ones. Marcie, Kyle. They may think their prospects for getting rich just took a hit, and they may consider going somewhere else. You have to convince them that Everest won't miss a beat with you as chairman."

"I'll take care of that in the next few days." Gillette checked his watch. Today was jammed, but he didn't want to rush this man. "I need to talk to you about Troy."

Whitman glanced up. "What is it?"

"He's gone."

"Gone?"

"I fired him at the funeral reception."

"You're kidding. Why?"

"He was having sex with a woman who worked in the marketing department at one of our companies, a company Troy was chairman of."

Whitman rolled his eyes. "Oh, Jesus. So you were staring down the barrel of a massive sexual harassment lawsuit."

"Exactly."

"How did you find out?" Whitman asked.

"You don't want to know."

"As your biggest investor, I *need* to know. This'll get out, and I need to be able to support you with evidence. People will call and ask me about what you did to him."

Gillette's mind flashed back to the image of Mason on top of the young woman in the basement. "He invited her to the funeral reception, Miles. While you were talking to Senator Stockman on the first floor, they were in a basement bedroom."

"Christ!" Whitman banged the table. "What an idiot."

"Yeah. Like you said, that kind of crap could put us in court and cost us tens of millions of dollars."

"And a lot more than that in bad press," Whitman agreed. "You had no choice. But how do you know he was having sex with her?"

"I walked in on him."

Whitman stared at Gillette for a few moments without blinking. "How did you find out he was down there?" he finally asked.

"One of my people tipped me off."

"Who?"

"Kyle."

Whitman raised both eyebrows. "Really?"

"Yes."

"You figure Kyle saw an opportunity, a chance to get one of you guys out of the way so he could move up?"

"Probably."

"What did you give Mason in severance?"

"A million."

"What about his ups? Did you let him keep any?"

Gillette shook his head. "I don't want him associated with Everest at all."

"That's cold."

"He had it coming."

"Don't go out of your way to make enemies, Christian," Whitman advised. "You'll have plenty without even trying."

"I already do, and it doesn't bother me."

"A limousine blowing up doesn't bother you?"

"I'll be fine."

Whitman grimaced. "Be careful."

"I am." Gillette could tell Whitman wasn't convinced. "Look, Tom McGuire has people with me full-time now." As Everest's largest investor, Whitman was familiar with the portfolio companies, so he knew about McGuire & Company. "They sweep the limousines every few hours and rotate the vehicles constantly. They check my homes, the boats. Everything. And they're rerunning background checks on everyone at Everest. Tom's taking every precaution. I'm satisfied."

"Do you trust Tom?"

Gillette thought for a moment. "I have to trust someone." But maybe Whitman had a point. Maybe getting someone from the outside as well wouldn't be a bad idea.

"What do you think Mason will do?" Whitman asked.

"I don't know. I didn't talk about it with him."

"You should help him land on his feet. He's got a lot of information about Everest stored up in his head. Some you'd probably rather have him keep quiet. You don't want him showing up at one of your competitors spilling his guts. Remember, control every string. That's the key in your world." Whitman adjusted his bow tie again. "So, let's get to the main attraction. What's the real reason you came to see me this morning?"

Gillette nodded. "Okay. Well, look, NAG has always been one of our biggest backers. You've been an anchor tenant in each of our seven funds."

"Yep. We committed three million bucks to the first fund Bill put together twenty years ago. I remember presenting that to the investment committee like it was yesterday."

"And now you *are* NAG's investment committee. You make all the big decisions around here."

"Don't remind me," Whitman pleaded with a groan. "Why do you think my hair's so white? What did I commit to your last fund? To Everest Seven."

"Four hundred million."

Whitman whistled and grinned. "Four hundred million. That's a lot of money, Christian. Somebody might think I actually had faith in you guys."

"And now I'm asking you for more."

"What a surprise."

"At this point we've invested over half of the 6.5 billion of the seventh fund, so I'm getting ready to raise the next one. Our eighth."

"Didn't Bill usually wait until the current fund was at least 75 percent invested before he started raising the next one?"

"He did, but my target for this fund is ten billion," Gillette explained.

"Ten billion?"

"Yes. I'm going to need extra time to raise that much."

Whitman hooked his forefinger over his lower lip. "That's odd," he murmured through his hand.

"What is?"

"Paul Strazzi was in here yesterday. He's going to start raising his next fund, too. His target is the same as yours. Ten billion."

Paul Strazzi ran Apex Capital, the largest private equity firm in the world. Apex was also based in Manhattan. Apex and Everest had been rivals for years.

Thirty years ago, Bill Donovan and Paul Strazzi had worked together at Morgan Stanley, a high-powered New York investment bank. They'd been in the same associate class and started out as friends, but the relationship had soured as they constantly competed for promotions, raises, and bonuses. Ultimately, they'd each gone off on their own in the early eighties to start private equity firms, guiding their respective entities to the top of the financial food chain, competing for investors and performance as viciously as they had for promotions and bonuses at Morgan Stanley. Now Apex and Everest were the number one and two private equity firms in the world.

"Strazzi was here yesterday?" Gillette asked.

"Yeah. He called me first thing yesterday morning. Wanted to see me right away. Took me to lunch and laid the same thing on me. Ten billion dollars of a new fund. Apex's last fund was seven billion. We invested four hundred million in that one, too."

"Donovan wasn't happy about that."

Whitman shrugged. "Hey, Strazzi's performance has been excellent over the years. Just like you guys. There's no rule against me investing with both of you."

Gillette thought for a moment. "That's a hell of a coincidence. Strazzi coming in yesterday, I mean."

"Maybe it isn't a coincidence."

"Maybe not. But, Miles, the question is at what level will you support my new fund?"

Whitman hesitated. "I have an idea."

"What?"

"Increase your target to fifteen billion."

"*Fifteen?*"

"Yes."

Gillette clasped his hands together and rested them on the table. "Miles, that would be the largest private equity fund ever raised. By far."

Whitman's eyes danced. "I know."

"Do you think there's enough capacity in the market to fill a fifteen-billion-dollar fund *and* a ten-billion-dollar fund at the same time?"

Whitman shook his head. "No way. There's probably several hundred billion dollars committed to hundreds of private equity firms around the country, but there's not enough in the institutional coffers for two funds that size being raised simultaneously. Our total portfolio here at NAG is three trillion, but we only allocate 2 percent of that to private equity. That's sixty billion, and that's the maximum we commit to the *entire sector* of private equity. Which is probably about a hundred funds right now."

"Then why are you suggesting I increase the size of Everest Eight to fifteen?"

"Because I don't think there's enough capacity for two *ten*-billion-dollar funds, either. Not being raised at the same time, anyway. But there is capacity for one fifteen-billion-dollar fund. More important, I think it's time for one of you to take over. Having two firms this size just bids up prices you both ultimately have to pay for the companies you buy. So make the play, Christian. Head-to-head with Paul Strazzi. Everest raises the largest private equity fund ever." Whitman paused. "Or Apex does."

"I'll think about it, Miles, but the question still stands. At what level will you support me."

"A billion dollars." Whitman let out a heavy breath. "Along with our commitments to Everest's other funds, that'll be over two billion to you guys." He looked up, his expression darkening. "That's a lot of money for me to have with one private equity firm. Probably too much. The CEO will question me hard, but I have faith in your ability, young man." He pointed at Gillette. "Don't disappoint me."

"Don't worry," Gillette answered calmly.

"Your portfolio companies will have to be squeaky-clean during the fund-raising, Christian. No bankruptcies or scandals of any kind."

"Of course."

"I can't stress that enough."

"I hear you."

"How is the portfolio doing?" Whitman wanted to know.

"Overall, fine. In line with our historical performance. We're on track to generate 50 percent returns with the seventh fund. We've got a couple of investments that aren't doing as well as we'd like," Gillette admitted. "The power-tool company, for one. But that's natural. You can't bat a thousand when you control twenty-seven companies."

"Blalock Industries. That's the power-tool company, right?"

"Right."

"Roger Nolan runs it."

"Not anymore."

Whitman glanced up.

"I fired him," Gillette explained.

"You've been a busy man. Do you carry an ax with you at all times?"

"He never hit his budgets, Miles, and he whined about foreign competition. Yesterday I promoted Fred Cantwell to CEO. Fred had been the chief operating officer."

"Roger and Bill Donovan were good friends, weren't they?"

"I don't care. I can't let personal relationships influence my business decisions."

Whitman nodded approvingly. "Good for you, son. Too many people do. I think you're going to do just fine as chairman."

"Thanks."

"But whatever you do, don't let any of your companies fail while you're raising this next fund," Whitman advised strongly. "Keep them on life support if you have to. Put in more dollars even if you don't think you'll ever see the money again. Just don't let a single company go down. That would spook the investors."

"I don't believe in throwing good money after bad," countered Gillette. "We've always been careful about that at Everest. We've only had a few companies go down in twenty years, which is damn good. But the reality of this game is if you're in it long enough, sooner or later you're going to have companies blow up. You know that, Miles. Fortunately, we've had a lot more winners than losers. As a result, you and our other investors have done well."

"*Quite* well," Whitman agreed. "But this is fifteen billion dollars, Christian. Twice as much as anyone's ever tried to raise for this kind of fund. Take my advice. Don't screw up. No bankruptcies, no scandals, and keep the companies running at all costs. Once you've raised the fund, fine, back to financial Darwinism. But not until you have fifteen billion dollars of signed subscription agreements sitting in your lawyer's office. Understand, *amigo?*"

"I understand."

"How long do you think it'll take to raise Everest Eight?" Whitman asked.

"A year."

"That's probably right," the older man agreed. "Maybe a little faster with a break or two."

Gillette glanced over at Whitman. "I assume that because you're supporting me, you won't support Paul Strazzi's new fund."

"Bad assumption," Whitman replied sharply. "I'll give Strazzi an early soft commitment of a billion dollars, too. Whoever gets to fifteen first, that's who I'll go with."

Gillette had anticipated that answer, but it had been worth a shot. Getting North America Guaranty out of the market would have been a critical blow to Strazzi.

Whitman smiled. "Let the games begin."

"I'll get to fifteen first," Gillette promised firmly.

"I don't doubt it, Christian. When you focus on something, you seem to make it happen. Even something huge like this." Whitman shook his head. "But Paul Strazzi is a street fighter. He grew up in a rough part of Brooklyn, not Beverly Hills," Whitman said pointedly. "Paul has the toys now. Boats, cars, and planes. But he hasn't forgotten where he came from. He'll do whatever he can to screw you. He'll be out to prove a hard lesson to a young gun. There won't be any rules, I guarantee you. That's the essence of Strazzi's success. He'll do anything to win."

"So will I," Gillette said flatly.

Whitman chuckled. "Look at you. I just gave you a billion-dollar commitment, and it's like we're talking about the weather. No big deal. In fact, it's almost like you're disappointed."

"I wanted *two* billion."

Whitman laughed. "I admire you, Christian. If I could do it over again, I'd do private equity." He took a deep breath. "A fifteen-billion-dollar fund. It's really amazing."

"You manage *trillions*," Gillette pointed out.

"Yeah, but most of it is in bank CDs and U.S. government securities.

How exciting is that? Where's the risk? You're the one buying and selling entire companies," Whitman said wistfully.

Gillette stood up. He needed to get going, and he had what he'd
come for. "I appreciate your support, Miles," he said, shaking the older
man's hand.

"Of course."

"I'll be in touch."

"Christian," Whitman called as Gillette reached the conference
room door.

"Yes?"

"I'm a big football fan."

"I know."

"Well, the Super Bowl's coming up. I'd *really* like to get my hands on
four tickets to it. Good ones. Don't you have a connection with the
family that owns the Giants?"

"I do," Gillette confirmed. "And I'll get you four box seats on the
fifty-yard line. But, in return, if I get to 14.5 billion first, I want another
five hundred million from you. I want a billion five in total. Is it a deal?"

Whitman thought for a moment. "Deal."

"Good."

"One more thing," Whitman called.

"What?"

"How much key man life insurance is Ben Cohen carrying on you?"

"Five million."

"Tell him to triple that."

7

Enemies. *They are everywhere.*

"MR. STRAZZI WILL BE WITH you in a moment."

The young woman wore a revealing top and a pleated skirt that rose high on her tanned, tapered legs. Mason tried not to look, but his eyes kept flickering to her bare skin.

"Would you like something to drink while you wait?"

Mason snapped himself out of it, remembering how cold the barrel of the pistol had felt against his temple that night after the funeral reception. He'd been just about to pull the trigger when Strazzi called. "Water's fine."

"Okay." She hesitated, her full lips breaking into a smile.

A suggestive smile, he was certain. He tried to fight it but smiled back. It was instinct.

"I'll be right back."

Mason cursed under his breath when she was gone. He couldn't keep going on like this. At some point, there wouldn't be any more chances.

"Here you are," she said, returning to the office a few moments later with bottled water and a glass of ice. She put the glass down on a table beside the leather chair and poured.

"Thanks."

"Oh, sure," she said, doing a double take.

"What is it?" he asked, catching the hint of recognition on her face. He'd seen that same look on the faces of other women before.

"Has anyone ever told you that you look a little like Brad Pitt?"

"Um, no."

"Oh, I doubt that." She put the bottle down beside the glass. "Why don't you stop by on your way out," she suggested. "I'm right down the hall. My name's Vicky."

Her hand hung suspended in front of him—sinewy fingers and long nails highlighted at the tips by a perfect French manicure. "Hi, Vicky." His fingers closed around hers. "I'm Troy."

"Troy *Mason*, right?"

"Right."

"Paul's been looking forward to meeting with you."

"He has?"

"Oh yes." She gave him another smile, then twirled around and headed out of the office. "See you in a little while," she called over her shoulder.

Mason watched until she disappeared, allowing himself a few seconds of vulgar fantasy. The hell with it. Dogs had to hunt.

"You like that?" a loud voice boomed into the office.

Mason's eyes snapped toward the voice. Paul Strazzi stood in the doorway opposite the one Vicky had just gone through.

"She's smart, too," Strazzi continued, sitting down behind his desk without shaking hands. "Not just a pretty face."

Mason said nothing, thinking about what a terrible first impression he'd made.

"Glad you could come by this morning, Troy." Strazzi was a bear of a man. Six six and 240 pounds with a barrel chest and a massive skull covered by a full head of short-cropped gray hair. Still in decent shape for a fifty-seven-year-old. "No need to be so dressed up," he said, gesturing at Mason's necktie. "We're business casual here at Apex. One small way out of many that we're different from Everest."

"Different from Everest. I like the sound of that."

"I'm sure you do." Strazzi gestured again. "So take it off."

"What?"

"The tie. Take it off."

Mason slowly undid the knot, then slid the tie from around his neck and draped it over the arm of the chair.

"Undo the top button of your shirt, too."

Mason obeyed.

"That's better," Strazzi said. "Now we can relax."

Mason had never met Strazzi, but he'd heard the man was eccentric—and dictatorial. That he ran Apex Capital with an iron fist. That no decision was made without his input. From which companies they bought to the brand of paper clips they used.

"So your partner, Chris Gillette, fires you the day after he takes control of Everest." Strazzi sneered. "That's a hell of a thing."

The image of taillights gliding away into the darkness at the Donovan estate was etched into Mason's memory. Gliding away as he picked himself up off the asphalt. "Yes, it is."

"You should have expected it."

Mason recoiled slightly. "Why? He was my friend. At least I thought he was."

"He did what any alpha wolf would do. He drove out his closest rival when he took control. Friend or not." Strazzi nodded at the door Vicky had left open. "Shut that."

Mason stood up deliberately, forcing irritation into his expression, aware that being told what to do was all part of a mind game. Unfortunately he had no choice but to obey Strazzi's order. He needed this job.

"How did he do it?" Strazzi asked when Mason was seated again.

"What do you mean?"

"How did Gillette get you out of Everest so fast without a fight?"

Mason had anticipated this coming up. Just not so soon. "He caught me having sex with a woman who worked for me at one of our portfolio companies." Maybe he could move to Vermont and open an ice-cream shop on the main street of a little town. Maybe then he and his wife could start over.

Strazzi rubbed his large Roman nose. "Good, Troy. I thought it would take us a while to get to the bottom line, but I guess you're desperate."

"You guessed right," Mason agreed, grabbing his tie. He assumed the meeting was over.

"Gillette gave you a million bucks but he stripped you of your ups. Right?"

Mason hesitated, gazing at Strazzi.

Strazzi nodded. "Yeah, I know the deal." He pointed at the tie hanging from Mason's hand. "Put that down. You're not going anywhere."

"How do you know the deal?"

"I have a source inside Everest."

Mason's eyes narrowed. "Who is it?"

Strazzi shook his head. "I'm not telling you. Not yet anyway." He pulled a cigar from a desk drawer and lit it. "Would you rather be loved or respected, Troy?" Strazzi blew out the match and tossed it in a trash can.

"Do you mean—"

"No qualifiers, son. Just answer the question. Loved or respected?"

Mason paused. The answer Strazzi was looking for wasn't clear. His first instinct was to say "respect." Strazzi was a hard-nosed man with a fiery temper. He axed people at will and let attorneys and courts deal with the details. But he was a passionate man, too. A family man with ten grandchildren. "Loved."

"Why?" Strazzi demanded, exhaling a cumulonimbus cloud of smoke.

Mason shrugged, wishing suddenly that he could be true to his wife, that he wasn't so tempted by other women. "Isn't that what we all want?" he asked, surprised at the conversation. He'd anticipated that this would be about his background, and what he could do for Apex.

Strazzi put the cigar down in a large, circular ashtray. "Right answer, wrong reason. A man who's respected gets cards on his birthday and a gold watch at sixty-five. But a man who's loved can inspire others to do incredible things, and those of us who inspire can take advantage of those incredible things." Strazzi's expression hardened. "Of course you could say the same thing about hate. Hate can inspire people to do incredible things, too." Strazzi picked up the cigar again. "And sometimes hate becomes love. Sometimes hate really is love."

Mason understood. He'd hated his Stanford football coach for three long seasons, detested the brutal practices and the tongue-lashings he'd endured in front of the entire team for minor mistakes. Then the man had made him captain his senior year, and they'd won the Rose Bowl and ended up ranked fifth in the nation. They'd accomplished an incredible thing. Despite his heavily bandaged knee, Mason had hobbled up to the man when the game was over, hugged him, and told him he loved him.

"I hated most people at Morgan Stanley when I started work there right out of City College," Strazzi spoke up. "They were all punks who'd gone to Princeton, Harvard, and Stanford. I was just a social 'project' to them. I had the wrong last name and I'd gone to a minor-league school.

I figured I was around just to remind them of how much better they were than me.

"But this one guy took me under his wing," Strazzi continued, taking another puff on the cigar. "He convinced me I could go through the white-shoe set like a bullet through rotten flesh. He convinced me they didn't have something I had—the drive to do whatever it took to get what I wanted. I'll never forget that man as long as I live. He's the one person I'll *never* turn my back on."

Mason thought about asking who that person was. But, like the question about Strazzi's source inside Everest, he assumed he wouldn't get an answer.

Strazzi put his feet up on the desk. "Where did you go to school, Troy?"

For the second time, Mason assumed his answer would end the conversation. "Stanford undergrad and Harvard Business School."

"Best of the best." Strazzi sneered.

"Yeah, well . . ."

"Didn't want to tell me that, either, did you?"

"No."

"Do you hate Chris Gillette?" Strazzi asked, suddenly slamming his feet to the floor, leaning over the desk, and pointing the smoking cigar at Mason. "Or do you just dislike him?"

Mason stared into Strazzi's burning eyes. This was an easy one. "I hate him."

"Good. So do I, and I want to take him down. I want to take his whole damn firm down. I want to destroy Bill Donovan's legacy." Strazzi puffed on the cigar. "Will you help me?"

Mason felt emotion surge through his body. "Oh yeah."

"And are you willing to do whatever it takes?"

"Yes."

"*Anything*? Anything at all?"

Mason gazed at Strazzi intently, trying to understand exactly what the other man meant. But maybe there was nothing to analyze. Maybe there were no boundaries. Maybe it was just that simple. "Yes."

"All right, then. Welcome aboard. Let's talk compensation."

"One question, first."

"What?"

"How did you know to call me so fast?"

"What do you mean?"

"You called me at home after Donovan's funeral, only a few hours after Gillette canned me. How did you know?"

Strazzi smiled. "I told you. Chris Gillette has enemies he thinks are allies."

The bodyguard trotted across the sidewalk and opened the limousine door. Gillette spotted the handle of a pistol protruding from the man's shoulder holster as he bent down and slipped into the vehicle. "Thanks."

"You're welcome, sir."

Cohen was waiting inside, scribbling notes on a legal pad. "How did it go?" he asked, looking up.

Gillette relaxed onto the seat beside Cohen. "Miles committed NAG to a billion five," he answered, omitting the fact that the commitment was conditional. That it was only going to the firm that raised thirteen and a half billion first.

"A *billion five*? That's incredible, Christian. Congratulations."

"Thanks." Gillette watched the bodyguard get in beside the driver. "The rest of the raise won't be that easy."

The small cell phone Gillette carried in his suit jacket began vibrating. He used the Blackberry strictly for business calls. This phone was for social calls.

He pulled the phone from his pocket, loving the way it fit snugly in the palm of his hand. He'd become a techno-junkie over the past few years, always looking for the latest gadget. "Hello," he said, not recognizing the number on the tiny screen.

"Hi."

It was Faith. He recognized her voice immediately. "How are you this morning?" He was aware that Cohen was listening intently.

"Great. I still have that glow. I had a wonderful time last night."

"Me, too."

"Listen, I have to go to Los Angeles this afternoon to do some PR stuff. You know, drop by a few stores and sign some CDs. Why don't you come with me? It would be a lot of fun."

Gillette hesitated, remembering how good it felt to be with her. "I'm sure it would be fun, but I'm stacked up over the next few days with Everest stuff."

"Disappointing me already," she said, her voice turning sad.

"Hey, look, I—"

"I'm just kidding," she interrupted. "I know you've got even more going on now that you're chairman. I just thought I'd take a chance."

"When are you back?"

"It's a quick trip. Tomorrow or the day after."

"Call me tonight," he suggested. "We'll get together when you get back."

"Okay." Faith hesitated. "Say something nice, Christian, please."

"Have a safe trip."

"That's not what I meant."

"Call me tonight," he repeated, catching the beginning of her frustrated groan as he cut the call off. "Bye."

"Was that Faith?" Cohen wanted to know.

Gillette slipped the phone back into his pocket.

"Did you sleep with her?" Cohen pushed when he didn't get an answer.

"None of your business."

"It is when you fire Troy for doing the same thing."

Gillette turned slowly on the seat. "It isn't the same thing, Ben," he said evenly. "And don't ever be disloyal to—"

"It's *exactly* the same thing. Ultimately, Faith Cassidy works for you. And I'm not being disloyal, damn it, I'm trying to *protect* you. Who the hell do you think decoyed the paparazzi away from your front door this morning?"

Gillette stared at the small man for a few seconds. "I appreciate that," he said quietly, realizing suddenly that maybe he shouldn't take Cohen for granted, that Cohen could be more than just a numbers guy. "Have you found out whether or not that woman who was killed in front of the church had children?"

"She had three."

"How old were they?"

"Nine, seven, and four. Two girls and a boy. She was divorced, and the kids have gone to live with her sister on Long Island. There's child support from the ex, but it isn't much, and the sister has a full plate with four kids of her own."

Gillette glanced out at the Brooklyn Bridge as they headed north on the FDR toward midtown. "Give each child a quarter of a million."

"That's a lot of money," Cohen said. "It isn't our fault she was—"

"They're kids, Ben. Young kids. It doesn't matter whose fault it is."

Isabelle's image drifted suddenly through Gillette's mind: long black hair, sculpted cheekbones, smooth, honey-brown skin, and dark eyes. There was something about her that haunted him, something he couldn't shake. Thinking about her was distracting, and he hated being distracted.

He'd only spoken to her for a few moments in Jose and Selma's kitchen. Not long enough to really even draw a first impression. But here he was, thinking about her—again.

"Take it out of my bonus," Gillette instructed.

"Okay, okay. I agree." Cohen put his hands up, giving in. "We need to do the right thing here. I'll make the arrangements, and we'll *all* share the burden. Not just you."

Fifteen minutes later the limousine eased to a stop in front of the Everest building.

"I have a few more things I want to cover," Cohen said, "but I guess they can wait until we get upstairs."

"We're stopping here for you," explained Gillette. "I'm on my way to see Tom McGuire, then I'm having lunch with Senator Stockman. What do you want to cover?"

Cohen checked the list of items scrawled on the legal pad resting on his knees. "We need to talk about all the companies you're chairman of now. All twenty-seven of our control investments, with Bill dead and Troy fired. You can't possibly handle that many chairs *and* raise ten billion dollars."

"I agree, and the target isn't ten billion anymore. It's fifteen."

"*Fifteen?*" Cohen asked, squinting.

"Miles convinced me to go for that much. He wanted to commit a billion five." An exaggeration of the number and not the real reason Whitman wanted Gillette to raise the target. But Cohen needed confidence. "But he can't be more than 10 percent of any individual fund. That's an internal NAG limit."

"Jesus," Cohen muttered under his breath. "I hope we can raise that much."

"I have no doubt we can," Gillette said. "Okay. Let's talk about the chairmanships. What's your recommendation?" He saw that Cohen had been taken off guard.

"Well, I . . . I guess I would—"

"From now on," Gillette interrupted, "when you bring up an issue, do it along with a recommendation. I may not agree, but I always want a recommendation."

"Okay." Cohen paused. "Um, how about this? You keep fifteen chairs and split the balance between Faraday and me. That would be six each for the two of us."

Gillette shook his head. "Nigel's going to be focused on raising the new fund. That'll be a full-time project. And I need you to run the office."

"So you aren't going to give me a single portfolio company?"

The cell phone vibrated again. Gillette pulled it out and flipped it open. It was Jeremy Cole. "Hi, Jeremy," he said, holding up his hand to Cohen.

"Hey, I got a message that you called. What's up?"

"I talked to the Giants yesterday. They'll be contacting your agent in the next few hours, if they haven't already. They'll be offering you six million per for five years with a $10 million signing bonus. Take it. Don't let your agent get greedy," Gillette warned. "I've gotten everything there is to get. Understand?"

"I . . . I understand. My God, Christian, how did you do that?"

"Don't worry about it. Now I need a favor."

"Anything. Just name it."

"I need tickets to the Super Bowl. Whether you and the Giants get there or not." Gillette could have called the owner's son, but he wanted Cole to step up. "It's in New Orleans this year, right?"

"Right."

"Okay. I need four seats. Good ones, too. It's for a very important friend."

"Done. I'll make the arrangements right away. For all the other stuff, too: passes to the parties and as many luxury suites as you need at the best hotel in the French Quarter. I'll take care of everything."

"Good. By the way, how's Faith Cassidy? Weren't you two supposed to see each other this week."

"How did you know?"

"Word travels."

"Uh-huh. Well, she canceled on me," Cole grumbled. "Something about having to go to L.A., but she wouldn't reschedule. That hasn't happened to me in a while." He laughed. "Maybe you could help me with that, too."

Faith had done exactly as she'd been told. Power was a beautiful thing. "Maybe," Gillette said. "Look, I've got to get going. Remember, tell your agent not to get greedy. If he does, I can't help."

"I'm calling him right now."

Gillette closed the phone, ending the call.

"Is it Miles who wants Super Bowl tickets?" asked Cohen.

Gillette nodded. "Let's get back to the chair positions. Here's what I'm going to do. I'm going to promote Marcie and Kyle to managing partner. Both of them are already board members at several of our portfolio companies. They'll replace me as chairman at those companies, and I'll appoint them to chair positions at a few others as well. As you suggested, I'll keep fifteen and split the remaining twelve between Marcie and Kyle. Of course, you, Nigel, and I need to talk about how much of the ups we're going to give Marcie and Kyle. I'm leaning toward splitting 10 of Mason's 25 percent between them: 5 and 5. We'll keep the other 15. At least for now."

"You're not even going to give me one chairman seat?" Cohen asked angrily.

"I told you. I need you focused internally."

"Just one, Christian. Being chairman of a company is something you've always taken for granted because you've always had lots of those positions. I just want to be able to tell my daughters I'm chairman of one of our companies. Please."

"No, Ben. And don't beg. It's pitiful."

"Hi, Vicky." Mason leaned into the young woman's small office.

Vicky looked up from her desk. "Are you and Paul done?"

"Yes."

She smiled self-consciously, starting to say something, then stopping.

"What is it?" he asked.

"Nothing."

"*Come on.*"

"I don't usually do this."

"*What?*"

"I was going to ask you to lunch, but you're probably already busy," she added quickly.

Mason's eyes ran down the plunging lines of her top. "No, I'm free. Let's go."

His cell phone rang as they headed toward the door. It was his wife. He shut it off without answering.

Paul Strazzi watched Mason and Vicky move toward the elevators. He loved how predictable a man like Mason was. It made the pursuit of money so much easier.

8

Unconditional Trust. In a world dominated by the cutthroat race to extraordinary financial gain, unconditional trust is nonexistent. In the end, a private equity professional must assume that those circling around him are ultimately driven by money—and nothing else. Otherwise, he's setting himself up for failure.

TOM MCGUIRE MOVED INTO THE back of the limousine, letting out an exasperated breath as he eased onto the seat beside Gillette. He'd been standing on the corner of Eighth Avenue and Fifty-seventh Street for the last twenty minutes—cooling his heels.

Gillette knew the heavy breath was meant to let him know McGuire was angry, but he didn't care. He didn't have time for egos. It was all about what was best for Everest. "Hi, Tom. I'm having lunch over on Fifth, so we'll talk while we ride. The driver can take you wherever you want to go after he drops me off."

Tall and lanky with gray, unkempt hair and round, tortoiseshell glasses, McGuire reminded Gillette of several of his Princeton professors. He always seemed disheveled in his unpressed, button-down shirts, khakis, and rumpled sports jackets with elbow patches.

Vince, Tom's younger brother by four years, was the opposite. Short and muscular, he wore crisp turtlenecks, designer jeans, and cowboy boots. And while Tom had an easygoing manner about him, Vince was intense.

They were night and day, black and white, but they made an excellent team. Tom the brains, Vince the muscle. The perfect combination to run a global security company. They were co-CEOs, and they'd doubled the company's revenues since Everest Capital had bought the company three years ago.

Bill Donovan had been chairman of McGuire & Company, and now Gillette was taking over. It would be one of the fifteen chairs Gillette would keep. He'd been the other Everest board member since the beginning, so he'd known the McGuire brothers since the beginning.

McGuire nodded subtly to the bodyguard peering back at them over his shoulder from the passenger seat. "You're meeting with Senator Stockman, right?"

"Yes." Gillette glanced from the bodyguard to McGuire, catching the exchange. "You dig up anything else on Stockman?"

McGuire winced.

"What's wrong?"

"I hate this crap."

"What do you mean?"

"It's so predictable." McGuire reached for the console on the limousine door, and pushed the button that raised the panel between the front and back seats. "I found out this morning that Stockman's having an affair with a woman who works for him. Her name's Rita Jones. She's twenty-four and pretty," McGuire stifled a chuckle, "in her own way."

"What's so funny?"

"She's black. It kills me when these lily-white guys like Stockman get the jungle fever because they—"

"Enough," Gillette interrupted. McGuire didn't air his prejudices publicly, but once in a while he let loose with a comment Gillette didn't appreciate. And there were no African-American senior executives at McGuire & Company, a situation Gillette was going to change now that he was in charge because there were plenty of deserving candidates in middle management. "Just tell me what's happening."

McGuire rolled his eyes, irritated. "The affair's been going on for six months. Stockman uses an apartment in Queens a couple of nights a week. One of his aides pays for it so there's no direct money link. He's also brought Jones down to Washington a couple of times. His wife has no idea what's going on, not, at least, from what we can tell."

Good. It was something he could use, especially if Stockman's wife didn't know. "How do you find this stuff out, Tom?"

"Hang out in the gutter long enough and eventually all the garbage flows past you."

The McGuire network was broad and deep. Gillette had checked on that before Everest made the investment. He'd found that the brothers knew a lot of people in a lot of different places, not just the gutter. "Take me through Stockman's background one more time, will you?"

"Sure. He's from upstate New York, near Albany. Cornell undergraduate, then the Wharton Business School at the University of Pennsylvania after two years as a Chase Manhattan corporate banking trainee. After business school he worked as an investment banker at Morgan Stanley for ten years, then went into politics. Served a couple of terms as a state senator before moving on to the big time in D.C."

"Wealthy?"

McGuire shook his head. "Not really. No major money in his or his wife's family. Both families belong to all the right clubs, but that's because they settled in the area two hundred years ago, so they know everybody. Stockman made some bucks at Morgan Stanley, but he put a lot of that into his campaigns. And his investment portfolio got dinged pretty bad when the tech stocks got crushed in 2001. It hasn't come back."

"Anything else?"

"No, but we're still looking."

"What about Donovan?" Gillette asked. "Any more news there?"

"Yeah, one of Vince's guys spoke to somebody he knows at the coroner's office in Connecticut. There were bruises on Donovan's body consistent with a struggle," McGuire explained. "No heart attack, either. Bill's ticker was fine, but the cops are still calling it an accidental drowning. They aren't following up. We don't know why."

"Could they be involved? Paid off, maybe?"

"With the stakes as high as they are, anything's possible at this point."

"But who would want Donovan dead?"

McGuire ran a finger inside his collar. His shirts always hung loosely around his thin neck. "I might have an idea."

"Talk to me."

"Well . . ." McGuire hesitated. "I don't know if I want to—"

"Come on, Tom."

McGuire gazed out the window for a moment. "For starters, how about the guy you're having lunch with?"

"Stockman?"

"Yeah."

"Why would Stockman want Bill Donovan dead?"

McGuire flashed Gillette an odd look. "You don't know?"

"No."

"Oh."

Gillette cleared his throat, making certain McGuire heard his frustration. "Tom."

"I just assumed Bill told you this stuff. After all, you were his partner."

"Don't assume anything."

"Look, here's the thing. Bill told Stockman a few months ago he'd do whatever he could to keep him out of the White House, said he'd spend a ton of dough on negative ads himself. Call people. Anything."

"Why?"

"*That* I don't know. Bill told me he'd found out something about Stockman that really pissed him off, but he wouldn't tell me what."

"You think it was the affair with the Jones woman?"

McGuire chuckled. "Ah, no."

"Maybe it was just that Stockman's a Democrat and Donovan was a big Republican."

McGuire shook his head. "I don't think that was it, either."

"Well, it seems like a stretch to me that Stockman would go as far as having Donovan killed."

"I know for a fact that Donovan was going to try to derail Stockman's campaign."

"Yeah, but who knows if he really could have."

McGuire smirked. "You're selling Bill short. Even though he was a Republican, he was *very* connected on both sides of the political aisle. He could have made things tough for Stockman, and he had the economic muscle to get his message out. Particularly with that network of radio and television stations Everest owns." McGuire hesitated. "Believe me, they hated each other from a long time back."

"Still, it seems like a long shot."

McGuire shrugged. "Hey, *you* asked *me* to speculate."

"Who else?" Gillette asked as the limousine turned right onto Park Avenue.

"Bill's widow," McGuire replied bluntly.

"*What?*"

"Boy, I never gave Bill enough credit," McGuire said, shaking his head. "I figured you guys would have known about this, too. I never thought Bill could keep a secret, but I guess I was wrong."

"Known about what?" Gillette demanded.

"He's dead, so it doesn't really matter," McGuire muttered.

Gillette was getting frustrated. "*Tom.*"

"All right, all right. Bill liked younger women. The same way Stockman does."

"Really?" Gillette never had a clue, never even caught Donovan looking at a woman that way.

"That's why I don't think Bill would have cared about Stockman's affair," McGuire continued. "Bill was old school about all that. He thought powerful men deserved distractions. As compensation for all the stress."

"I assume Ann wasn't on the same page."

"Not even the same book."

Gillette hadn't realized until just now how close Bill Donovan and Tom McGuire were, and it struck him as strange that McGuire would air the dirty laundry so fast. There had to be another motive here. "Did Ann know what Bill was doing?"

"She probably suspected for a while, but I don't think she knew for sure until a few months ago."

"What happened?"

"There was an incident at the mansion. Ann was traveling in Europe with an old girlfriend from college and came back a few days early. She wanted to surprise Bill, and she sure as hell did. Caught him with a twenty-three-year-old in their bedroom. World War Three broke out. Bill had to spend a bunch of money to put the place back together. He told me they reconciled, but maybe Ann was just taking her time."

"That's hard to believe."

"You've known Ann longer than I have, Christian, but you haven't spent as much time with her. She's a spitfire. She might seem quiet on the outside, but there's a temper and a mean streak in there." McGuire laughed harshly. "And Bill was relentless. Maybe Ann found out a while ago, and the thing in the mansion was the straw that broke the camel's back. Did you know he tried to tag Faith Cassidy one night?"

Gillette looked up.

"Yup. It was about six months ago," McGuire continued. "Took her to dinner in Manhattan, supposedly to talk about her next contract. Basically attacked her in the limousine on the way back to her apartment. She had to fight her way out of it, then catch a cab."

"Jesus."

"Bill put her contract negotiations on hold the next morning, and ordered the record label to cut back on marketing dollars for her next album."

The limousine pulled to a stop at a traffic light. They were only a few blocks from the Racquet Club.

Gillette gazed at McGuire. Now it was beginning to make sense. Why Faith had been so tight-lipped about what was going on with her second album. She probably thought his ultimate loyalty would be to Donovan, that he wouldn't believe some story about Donovan coming on to her in the back of a limousine. That he'd figure it was just a pathetic attempt to extort marketing money out of the record label.

"How do you know all this?" Gillette asked. He made a mental note to check into Faith's contract negotiations this afternoon. And to check the amount of ad dollars she was getting.

"I guess I was the one Bill told his secrets to," McGuire said. "The *only* one, I'm finding out. I suppose Bill needed to tell someone these things. Obviously, he couldn't tell Ann." He smiled. "In the end, most human beings need to tell someone their secrets. If they didn't, my job would be a whole lot harder."

"Does Vince know about this stuff?"

"Yes," McGuire answered directly. "He and I tell each other everything. We keep each others' secrets."

Gillette took a deep breath. He wanted to see if Tom thought there were others who had motive, but he'd have to follow up on that later. There was something else they needed to talk about before his meeting with Stockman, and he was already forty minutes late. "What about the limousine, Tom? Any more information on the explosion?"

"Yeah, we're pretty sure the bomb was set off by a remote control device and not a timing mechanism. One of Vince's boys got that from his contacts inside the NYPD crime lab."

As they pulled to a stop in front of the Racquet Club, Gillette rubbed his eyes. His contacts were beginning to burn. He was supposed to have picked up new ones last week, but there hadn't been enough time. And he hated asking Debbie to do things like that. "So someone was watching me that day," he said quietly.

"Apparently."

"Then why—"

"It must have been a warning, Christian," McGuire interrupted. "Probably meant to scare you. Maybe from being chairman."

Gillette stared at McGuire for several moments, then patted the other man's knee. "Good work, Tom. Thanks. Let's talk again later today or tomorrow. What's your schedule?"

"I'm around for a day or so, then I'm flying to London Thursday afternoon."

The bodyguard opened Gillette's door, allowing bright sunshine to stream in.

"Okay," Gillette said, shading his eyes. "I'll call you later."

"Christian."

Gillette turned back around. "Yes?"

"There's something else I want to talk about."

"I'm really late, Tom."

"It's important. Please."

Gillette nodded to the bodyguard, who shut the door. "What is it?"

"I want to talk to you about the firm," McGuire began. "About McGuire & Company."

Maybe he was about to find out why Tom McGuire had been so open about Bill Donovan's secrets, Gillette thought. Maybe that had all been bridge building leading up to this. "What about it?"

"Vince and I want to buy McGuire & Company back from you."

And that explained everything. "That's interesting," Gillette said slowly. "Obviously, it's a surprise and I need time to think about it."

Everest had acquired McGuire & Company three years ago for a hundred and fifty million dollars. Tom and Vince had done well in the original buyout, grossing five million each, but the venture capital firm that had originally backed the brothers had raked in the lion's share of the payout. Tom and Vince were comfortable now, but not wealthy. After paying taxes and what they owed on several personal loans, they'd netted a million each in cash. A decent sum, but not enough to retire on.

So they hadn't. They'd stayed on after the transaction to run the company for Everest, signing long-term contracts to be co-CEOs. And they'd run it well, doubling revenues and tripling profits in the last three years. Now they wanted the big payoff. They wanted to cash in on the stock options Everest had given them as part of the contracts to stay on after the acquisition. The options were worth tens of millions on paper, but nothing in cash because the firm was private and the shareholder agreement didn't allow them to exercise the options and sell the underlying shares unless Everest consented. Gillette could see that money-hungry look burning in Tom McGuire's eyes.

"You and Vince have done a great job running this thing, Tom. You know how much we at Everest appreciate that."

"Then let's agree on a price and do a deal," urged McGuire.

Gillette didn't want to have this discussion now. As the widow had counseled him at the funeral reception, he wanted to negotiate on his terms, at his time. But he didn't want to irritate Tom McGuire, either. The man was directly responsible for his personal security. "Where would you get the money?"

"We have a backer," McGuire answered quickly, giving away nothing specific. "Someone who'll supply the funds and give us 50 percent of the stock to manage the company. And we don't have to put up a dime."

"*Fifty percent?*"

"Yeah."

"When did this person approach you?"

"A few weeks ago."

"Did you tell Donovan?"

"Of course. Right away. Bill thought it was a great idea. I'm surprised he didn't tell you."

"Me, too." There was no way to know if McGuire was telling the truth about that. The McGuire brothers were different in many ways, but they shared a poker face a Vegas high roller would have cut off a hand for. "Who is this person?"

"Asked me not to say yet. Not until we've agreed on a price."

"Why?"

McGuire shrugged. "Beats the hell out of me. You probably have a better idea than I do why there's so much concern about staying anonymous. You finance guys are more paranoid about secrecy than we are in the security business."

This was a problem, Gillette realized. A *huge* problem. He needed the McGuires on his side. He needed to be able to trust them—with his life, given everything that was going on. But if he didn't negotiate with them, they'd be furious. Then how safe would he be? "How much were you thinking about paying?"

McGuire smiled. "I was thinking you'd tell me. You're the money man. I don't know much about this financial stuff. I'm just a security guy."

McGuire was trying to be cagey, trying to get the other side to talk first so he wouldn't leave anything on the table, but it wasn't going to work. Gillette had a lot more experience in this kind of chess match than McGuire. "I'm sure your backer gave you some indication of what he'd pay."

"Well . . ." McGuire's voice trailed off.

Gillette saw McGuire struggling. "When he does, let me know." Gillette turned to open the limousine door.

"Three hundred million," McGuire blurted out. "That's twice what you guys paid three years ago. That's very fair."

Maybe in a normal scenario, Gillette thought to himself, but with the threat of terrorism heightened around the world, the security space was hot, especially for a multiservice global firm such as McGuire & Company. Two top investment banks had approached Everest several months ago about taking McGuire & Company public, and the price talk from the Wall Street firms was five hundred million—which was why Gillette doubted Donovan would have thought a Tom and Vince McGuire–led buyout would have been such a great idea. The IPO would be a nice payday for the McGuires, but the public market would never give the brothers 50 percent of the company for no money down. Which was what they really wanted. That was how they could ultimately make *hundreds* of millions, not just tens.

"When are you back from London, Tom?" asked Gillette. He was very close to signing an underwriting agreement with one of the investment banks—basically agreeing to do the IPO. Which Tom would quickly find out about because, once the agreement was signed, the investment bank would immediately start the due diligence process, digging deeply into the company's records to confirm figures and legal issues. It was the first step in the IPO process, and Tom and Vince would have to be intimately involved in it as CEOs of the business.

"Sunday," McGuire answered.

"Okay, if for some reason we don't hook up in the next couple of days, let's get together early next week and talk."

"But give me your initial reaction now, Christian. I want to be able to tell Vince and our backer what you thought."

Gillette hesitated. "It sounds good. I'm inclined to start talking to you seriously about it, but let me run it by a few of my guys at Everest." Never let the other side think that you can make the decision on your own—even if you can. "All right?"

McGuire shook Gillette's hand warmly. "That's great, Christian. I appreciate it very much."

"Sure."

Gillette would never leave two hundred million on the table—the difference between the IPO price and what the McGuires were offering. He'd have to find a way to string McGuire along without letting him know about the discussions he was having with the investment bankers about taking McGuire & Company public. At least for a little while.

He was still fifty miles from the nearest town, still out in the middle of nowhere, creeping through the pitch black and the driving snow because the Explorer's headlights had given out ten minutes ago, along with the windshield wipers and the defroster. Now the engine was beginning to falter, slowly losing power like everything else in the vehicle already had.

The man tried punching the accelerator, but it didn't help. It was just a matter of time before the truck would be done, and he cursed himself for knowing nothing about engines. He'd been warned to have at least a basic knowledge of how the things worked, but, in all the years, he'd never gotten around to it.

A few minutes later the engine died and the Explorer drifted to a halt. "Damn it!" The man banged the steering wheel as he turned the key over and over again in the ignition, trying in vain to restart the engine. But no amount of urging was going to make it start again. There was nothing to do but wait for help, which could take days. Especially if the snow kept falling heavily. He might be dead by then.

He switched on a flashlight hanging from the rearview mirror, then picked up several photographs of his two children that were lying on the passenger seat and gazed at them. Bill Jr., thirteen. Cindy, eleven. They lived with their mother in Houston. She'd gotten custody of them two years ago in the divorce. He could still remember the judge shaking her head when she heard how much time he spent away from the family.

He touched Cindy's face. Now he saw them two weeks a year. It didn't need to be this way.

As he was staring at the pictures, the driver-side door flew open, and, before he knew what was happening, he was facedown in the snow beside the truck. Still grasping the photographs.

Two men held him down in the drift while a third reached onto the floor in front of the passenger seat, picked up the box containing the seismic tapes, and switched it for another box. "Got 'em."

They tied his hands behind his back, picked him up roughly, and hustled him into another truck—snow covering his beard and mustache—then drove a mile to the lake. There, they pulled him outside into the blizzard again, untied his hands, and tossed him into a large hole they'd cut in the foot-thick ice. He tried, over and over, to pull himself from the water, but each time he clutched at the ice, one of the men stepped on his fingers. He'd scream in pain each time a finger snapped, but there was no mercy.

Finally, he slipped below the surface—and the darkness closed around him for the last time.

Confrontation. *Most people hate confrontation in any form—standing up to the boss in person, fighting an unauthorized credit card charge over the phone, or calling a neighbor out for something her child did to yours. People shrink from confrontation like vampires from the sun, putting off the battle until it becomes unavoidable. Oftentimes they'll roll over at the last moment rather than face the enemy.*

And people hate confrontation for good reason. It causes their palms to perspire, brings on shortness of breath, makes their hearts race like there's no tomorrow. It isn't natural to like confrontation.

But a private equity professional must embrace confrontation—almost seek it. Because, ultimately, confrontation leads to progress—one way or the other. And any progress is better than no progress. So, the sooner the better.

After all, time is money.

"YOU'RE FORTY-FIVE MINUTES LATE."

Gillette sat down beside Senator Stockman at a table in a quiet corner of the Racquet Club's large dining room. "It couldn't be helped." He glanced at the glass in front of Stockman. It was half full of a clear liquid, but he couldn't tell if the liquid was alcohol.

"You should have at least called the club to let me know what was going on," Stockman sniped. "My time is *extremely* valuable."

Gillette noticed several sidelong glances coming from the other tables. Stockman was instantly recognizable at this point. He hadn't officially announced his campaign yet, but his aides were setting up photo ops everywhere. Here in New York and down in Washington. Local news and national. Everywhere and anywhere they could get airtime. "So is mine," Gillette said firmly.

"May I get you a drink, sir?" A waiter in a white dinner jacket and tuxedo pants appeared at the table.

"What are you having, Senator?"

"A little something to take the edge off."

Gillette glanced up at the waiter.

"Beefeaters and tonic," the young man replied.

"Two," Gillette ordered, glad he always tipped well. "Another for my guest and one for me. Bring us water, too, will you?"

The waiter gestured to a busboy as he moved off to get the drinks.

"When will you officially announce your campaign?" Gillette asked softly, watching the busboy pour.

Stockman finished what was left of his drink. "This week. The plans are already made."

"I'm surprised all this hasn't leaked to the press."

"My inner circle's very loyal to me."

"Only eleven months until the election, Senator. You've waited till the last minute, haven't you?"

"A conscious decision, Christian. I wanted to let the other eight jokers make idiots of themselves in the first televised debate before I declared. Makes me the clear choice very quickly."

"It gives you less time to raise your war chest, too," Gillette pointed out, remembering from Tom McGuire's report that Stockman wasn't wealthy.

"Money won't be a problem."

He'd said it confidently, Gillette noticed.

The waiter was back quickly, placing the drinks down on the table.

Gillette picked up his glass. "Here's to your campaign, Senator. I wish you the best."

Stockman picked up his glass, too. "Thank you." He took a sip. "I'm surprised, Christian."

"Why?"

"I thought you stayed away from alcohol."

Gillette glared at Stockman for a moment. So the senator had his own Tom McGuire combing through backgrounds. "I usually do, but I'm making an exception today." Ordering alcohol was standard procedure when he wanted to get information out of someone at lunch or dinner. To make the other person think he was drinking, too. That way they felt more comfortable, and most people didn't notice that his glass stayed full. "This is a special occasion."

"You better drink it," the senator said, raising an eyebrow. "Otherwise, I'll wonder about your motives."

Gillette took a healthy swig. "Satisfied?"

Stockman glanced around, making certain people at the other tables weren't trying to listen. "Let's talk," he said, leaning toward Gillette.

Gillette leaned forward, too, aware of the gin already seeping into his bloodstream. He hated how he loved the feeling. How the alcohol made him relax so fast. Made him less worried about all the critical decisions facing him. And made him less competent, which was a problem. A small lapse in judgment could cost millions.

"Tell me about the companies in the Everest portfolio," the senator said.

"What do you want to know?"

"What kind of companies are they?"

"All different kinds."

"Give me a few examples."

"We own a food company that—"

"Where's it based?"

"Boston."

"What do they make?"

"Frozen entrées, cookies, rolls—"

"What else?" Stockman interrupted.

Gillette took a sip of water, aware that Stockman was paying close attention to which glass he chose. "A power-tool manufacturer in Philadelphia, a waste management company based in Cleveland, a—"

"Anything in California?"

Gillette nodded. "An information management company."

"What do they do?"

"They maintain data files for state governments: driving records, criminal records, credit information. That kind of stuff."

"Personal information?"

"Very personal."

"Now that could be valuable," Stockman commented. "How about Texas? Anything down there?"

"We own a couple of businesses in Texas: the third largest rental car company in the country, and one of the largest grocery chains in the western half of the U.S." Gillette watched the senator's eyes bulge. "All that information is on our website."

"I don't have time for research, Christian. People do that for me," Stockman said curtly. "I assume these companies you own have operations all over the place."

"That's right. The waste management company is based in Cleveland, but it operates landfills and hauling companies in twenty-one states. The food company has facilities up and down both coasts, and in Chicago and St. Louis. I believe, in total, with the twenty-seven companies in the portfolio, we have offices, plants, and distribution centers in all fifty states."

"Excellent."

"Why?"

"As I told you at Donovan's funeral reception, I want votes from you, Christian. Those million employees at your portfolio companies as well as their families and friends. I want you to let me talk to them, then I want you to follow up with memos and videotapes that support me."

"Senator, I don't—"

"And, over the next year, I want to make announcements and speeches from your factories and offices. You know, with lots of cheering people in front of me while the TV cameras are on. In return, you'll have a friend in Washington who has lots of other friends in Washington. Understand?"

The waiter was headed toward their table, but Gillette waved him off. "I appreciate that offer, Senator."

"Good," Stockman said, continuing quickly. "I know one of the companies in your portfolio is a media company. Newspapers, magazines, and a string of radio and television stations. NBC affiliates on the TV side. Correct?"

"That's right."

"Which will be very helpful. You should work with my PR people on ideas there. Point is you need to do everything and anything you can to get me elected."

"I'm not prepared to go that far," said Gillette flatly. He didn't like

Stockman now that he'd had a chance to spend some time with him, but he could have gotten past that. He did business with plenty of people he didn't like—and who didn't like him. But he didn't believe in trying to influence people at their workplace. Even so, he could have figured out a way to string the senator along without committing to anything so as not to make an enemy—at least, not right away. The reason for his up-front refusal was that he *wanted* to provoke a reaction. He wanted the confrontation because he wanted to know why Stockman had dug so deeply into his background. Why the senator was going after Everest—and him—so hard. Maybe it really was just for votes, but Gillette suspected there was something else. "I'm not letting Everest Capital get dragged into all that."

"*Dragged?*"

"You heard me."

Stockman straightened up in his chair and paused, moving his lips without speaking. Silently counting to ten to let off steam. "Do you understand what will happen if you don't cooperate with me?" he asked. "Do you understand how powerful I am?"

Gillette remained silent.

"You'll have an *enemy* in Washington instead of an ally."

"I hear you."

"Is that good business?"

"Maybe not, but I'm chairman of Everest, and I have to do what I think is best in the long run. And I think it's best to stay out of this."

Stockman smiled. A fake smile. Like he had a pain in his side but was trying not to let on. "I hear Everest Capital is going to be raising a new fund soon."

Gillette looked up slowly from the table. "How did you hear that?"

"I hear lots of things. Which is why you'd be a fool not to work with me."

Gillette ticked off the different ways Stockman could have gotten that information. Remembering who he'd told about his plans for the new fund. "What are you saying?"

"You still own shares of companies you've taken public. Don't you, Christian?"

When private equity firms sold companies to the public, they didn't sell all their holdings in the initial public offering. The investment bankers—who distributed the new shares to their individual and institutional clients—wanted the private equity firms to retain at least some of their ownership after the IPO. As a sign of good faith. So the new investors would feel like the existing owners had continuing confidence in the business's prospects. That they weren't getting out at the top. And, once a company was trading publicly, there were strict rules governing how and when the original owners could sell their shares.

"That's right," Gillette agreed. "We own some publicly traded stuff." Which was no secret. Stockman's aides could have found that information in the mandatory SEC filings available on the Internet. "But we don't count those as portfolio companies. Not like the twenty-seven we control."

"One of those public companies you still own a piece of is Dominion Savings & Loan down in Virginia," Stockman continued. "It's headquartered across the Potomac River from Washington in Alexandria, but it has branches in the District. I see them all over the place on my way in to the Capitol from my apartment in Georgetown."

"Yeah, so?"

"What if the federal regulators were to uncover problems at Dominion?"

"Dominion's squeaky-clean. There's nothing—"

"Still, what if they did? Would that be a problem?"

"It's a waste of time to talk hypothetically. At least, in this case."

The senator smiled thinly. "Humor me, Christian."

"What are you trying to tell me?"

Stockman spread his arms, shrugged, and gave Gillette a quizzical look. "I don't know what you mean," he said. "It's just a simple question. If the feds start a probe into Dominion's IPO, would that be a problem for Everest?"

"Depends on what they find," Gillette said bluntly.

"My aides tell me Everest took in two billion dollars on that IPO. After investing just two hundred million three years ago," Stockman added.

"Our profit on the deal was a billion eight," Gillette acknowledged. "It was a great transaction. And, like I said, we scrubbed Dominion with Ajax and steel wool for ninety days before the SEC came on the scene. Then they were in our shorts for months before the IPO."

"All the same, if an investigation was announced, it wouldn't be good for your next fund, would it? Might make your partners wonder what was going on at Everest. Might even make them not invest."

Dominion's loan portfolio was almost forty billion dollars. In a loan portfolio that huge, there were bound to be problems, especially when the portfolio was grown quickly. And Gillette knew that to maximize the value of the transaction, to get that billion eight profit, Donovan' had grown the Dominion loan portfolio *very* quickly during the year before the IPO. Gillette also knew that Donovan had given Dominion's employees huge bonuses to grow the business, even the credit officers— the people charged with making certain the loans Dominion made were good-quality loans, loans that were likely to be repaid—had gotten something. Which was a tremendous conflict—to pay credit officers to *grow* a portfolio rather than *protect* it.

Donovan had been chairman of Dominion while Everest controlled it, and Marcie Reed had been his second—like at Blalock. She and Donovan hadn't told the other managing partners much about what was going on, but Gillette knew that the general strategy had been to grow Dominion as fast as possible. Suddenly he was concerned that Stockman's threats might be backed up by credible information.

"One of the Big Four accounting firms audits Dominion," Gillette pointed out, "and has since before it was public. I'm comfortable everything is fine there."

Stockman chuckled snidely. "Are you now?"

"Yes." Not really. As Donovan had gotten older, he'd developed a bulletproof mentality, as if he thought he was somehow above the law. It wouldn't surprise Gillette at all if Donovan had done something shady at Dominion to assure Everest of that huge payday.

The senator drew himself up in his chair, his forced smile fading. "Are you going to support me, Christian?"

"Senator Stockman, I think we should—"

"Answer the question."

"Not to the extent you're talking about. Now, I'm willing to consider—"

"Thank you for the drinks," Stockman said, standing up abruptly. "Unfortunately, I don't have time for lunch thanks to your being so late. I wish you all the best as the new chairman of Everest Capital." He smiled again. "For as long as you *are* chairman, anyway."

Gillette watched the senator move off, stopping to shake hands at several tables as he worked his way toward the door, smiling and chatting with people as if his nasty exchange with Gillette hadn't happened.

Tom McGuire knew that Bill Donovan had found out something about Stockman. Something so significant that, in McGuire's judgment, Stockman would have wanted Donovan dead. And, by extension, now would want him dead.

Gillette had been tempted to tell Stockman that he knew about Rita Jones, but he'd held off. It was something he could use more powerfully later. Especially if he could get evidence.

He eased back into the chair, pulled out his Blackberry, and began scrolling through his e-mails. It was Stockman's move now.

Gillette punched in Jeremy Cole's number on his cell phone as he steered the rented Taurus south on the Jersey Turnpike. McGuire was going to be pissed. Pissed that Gillette had given his security detail the slip and gone out on his own. But it had to be this way. He didn't want McGuire—or anybody else—knowing about this trip. He checked the rearview mirror as the line rang in his ear. He hadn't noticed anyone following him.

"Hello."

"Jeremy, it's Christian Gillette."

"Hey, Christian. How are you?"

"Fine. Glad I caught you. I thought you might be at practice."

"Nah, we've done our field work for the day. Gotta go watch films in a few minutes. Pain in the ass, but, hey, gotta do what you gotta do, you know?"

Gillette guided the car off at Exit 8 and headed west toward Princeton. He'd been out of New York City for an hour. "Did your agent hook up with the Giants yet?"

"Yeah. The deal's gonna be announced tomorrow. The lawyers are making a few last-minute tweaks, but it's basically done. I can't tell you how much I appreciate it. That was amazing. Thanks."

"No problem." Gillette handed the woman in the toll booth a five, then drove through the gate without waiting for the nickel change. "I need a favor."

"Name it. Anything."

"I need a bodyguard. Know where I can get one?"

Cole thought for a moment. "Some of the guys on the team use them. A couple of the running backs and one of the wide receivers. You know, the megabuck guys."

"Yeah, like you now."

Cole hesitated. "God, you're right. I hadn't even thought about that."

"Talk to those guys and find out who they use, then call me back. All right, Jeremy? As soon as you can."

"Of course. I'll get back to you tonight. Tomorrow morning at the latest."

Gillette tossed the cell phone onto the passenger seat and picked up his Blackberry, scrolling down the small screen as he drove. Thinking about how he needed to hire his own security detail, not one arranged for and managed by Tom McGuire, who was going to be mad as hell when he found out he wasn't going to be able to buy his company back from Everest. Not without a lot more than three hundred million, anyway.

A horn blared and Gillette's eyes flashed up from the tiny screen. While he'd been focused on the Blackberry, the Taurus had drifted into the oncoming lane. He jerked the steering wheel right, barely avoiding the dump truck bearing down on him, then to the left to miss a telephone pole. Finally, he skidded to a stop on the gravel shoulder.

Gillette put his head back, closed his eyes, and let out a long breath.

Twenty minutes later he swung the Taurus into Jose Medilla's driveway. For the first few minutes after the close call with the truck, he'd been able to stay focused on the road, able to keep his fingers off the cell phone and the Blackberry. But the shock had worn off quickly and his fingers had gotten itchy. After one last scroll through the screen, Gillette put the Blackberry onto the seat beside the phone, climbed out of the car, and headed toward the house.

Isabelle opened the door before Gillette even knocked. He froze. He'd been expecting Selma.

She gave him a wide smile. "*Buenos dias, Señor* Gillette."

"*Buenos dias.*" She was even prettier than he remembered. Delicate features. Beautiful black hair. Those huge brown eyes. A vulnerability hiding behind the long, curved lashes that naturally made him want to protect her. "May I come—" Gillette stopped himself, searching for the words in Spanish. College, just to the west of here, seemed so long ago. He'd been good with Spanish back then, but had forgotten a lot since. "Um, *los siento. Puedo entrar—*"

Isabella opened the door wide. "*Sí.* Come in. Selma's expecting you. She's upstairs with Maria."

"Oh," he said, stepping into the foyer, "you speak English."

She held her hand out, turning it from side to side. "I'm pretty okay. We grew up speaking Spanish and English in Puerto Rico. My father said it would come in handy one day to know English. I guess he was right."

"He was definitely right."

"Chreeees!"

Maria bounded down the stairs, followed by another little girl Gillette didn't recognize. "Who's this?" he asked, picking up Maria. Watching Isabelle move off toward the kitchen.

"This is Julie," Selma explained. "She's Alex's youngest. Alex and his wife are down here today buying furniture. I'm sure Alex's wife will have them shopping until the stores close." Selma kissed Gillette gently on the cheek. "You're wonderful. I've never seen Jose and Alex closer. This has been an amazing experience for them."

Maria threw her short arms around Gillette's neck and kissed his other cheek. "You like me better than Mommy, don't you, Chris?"

"I like you better than anyone." He spotted Isabelle in the kitchen, putting something away in a cabinet. "When will Jose be home?" It was almost five o'clock.

"He should be here in a few minutes. Come in and I'll fix you something to eat."

"No, I'm fine," he said, following Selma toward the kitchen, Maria still in his arms. "I'm not hungry."

"Don't be silly. It's cold out. A plate of my rice and beans will do you good."

Isabelle was coming the other way. She had on a pink sweater and jeans, and it occurred to Gillette that he hadn't noticed what she was wearing when she first opened the door. Usually he noticed things like that. "Where are you going?" he asked her, putting Maria down beside Julie as she passed by.

"Upstairs to read."

"Why don't you stay down here and talk?" he called after her.

"I'll come down later," she called back, trotting up the stairs.

"Come on, Chris." The two little girls pulled Gillette toward the living room. "Play with us."

"You two let him go," Selma ordered. "Maybe he'll come in there with you in a few minutes. Go on."

Gillette eased into a chair at the kitchen table as Selma shooed the girls away.

"You should ask Isabelle to dinner," Selma suggested, pulling a bowl from the refrigerator and turning on the oven.

"Oh, I don't know."

"I see the way you look at her."

"Well, she's pretty easy on the eyes." He glanced out through the French doors at the house he'd just bought for Alex. "But I doubt we'd have anything in common, and she seems kind of shy."

"You'd be surprised. She's quiet at first, but there's a lot to her once you get to know her."

"How old is she?"

"Twenty-six."

The same age as Faith. He'd thought she was younger. "How long is she visiting?"

"We're trying to get her into the local community college. If we do, she'll stay with us until she has a chance to get on her feet and get a place of her own. I don't want her going back to Puerto Rico. There's nothing for her there."

Gillette heard a car pull up outside. Jose. "Would she go out with me if I asked?"

Selma laughed. "I don't know. Ask her and find out."

Gillette spotted Isabelle as soon as he and Jose emerged from the small study off the living room. She was sitting at the kitchen table, reading. "Thank you, *Señor* Medilla," he said, shaking Jose's hand.

"Sure." Jose's voice was low.

Gillette could tell that what they'd discussed was still sinking in.

"I always told you I'd do anything you asked," Jose spoke up. "And I meant it. I'll talk to Alex when he gets home."

"Good." Gillette spotted Selma coming down the stairs. "I hope Alex and his wife had a nice time shopping tonight," he said. "The bills for their credit cards will come directly to me. The same way it works for you and Selma."

Jose shook Gillette's hand warmly. "Thank you, Christian. I don't know what to say. Your kindness is very great."

"Don't say anything. It all evens out in the end."

"I guess you're right," Jose agreed quietly. "Would you like something to eat?"

Gillette smiled. They were always trying to feed him. "No thanks."

"Honey, I need you upstairs for a few minutes," Selma said, moving beside her husband.

"Why?"

"There's a lightbulb out in the bedroom."

"I'll take care of it later. I want to talk to Isabelle about something."

"You'll take care of it *now*," Selma ordered, taking Jose's arm and tugging him toward the stairs. "Bye, Christian," she called.

Gillette hesitated as Jose and Selma climbed the steps. He could hear Jose grumbling, then there was silence.

He took a deep breath. He could deliver Bill Donovan's eulogy to a congregation packed full of Manhattan luminaries and hold them spellbound. Fire the CEO of a $3 billion company and barely feel his heart rate change. Take a pop star to dinner and charm her. But suddenly, standing in this middle-class home in central New Jersey, his palms were clammy.

"What are you reading?" he asked, moving into the kitchen and sitting down across from Isabelle. She had the book in her lap.

"*Gone with the Wind*." She held the book up so he could see the cover.

"Wow. That's a big project." He couldn't think of anything else to say. "You know, you have very pretty eyes."

"*Gracias*. I mean . . . thank you."

He gazed at her. Her whole face lit up when she smiled. "So, what do you do for fun around here?" He chuckled to himself. A silly thing to ask, but he was a little on edge. His natural ability to make conversation was jammed by her incredible beauty. Something he wasn't accustomed to.

"Not much," she answered, putting the book down.

She still hadn't looked directly into his eyes, he realized. "Want some dinner?"

She shook her head. "I'm not hungry but I can fix you for something."

He laughed. "No, you don't understand." Her eyes raced to his for the first time, and he saw a flash of anger, as if she thought he was making fun of her grammar. "I mean, I didn't explain myself very well."

"Oh," she said softly, her anger evaporating as quickly as it had condensed. "What *did* you mean?"

"I'd like to take you *out* for dinner."

Her gaze fell to her lap again.

"Don't get so excited. All that jumping up and down might be tough on your heart."

"Sorry."

"I'm kidding. I was just hoping for a different reaction."

"I don't think it would be a good idea to go out for us," she said quietly.

"Not even for a quick bite?" he asked, holding back a smile at the way she had mixed her words a second time.

"No," she answered, standing up, "but thank you. I'll tell Jose you're leaving," she said, heading quickly out of the kitchen.

"Isabelle," he called after her, rising from his chair.

But she was gone.

Gillette scrolled through his e-mails as he waited at the stoplight. The New Jersey Turnpike, on the other side of the small village of Hightstown, was only a couple miles away. Ahead of him, Route 1 lay across the road he was on. He'd be back in Manhattan in an hour.

He looked up, through the darkness. The light was still red. He shook his head. Isabelle had turned him down flat. That hadn't happened in a long time.

"Oh, well," he sighed, glancing back down at the now darkened Blackberry screen. "Never up, never in."

He pressed a button on the tiny keyboard, illuminating the screen. In the eerie blue florescent light he saw that one new message had just arrived. He didn't recognize the sender's address, but the subject line blared "READ ME NOW." Most likely an add for a dating service or a travel agency. The spam was constant, but there was nothing else to do while he waited, so he pulled the full text up on the screen.

His eyes narrowed as he scanned the words:

Don't stop for *anything* until you're back in the city. They may try again tonight.

Gillette glanced at the sender's address again. User7@ECoffee.com.

A moment later there was a tap on the bumper and the Taurus lurched forward. Gillette's eyes flashed to the rearview mirror. The car behind his had hit him. Not hard, but enough to get his attention. He opened the door and rose quickly from behind the wheel. The woman who'd hit him was getting out of her car, too.

He glanced around the intersection. There were three cars in front of him waiting at the red light. Lots of cars flashed by in both directions out on Route 1. A strip mall to his left with a bakery, a liquor store, and a dry cleaner. Several people inside. Visible through the glass.

"I'm so sorry," the woman called, trotting toward him. She seemed sincerely upset. "Are you all right?"

Gillette checked the passenger seat of her car. Empty. He glanced back at her as she moved toward him. Middle-aged, wearing a nice dress and tennis shoes. Probably on the way home from work. Walking in the oncoming lane, he noticed. On the other side of the double yellow line. She seemed to be watching something as she came toward him. Something over his shoulder.

He sprinted forward two steps and dove over the Taurus's trunk just as the sound of gunshots crackled in his ears. He tumbled to the asphalt on the other side of the car, then scrambled to his feet and sprinted toward a gas station fifty yards away. Zigzagging as he ran.

Two more shots. Like firecrackers on the Fourth of July.

A setup.

Without the e-mail, he'd be dead.

A bullet slammed into a telephone pole as he raced past it, and he glanced over his shoulder. A guy with a pistol was chasing him. The woman was still standing by the Taurus.

Gillette headed toward the gas station, but the attendant inside had seen what was happening and rushed out from behind the counter to bolt the door. Another bullet zipped by and slammed into the large window in the front of the building, shattering it. Gillette ran past the station and around back.

There was a wide, empty parking lot behind the station. With a full moon hanging in the sky like a beacon, the guy would have a clear shot at him. So Gillette stopped as he turned the corner of the building and backed up to the cement wall, sucking in air. Then he noticed the rest-rooms a few feet away and darted for them. The first door was locked, but the second was open and he hurried inside, leaving it slightly ajar. Climbing up on the toilet beside the door and holding his breath.

Gillette could hear the man outside, breathing hard. The guy would have to do something fast. No doubt the attendant inside the station had already called the cops—unless he'd been shot.

The man reached inside for the light switch and flicked it up and down, but the bulb was burned out. Gillette could hear the switch click-ing.

Suddenly the man burst into the pitch-black restroom, shooting blindly, bullets screaming and echoing around the small, enclosed space.

Gillette grabbed the beam above him with both hands and kicked, slamming one of his hard-soled shoes into the side of the man's head. The gun flew from the man's hand and clattered against the far wall as he crumpled to the floor. But he was up again instantly, racing away.

Gillette dropped down, searching for the gun in the gloom, finally spotting it under the sink. He bent down, grabbed it, and headed out the door. As he came around the side of the building, the assailant and the woman were jumping into the car ahead of the Taurus. Too late. No chance to get them.

He bent over and grabbed his knees, sucking in air. He needed to hire an outside security firm as soon as possible.

10

Economic Incentive. *If you believe that those around you are ultimately driven by what's in their best economic interest, you have only one choice if you want their best: pay them well. More than they could earn anywhere else.*

It's called capitalism.

It's also called common sense.

"CHRISTIAN."

Gillette glanced up from the computer screen at his assistant, Debbie Long. She was standing in his office doorway, leaning on the knob, a pen and notepad in hand.

Debbie was young and cute—twenty-eight, with short brown hair and a trim figure. She was also a lesbian. Tom McGuire had confirmed that before Gillette hired her. So there was no sexual tension between them, which was exactly how Gillette wanted it. A perfect business relationship. No chance of her developing some silly crush on him, or of him getting any stupid ideas of his own.

Debbie was very good at her job, too. Efficient, loyal, and willing to put in the time. She often worked fifty to sixty hours a week—and never complained. She had the most positive attitude of anyone he'd ever met. She never seemed to have a bad day. If she did, she didn't show it. In short, she was perfect.

So Gillette paid her well: a hundred thousand dollars in salary and last year a fifty-thousand-dollar bonus. Which, even in New York, was good money for an executive assistant who didn't occasionally use the boss's toothbrush in the morning. He'd probably pay her a seventy-five-thousand-dollar bonus this January so she'd understand that the deal would keep getting better—as long as she kept performing. He might even give her a small portion of the ups. Which Cohen and Faraday would scream about, but he didn't care. This was his show now.

"What's up?" he asked gruffly.

"And a *very* good morning to you, too."

He was still distracted by the incident in New Jersey last night, but he intended to do something about it this morning. "Debbie, I—"

"Come on, Chris," she interrupted. "Perk up."

Gillette's eyes moved deliberately to hers. "Someday we'll go to dinner and talk about how you stay so sickeningly positive." They'd never been together outside the office. Part of their unspoken pact to keep everything business.

"No, we won't," Debbie replied flatly.

"Why not?"

"You wouldn't be able to handle what I'd tell you."

"I can handle any—"

"Your ten o'clock is here," she cut in.

Gillette shook his head and smiled. Glad she wasn't going to let their relationship go any further. "Fine. Show him in."

Debbie moved to one side and waved the visitor on.

A moment later a well-built African-American man moved past her. He was dressed in black—jacket, turtleneck, slacks, and shoes. Cut and sleek looking, he had a cool, confident air about him. As if nothing in his world moved faster than he wanted it to.

Gillette gestured toward a corner of the office and several comfortable high-backed chairs arranged around a coffee table. "We'll meet over there." He looked back at Debbie. "Keep everyone away from here until I'm finished. No exceptions."

She nodded, her expression turning serious when she heard Gillette's tone change. "Right."

Gillette waited until Debbie had closed the door, then moved to where the man stood. As they shook hands, Gillette felt immense physical strength in his grip. "I'm Christian Gillette."

"Quentin Stiles."

"Have a seat." Gillette pointed to one of the chairs. "Would you like something to drink?"

"No."

"I appreciate Jeremy Cole putting us in touch," Gillette said when they were both seated. Cole had called late last night to tell Gillette he'd found someone with an excellent reputation. "Thanks for coming to see me on such short notice."

"No problem. My company is based in Manhattan."

Gillette picked up a bottled water from the table. "What's your background, Quentin?"

"Five years with the Army Rangers, then three with the Secret Service. The last five I've been on my own in the private sector."

"What's the name of your company?"

"QS Security."

"Clients?"

"The president of the United States, for one."

"I mean, *after* you quit the Secret Service."

"The Saudi royal family when they come to Manhattan. Madonna. Michael Jordan. Several high-profile football players. Jeremy Cole, for one. Now that you got him that big contract. Others you'd recognize."

"How many people at QS?"

"Forty. And I'm not one of those guys who hires temporary help if I get a couple of big jobs at the same time. I only take the number of jobs I can handle with the people I've trained. People who understand how I do things."

"Ever lost a client?" Gillette asked, drinking some water.

"Never."

"Close?"

"Define 'close.' "

"Anyone you've been protecting ever been hurt?"

"No."

"Attacked?"

"Sure."

"You ever been shot?"

"Yup," Stiles replied, pulling back his jacket and lifting up his shirt to point at a nasty scar beside his navel, then to another one on the left side of his rib cage.

Gillette gazed at the wounds, wondering how it would have felt if one of the bullets had hit him last night. "Why'd you quit the Secret Service?"

"They didn't pay very well."

"What do you charge?"

"Two thousand a day, plus expenses. Another thousand a day for each additional person."

Gillette whistled. "You must be good."

"*Very* good."

"You don't talk much, do you, Quentin?"

"My clients don't usually care about talk. They care about being safe." Stiles glanced around the office. "If you're *really* looking for companionship, I can put you in touch with another kind of firm. High end. No questions asked."

"Thank you, no." Gillette took another drink of water. "Get some references to my assistant, will you?" But he already knew he was going to hire Stiles. Something about the man impressed him. And, as analytical as he was, Gillette had learned over the years to trust his instincts, too.

"I'll leave telephone numbers with her on my way out, numbers of people I've worked with."

"Good."

"What's the job?" Stiles wanted to know.

"Protecting me full-time."

"How long?"

"I don't know."

"Then it's *three* thousand dollars a day. I charge an extra grand when it's open-ended."

Gillette did some quick calculations. Almost a hundred thousand a month just for Stiles. Plus another thousand bucks a day for anyone else Stiles used. A lot, but so be it. "Okay."

"Why?" Stiles asked after a few moments.

"Why what?"

"Why do you need protection?"

"Someone blew up my limousine." He didn't want to mention last night yet.

Stiles's eyes flashed to Gillette's. "The one that exploded in front of a church over on Park Avenue?"

"Yes."

"I heard about that." Stiles shook his head. "And you waited *three days* to get in touch with someone like me?"

Gillette shook his head. "No. We own a firm that provides executive protection. The CEO of that firm has people with me."

"What firm are you talking about?"

"McGuire & Company. You familiar with them?"

"Of course." A quizzical expression ran across Stiles's face. "If you own them, and Tom McGuire already has someone with you, why did you call me?"

Gillette liked the fact that Stiles was familiar with McGuire & Company, particularly that he knew who Tom McGuire was. "Last night I was attacked," he said quietly. "A woman—"

"Stop talking," Stiles ordered, scooping up the television remote from the table. He pointed it at the set in the far corner of the room and clicked. When it was on, he turned the volume up high, then pulled his chair close to Gillette's. "Go ahead, but keep your voice down."

"What's the problem?" But Gillette knew what Stiles was thinking. And he liked how suspicious the guy was.

"Keep your voice down, *please*."

Gillette leaned toward Stiles. "What's the problem?" he repeated innocently.

"Where was the McGuire guy last night when you were attacked?"

"Not around."

"So the guy who's supposed to protect you isn't around when you're attacked." Stiles placed the remote back down on the table.

"I gave him the slip here in Manhattan. I'm a pretty good driver when I want to be."

"Then I have a question and an observation."

"Go ahead."

"First, the question."

"Okay."

"Why did you want to *slip* away?"

"I had personal business."

Stiles gave Gillette a frustrated look. "Mr. Gillette, if I'm going to protect you, there can't be any secrets between us. I have to know everything about you. But I will promise you this," Stiles said, holding up his right hand as though he were about to take an oath. "No one will ever know what I know. *No one*."

Gillette stared hard at Stiles. He had that air about him that made you trust him. "It involved a woman," Gillette explained. A partial truth, but probably enough to satisfy Stiles's curiosity.

"Okay. Now, here's my observation. Just the fact that you were *able* to slip away tells me something. With all due respect to your driving skills, I can assure you right now that you wouldn't be able to slip away from me or any of my men under any circumstances. Do you understand?"

Gillette was already feeling safer. "Yes." And it had occurred to him that he'd been able to lose the McGuire guy easily, too.

"Good. Now why would someone want to blow up your limousine?"

"Don't know."

"Speculate."

For the next five minutes Gillette described Everest Capital and the events of the last week. What the firm did and the massive amount of money it—*he*—controlled. Bill Donovan dying suspiciously at the estate. How Gillette had been elected the new chairman of Everest by one vote. How there were a number of people who might want him dead. And how there were very few people he could trust at this point. Maybe no one.

"Tell me exactly what happened last night," Stiles requested when Gillette was finished. "When you were shot at."

Gillette took several more minutes to explain the incident in New Jersey. "I guess it could have been a random carjacking," he said, finishing the story.

"What kind of car were you driving?"

"A rented Taurus."

Stiles shook his head. "People don't go out of their way to steal a Taurus. And a carjacking? I seriously doubt that. Particularly if there were two vehicles working together, and they shot at you *before* driving you to an ATM. It makes no sense. No, they were after you. Plain and simple." Stiles paused. "How much are you worth, Mr. Gillette?"

"A lot," he answered. "And, with Donovan dead, I could be worth a lot more."

Stiles pointed at Gillette. "In other words, as far as Donovan goes, you had motive, too."

Gillette gave Stiles a strange look. "I like how you try so hard to ingratiate yourself a potential client, Quentin."

"I call it as I see it," Stiles replied firmly.

"While you're at it, call me Christian."

"I don't get close to my clients. Now answer my question. How much are you worth?"

"Around seventy million." In addition to his stake in the funds, which Cohen estimated was worth sixty, Gillette had banked ten during his career at Everest, thanks to the salaries, bonuses, and payouts on the ups he'd earned on earlier funds.

Stiles's expression didn't change. "And, as a result of Donovan's death, how much could you be worth?"

"Billions." Again, Stiles's expression didn't change. Which Gillette liked.

"Just by virtue of being chairman of Everest."

"If I'm chairman long enough."

"So, if someone else were in your position, they could be worth billions, too?"

"Yes."

Stiles picked up the remote and turned the television off, then stood up and extended his hand. "Nice to meet you, Mr. Gillette. I'll give your assistant those telephone numbers on my way out, and I'll wait to hear from you."

Gillette stood up, too, and shook Stiles's hand. "Can I look at your gun?" He'd seen it when Stiles had shown him the bullet scars.

Stiles pulled his jacket back, revealing a shoulder holster and the black handle of a pistol.

"What kind is it?" asked Gillette.

"Glock forty cal."

"Let me have it."

Stiles withdrew the weapon from the holster and popped the clip, then handed the gun to Gillette.

"Not going to let me have it loaded, huh?"

"No."

Gillette held the Glock for a few moments. He liked the way it looked and the way it felt in his palm. He handed it back to Stiles, who reinserted the clip and slid the weapon smoothly back into the holster. "You're hired, Quentin." Stiles was heading toward the door. "I want you to start immediately."

Stiles turned back around to face Gillette. "Sorry, Mr. Gillette, but I have a few things to take care of first."

"Get one of your people on them."

"I can't. I have to—"

"I'll pay you five grand a day plus two for each additional man. But you have to start *right* now."

Stiles eyed Gillette for a few moments, then glanced around the office. As if he was trying to figure out whether or not all this was real.

"Okay," Stiles agreed, moving back to where Gillette stood and handing him a business card. "I'll be with your executive assistant for the next half hour, going over your schedule and your routine. Before the end of the day, I'll need fifteen minutes to sweep your office for listening devices. Call if you need me," he said. Then he was gone.

Gillette went to his desk. "Debbie, have Ben come in," he instructed through the intercom. "And give Mr. Stiles any information he needs."

"Anything?"

"Anything," Gillette confirmed, checking stock prices on Bloomberg. Dominion S&L was off 3 percent in early trading, but the overall market was up. There might be a fly in the ointment, a silver-haired one with designs on the Oval Office.

A few minutes later, Cohen entered Gillette's office and sat down. "Who's out there with Debbie?" he asked.

"A guy named Quentin Stiles. He'll be my personal bodyguard from now on. We'll pay him five thousand a day plus expenses."

"Five thousand?"

"And two thousand a day for any additional people he uses. He'll have a contract to you this afternoon."

"But Tom McGuire has people with you," Cohen protested.

"I need my own person," Gillette said firmly. "Not Tom's, not yours, not anyone else's. Just mine."

"That seems like a pretty big *non sequitur* to me."

Gillette drew himself up in his chair, tempted to forbid the use of Latin at Everest, but he controlled himself. "No more questions about this." He wasn't going to tell Cohen about last night's shooting. There was no need for him to justify anything to Cohen. Or anyone else for that matter. "Got it?"

Cohen squinted. "Got it."

"Good." Gillette checked Bloomberg again. Dominion's share price had fallen another twenty cents in the last few minutes. "Have you gotten the money to those kids yet?"

"It's all taken care of."

"Thank you."

"Sure."

"How about those questions I had about Faith?" Gillette asked. Yesterday afternoon he'd tasked Cohen with following up on what Tom McGuire had relayed about Faith Cassidy. "Anything?"

"Yeah." Cohen flipped back several pages in his pad. "Sales of her latest album are off 30 percent from her first one—when you compare where the first one was after the same number of release weeks."

"When was that last album released?"

"A few weeks ago."

"And her contract negotiations have been on hold for a while?"

"Yes," Cohen confirmed. "According to the chief counsel at her record label, anyway."

"Did he give you specifics on the marketing dollars the label committed to that album versus the first one?" asked Gillette.

Cohen nodded deliberately. "Fifty percent less."

"*Fifty percent?* Did he tell you why?"

"He's still checking."

"That prick," Gillette muttered under his breath.

"What was that?" Cohen asked quickly.

"Nothing." The situation was exactly as McGuire had described it. Donovan was getting back at Faith for not letting him have what he wanted in the limousine. This was all about revenge.

"When are you seeing her again?" Cohen wanted to know.

"She's on the West Coast doing some PR. She's supposed to be back tonight or tomorrow."

"Be careful," Cohen warned.

"Don't worry, Ben." Gillette checked another stock quote. "You were going to give me the latest on Laurel Energy, right? Did they finish shooting seismic up there yet?"

"Yeah, but it's strange," Cohen said, shaking his head.

Gillette glanced up from the computer. "What is?"

"Last night they found the team leader's SUV abandoned fifty miles north of this no-phone, one-horse town called Amachuck. The tapes from the shoot were in the front seat, but he was gone. There was no sign of him."

"Did we get the tapes to the lab?"

"They're analyzing them as we speak."

"Any idea what happened to the guy?"

Cohen shrugged. "The truck died. There were heavy snows up there yesterday. Our people think he must have tried to make it out on foot. But he'd been up there quite a few times. He would have known that he was still fifty miles from town. He should have just stayed in the truck. That was his best shot."

Gillette peered at Cohen for a few moments, thinking. "You said the truck's battery died?"

Cohen checked his notes. "That's what I was told. The key was in the truck when the guys found it. They tried to start it but it wouldn't go."

"How does a battery die out in the middle of nowhere? I mean, once the engine starts, the battery doesn't matter anymore, right?"

"I guess. I don't know much about cars."

"Why would you turn the engine off and let the battery die?"

Cohen shrugged. "Beats the hell out of me."

"Let me know as soon as the lab calls," Gillette instructed.

"Of course."

"Have we heard from the U.S. Petroleum lawyers?" asked Gillette.

"They called our attorneys about the oil field service division yesterday. Richard Harris must really want Laurel."

"Yeah," Gillette agreed. "Maybe he knows something we don't."

"You really think so?"

"Maybe. Listen, you, Faraday, and I are getting together later to talk about promoting Kyle and Marcie."

"What's to talk about?" Cohen grumbled. "You've already made the decision."

Gillette nodded. "Yes, I have."

"And you aren't going to let me be the chairman of even one company."

"We've been over that, Ben," Gillette said firmly. "You're going to be focused internally. You're going to be in charge of what goes on here at Everest. I need you to do that for me while I run most of our portfolio companies and help Faraday raise the next fund."

"Okay," Cohen said quietly after a few moments. "I don't like it, but I accept it."

"Good."

"And you know I'll do the best job I can."

That was true, Gillette thought to himself. That was Cohen. If he accepted a job, he did the best he could. Whether he was excited about it or not. "I do."

"But if that's how it's going to be, I need people around here to know I'm in charge."

"I'll make an announcement tomorrow," Gillette assured him.

"I need more than that," Cohen pressed.

"What do you mean?"

"I need a title."

"A *title?*"

"Yes."

"But you're already a managing partner."

"I need to be the chief operating officer."

Gillette pushed out his lower lip. That didn't seem like a big deal. If Cohen wanted to be COO of Everest, so be it. He almost felt grateful to Cohen for coming up with a solution that gave them both what they wanted. "You got it. From now on, Ben, you're COO."

Richard Harris stood on a crowded Dallas street corner, waiting for the light to change. He could have sent his executive assistant to pick up his roast beef and provolone sandwich, but the deli was only a few blocks away from U.S. Petroleum's shiny new sixty-seven-story headquarters building and it was a beautiful day. The exercise would do him good. Make him feel better about having potato salad with his sandwich.

Harris glanced back over his right shoulder at the skyscraper that had been his pet project for the last two years. It was an impressive structure, dominating the Dallas skyline. In thirty days he'd have Laurel Energy to add to the trophy case, he thought to himself, smiling. Christian Gillette thought of himself as a master negotiator, but the young buck still had a lot to learn about red herrings and hidden agendas. Someday he'd be as good as Donovan, but not today.

As the Metro bus barreled along beside the curb, a man in the crowd on the corner slipped behind Harris and pushed. Not hard. Just a subtle shoulder to Harris's back. Just enough to make him stumble into the street with the bus ten feet away.

One moment Harris was on the street in front of the crowd. The next he was gone. Cartwheeling across the intersection like a rag doll. Dead before his body stopped tumbling—three hundred feet from where he'd been struck.

In the ensuing chaos the man who had pushed Harris walked calmly away into the Dallas afternoon.

Last night, he'd missed. Gillette was still alive. But today had been a different story. Harris was dead.

Now it was time to finish off Gillette.

Partners. *The hardest things in life to have.*

"LET'S GO." GILLETTE MOTIONED FOR Debbie to close the door of the small conference room outside Donovan's old office. Where Donovan and the managing partners had always met.

It seemed strange not to have the old man here, Gillette thought to himself. Even stranger that he'd thought about it. He wasn't a sentimental man.

He'd already had the personal items in Donovan's office boxed and sent to the estate, and all Everest-related information in Donovan's desk and credenzas catalogued and filed. He'd move in this weekend. Not that he liked the office very much, but he *had* to take it. It was the alpha office, and everyone needed to know he was the alpha dog.

"We've got a lot to cover," he continued as Debbie sat down beside him. He was pushing things forward the same way Donovan would have. The only other people in the room were Cohen and Faraday. It was the first time they'd met as a group since the funeral.

"What's she doing here?" Faraday demanded, his British accent more pronounced than usual.

Over time, Gillette had come to recognize what flare-ups of Faraday's accent meant. Faraday was irritated. "She's taking the minutes of the meeting."

"Bill never brought *his* assistant in to take minutes."

"Maybe he should have." Gillette glanced across the small table at Faraday, glad he'd made time earlier to go out and pick up the new contacts. No more blurry images. And it had given him a chance to see Stiles in action, which had impressed him. "Don't be afraid of change, Nigel," he counseled, noticing that today's razor cut was on Faraday's chin.

"Speaking of that," Faraday piped up, "I vote we go business casual now that Bill's gone. Everybody else in New York is, and I'm sick of wearing suits and ties."

Gillette shook his head. He liked formality. The same way Donovan had. It made people serious. "No."

"Don't be afraid of change, Christian," Faraday said sarcastically, giving Gillette an irritated stare, then looking over at Cohen. "What do you think, Moses? Want to go casual?"

"It's Christian's decision."

"Yeah, but what do *you* think?"

Cohen shrugged. "It doesn't matter to me."

Faraday groaned. "Have your own opinion once in a while, will you?"

"Hey, I—"

"Who's the black guy hanging around today?" Faraday continued, switching subjects. "The one who looks like he could break me in half with two fingers."

"Quentin Stiles," Gillette replied, amused at the way Faraday had easily segued from topic to topic. He was the consummate salesman. "My new bodyguard." The fact that Faraday had asked about Stiles indicated that Cohen and Faraday hadn't buddied up since they'd been passed over for chairman. Cohen had known since this morning about Stiles but apparently hadn't told Faraday. They'd never been close, but Gillette figured they might form some kind of alliance after the events of the last week. He was glad they hadn't. "Stiles will be with me full-time from now on."

"I thought Tom McGuire was taking care of your personal security," Faraday said.

"I needed another set of eyes and ears, given what's happened."

"Hmm. Hey, what about Bill's old office? You going to take it?" Faraday wanted to know. "Because if you don't, I will," he volunteered quickly. "In fact, I *should* get it. I'm the lead money-raiser around here. I deal with investors more than anyone else. It makes sense for me to have it. Always good to impress the investors with the best digs."

"I'm taking it," Gillette said firmly. "But thanks for bringing up our investors and getting us to the first agenda item. Which is the new fund."

"New fund?" Faraday asked.

"Yes. Everest Capital Partners Eight."

"I thought Seven was only 50 percent invested."

"*Over* 50 percent," Gillette made clear. "Which means I can start raising Eight whenever I want to."

Faraday turned to Cohen. "Is that right?"

"Yes."

"I've already started the raise, Nigel," Gillette continued. "I met with Miles Whitman over at North America Guaranty yesterday morning."

Faraday sat back in his chair and folded his arms tightly across his chest. "Thanks for telling me," he muttered.

"I wanted to get things kicked off as soon as possible. Miles was available on short notice. He committed a billion five."

"A billion five?" Faraday asked incredulously.

"Yes. And, Nigel, there's no need for you to follow up with Miles. I'll deal directly with him on this."

"But, I—"

"Don't sweat it," Gillette broke in, hearing the insecurity in Faraday's tone loud and clear. "You're going to have your hands full bringing in the other thirteen and a half billion."

"*Thirteen and a half?*"

"That's right."

"*Holy shit.* You mean we're going to try to raise fifteen fucking billion?"

"Yes."

"No one's ever raised a private equity fund that big."

"We'll be the first," Gillette said matter-of-factly. "By the way, Paul Strazzi is going to be in the market raising a $10 billion fund for Apex at the same time."

"That's comforting news."

"Have confidence, Nigel."

Faraday gave Gillette a quick salute. "Aye, aye, Captain. But in the future, could you at least let me know when you're going to talk to one of our big investors? We'll look like fucking amateurs if I call one of these guys and he says you've already been in touch."

"Of course," Gillette agreed. "Let's get together later and talk specifics. You're going to need to hire at least one more person. Maybe two."

"Maybe three."

"Like I said, let's talk later." Gillette looked around. "Next topic. I've agreed to sell Laurel Energy to U.S. Petroleum for a billion dollars. We invested three hundred million in that business, so it's an excellent transaction for us: a seven-hundred-million-dollar profit. And we know the buyer's good for the money. There'll be no financing contingency." He glanced at Cohen. "Ben, I've asked Kyle to take the lead on this one."

"Right!" Cohen jotted down a note to himself.

"I want to close the transaction quickly," Gillette continued. "No earlier than January first, though. We don't want our partners getting hit with capital gains taxes this year."

"Whoa," Faraday spoke up. "At least Bill let us have some discussion about selling a portfolio company before he made his decision."

"The offer came out of nowhere," Gillette explained. "Directly from Richard Harris, the CEO of U.S. Petroleum, at Bill's funeral reception. I had to make a decision right there." Here was another sign that Cohen wasn't running to Faraday to tell him about what was going on. "Ben was in the room with me when Harris made the offer."

"Shouldn't we get info on the seismic tests in Canada before we commit to Harris?" Faraday asked.

"We'll get those next week," Gillette answered. "If we win the lotto, we'll renegotiate. Any more questions?"

"Yeah," Faraday said. "Why does Cohen already know everything?"

"I've promoted Ben to chief operating officer," Gillette answered without hesitation. "Things happened fast in the last few days, and I needed someone with me while I negotiated. I'm going to need someone focused internally, too. Ben's the best suited for that job."

Faraday shoved his hands in his pockets and slouched back in his chair, annoyed. "What about our portfolio companies?" he asked, the edge in his tone sharpening. "Who's getting the chair positions now that Donovan and Mason are gone?"

"I'll chair fifteen of the twenty-seven. Kyle and Marcie will split the other twelve, six and six."

Faraday was quiet for a few moments. Finally he looked over at Cohen. "Did you know about this, too?"

Cohen looked away.

"Yes, he did," Gillette admitted.

"Christ!" Faraday shouted, yanking one hand out of his pocket and banging the table.

"Oh, God." Debbie dropped the pen and put her hands to her chest. She'd been focused on taking minutes and hadn't seen Faraday's explosion coming.

"Easy, Nigel," Gillette warned.

"*Easy?* Damn it, Chris. You're making major decisions, and I'm hearing about them days later. But Cohen's in on everything real time. I'm a managing partner here, too. And you tell me to be *easy?*"

"I have to do what's best for the firm," said Gillette calmly. "I'm the chairman."

"Good for fucking you."

"Nigel, I don't think—"

"I didn't even find out first from you that you'd axed Mason." Faraday wasn't finished with his tirade.

Gillette's eyes narrowed. "So, how *did* you find out?"

"Troy called me." Faraday raised one eyebrow. "Did you know that Paul Strazzi hired him?"

Gillette stared back at Faraday but said nothing.

"Ha," Faraday crowed triumphantly. "You *didn't* know."

"When did this happen?" Gillette demanded.

"Yesterday. Strazzi called Mason at his apartment after the funeral reception to set up a meeting. Strazzi knew what happened before I did, for Christ's sake. Before any of us but you, apparently."

So there *was* a rat inside Everest. Miles Whitman had warned him that Strazzi would do anything to get an advantage, and having someone inside Everest would be the best way to do it. Now he knew for sure Whitman was right, and he needed to ID the traitor immediately. Quentin Stiles could help. And he could help find out who e-mailed him last night just before the attack in front of the gas station.

"And you aren't going to let Moses or me have even one chair position," Faraday continued, ranting. "You're going to promote Kyle and

Marcie to managing partner and let them have the chairs right away. This is fucking bullshit!"

Gillette glanced at Cohen. So Ben was filling in Faraday after all. At least on some things. Probably things he was pissed off about, such as Kyle and Marcie's promotions. "Yes," he confirmed. "I'm going to promote them. And I'm going to give each of them 5 percent of the ups."

"That's ridiculous!" yelled Faraday, springing out of his chair. "They don't deserve 5 percent."

"Shut up, Nigel," Gillette snapped. "Kyle and Marcie are *extremely* talented. Tom McGuire tells me Kyle's been approached several times in the last six months by other private equity firms." He glanced at Cohen. "Marcie, too. Right?"

Cohen nodded.

"So, if I don't promote them and give them a piece of the action, they'll leave. Then we'd have to hire people from the outside who'd squeeze us for more than 10 percent. People we wouldn't know." Gillette paused. "Sit down, Nigel."

Faraday sank slowly back into his chair, teeth gritted.

"I'm going to meet with Marcie and Kyle after this," Gillette explained. "I'll write an e-mail to the rest of the firm in the morning making the announcement."

"How much of the ups of Fund Eight are you going to give Cohen and me?" Faraday blurted out angrily, unable to control himself.

"Jesus, Nigel. Don't be so pushy," Cohen urged.

"Fuck you, Moses. He's going to screw us. I know it."

"I'm going to give you what you deserve, Nigel," Gillette said calmly. "If you raise the fund quickly, you'll do well. If not, you'll be disappointed."

"How much are you going to keep for yourself?" Faraday demanded.

"I haven't decided."

"More than twenty-fucking-five percent, I'll bet."

"Like I said, I haven't—" Gillette stopped talking as the door opened and Cohen's assistant entered the room.

She leaned down and whispered something into Cohen's ear. Cohen's jaw slowly dropped.

"What is it?" Gillette demanded.

Cohen didn't answer right away.

"Ben."

Cohen shook his head. "Richard Harris was killed this afternoon in Dallas," he murmured. "Three blocks from U.S. Petroleum's head-quarters."

Gillette felt his mouth go dry. "How?"

Cohen glanced up at his assistant, then back at Gillette. "He was run down near his office.

Cohen's face blurred in front of Gillette's eyes. First Donovan. Then the guy up in Canada. Now Harris.

12

The Government. *Serving and protecting, faithfully.*

Until the evil in those who wield power deem the probability of their crimes being discovered small enough to abuse their positions for personal gain. Or, worse, they're blinded by ambition.

If you've never been the target of a government conspiracy, you can't truly comprehend the frustration—and, ultimately, the fear—involved. If you have, you know that despite your innocence, you're very vulnerable. Because the government can do almost anything it wants in its pursuit of you—legal or not. And you can do almost nothing to stop it.

*Then, even if you've been an atheist all your life, you suddenly believe in God. Because, at that point, he's your best chance. Your **only** chance.*

TYPICALLY, PAUL STRAZZI SURROUNDED HIMSELF with his success: His office at Apex filled with elegant furniture and antiques. A Rolls-Royce limousine. His five-bedroom penthouse atop the most prestigious apartment building in Manhattan, a sprawling East Hampton estate, fine wines from France, and cigars imported from Havana by an old friend who knew his way around customs at Newark Airport.

Opulence. Everywhere, all the time.

But this office was bare-bones: ten by ten and windowless—a prison cell. Walls unpainted. Furnished with just a metal desk and two spindly chairs. Tucked into one corner of a run-down warehouse located in a war-zone section of the Bronx.

It reminded Strazzi of the East New York hellhole tenement he'd grown up in. Despite how much he abhorred its appearance, it did serve one extremely important purpose. It provided him a place to meet with someone in secrecy. When that person was a U. S. senator, it took on an even greater importance.

He glanced to his left at the lone decoration on the wall. The only item he'd kept all these years as a reminder of a childhood he despised. Hanging by a twisted wire from a single nail, encased by a simple black frame—the letter from the insurance company denying his mother the money she needed to fight her cancer.

At the time the doctor discovered her sickness, she'd missed four monthly premiums in a row because she'd had to use the money she usually set aside for health insurance to put food on the table for her three boys. The man she worked for as a maid in Manhattan had repeatedly stiffed her, always telling her he'd pay her next week. Finally she'd realized that he had no intention of ever paying. And because she was a single mother—Strazzi's father had abandoned them years ago—there was no other source of income.

There had been no compassion from the insurance company. The pleas for making an exception this one time had fallen on deaf ears, and she'd died in her bedroom on a hot summer afternoon.

It had taught Strazzi the most important lesson of his life: Most people have no compassion for those they don't know—even for many they do. In the end everything comes down to money.

So, he'd learned to have no compassion himself—except for those very few he was closest to. He'd learned to bring it down to money, just like everyone else did. To use all those he wasn't close to for personal gain.

Now, because of the sense of purpose and focus the lesson had instilled, he was worth billions. Sometimes he wondered if he would have traded it all for a loving father and a normal childhood.

Strazzi gazed at the name at the bottom of the letter from the insurance company. Harold Bleaker. The man who'd denied his mother coverage, a chance at living. Fifteen years ago, he'd ruined Bleaker's life, destroyed the one-shop dry-cleaning business Bleaker had poured his life savings into after he'd tired of the insurance business. Strazzi had opened his own shop, next door to Bleaker's, charging half of what Bleaker charged for everything, put Bleaker out of business in three months. He also paid an attractive young woman to approach Bleaker one night in a bar as his business was collapsing, get him drunk, and take him to a hotel, where their encounter was secretly recorded. Then Strazzi had the tape delivered anonymously to Mrs. Bleaker. He did the same thing to Bleaker's married son, using the same woman.

Strazzi smiled as he stared at Bleaker's signature. Whoever said revenge didn't taste sweet was a pussy. It was sweeter than honey, and he'd loved every second of it.

There was a light tap on the door and Strazzi rose from his chair, passing one large hand over his gray crew cut, musing at how a powerful person could knock so meekly.

He opened the door and Stockman moved quickly past him into the office, as if something was chasing him. Strazzi leaned into the dimly lit corridor and glanced around. Satisfied no one was there, he closed and relocked the door. Stockman had already removed his coat and taken a seat in front of the desk.

"Morning, George."

"Hello, Paul." Stockman checked the letter hanging on the wall to his right, peering at it hard so he could read the small print. He abandoned the effort when he realized it was one of those artifacts that held significance only for the person who had hung it. "Nice place," he said sarcastically, gesturing around.

"It serves its purpose."

"Uh-huh. So, why did you have me come here?"

Strazzi chuckled. "I figured you didn't make it to this section of the Bronx very often, and I thought it might do you some good to see how your constituents live."

"Thanks for the educational opportunity," Stockman replied drily. "What did you want to talk about?"

"Let's start with Donovan's widow."

"I made the call," Stockman confirmed. "I told her I had information from a reliable source that there were significant problems in the Everest portfolio. As we agreed."

"I know you did," Strazzi confirmed.

"You do?"

"Yup."

"How?"

"She called to tell me that she plans on seeing Gillette this after-noon."

"Oh, good."

"And once the information on Dominion Savings & Loan is re-leased to the public through your friend in the House, she'll sell out to me immediately. She'll roll over on Gillette so fast he won't have a chance to react. As soon as Pete Allen has his press conference."

Peter Allen, the senior congressman from Idaho, was vice chairman of the House Select Committee on Corporate Abuse. A man Stockman controlled.

Stockman flicked a piece of lint from his pants. "Are you worried that it won't be enough?"

"That *what* won't be enough?"

"What we're going to claim is wrong at Dominion."

"Enough to what?"

"To make the widow sell her stake in Everest to you," Stockman an-swered, irritated that Strazzi wasn't seeing things as clearly as he was.

"You spoke to her. You heard her voice. She's a cat on a hot tin roof. She's looking for an excuse to sell. Why wouldn't it be enough? The newspapers will be all over it. She'll be out of her mind. She'll think her whole net worth is about to evaporate."

"Everest doesn't control Dominion anymore," Stockman pointed out. "They only own about 10 percent of it now that it's public. Gillette might be able to deflect the heat so there's no real damage to Everest."

"But what we're saying we have on them would have happened *while they did control Dominion*," Strazzi countered. "And Allen *has to* point that out in the news conference. He *has* to say that we have documents that show Everest's direct involvement."

"He will," Stockman assured Strazzi.

Strazzi leaned back in his chair, not satisfied. Of course, he never was satisfied in situations like this. Not until he actually saw the scenario play out and everybody did what they were supposed to do. "Are we still on for Friday?"

Stockman nodded. "Allen will hold the press conference sometime around noon."

"You sure he's going to do this?"

"Absolutely. I'm his godfather in the Senate. He needs me."

"Has Allen pushed you at all on whether or not the information is credible? Has he asked to see documentation?"

"No. And he won't. He knows better than that. I helped him with a tough situation he had a while back. Something that could have snowballed and destroyed him. Everything's good."

Strazzi broke into a broad smile. He couldn't help himself. "Gillette will have to abort his try at that next fund before it even gets off the ground. And the widow will sell me her stake in Everest. I'll call for a vote of the limited partners right away and have Gillette thrown out on his ass. Then I'll install my person as chairman." His smile grew broader. "Me. Hell, with 25 percent of the vote in my back pocket, it'll be a lock. Gillette only won by one vote the other day, and there wasn't even a scandal at that point. I'll probably get a hundred percent."

"It would be nice if you had something on Gillette personally," Stockman pointed out. "Because we won't be able to pin Dominion on him. We'll be able to pin it on Everest, but not him specifically. He'd be able to prove very quickly that he wasn't involved. That it was just Donovan and Marcie Reed who worked on the Dominion IPO. I mean that's the whole reason for using it—because he *wasn't* close to it. So he won't be able to figure out what we're doing."

"I'm working on that," Strazzi answered.

"What are you doing?"

"I hired the Everest managing partner Gillette fired last weekend. His name's Troy Mason. If there's anyone who can give us dirt on Gillette or the companies he works with directly, it's Mason. He'll know where the bodies at Everest are buried." Strazzi paused. "When will you announce your candidacy, George?"

"Right after Allen's press conference on Everest. Right after he tells the world he's going to investigate them."

"Nice symmetry." Strazzi nodded approvingly. "Once we have control of Everest, you'll have yourself another couple million votes—and my checkbook," he added.

"And, because of my help, you'll control twice as much private equity," Stockman countered. "The two most powerful private equity firms in the world. It goes both ways, Paul."

Strazzi nodded slowly. He already had his empire but, very shortly, he'd double the size of it, and destroy Donovan's legacy at the same time. Very quickly he'd wipe the man off the face of the private equity map.

"How are you going to pay for all this?" Stockman wanted to know. "The widow's share of Everest and my campaign, I mean. You told me her stake is going to cost at least two billion, which is what I told her someone might offer her. Like you told me to do on the call. And you promised me a hundred million for my campaign."

Strazzi glanced over at Stockman. He didn't really have to tell anyone how he was going to pay for anything. It was none of Stockman's business. But he wanted the senator to be confident about everything when he gave Pete Allen the go-ahead to hold the press conference on Friday. "My stake in Apex is worth almost 5 billion. I've already had discussions with several of my personal bankers about using it as collateral. I haven't told them what for yet, but it won't be a problem to get at least two billion in cash out of that. I might even be able to use the Everest stake as collateral, too. But if the bankers think there are problems with that portfolio, I won't get much." He paused. "Plus, I'm going to negotiate with the widow."

"What do you mean?" Stockman asked.

"I mean I'm going to try to use her as the bank, too."

"I don't understand."

"When I meet with her to talk about buying her stake, I'm going to tell her I'll pay her a billion in cash and the other billion over five years. Two hundred million a year."

"She might not agree to that," Stockman said worriedly. "Don't blow this, Paul."

Strazzi let out an exasperated breath. Politicians. Idiots, most of them because they never actually had to make money. They lived off others. They didn't understand that everything in business was a negotiation. Right down to the price of paper clips. "Relax, George. It'll be fine."

"What about my campaign? Let's say the widow holds out for all cash up front and you have to come up with two billion. How are you going to pay for my campaign then?"

"I've got three hundred million in CDs, my friend." Strazzi saw relief spread across the senator's face. "It won't be a problem. Trust me."

"And you're going to let me use your portfolio companies as places for speeches and announcements. At Apex *and* Everest, right?"

"Just like we talked about. Don't worry."

"I want access to that media company Everest owns right away," Stockman kept on. "I want the TV and radio stations."

"You'll have it."

They were silent for a while, and Strazzi thought about what he was so close to.

Finally Stockman spoke up. "Are you sure that guy you just hired from Everest is on our side?"

"What do you mean?"

"I hate to admit it, but Gillette's pretty cagey. Maybe he cut the guy loose as a ploy, knowing you'd go after him immediately. Maybe the guy's a Trojan horse. Maybe he's still working for Gillette."

Strazzi's eyes narrowed. Stupid as most politicians were about business, they understood intrigue. "That thought crossed my mind," he admitted, "but I have an insurance policy. Mason's on our side. I'm positive."

Stockman took a deep breath. "Okay."

Strazzi reached into the desk's top drawer, pulled out a cigar, and ran the length of it slowly under his nose. "Do you think Donovan ever told Gillette he found out you and I were working together?"

Donovan had discovered what was going on thanks to an aide in Stockman's office who he had on the payroll, an aide who was quickly dismissed.

"I don't think so," Stockman answered. "He and Gillette weren't very close the last couple of years. At least, according to your contact."

Strazzi lit the cigar and took several puffs. "I think that's right." He shook his head. "It wouldn't be good for us if Donovan had. Gillette might see through this thing very quickly."

Stockman cleared his throat. "Do you think Bill Donovan was murdered?"

Strazzi's eyes flashed to Stockman's. "How would I know?" he demanded.

"The timing of his death certainly worked out well for us."

Strazzi glared at Stockman, thinking about how the senator wasn't really risking much in this but was getting a great deal in return. Really, he was risking nothing. Just providing access to Congressman Allen and the House Select Committee on Corporate Abuse. In return he was getting a campaign war chest, votes at Apex and Everest, a radio and television network, and corporate venues for speeches in front of thousands of cheering employees, which would be made into wonderful video bites for the evening news.

"Do you think he was murdered?" Stockman asked again.

"I told you," Strazzi said quietly, "I have no idea."

"What about Gillette?"

"What about him?" Strazzi asked curtly. It irritated him to think that Stockman was getting the better end of this deal. He took it personally when anyone got the better of him in *any* situation.

"What about his limousine blowing up outside the church at Donovan's funeral? What do you think of that?"

"I think Gillette has enemies. I think he'd better watch his step if he wants to kiss his girl at midnight on New Year's Eve."

Jimmy Holt hurried along the corridor, head down, hands jammed in his pockets, the report clutched tightly under one arm. He was a senior energy analyst at the engineering firm of Pullen, Marks of Houston—and his heart was in his throat. The tapes had just finished telling him an amazing tale.

"Hey, Jimmy."

Holt spun around, toward the voice. Sam Abernathy, another analyst at the firm, was leaning through his office doorway into the corridor. "What?" Holt snapped. "What do you want?"

"Jesus." Abernathy ambled up to Holt. "You all right, Jimmy?"

"Of course." Holt took a deep breath, aware that he needed to relax, that Abernathy might somehow make a connection between his anxiety and the report if he wasn't careful. "Why?" he asked as casually as he could.

Abernathy shook his head. "You seem nervous."

Holt turned around quickly and hurried away. In the same direction he'd been headed before the interruption. It was the best thing to do. Otherwise, Abernathy would see how nervous he was.

"Hey, you wanna have lunch today?" Abernathy called.

"Yeah, sure. Buzz me in an hour."

Moments later, Holt knocked on his boss's door.

"Jimmy?"

"Yeah."

"Come in, come in." Bill Perkins ushered Holt inside, then quickly shut the door after him. "Well?"

Holt held the report out. "It's incredible. It's one of the largest untapped oil and gas fields in the world."

Perkins snatched the manila folder from Holt's hand and quickly reviewed the summary page Holt had prepared.

"The thing is worth megabillions," Holt continued. "I've never seen anything like it."

"You didn't tell anybody, right?" Perkins's voice was shaking.

"Right. Just like you told me. I came straight to you."

Perkins nodded. "Good." He hesitated. "Now forget you know anything about it. You understand me?"

Holt shook his head. "What's this about, Bill?"

"Don't ask. Don't ask and don't tell. That's the best advice I can give you." Perkins nodded toward the door. "Now, get out of here."

13

Subordinates. *Only slightly less difficult to deal with than partners.*

NICKNAMED "POISON" BY THE YOUNGER men at Everest, Marcie Reed had emerged from the womb destined for private equity. A master manipulator, Marcie was as aggressive as they came, easily intimidating CEOs with her cold, steel blue eyes, a knack for numbers, and her comfort with confrontation. She *demanded* results—and got them.

Marcie was five eight and slim, with shoulder-length blond hair, a thin face, and long, tapered legs. She rarely wore panty hose under her short skirts and dresses, and she always sported high, high heels. She knew what she had and didn't hesitate to use it.

When she tasked the younger men at Everest, they quickly put aside other assignments—even projects Donovan had given them—hoping that the bedroom smile and light touch to the back of their hand meant something more than just thank you. That maybe, just maybe, after a few drinks at the bar downstairs, she'd take them home to her sprawling loft in SoHo. Then they might be able to confirm that rumor about a sexy tattoo on the small of her back.

Thirty-two and single, Marcie had been around money all her life—and it showed. Nothing impressed her. Her father, the CEO of a multinational drug company, had taught her the value of thinking from forty thousand feet, of always seeing the bigger picture. And her mother had given her style and grace. So she had that deadly combination of beauty, brains, and sophistication—and she knew it.

Which Gillette intended to capitalize on.

He'd suggested to Donovan that Marcie be promoted to managing partner six months ago, but the old man had balked, telling him to pound salt and keep his mouth shut. Still psychologically mired in a bygone era, Donovan didn't want a female partner. But Gillette saw opportunity and now he could do what he wanted.

"Hello, Marcie." Gillette checked Dominion's stock price—off another thirty cents this afternoon. Donovan had been the chairman while Everest controlled Dominion, and Marcie his second. A board member and the Everest person most active at Dominion on a day-to-day basis, Marcie had been in charge of the initial public offering on which Everest had made one of its biggest killings. "Busy today?"

"Of course." She sat on the other side of his desk, twirling her blond hair impatiently. Marcie understood efficiency. Donovan's obsession with it had rubbed off on her, too. "I'm always busy. You know that."

"Right. Well, look, obviously there've been a lot of changes in the last few days. Unfortunately, Bill's gone, and—"

"Not unfortunately for you," she cut in.

"And, as I'm sure you know by now," he continued, unfazed by her comment, "I fired Troy."

"And Paul Strazzi hired Troy over at Apex," she said. "Rumor going around is that Strazzi's paying him three million a year."

"Don't get any ideas," Gillette warned, rifling through his e-mails while they talked, slowing up when he saw that an old friend was blasting out to everyone that he had a new cell phone number—a sure sign the guy was ending an affair because these days you could keep your number even if you lost your phone or switched providers. "Understand?"

"I can't help having ideas," Marcie retorted. "It's what I do."

"Strazzi did hire Troy," Gillette confirmed. "I don't know what they're paying him, but I doubt it's three million." He shook his head. "I'm sorry Troy had to go, but I had no choice."

Marcie laughed harshly. "Troy's an asshole. He was always asking me to dinner, trying to get me in bed. I'm glad he's gone." She glanced around the office impatiently, then refocused on Gillette. "By the way, congratulations . . . Mr. Chairman."

"Thanks."

"You deserved it."

She was good, Gillette thought to himself. She was completely insincere, but the remark sounded pure and honest coming from her mouth. He almost smiled as he thought about how that ability was going to make his stake in Everest worth much more. How easily she could wrap men around her little finger—even experienced executives. He'd seen it firsthand.

"What do you make in salary as chairman?" Marcie asked.

Gillette glanced up. She always asked pointed questions out of the blue. "Five million," he answered directly. He was about to make her a managing partner. With the promotion she'd have access to all of Everest's internal numbers, so there was no reason to be coy.

"Jesus. What does that come out to an hour?"

"Around seven hundred bucks."

Her expression turned serious for a moment, then relaxed as she quickly finished the calculation. "Oh, I get it. Twenty-four—seven—three-sixty-five less about four or five hours of sleep a night. Seven hundred an hour."

"Exactly." Gillette nodded approvingly. "Which isn't outrageous. Plenty of lawyers in Manhattan charge more than that."

"But that doesn't include your bonus."

"So?"

"What's that going to be this year?"

"Probably another five."

Marcie whistled. "That certainly helps the hourly—"

"Let's get to why I called you in here," Gillette interrupted. "I'm promoting you to managing partner and giving you 5 percent of the ups in the next fund, which, by the way, I've already started raising."

"Oh?"

"And the target for Eight is fifteen billion." Gillette made certain to look away as Marcie crossed her legs at the knees. She was wearing a skirt that was even shorter than usual, and she'd lifted one leg very high as she'd crossed it over the other. "Miles Whitman at North America Guaranty has already committed a billion five."

"Good," she said, her voice emotionless.

"I know you're busy with your portfolio companies, but I want you to get involved in the money raise this time around, too."

She nodded enthusiastically. "See, Christian, that's why the limited partners elected you chairman. You just want to get your hands on fifteen billion as fast as possible. You aren't caught up in the whole male domination thing like Bill was." She leaned forward. "You know the gatekeepers at the insurance companies and the pension funds will love to see me walk through their doors." Her eyes were flashing. "You know they'll be more likely to commit big bucks if they think they get to take me to dinner once a quarter to give them an update." She smiled slyly. "You have no problem using me. I like it."

"Good. I think you'll like this, too. I'm taking your salary from five hundred thousand to a million starting January first. And, like I said, you'll get 5 percent of the ups of Everest VIII."

She nodded again.

But not enthusiastically, he noticed. It was as if she expected it, as if she was even a little disappointed at the number. The same way he'd reacted to Miles Whitman's commitment to Everest VIII. Like they were talking about the weather and the forecast wasn't great. Which was exactly why he was promoting her, he reminded himself. She was so good. Of course she was excited; she just wasn't showing it. "You're going to chair six of our companies," he continued. "I'll send you an e-mail on that by close of business tomorrow. I haven't made all the decisions on which companies you'll have yet."

"Are you keeping the other twenty-one? You can't possibly—"

"No, I'm going to chair fifteen."

"Who's getting the other six?"

"Kyle."

Marcie stopped twirling her hair. "You're promoting Kyle to managing partner, too?"

"Yes." She wasn't happy, that was obvious. Clearly she'd wanted this to be a solo deal. She didn't want to share the spotlight with Kyle Lefors when Everest published the announcement of her promotion in *The Wall Street Journal*.

"What about Cohen and Faraday?" she asked.

"Ben will be focused internally. I've promoted him to chief operating officer."

"I bet he was *real* happy about that," Marcie said sarcastically.

"Why do you say it like that?"

"He's dying to be chairman of at least one of our companies. Faraday, too. They've been pissed off for a while that Donovan kept those positions for just you and Mason."

"Too bad. We all need to focus on what we do best. That's the bottom line. Ben needs to run the shop, and Nigel needs to raise the next fund. Both of those jobs are critically important if we're going to become the most dominant private equity firm in the world."

"I like the sound of that."

"You should. You'll be very rich if we're successful."

Marcie shrugged. "Just serve me up as an appetizer on the fundraising side, Mr. Chairman. I'll make Nigel's job a lot easier."

Gillette checked Dominion's ticker one more time. The price had dropped another ten cents. "I need to ask you a question," he said, still gazing at the screen.

"Okay."

His eyes moved to hers. "When you were running the IPO diligence for Dominion, did you ever get a sense that there was anything wrong?"

"Like what?"

"Like the loan portfolio might not be as clean as we and the investment bankers claimed it was in the offering documents, like the Dominion senior executives might have been playing shell games with the files to hide that."

Marcie tugged at her skirt, pulling it toward her knees. "No. Why?"

"Just curious."

"Oh, no. You don't just ask questions like that, Christian. Come on, what did you mean?"

Gillette stood up. "The stock's been off the last few days, but the overall market's been strong," he explained, moving out from behind the desk. "Seems like something's going on."

"I'm supposed to believe that the trading pattern over the last few days would make you think the Dominion senior executives were playing shell games with the loan portfolio when the IPO went off months ago?" she asked, standing up to block his path to the door. "Come on."

"Okay. Somebody told me there might be a problem."

"Who?"

"I can't say."

"Tell me, Christian."

"No."

They stared at each other for a few moments, their faces close.

Finally, Marcie walked to the door, hesitating there a moment. "Watch out for Kyle, Christian."

"Why?"

"There's something about him I don't trust."

"Good job today."

"Thank you."

"I've heard nothing about anyone at the scene seeing anything unusual. The Dallas cops are calling it an accident."

"Couldn't have gone any smoother."

Tom McGuire lit a cigarette and tossed the match into an ashtray. Gillette thought he didn't know about the investment bankers who wanted to take McGuire & Company public at a much higher price than his backer was willing to pay. McGuire took a puff. Gillette had proven to be a tough adversary, but he wasn't as smart as he thought he was.

"Where are you?" McGuire asked.

"Still at LaGuardia Airport. I landed a few minutes ago."

"You're calling me on a pay phone, right?"

"Of course. Like I'm supposed to."

"So you'll be trying again soon?"

"Yeah."

McGuire hesitated. "There's one thing you should know."

"What?"

"Gillette's hired another bodyguard. A man named Quentin Stiles. I've checked him out. He's good."

Kyle Lefors's nickname at Everest was G-2. Short for Gillette-2. Thirty-one, he resembled Gillette in many ways: physically, with his dark hair and gray eyes, and in the way he approached problems—analytically and from all angles. Gillette could still remember Donovan laughing the day he'd hired Lefors out of Harvard Business School five years ago. How the old man had called it the second coming of Jesus.

In those days Gillette was Jesus, the favorite son, the one who got the best assignments, the one who served as Donovan's deputy at the high-profile portfolio companies. In those days, Mason had run a distant second.

But all that changed a few years ago when Donovan proposed purchasing a Michigan-based manufacturer of bath and shower products. A company that, in Gillette's opinion, Everest should have stayed far away from. It owned tired brands in the twilight of their life cycles, and the purchase price was outrageous—thirty times earnings. Earnings that were spiraling further down every month.

The deeper Gillette dug into the company's operations, the more he objected to the transaction. And the more irritated Donovan became, finally sticking a finger in Gillette's face one night and telling him to back off or find another job.

Gillette didn't understand. Donovan never irrationally fell in love with companies the way some gunslingers did—convincing themselves they could work miracles with rusty assets that were at the scrap heap gate. Donovan stayed stone cold sober when it came to investing, never thinking with his heart.

Gillette didn't understand until he found out that the company's largest shareholder was one of Donovan's oldest friends, a man Donovan had known for thirty years who'd recently lost everything in an ugly divorce. Everything except his ownership in the company because the wife's attorney had convinced her it wasn't worth anything. That it made sense to trade it for everything else in the estate because no one in their right mind would buy the company.

Enter Donovan. Paying a hundred million for his friend's share of the company alone. He'd known the company was teetering on the brink of insolvency, but hadn't cared. He was saving an old friend—who'd ultimately taken twenty million of the hundred and bought Donovan a twelve-thousand-square-foot beachfront mansion in the Caymans with fifteen acres of land along with it. It had been a slick way for Donovan to slip eighty million dollars out of Everest to an old friend—and twenty million to himself.

After figuring out the real deal, Gillette had stopped objecting. Dutifully processing the due diligence information and drafting a memo to Everest's limited partners describing the acquisition and the "solid" opportunity it represented. In his heart believing the company wouldn't survive more than two years. He'd been wrong. It had gone bankrupt in less than one. Ten months after acquiring the company, Everest had been forced to write off its entire three-hundred-million-dollar investment. In twenty years, it was one of only a handful of companies Everest had bought that crashed and burned.

But, in the end, it hadn't mattered at all. Not one iota. Because the rest of the companies in the fund had been huge winners and the limited partners barely noticed the three-hundred-million-dollar write-off. It was just a footnote and a ha-ha during the annual partners' meeting at the Plaza. No one even questioned Donovan's motives. Instead, they'd thanked him profusely for being their most successful gunslinger.

After that, Gillette's relationship with Donovan was never the same. They hadn't spoken for weeks after closing the deal, and for months after that it had been difficult for Gillette to even be around the old man. He hadn't said a word when the bankruptcy hit, and Donovan never acknowledged the mistake. Instead, he subtly blamed the bomb on Gillette at the partners' meeting. Over time, they'd reestablished a working relationship, but it had never been like the old days.

And Troy Mason had become the messiah. The one who would ultimately run Everest Capital.

Until Donovan had met an untimely death on a Connecticut stream.

"Hello, Kyle." Gillette was the only one at Everest who didn't call Lefors by his Donovan-given nickname. He'd never liked it. "What's up?"

"Just putting chicken in the bucket for the man," Lefors answered smoothly. "Punching that Everest time clock."

While Marcie was relentlessly aggressive—a bull in a china shop— Lefors was smooth. He was always ready with an amusing story or an engaging remark to put others at ease. Calmly, almost imperceptibly taking center stage when he wanted to, he never appeared rushed or uncomfortable.

Marcie and Lefors were different in their methods, but equally effective. And, down deep, they both craved their own empires. Which Gillette was wary of because, sooner or later, they'd both want to break away from Everest and start their own firms. It was the natural progression.

"Did you hear about Richard Harris?" Lefors asked casually.

"Yeah."

Lefors opened a bag of potato chips that was lying in his lap. He inhaled junk food constantly, but never gained weight. "Think he was murdered?"

Gillette glanced up from his computer. Dominion had come back a little at the closing bell but had drifted lower again in after-hours trading. "Why do you ask?"

Lefors shrugged. "A man like Harris probably had lots of enemies. You don't get to be CEO of U.S. Petroleum without ruining a few careers. I never met him, but I heard he was a deliberate man. Deliberate men don't step in front of buses. That's why."

"It was an accident," Gillette said. "At least, that's what I was told. No one at the scene saw anything suspicious."

"I'm considering all the possibilities," Lefors said, munching on a chip. "Like you've taught me."

"Just make sure Harris's death doesn't throw a wrench into our deals with U.S. Petroleum."

"I've already talked to the business development guy there who's handling everything," Lefors answered. "I reminded him that we still expect to close both transactions no later than January tenth. He started backpedaling at first. Said things would probably go on hold with Harris's death, so I reminded him of the five-million-dollar no-go fee I put in the letter of intent I made him sign."

"What if *we* crater the deal?" asked Gillette. "Does the no-go fee go both ways?"

"No," Lefors replied proudly. "We don't pay a cent if we cut off negotiations."

"Good."

Lefors wiped his mouth with a paper napkin. "So, why did you want to see me?"

"I'm promoting you to managing partner."

Lefors stuffed several more chips in his mouth. "Do I at least get a cost-of-living increase?" he asked through a mouthful.

"More than that," Gillette said straight-faced. "Six percent."

"You're a generous man."

"I'm kidding," Gillette said, breaking into a grin. "You'll make a million a year, up from the five hundred grand you make now. And I'm going to make you chairman of six of our companies."

Lefors tossed his tie over his shoulder and brushed crumbs off his shirt. "What about incentive comp? I heard we were raising a new fund. You going to spread some of the ups around now that Donovan and Mason are out of the picture?"

"How did you find out we were raising a new fund?" Gillette wanted to know, irritated. Nobody in New York could keep a damn secret. For such a big city, sometimes it seemed like a small town.

"I gotta plead the Fifth on this one, Christian. I can't give away my sources. My network would fall apart if it got out that I didn't keep things confidential."

"This time you're going to make an exception, Kyle," Gillette said. "Tell me."

"All right, all right." Lefors closed the bag of chips and dropped it on the floor. "A buddy of mine over at North America Guaranty & Life told me. I went to business school with him. He's putting together some kind of investment memo on us for the Mac Daddy over there. For Miles Whitman."

"I know who the Mac Daddy at NAG is."

"You know who *all* the Mac Daddies in New York are, Christian. That's why I like hanging with you." Lefors shook his head. "Thirty-six and chairman of Everest Capital. Did you wake up this morning and pinch yourself to make sure you weren't dreaming? I mean, where do you go from here? Hell, you *are* one of the Mac Daddies now."

Lefors could charm a leopard out of his spots, so you couldn't assume he was being sincere. Still, it was nice to hear that someone understood what he'd accomplished. Marcie had congratulated him, but only because that made sense from a political perspective. There was no doubt that her congratulations were insincere. But you never knew with Lefors. He might actually mean it. Which made him more unpredictable than Marcie. And, therefore, more dangerous. "I'm giving you 5 percent of the ups on the next fund."

"What's the target raise?"

"Fifteen billion."

Lefors let out a low whistle. "Hey, I might actually be worth something someday. No more filling chicken buckets. *If* you can raise that much," he added.

"I can and I will."

"Is this the same deal Marcie's getting?"

Gillette knew what was coming. Lefors was a natural negotiator, a man who always assumed that no one started with their best offer. Which wasn't necessarily a bad assumption. But in this case, he was wrong. "Yeah, and don't think you're going to get any more. You aren't."

"I want two million a year in salary and 10 percent of the ups."

·"Then I'll promote Danny Wagner instead of you." Wagner was another Everest managing director.

"Wagner." Lefors laughed. "What a joke. You wouldn't promote him if he was the last private equity guy on earth. He's okay at blocking and tackling, like Cohen, but he can't *get* people, you know? Which is what really sets a private equity person apart. What sets *you* apart. You take control of a situation whenever you want to. It's a gift. Not many people have it."

Gillette passed a finger slowly over his lower lip. Lefors was right. The bluff had been called. Wagner would never be a managing partner. "Or I could go outside the firm."

Lefors shook his head. "Look, in the last six months I've been approached by three other private equity firms. They're all offering me nice packages, better than what you just did. Of course, you already know that. From Tom McGuire. And here's how I know you know." He pulled the tie from over his shoulder and laid it down over the buttons of his shirt. "So I'm having lunch with a senior partner at one of these firms a few weeks ago, and I notice two guys a few tables over. One of them looks real familiar. I can't place him for a while, then suddenly I remember. A couple of months ago I rode out to Kennedy Airport with Donovan. I was briefing him on developments at a couple of our portfolio companies. He was on his way to Africa for that presidential delegation, remember? And I was with him because you know how he always had to be doing ten things at once? Anyway, he's dragging a McGuire bodyguard with him, too. The guy's sitting in the front seat with the driver. Turns out, it was the same guy who was watching me eat lunch." Lefors hesitated. "And he didn't touch his food the whole time. He was just watching. Like he was trying to read my lips."

"I know you've been approached," Gillette acknowledged quietly, "but I don't care. The deal I presented to you is the deal. There's nothing more."

Lefors said nothing.

It was time to deliver the knockout punch. If there was one person in the firm who was economically motivated, it was Lefors. He'd made it into Yale undergraduate by conning the university's admissions office. He'd grown up in a Louisiana trailer park outside a small town thirty miles north of Baton Rouge called McManus. His real high school transcript was a train wreck because he hadn't tried, but he'd made 1580 on his SATs, then submitted a fraudulent application to Yale—third in his class with a 3.96 GPA, captain of the football team, student council. All bogus claims. But Yale had fallen in love with the SAT scores and were too frothy to have a kid from rural Louisiana that actually fit their admissions standards. Lefors had conned them perfectly. And, Gillette knew, for a con man, it always came down to money.

"Kyle, I know which three firms are recruiting you. They're nice firms, but the biggest fund any of them has is nine hundred million. You'll make a lot more owning 5 percent of the ups of a fifteen-billion-dollar fund than you ever would owning even 50 percent of a nine-hundred-million-dollar fund. Which, of course, you won't get. You'd get ten at most. And, if you keep doing well here, you'll get more. Don't be stupid."

They stared at each other over Gillette's desk for several moments.

Finally, Lefors nodded. "Okay, fine." He laughed. Nervously this time.

Which Gillette picked up on instantly. He'd only seen Lefors nervous a few times.

"No hard feelings, right?" Lefors asked. "I mean, you'd expect me to negotiate because I—"

"How did you know Troy was in the basement with the Hays woman?" Gillette interrupted, changing tracks. "At Donovan's funeral reception."

"Marcie told me," Lefors answered quickly.

"*What?*"

"Sure. Marcie always watched Troy like a hawk. Personally, I think they had something going on. She was pissed he was down there."

And Marcie had made it seem like she couldn't stand Troy. "Why did you tell me Troy was in the basement with Ms. Hays?"

"I thought Troy was out of control for a while. I heard he was banging women at all his portfolio companies. I was worried it could hurt us big-time." Lefors hesitated. "And . . ." His voice drifted off.

"And *what?*" Gillette pressed.

"And I figured if I told you, it might create a spot for me." Lefors looked around. "Guess what? It did."

Gillette gazed at Lefors for a moment without responding. It had just hit him. Lefors was from a tiny, backwoods Louisiana town, but he didn't have a trace of a southern accent. In the five years Lefors had been at Everest, Gillette couldn't remember a single time he'd heard even the slightest twang. Lefors ought to have an accent thick enough to cut, but he didn't. He'd erased it because he knew it wouldn't go over well in the New York private equity world. Or maybe he wasn't really from Louisiana.

"Christian." Debbie's voice crackled through the intercom.

"Yes?"

"Ann Donovan is here to see you."

14

The Wild Card. *You never know.*

"PLEASE, COME IN." DONOVAN'S WIDOW looked much better than she had the day of the funeral. There was color to her face, and her lips weren't as drawn and tight. "Let's go over here." He took her gently by the arm and guided her to the chairs around the coffee table, where he'd interviewed Quentin Stiles. "Would you like something to drink?"

"No, thank you," she said, her head shaking slightly. She was in the early stages of Parkinson's. "I'm sorry to drop in on you like this without calling ahead."

"No problem." Gillette settled into a chair beside hers. "How are you?"

"Better."

"I'm sure it's been difficult. If there's anything I can do . . ."

The widow patted his hand. "Thank you, dear," she said softly.

"Everyone around here misses Bill very much. It hasn't been the same without him."

Her lips formed a wry smile and she pulled a tissue from her black purse. "I'm sure not *everyone* misses him. I'm not naïve, Christian."

"Of course you aren't."

"Bill wasn't an easy person to deal with."

"Well, he . . ." Gillette's voice trailed off again.

The widow glanced into Gillette's eyes. "I'm sure it was terrible when he turned his back on you, when he started favoring Troy. You must have hated him for that."

"I never hated him."

"It was despicable what he did," she muttered. "Stealing money from Everest to help a friend. And himself," she added. "A friend who was a horrible person anyway, trying to bed every woman he could," she continued, her voice beginning to tremble. "You'd think a man in his fifties wouldn't have to chase twenty-year-olds."

Gillette knew her bitter tone wasn't really directed at Donovan's friend.

"But Bill helped him," the widow continued, sniffing. "Got him all that money after his wife finally wised up and took him for everything he had. Or so she and I thought." She shut her eyes tightly. "He ended up with more money *after* the divorce because of Bill, and Bill's fee was that mansion in the Caymans."

Gillette hesitated. "How did you know?"

"I overheard him on the phone one night laughing about it."

"Oh."

"Bill thought I was out, or off in another wing, I suppose." The widow dabbed at the corners of her eyes with the tissue. "He didn't keep track of me very closely for the last few years of our marriage. But he should have."

It was better to say nothing. Gillette understood what she meant thanks to Tom McGuire.

She drew a deep breath, her head shaking more noticeably. "Bill did leave me quite a fortune."

"Yes, he did."

"And I intend to protect it."

"Of course."

"Most of that fortune is tied up in my ownership stake in Everest."

Gillette sensed there was more coming. That the widow hadn't dropped by just to tell him what he already knew.

"How are the portfolio companies doing?" she asked.

"Most of them are doing fine. We have problems with a few, but that's normal, Ann. I'm sure Bill told you stories about things that happened to our companies."

"No, he didn't."

"Oh."

"Are there any *big* problems the world hasn't heard about?"

There were always problems, but she didn't need to hear about them. "No."

"What about the companies that were taken public? The ones that trade on the stock exchanges and Everest still owns shares of?"

Gillette felt his pulse tick up slightly. "They're all fine," he said calmly. "Why?"

"I heard there might be problems."

"Heard?"

"From someone."

"Someone?" Gillette leaned forward in his chair. Stockman was already at work. "Who was it?" He wanted her to confirm his suspicions.

"It doesn't matter," she said quickly. "What *does* matter is that I've been offered a lot of money for my ownership stake. A *lot* of money," she repeated. "Not as much as I'd get by holding on to it until you sell all the portfolio companies over the next few years. But of course that assumes there aren't any problems with the portfolio, too. That assumes everything goes smoothly and that you can sell all those companies for big price tags. But if it turns out there *are* problems, I'll be very sorry I didn't accept this offer."

Gillette sat in his office staring at the ceiling. It was seven o'clock and the only light in the office came from the computer screen.

He ran his hands through his hair and exhaled heavily. The widow wouldn't say who had told her there were problems in the Everest portfolio and that she ought to get out now for a discounted price, but he was certain Stockman was involved. The timing was too coincidental. If it turned out Marcie hadn't been diligent enough while Everest controlled Dominion and there were problems with the loan portfolio—or, worse, there was fraud—the fallout would rain down on Everest. Gillette could see the headlines: "Market Manipulation." "Insider Dealings." Raising a $15 billion fund—any fund—would quickly become impossible.

The problem was he didn't know who to believe: Stockman or Marcie. The auditors had been all over Dominion before the IPO, but in a

$40 billion loan portfolio, experienced auditors could still miss things. Lots of things. Even if Stockman was bluffing, it might not matter. In the Internet age, rumors could be just as devastating as facts.

Maybe Stockman hadn't been the one to actually approach the widow, Gillette thought to himself. Maybe it had been one of his aides or someone involved in the campaign. Maybe Stockman had made the call to Ann Donovan to set up the meeting with whoever had actually delivered the message so it didn't look like he knew anything. Just him doing her a favor. He and Ann had known each other socially for a long time, and it would be appropriate for him to help her if he happened to hear important information. Even though Stockman and Bill Donovan had hated each other, Stockman and the widow always got along—probably because they shared a common loathing. The outside world didn't know the extent of the animosity between the two men. In public, at the never-ending string of charity functions, they behaved as though they were friends. But, down deep, they despised each other.

The widow was seriously considering selling her Everest stake. Gillette had no doubt of that after their conversation today. Which created a *huge* problem. If she sold it, that 25 percent voting block she controlled would fall into someone else's hands, someone who would undoubtedly want to install his own chairman.

If Stockman was responsible for putting the fear of Jesus into the widow, then he had to be working with someone else. He didn't have the resources to buy her position—$2 billion assuming a 50 percent discount to Cohen's $4 billion estimate of its value. In fact, there were very few people who did have that kind of wherewithal *and* would have an interest in buying it. Gillette could count on the fingers of one hand who it might be—and Paul Strazzi was at the top of the list. And Strazzi's call to Troy Mason right after the funeral reception proved he had a mole inside Everest.

Gillette hadn't heard any rumors of a Strazzi-Stockman connection, and, if you'd been at the top of the financial food chain long enough, you usually would. He considered putting Tom McGuire on it—to confirm a Strazzi-Stockman connection. Tom had already done all the background work on Stockman, so it would be easier. But he didn't know if he could trust Tom anymore. It would have to be Stiles.

Maybe it made sense to sell McGuire & Company back to Tom and his brother cheaply, Gillette thought to himself. Maybe then he could trust them again. Maybe it was worth $200 million after all.

Gillette groaned as he dropped his feet to the floor. These were the tough times. When there was no one to trust.

There was a sharp knock on the door.

"Come in," Gillette called. Despite the feeble light, he recognized Faraday's round face at the doorway. "Have a seat."

"Yes, sir," Faraday shot back sarcastically, moving into the office and dropping heavily into a chair in front of the desk.

"What's the problem, Nigel?"

"What do you mean?"

"Why the hostility?"

"Fuck off."

"You been drinking?"

"I was downstairs for a while," Faraday admitted, slurring his words.

"Downstairs" meant the steak place on the first floor. In the back of the restaurant there was a pub with dark paneled walls and friendly bartenders. All of whom Faraday knew well.

"How many scotches?"

"None of your fucking business."

"Nigel, we can't work this way. I know why you're pissed off, but there's nothing I can do about it. The limited partners elected me. You've got to get past it."

"You could give me one company to be chairman of, Christian. Just one. That would help."

"Look, I—"

"And you didn't have to tell Marcie Reed she was going to run the money-raise for Fund VIII."

"*What?*"

"She came into my office a few hours ago looking for our investor lists. Said when you promoted her to managing partner, you made her chairwoman of six of our companies *and* told her she could co-raise the new fund with me."

Gillette rolled his eyes. Marcie only knew one speed and one direction—full ahead. "I never told her that. What I told her was that in a few cases she could help. I hope you didn't give her the lists."

"Of course not."

Managing thirty type-A personalities was going to be hell. That was clear. "Let's talk about Fund VIII," Gillette suggested. "You're going to need to hire at least two people, and probably—"

"I want a company," Faraday interrupted, his voice a monotone.

"Nigel, let it go."

"*I want a company*," he repeated, standing up. "I deserve one."

"It's not about *deserving* one. It's about knowing how to run one. You don't. You're the fund-raiser at Everest. You're the expert at that."

"I don't care about raising money right now." He took a step around the desk. "I want a company, damn it."

Gillette stood up. Over the Brit's shoulder, he saw Stiles at the door. But he shook him off. He wouldn't need help with Faraday. "Don't do this, Nigel. You'll regret it."

Faraday stopped a few feet away. "What are you gonna do, Christian, fire me, too? Like you did Troy. You gonna get rid of all of us?"

"Don't let the scotch talk you into a mistake."

"You think you're so fucking superior, Chris." Faraday blinked slowly, his eyes glassy. "Now, are you going to make me chairman of at least one company?"

"No."

"You fucking son-of-a-bitch!" Faraday lunged, aiming for Gillette's chin.

He was faster than Gillette had anticipated, but nowhere nearly fast enough. Gillette avoided the punch easily and landed a swift, straight blow to Faraday's stomach, catching the Brit by the throat as he doubled over, thumb and forefinger closing tightly around the soft skin of the man's pudgy neck. As Faraday slumped to his knees, Gillette grabbed the other man's right wrist, rotated it inward and brought it up almost to the back of his neck. Then he forced Faraday's face against the wall.

"Let me go," Faraday gasped.

"I warned you, Nigel." Gillette jerked him to his feet, bringing his wrist to the small of his back, then pushed him toward the door. Finally, he shoved him through the doorway roughly. "Go home and sleep it off," Gillette called as Faraday stumbled toward the lobby. He glanced over at Stiles, who was grinning. "What's your problem?"

"Where'd you learn that?"

"Green Berets."

"Yeah, sure. You didn't—"

"Come in for a second," Gillette interrupted, heading back into his office. "I need to talk to you."

"Okay."

"I need you to check out something else for me," Gillette said when the door was closed.

"In addition to identifying the Strazzi mole and finding out who sent you the e-mail last night right before you were attacked?"

Gillette had spoken to Stiles about those things after his meeting with Marcie Reed. "Yeah."

"What else you need?"

"The guy I just promoted this afternoon."

"Kyle Lefors."

"Right." Gillette liked the way Stiles was on top of everything. "Check out his background."

A confused expression came to Stiles's face. "I thought I read that he's been here for five years."

"That's right."

"Why check out his background now?"

"I need to know if he really grew up in Louisiana." Gillette looked up. "Oh, and one other thing."

"George."

"Yes?"

"It's me. Paul."

"Yes?"

"The widow met with Gillette this afternoon and delivered the news. It went off perfectly. She's very scared."

"How do you know? Did she call?"

"No," answered Strazzi.

"Then how do you know?"

Strazzi realized he shouldn't be saying this on a cell phone, but he couldn't help himself. He had to tell someone. "I have a contact inside Everest."

"You have every angle covered, don't you, Paul?"

"Always."

. . .

Gillette and Whitman were meeting in the same conference room they had met in before. In all the time Gillette had known Whitman, they'd never met in his office. Gillette knew it was precautionary on Whitman's part. As the chief investment officer of the country's largest insurance company, Whitman was constantly in the middle of confidential transactions—often as the money backing one side of a hostile takeover. Whitman couldn't afford to have outsiders see something sensitive on his desk or credenza and word of a big public transaction leaking out. So he always met with people in conference rooms.

"Thanks for getting together with me on such short notice, Miles."

"No problem. What's up?"

"I need your advice, and maybe your help."

"What about?"

"Donovan's widow."

"Oh?" Whitman straightened up in his chair.

"She came by my office today to let me know that her stake in Everest was very important to her."

Whitman spread his hands. "And this was a surprise to you? I don't see the significance. Don't take this the wrong way, Christian, but I've got to get out of here as soon as I can. I'm late for a—"

"Someone's been telling her there are problems with the Everest portfolio."

Whitman stopped talking and stared.

"So she's concerned," Gillette continued, glancing at Whitman's bow tie. A conservative dark blue today.

"*Are* there problems with the portfolio?" asked Whitman quietly.

"You know how these things go," Gillette answered. "Portfolio companies are like children. There are always problems."

"Any *big* problems?"

"Not that I know of, but the widow's spooked."

"Tell her everything's fine and send her a box of candy. There's nothing she can really do about it."

"She was talking about selling her piece of Everest."

Whitman's eyes flashed to Gillette's. "*What?*"

"Yeah. With that big fat 25 percent voting bloc."

Whitman pointed at Gillette. "You can't let her do that, you hear me? You *cannot* let that happen."

"I hear you, Miles. Believe me. I don't want to be out on my ass."

Whitman settled back in his chair. "Right. Of course you don't." He glanced around. "Have you made any organizational changes yet?"

"What do you mean?"

"Promotions."

"I'm going to promote Kyle and Marcie to managing partner. I told you that."

"Yeah, sure. Anything else?"

Gillette thought for a moment. "Well, I'm going to make Cohen the chief operating officer. That's really more an internal thing than anything else. So the troops know he's in charge."

"Oh? When does that take effect?"

"I just need to send out an e-mail tomorrow morning."

Whitman nodded. "Good move. He seems like a decent guy. Harmless, but decent. That kind of thing will probably make him happy. Wouldn't make you or me happy, but Cohen seems like the type who would appreciate it. And you want to keep turmoil to a minimum right now."

Kathy Hays eased the car to a stop after slowly negotiating the long, twisting driveway through the dense woods. She'd taken an extra day and a 300-mile detour to visit her family in Pittsburgh. There she had told them how she was starting a new life in Los Angeles—which was what she'd been told to say—but this was about as far from L.A. as you could get.

She stepped out of the car and gazed through the night at the tiny house that she'd call home for the next six months. That's what they'd said. Six months, then she could go on with her life. She shrugged as she started walking through the gloom toward the house, gravel crunching beneath her shoes. For what they were paying her—and what they were willing not to tell anyone—she could do anything for six months.

As she climbed the front steps to the porch, she reached into her purse for the house keys they'd given her, thinking about Troy Mason. How she'd gotten him fired. How he had a wife and a young child. It was awful. She shook her head. But they'd given her no choice. If she didn't work with them, they'd have told her parents and all of her parents' friends about her prostitution arrest in college at the University of New Mexico.

Kathy slid the key into the front door. So stupid. A one-time thing, but she'd solicited an undercover cop and he'd taken her straight to jail. She'd served ten days, paid a small fine, and that had been that—or so she'd thought. Until they approached her on the street that day to tell her they'd found out about it.

Kathy shuddered as she pushed the door open, thinking about what that news would do to her parents. Her mother was active in the neighborhood church and her father was suffering from high blood pressure. They'd always thought she'd been such an angel. And they were going to tell her parents that it hadn't been a one-time thing at all, that she'd been doing it for money for months.

She flipped on the living room light and took a deep breath. A musty smell came to her nostrils. This was definitely the best outcome. Good money, no worries about her parents finding out anything, and Troy Mason would catch on somewhere else. And they'd promised her no one was going to get hurt.

Kathy put her purse down on the table by the door and glanced around the room. Six months. It couldn't go fast enough.

She shivered as she stood a short distance down Fifth Avenue from the apartment building entrance, pulling the flimsy coat tightly around her body. She'd been waiting for three hours in the darkness—and the freezing cold. She'd never experienced anything like it. The trees across Fifth Avenue—at the eastern edge of Central Park—swayed from side to side against a sudden gust, and she tried pulling the coat even closer to her body.

A blue sedan eased to a stop in front of the apartment building and two men got out. One of them hurried up the steps and through the doorway, while the other remained outside, checking the sidewalk in both directions. It was almost ten o'clock and, because of the wind and cold, there was no one on the street. So he spotted her right away and moved directly toward her.

"Why are you standing here?" he demanded.

"I'm waiting for someone."

"Who?"

"A friend."

"Well, move off for now, miss," he said politely.

"Why?"

"Just do it."

Then she saw a limousine approaching. He had to be in there.

"Move off now," the man ordered, his voice intensifying.

Isabelle took a few steps down the street, as if she were obeying, then spun around and tried to dart past him. But he caught her easily, gathering her slender body up in his huge arms and carrying her away from the entrance as Gillette's limousine pulled to a stop.

She tried to break free, slapping the man about the face and shoulders, but he was too strong for her.

When they were far enough away from the entrance, he put her down and held her against the wall. Trying to be as gentle as possible, he pulled her wrists behind her back and held them together with one hand while he frisked her with the other.

"What's this?" he demanded, yanking a steak knife from her coat pocket and holding it in front of her face.

"Protection."

"Uh-huh. Sure." The man grabbed his radio phone. "Stiles!"

"Yeah."

"Get Gillette inside! Fast!"

Reggie's was the best pool hall in Harlem, best from the standpoint of the caliber of play. But it was a rough place, too. Much rougher than the place he'd been in the night of the funeral reception.

Gillette had worked his way into a game with a tough opponent, again able to convince the gate he was good for the five grand without actually putting it up. All he had on him was a pair of twenties for the cab home.

There was nothing left on the table but the eight and the cue ball. The eight was against one side, a few inches from a corner pocket, and the cue ball was all the way at the other end of the table. Lots of felt to cover, but it was an easy shot, one Gillette had executed a thousand times. Hit the side of the table and the eight at the same time and the eight would roll straight into the corner pocket. Game over, pay me five grand.

He leaned over the table, and lined up the shot, drawing the stick smoothly back through his fingers, seconds from the win.

But suddenly he needed something more. He could feel it. Sinking the shot and taking the five grand wasn't going to do it for him. Not this time.

He hit down on the cue ball, shooting it across the table toward the eight with tremendous backspin. The eight slammed into the corner pocket, but the cue ball rolled back toward Gillette, toward the opposite corner pocket—and dropped in. Scratch. Game over, pay *him* five grand.

The crowd erupted and Gillette glanced up at his opponent. There was a broad smile on the man's face.

"Five grand," the man demanded over the din, sauntering toward Gillette. "Fork it up, rich boy."

"Double or nothing," Gillette offered.

"No way. I want five grand, and I want it now."

Gillette glanced around. If he couldn't convince the man to play again, things were going to get bad. A few of the man's friends were in the crowd, guys who looked like they might enjoy beating up a Manhattan punk dressed in expensive clothes.

Gillette's eyes flicked to the gate, who was fidgeting, nervous that he'd misjudged the rich boy's ability to produce the dough and might end up having the shit kicked out of him, too. Gillette looked back at his opponent, feeling a rush in his head and chest. He'd put himself in a terrible jam—and it felt awesome.

"How about I give you two-to-one odds on ten grand?" Gillette suggested.

The man gave Gillette a curious look. "What do you mean?"

"If you win, I pay you twenty grand. If I win, I get ten grand. Netted against the five I just lost, you'd only owe me five if I win. Five to win twenty. That's a damn good deal." He could see he'd gotten the man's attention.

"Four-to-one."

People were so damn predictable when it came to money. "No. Two on ten. That's it."

"Let me see the money."

Gillette pointed at the man's friends. "You really think I'd risk getting into it with them?"

"People don't usually carry that much cash around. I want to see it."

"They do if they want to play big stakes pool in this place," Gillette said calmly, "and live." He could see the gears in the man's head spinning as he tried to figure out what to do.

Thirty minutes later Gillette walked out of the pool hall onto 134th Street, five thousand dollars richer and very satisfied. As he emerged onto the sidewalk, he stopped and handed five hundred dollars to a woman pushing a baby carriage. Her eyes widened when she saw how much it was. Gillette simply nodded, then moved toward the curb, glancing around for a cab. It wasn't going to be easy getting one up here. He might have to take the subway.

"Hey, you really thought you gave us the slip?"

Gillette spun around, startled. Relieved when he saw Quentin Stiles standing beside a black sedan parked twenty feet away.

Stiles walked up to Gillette deliberately and tapped him on the chest. "Don't ever do that again," he warned sternly. "You do and I drop this assignment. Understand?"

Gillette nodded, suddenly feeling very safe. "Okay."

Stiles motioned toward the car. "Come on, let's go. I don't want you out on the street like this." He took a few steps and looked back over his shoulder. "By the way, nice playing in there. You might even give me a game."

15

Infatuation. So powerful sometimes. Powerful enough to distract a man who prides himself on never being distracted.

"NO. I'M NOT GONNA LET you to go in there without me." Stiles stood between Gillette and the hotel room door, arms crossed defiantly over his maroon turtleneck and a sharp wool blazer.

"Quentin, it's all right. I'm telling you."

"I said no."

"She's harmless. There's no reason to be suspicious."

"I'm *paid* to be suspicious."

"And *I'm* the one paying you," Gillette reminded Stiles sternly. "You better let me go in there."

"You hired me to do a job, Christian. To protect you. I'll do that job as I see fit, no matter what."

"I could let you go."

"You mean fire me?"

"Sure."

"Fine," Stiles retorted.

Gillette glanced down the hall. A maid was picking up towels off a cart outside a room she was cleaning, trying hard to seem like she wasn't listening. "Gets you mad, huh?" He'd heard an edge in Stiles's voice, and he liked it. He wanted to see Stiles lose that signature cool.

"I don't get mad. Getting mad gets in the way."

"Okay. Then this won't get you mad. You're fired."

"Great. I'll alert the media. But I'm still not letting you in that room alone. Besides, Cohen already paid me for a month."

"I want my money back."

"No refunds. It's in the contract."

"You're making that up—"

"Page seven, paragraph two."

"Cohen would never have agreed to that."

"Well, he did."

Gillette gritted his teeth. "Quentin, I don't have time for this. I want to—"

Stiles put his hand on Gillette's shoulder. "Christian, my guy found a knife on her last night when she was outside your building."

"It was a steak knife, for Christ's sake."

"So what? That could do the job."

"No. That could be paranoia."

"We've been over this. You pay me to be paranoid."

"Quentin, listen. Isabelle wouldn't hurt anyone."

"You told me you just met her. How would you know?"

Stiles was right. "Look, she only came to this country a few weeks ago. She's never been to New York City. Her sister probably told her the city was dangerous and that she should have some protection on her."

"How did you meet Isabelle?" Stiles asked.

"It doesn't matter."

"Everything matters if I'm going to protect you. I keep telling you that. You *have* to buy into it if I'm going to keep you alive."

"I think you use that line as a device."

"A device?"

"So you can pry."

"*That's ridiculous.* I would never—"

"All right, all right," Gillette muttered, exasperated. "I work with Isabelle's family down in New Jersey. With her sister and brother-in-law. That's where I was coming back from the other night when I was attacked outside Hightstown."

"What does 'work with' them mean? You do business with them?"

"Not exactly."

"What, then?"

"I've helped them." Gillette suddenly realized that he'd never told anyone that, and it felt good to say it. Of course, he knew he'd exact a price someday. So it wasn't like Jose was getting anything free.

"How exactly have you *helped* them?"

"Financially. I moved them out of the Bronx and bought them a house in a good school district in central Jersey."

"Oh, I get it. They're like your personal social project. It makes you feel better about all that money you make." Stiles shook his head. "You've got that knight-in-shining-armor complex."

Gillette glanced up. The edge in Stiles's voice had sharpened, making him wonder about Stiles's background. "Maybe I do," he admitted. He'd never thought about it that way. "But so what?"

"It could bring you down."

"No way."

"Yeah, it could."

Gillette checked his watch. Seven thirty. Tom McGuire was going to be at Everest in an hour to talk about buying McGuire & Company. He had to move if he was going to be on time.

"Let me go in there and check it out first," Stiles suggested, aware of the time constraint. "If everything's okay, you go in. I'll stay by the door. Inside the suite, but you'll never know I'm there."

"You'll scare the hell out of her."

Stiles raised one eyebrow. "Why? Because I'm a big black guy?"

Gillette stared at Stiles for several moments, then broke into a wide grin. "Yep."

Stiles grinned back, then stepped to the side and pointed at the door. "Knock."

Isabelle opened the door immediately—as though she'd been waiting on the other side. She was wearing a white, terry-cloth robe that fell close to her ankles and had a script "W"—for Waldorf—on one lapel. Her hair was down and wet, presumably because she'd just stepped out of the shower. And she smelled wonderful, like a rose garden on a summer evening. He took a long look at her. She was so gorgeous.

"*Buenos dias, Isabelle.*"

She smiled up at him, her eyes dancing. "Hello, Christian."

She seemed happy to see him this morning. It was all over her face. "This is Quentin Stiles." He motioned toward Stiles. "Quentin works for me. He needs to spend a few minutes with you before I come in." Fear flashed across Isabelle's face, and Gillette reached for her hand to reassure her. "Don't worry," he said softly. "It'll be fine."

Stiles moved beside Gillette. "Ma'am." He pointed down the short hallway toward the suite's bedroom. "Please go sit on the bed," he instructed. "I'll be there in a minute. And you stay where you are," he said to Gillette as he moved past.

For several minutes Stiles searched the suite. "Okay," he called when he didn't find anything. "You can come in."

Gillette moved quickly down the hallway and into the bedroom. Isabelle was standing by the end of the bed.

"I'll be at the door," Stiles said quietly as they passed. "You need me, you yell."

Gillette glanced at Isabelle's slender frame. "Somehow I think I'll be able to take care of myself."

"Still."

"Quentin's very good at what he does," he said to her when Stiles was out of sight. "But sometimes he goes a little overboard."

She shrugged. "It's okay. He's just protecting you. I understand."

"Please sit down. Was everything all right last night?"

"Wonderful," she answered, sitting down on the end of the mattress.

After Stiles had reported the incident outside the apartment building and Gillette knew it was Isabelle they had detained, he'd instructed Stiles to put her up in the Waldorf for the night. And to tell her he'd stop by in the morning. Gillette had called Selma to tell her everything was all right, then left his apartment to play pool.

"I've never stayed in a place as nice as this," she told him as he sat down beside her on the bed. "It's incredible. They brought me these little chocolates last night before I went to sleep, and this bed is so comfortable. I've never slept on a mattress this soft. I feel like a princess."

Gillette studied her face for a few minutes. Physically she was a mature, beautiful woman. But she was still a child in many ways, too.

"Why did you come to the city last night?" he asked.

"To see you. I was hoping we could have that dinner you asked me to."

"Why didn't you just call me?" The robe fell open as she crossed her legs at the knee, exposing her thighs. Gillette glanced at her smooth brown skin for a moment, then away, not wanting to offend her. Aware that she'd noticed his glance. "Why were you waiting outside my building?"

"I didn't think you'd take my call," Isabelle murmured, looking down. "After the way I acted the other night."

"Why did you change your mind?"

She shook her head. "I didn't really change my mind."

"What do you mean?"

"I wanted to say 'yes' the other night when you were in New Jersey."

"Then why *didn't* you?"

Isabelle hesitated. "I don't know."

"Come on," he urged. "Tell me."

She took a deep breath. "I hear Selma and Jose talk about you all the time. How you went to really good schools, how you're an important person, how your father was a senator, how rich you are."

Gillette's dark eyebrows furrowed. "How do they know all that?" He'd made a point not to tell Jose and Selma much about himself, to stay as anonymous as possible. Maybe Stiles wasn't so paranoid after all. "I never told them about my father or where I went to school, and certainly not how much I'm worth."

"I think you mentioned the name of your firm to Jose one time. Selma went on the website and checked it out. Your background is on there, I think. I don't know how she found out who your father was."

Now that Isabelle mentioned it, he remembered telling Jose about Everest once. So the part about his background made sense. Everyone had a brief biography posted under the "Staff" section of the Everest website, and all the news clippings about his father's fatal accident would have mentioned children. If Selma had done a general Internet search of his name, she would have found out about his father. And, so far, he'd bought two houses for them. They would assume he was rich if he could do that.

"So you've heard them talk about me? So what?"

"Why would you want to spend time with someone like me?" Isabelle asked directly. "When you could spend time with more interesting people. People you have more in common with."

"I think you're *very* interesting," Gillette answered. "Now we just need to get to know each other a little. Right?"

"Why do you find me so interesting?"

"You left your country to come to a place you'd never been. That took a lot of courage. I find courage interesting." He smiled. "And any woman who hangs around my front door packing a knife has to be, well, *very* interesting."

She put her face in her hand, embarrassed. "I'm sorry about that."

He gazed at her face. So beautiful.

"The second reason I didn't say 'yes' the other night," she spoke up, "was that I didn't think Selma or Jose would want me to go with you. I thought they'd be angry if we went out."

"Why?"

Isabelle shrugged. "I don't know. Maybe because if we didn't work out they'd be afraid it would make their relationship with you bad. When I told Selma you asked me out and I said no, she got mad. Jose did, too." She folded her hands on her bare knees. "So, here I am."

"Okay, but I need to know why you had that knife in your pocket last night."

She shook her head. "Pretty silly, huh? I'm sorry about that, but I've heard a lot of bad things about New York City, that people rob you on the street in broad daylight with guns."

"A knife wouldn't do much good if you're being robbed by someone with a gun," Gillette pointed out.

"*Sí,* I guess I just wanted some kind of protection. It made me feel safer to have it with me."

"You hear that, Quentin?" Gillette called out loudly. They couldn't see Stiles from where they were sitting. "She just felt safer having it with her."

"Yeah, yeah," came the response.

Gillette winked at Isabelle. "And?" he called back.

"And we'll talk about it later," Stiles answered gruffly.

Gillette took her hand. "Well, look, the dinner invitation is still open. You'll probably have to go through a metal detector and be frisked before Quentin will let you within a hundred feet of me again," he said so Stiles could hear, "but if you're willing to deal with all that, I'd like to take you."

Isabelle turned and put her arms around him. "I'd love it."

He stiffened, uncomfortable with the hug. "How about tonight?" he asked, gently pulling her arms from around his neck. "You can stay in the city today. I'll have someone come by later this morning to take you shopping. Would you like that?"

"Shopping. Oh, no, please," Isabelle said, laughing. "I don't think I could handle all that torture." She looked up at him, her laugh fading. "I know this is obvious, but I'll say it anyway. You and I have different color skins. Is that a problem for you?"

"Not at all." He started to touch her cheek with the back of his fingers, then stopped. "Is it for you?"

"You still salty?"

Gillette looked up. He'd been jotting down notes on a small pad—making lists. It seemed like he was always making lists—and they kept getting longer and longer. *"Salty?"* He was headed to Everest to meet with McGuire, and Stiles was sitting beside him in the back of the Town Car. It was a different car than the one he'd ridden home in last night. Stiles was rotating vehicles constantly, having them searched meticulously before the driver opened a door or turned the key. Making it as hard as possible for anyone to plant another bomb. "What does 'salty' mean?"

"You know, angry."

"About what?"

"About me searching Isabelle's room. And her."

"How thoroughly did you search her? Did you make her take her robe off?"

Stiles held his hands up. "Of course not."

"That's not what I heard," Gillette teased.

"Hey, I'd never do something like that."

Gillette shrugged. "I was down the hall. I couldn't see."

"Christian," Stiles said, his voice rising, "I'm serious."

"Hey, where's that Quentin cool? I thought you *never* got angry."

Stiles eased back against the seat. "I'm not angry," he replied, his voice dropping back to normal. "It's just that I take my job seriously."

"You know what I think?"

Stiles glanced over. "What?"

"I think you were into seeing Isabelle again. I think you were impressed with what you saw last night and wanted her to see you in action. You like her."

"Hey, what's not to like?"

"I knew it."

"Ah, you don't know anything," Stiles muttered. "Listen, I've got a couple of updates for you."

"Oh? What?"

"First, Kyle Lefors is definitely from Louisiana. He grew up in a little town outside of Baton Rouge called McManus."

"Right. What else?"

Stiles hesitated. "Yesterday, Paul Strazzi met with Senator Stockman in a warehouse office up in the Bronx."

Gillette's eyes narrowed.

"Is that important?" asked Stiles.

"Oh yeah." Hiring Stiles was turning out to be one of the best moves he'd ever made. Even if the guy was stubborn as a mule. Maybe because of it.

"Why?"

"I'll tell you later." He was damn glad he'd ordered Stiles to put one of his men on Strazzi's tail. "What about that e-mail? The one I got right before I was attacked the other night in New Jersey."

"Not much yet," Stiles answered. "We know it was sent from an E-coffee store. You know, the chain that offers five minutes of free Internet time with each cup. We just don't know which of the company's five thousand locations it came from. You have to get to their servers to figure that out. I'm trying to run it down through a couple of contacts, but I don't know how far I'll get. And I'm not sure it would do us much good even if I could identify the outbound location. There'd be no way to know exactly who the sender was because customers don't pay for specific terminals."

"Try to figure out which location it came from," urged Gillette. "You never know. It might help."

"Okay, I'll stay on it."

"Good." Gillette tossed the notepad into his briefcase and relaxed into the leather seat. "Tell me about your childhood, Quentin."

Stiles looked over at Gillette. "Why?"

Gillette shrugged. "Looks like we're going to be spending a lot of time together. I'm interested."

"No, you're not."

"What's that supposed to mean?"

"You're just making conversation."

"Quentin, I'm a busy guy. I don't 'just make conversation.'"

"What do you want to know?" asked Stiles after a few moments. He was staring ahead intently at a street vendor pushing his cart.

"Where'd you grow up?"

"About sixty blocks north of here." Stiles relaxed as they passed the vendor without incident. "In Harlem."

Gillette broke into a grin. "So, you probably know that pool hall where you picked me up pretty well."

Stiles nodded. "Wasted more hours in there than I care to count."

"Are you really that good?"

"Oh yeah."

"Got any brothers or sisters?" Gillette asked, wishing he had time to play Stiles right now. It would be a hell of a lot of fun to take him for five grand.

"A half brother and a half sister. That's all I know about, anyway."

"Do you keep in touch with them?"

"No."

"Why not?"

"I just don't."

It was clear Stiles didn't want to talk about it. "Did you go to college?"

Stiles snickered. "I didn't even finish high school. Dropped out junior year."

But he had excellent grammar, Gillette realized. In fact, he spoke more clearly and concisely than a lot of people Gillette knew who had paid hundreds of thousands to play in the Ivy for four years. "But how did you—"

"My grandmother," Stiles interrupted.

"What about her?"

"She's the reason I'm where I am today. The answer to what you were about to ask."

"What did she do?"

"She raised me. She was my mom, my dad, and my best friend. She's a great person. I owe her a lot."

"Why did she have to raise you?"

Stiles was quiet for a while. "My mother was strung out most of the time," he finally answered, his voice barely audible. "She'd be gone for weeks at a time. We had no idea where she was. Then suddenly she'd show up at the door looking like shit and spend a couple of weeks on my grandmother's couch. Sleeping most of the time. Then she'd leave again without even saying good-bye. It was a constant cycle."

Gillette grimaced. "That must have been hell."

"It made me cry when I was a kid. When I was a teenager, it just pissed me off."

"Did you ever talk to her about it?" Gillette asked, thinking about the day he'd approached his mother about her drinking. He was sixteen, and he'd tried to talk to her calmly one afternoon in the kitchen. Getting out only a few words before she'd erupted in a violent rage, hurling pots and pans at him until he ran. His father had warned him that night not to try again, and he never had. He'd never told his father about how he'd saved her life that day she'd fallen in the pool, either. "Ever try to help her?"

"Once."

"What happened?"

"She pulled a gun on me, told me she never did drugs," Stiles replied. "Told me she'd kill me if I ever told anybody she did."

"Jesus."

"After that I joined a gang and dropped out of school."

"I doubt your grandmother was happy."

"She wasn't, but she couldn't control me when I was a teenager. Nobody could."

"Then why is she responsible for where you are today?"

"You know," Stiles said, pointing at Gillette. "You're like a dog on a bone. You just won't let things go."

"Thanks."

"Some things are personal. Sometimes you need to know when to back off."

"You want to tell me," Gillette said calmly. "We all want to tell our secrets to someone," he said, repeating what Tom McGuire had said.

"What are you, some kind of amateur psychiatrist?"

"I analyze people all the time, Quentin. It's the most important skill I have. I have to motivate people. You can't motivate them until you understand them."

"Don't you mean manipulate them? Isn't that really what you do?" Stiles looked over at Gillette. "Yeah, I've been watching."

"Call it what you want," Gillette said sharply, "but I have to be able to make people believe in themselves even when everything is falling down around them. If that takes a certain amount of manipulation, so be it. In the end, they're better off and so am I. Which is all that matters."

"Just because you think you can get inside other people's heads doesn't mean you can get inside mine."

"You told me about your mother's drug problem."

"Yeah, I did," Stiles murmured, looking out the window. "I haven't told anyone about that in a long time."

"So," Gillette pushed, "why is your grandmother responsible for where you are?"

Stiles checked the intersection while they waited for the light to change. "One day me and my boys get into it with a gang from a neighborhood a few blocks over, and I end up getting shot in the chest."

"One of the scars you showed me," Gillette said, pointing to the spot on his own chest. "Right?"

"Yeah. When I'm better, my grandmother has two neighbors drag me down to the Army recruiting office in Times Square and make me enlist. I was cursing and screaming all the way down in the cab, but it was the best thing that ever happened to me."

"They might have dragged you down there, Quentin, but they couldn't *make* you enlist. You had to do that yourself."

"True. But, while I'm standing there looking at this hard-assed-looking white guy with a high and tight haircut and a mean-motherfucker stare, I realize I have to get out of Harlem. Even though I hate the guy, I know he's my best shot at making something of myself. Otherwise there'll be another gang fight, and I'll end up getting shot again. Things might not have turned out all right that time."

"Is your grandmother still alive?" Gillette asked.

"Yup. She still lives in the same projects."

"How old is she?"

"Seventy-two."

"What about your mother? Do you keep in touch with her?"

"No."

"Why not?"

"She was killed a week after I left for basic. Shot by a cop in a drug bust at a crack house a few blocks from my grandmother's place."

Gillette looked away.

"What about you?" Stiles asked after a long pause. "Where'd you grow up?"

Gillette turned back around. He hadn't expected Stiles to be interested. "Beverly Hills."

Stiles groaned. "A 9-0-2-1-0 brat."

"You know it," Gillette said unapologetically. "Spent most of my time in high school at the beach playing volleyball and surfing."

"And chasing girls."

"Yep."

"What does your father do?"

Gillette looked out the window. "He's dead."

"Oh." Stiles hesitated. "How?"

"Plane crash."

"How long ago?"

"Fourteen years."

They were silent for a while.

"Before he died," Gillette finally spoke up, "he ran an L.A. investment bank. Made a killing when one of the big New York houses came in and paid way too much for it. Stayed on to run it for the New York people for two years after the deal, then went into politics. Won a seat as a United States congressman in his first campaign, then became a senator after one term in Congress."

"Never went without very much did you?"

"I can't remember ever going without *anything*," Gillette admitted matter-of-factly. "Christmas was just another day." Until he was twenty-two, anyway.

"I didn't know there *was* a Christmas until I was six and one of my friends told me about it."

"That's tough."

"Got any brothers and sisters?" Stiles wanted to know.

Gillette took a deep breath. He'd lied to Faith about this one, too. Not because he didn't trust Faith. He just didn't want to talk about it. But Stiles had revealed some painful things, and it wouldn't be fair to hold back. "I have an older brother and a younger sister."

"Keep in touch with them?"

Gillette shook his head.

"Why not?"

"I just don't."

"Where did you go to college?" Stiles continued, unfazed by the warning tone in Gillette's voice.

"Princeton."

"Figures. Dad get you in?"

"I think the performing arts building he paid for probably had something to do with it."

"And after Princeton?"

"Stanford Business School. Then I joined Goldman Sachs. That's an investment bank based here in New York."

Stiles grunted. "I *know* what Goldman Sachs is," he said, irritated.

"Oh. Well, I spent a couple of years in their mergers and acquisitions group before Bill Donovan offered me a job at Everest Capital."

"I thought Goldman Sachs was the most prestigious investment bank in the world. Why'd you leave?"

"Investment bankers are nothing but agents. All they do is take commissions. They make money off other people's sweat. They make good dough doing it, but I didn't like it. Besides, the real money is in private equity. So is the real satisfaction."

"Why's private equity so much more satisfying?"

"Because you take risks. Lots of risks. You put your money where your mouth is. Investment bankers risk other people's money."

"Is that what gets you off?"

"What?"

"Taking risks. Is that why you play pool in Harlem with no money in your pocket?"

Gillette closed his eyes and allowed his head to fall back against the seat. "Yeah," he admitted.

Stiles chuckled wryly. "How much money is enough, Christian? I mean, your family's already wealthy. Why do you need more? What good is one more beach house that you visit a couple of days a year? One more penthouse apartment in one more European city? Why not enjoy life, instead?"

Gillette stared hard at Stiles for a few moments, Isabelle's image running through his mind. Then Faith's. "It isn't really about the money."

"You just said it was."

"Not in the sense that I can buy more things with it. It's a scorecard. That's all."

"Ah." Stiles nodded. "Well, at least you understand that."

"What are you talking about?"

"It's all about the game for you, all about power and control, about being the puppet master. Making people do what you want and seeing how many balls you can keep in the air at once. Finding out how much capacity your brain really has. How much pressure you can take." Stiles checked the intersection ahead. They were only a few blocks from Everest. "It's all about finding your limits, isn't it?"

Stiles was exactly right, though Gillette wasn't going to admit it. "How would you know?"

"You aren't the first big-money guy I've protected, and you're mostly all the same. You work eighty-hour weeks for twenty years, then you wake up at forty and wonder where the hell your life has gone. So you take six months off to travel the world and spend time with your family. To really get to know them, you tell yourself. After about three months, you find out they aren't really that interesting. Or, worse, they don't find *you* very interesting. You realize you've *got* to get back in the game, so one morning you call an old friend who owns a small but growing financial firm and suddenly you're in the middle of it again and you couldn't be happier." Stiles glanced at a man standing on a corner near the Town Car as they waited at a red light. "It's a curse for guys like you. It's in your blood. You never get rid of it." He looked over at Gillette. "And don't let yourself believe that Isabelle is the answer."

"What are you talking about?"

"I saw the way you were looking at her this morning, and I heard a lot of your conversation. Don't let yourself think there's a fairy tale in all that, that you could be her knight in shining armor. Like I said, it's something you have to watch out for. I've seen it before with you rich guys."

"Quentin, I—"

"Rich, good-looking white boy plucks vulnerable Hispanic girl out of poverty and they end up riding off into the sunset together on a white horse. I know how you think the book reads. Seems romantic, but the reality is very different. She won't fit into your world. Both of you will end up being sorry."

"You're jumping the gun a little. I haven't even gone out with her."

"Don't."

Gillette chuckled. "Quentin, you're jealous. That's what this is all about."

"You're wrong. I'm just trying to give you good advice."

"I thought you didn't talk to your clients."

"I usually don't," Stiles agreed hesitantly.

"So, why me?"

"I don't know," he answered lamely.

"Well, she and I are going to dinner tonight."

Stiles shrugged. "Fine. I don't give a shit."

They were quiet for a few minutes.

"Are you married?" Gillette finally asked.

"Divorced."

"Kids?"

"No."

Gillette hesitated, thinking about the best way to ask the question, but there was only one way—directly. "Was your wife white?"

Stiles's expression remained impassive for a few moments, then he nodded.

"Was she wealthy?"

"Not like you, but her family lived in a nice part of town. You know, big brick houses and Mexican maids."

"Any black families in the area?"

"Not within a mile." Stiles looked over. "I checked."

So Stiles had experienced it firsthand. No wonder he was ringing the warning bell. "My mother was an alcoholic," Gillette said. "On good days she just scared the hell out of me stumbling around the house. On bad days she got her kicks chasing me with a belt."

"Really?"

"Yeah." Gillette paused. "When my father died, my mother cut me off from the family money. She closed my checking account, canceled my credit cards, everything." Gillette looked over and saw that Stiles was suddenly hanging on every word. "I was riding my motorcycle cross-country after graduating from Princeton when my father died. I got the word when I was in western Pennsylvania visiting my grandfather, my father's father. He was poor all his life until Dad made lots of money and made sure he was okay. But he stayed in the same little mining town even after Dad gave him the money. So I'm staying there when my mother called to tell my grandfather his son had died. She called to tell me I was off the payroll. That I was completely on my own. From that point on I had to beg and borrow until I got on my feet." He smiled grimly. "That's when I picked up pool. It took me almost six weeks to get back to California, and I played every day for food money. You get good fast when the price of losing is starving."

"Why did it take you six weeks to get back to the West Coast? I thought you said you had a motorcycle."

"The clutch burned out right as I got to my grandfather's place. It was in the shop when my mother called to cut me off. All I had on me was a hundred bucks, so I sold the thing for a grand to the mechanic who was working on it, and I road freight trains back to California."

Stiles gave Gillette a look that suggested he thought Gillette was truly insane. *"What?"*

"Yeah. There was a Conrail main line that went through my grandfather's town. I jumped on an empty box car one afternoon while the train was dropping off coal cars at the electric plant at the edge of town. Six weeks later, I was in L.A. I love trains now."

"Why didn't you ask your grandfather for cash? You said your father gave him money when he sold the investment bank."

Gillette shook his head. "He didn't know how things were between my mother and me. It would have killed him to find out. Besides, I don't ask *anyone* for money."

"Then how did you pay for Stanford Business School?"

"Worked two jobs and took out a student loan."

"But I thought you didn't ask anyone for money."

"When it's their business, I don't care."

"Uh-huh."

"And I paid back every cent of that loan. Early, too. I wasn't one of those kids who welshed." Gillette hesitated. "I'm telling you all this because I want you to know I've made everything I have on my own."

Stiles was quiet for a few moments. "Why did your mother do it?" he finally asked. "Why did she cut you off?"

Gillette took a deep breath. "Because she wasn't really my mother."

Stiles gave Gillette a confused look. "What do you mean?"

"You asked me if I kept in touch with my brother and sister. I told you that I didn't."

"Yeah, so?"

"They're actually my *half* brother and *half* sister," Gillette answered, his voice a whisper. "My father had an affair with a young Hollywood actress."

"And your *step*mother couldn't handle it."

"It drove her insane."

"Do you ever talk to your real mother?"

"I don't even know who she is," Gillette admitted. "All I know is that she's a star now."

As they turned onto Park Avenue from Fifty-first, a blue sedan darted alongside the Town Car, then slammed into the front passenger door of the vehicle, hurling Stiles into Gillette and Gillette against the door. Gillette's head hit the window hard, and for a few seconds his vision blurred. When it cleared, he looked up and out the window. Directly into the barrel of a gun.

There was a single gunshot just as Stiles threw himself in front of Gillette.

Gillette strained his neck to see over Stiles's shoulder, but the assassin was gone.

For a few moments Gillette heard someone moaning on the street outside the vehicle. Then nothing.

16

The Urge to Trust. *Even the most skeptical and cynical among us are, at times, vulnerable to deception. In the same way that we struggle to keep secrets to ourselves, we want to believe that those we've chosen to associate or partner with will not hurt us. Perhaps because we want to believe our ability to assess character is superior. Because we want to believe we are so endearing that others would hate to take advantage of us. Or because we desperately want to believe people are inherently good. For whatever reason, even the most experienced and savvy have their moments of vulnerability.*

It is then that the enemy can advance.

GILLETTE HUSTLED ACROSS THE SIDEWALK toward the entrance to the Everest building. Stiles was a few feet ahead of him; one of Stiles's men was close behind.

When they were through the revolving door and inside the elevator, Gillette leaned back against the car wall and let out a long breath. "Well, Quentin," he said, "I bet you didn't think the financial world would ever be this exciting."

Stiles motioned to his subordinate to stay behind in the lobby, then pressed the button for thirty-two. He and Gillette were the only people in the car. "No, I didn't," he admitted, shaking his head. "Which reminds me, my fee's going up."

"Oh, *I* see," Gillette shot back, his voice rising. "Things get a little rough and you bail on me."

"I'm not bailing on you," Stiles snapped. "I just want to get paid right for the risk. You understand that, don't you? Just like in finance. Risk, reward."

"What I understand is you're changing the deal on me."

"I didn't get all the information when I signed on."

"I told you about the limousine outside the church. That was all you needed to know."

Stiles pointed at Gillette. "I'm gonna guess that at some point you changed a deal on somebody."

"Well, I—"

"Besides, I'm not changing the deal," Stiles interrupted. "I'm in, as agreed. *And I will keep you alive.*" He slipped his hands into his pockets and leaned back against the wall, too. "You sure as hell pissed somebody off, or you've got something they want."

"I've got something they want."

"You're probably right. In your world people want money more than revenge."

As the elevator rose, Gillette's mind flashed back to the image of the pistol aimed at him from outside the window. Of how, for a split second, he'd thought he was dead. How, when he'd heard the gun go off, he'd expected a flash of excruciating pain, then nothing. Then he'd realized that the shot had come from the gun of one of the two men Stiles had trailing them in another vehicle, that the assassin had been hit.

For a brief moment afterward, he had lain sprawled on the seat, wondering if it was all worth it. Wondering if Faith and Stiles were right, if it was time to enjoy life a little. Maybe having an empire wasn't all it was cracked up to be.

"Hopefully the cops will get something out of the guy when he wakes up after surgery."

"If they do," Stiles answered, "they're miracle workers."

"Why?"

"He died in the ambulance."

"Oh." Death. So close. He could almost feel it.

The first two attacks had shaken Gillette, but hadn't made him consider getting out, or actually think about death. But now it was clear that whoever was behind the attacks wasn't going to stop until he was dead—or they were. And this time he'd stared right down the barrel of the gun.

"Maybe they can ID him and still find out something. Link him to whoever's behind this."

"Don't count on that, either," Stiles said dismissively. "My guess is they'll find out he was some random thug who got half the cash before and would have gotten the other half after."

"Your cup's running over with optimism."

"Comes with the turf."

The elevator slowed as it approached the thirty-second floor: Everest Capital.

"Quentin," Gillette spoke up as the doors parted. "I . . ." He dropped his voice. "I appreciate what you did in the car." He stopped outside the elevator. Far enough away from the Everest receptionist that she couldn't hear. "You put yourself between me and a bullet."

"Reflex," Stiles said firmly. "Nothing else."

"Still, I—"

"That's what you get from me, Christian. Execution." Stiles hesitated. "Look, somebody wants you dead, and that won't be the last time they try. Whoever *they* are," he added after a beat.

"How are we going to find out who *they* are?" Gillette asked, following Stiles as he headed toward the receptionist. "The cops haven't been able to."

As of yesterday afternoon, the New York City Police Department had no leads on who had blown up the limousine, and the New Jersey State Police were still coming up empty on the attack in Hightstown. The car the shooter had been driving in New Jersey—the one that had stopped directly ahead of Gillette's at the traffic light—had been left at the scene, but it was stolen.

"I'm working on it," Stiles answered. "Oh, by the way, I've implemented a new policy here at Everest." He acknowledged another of his men who was standing inside the lobby doorway. "And the guy waiting in your office won't be very happy about it. Also, from now on, I need to be informed at least thirty minutes in advance any time you plan to change locations. No exceptions. Got it?"

"What if I have to go to the head and I can't wait that long?"

"*Christian.*"

Gillette held up one hand. "All right."

Stiles shook his head. "You aren't taking this seriously enough. A guy just tried to kill you. I can't believe you—"

"*Quentin,*" said Gillette firmly, "I'm taking it *very* seriously. I'm just trying not to let it get to me." He patted Stiles on the shoulder. "And, again, thanks for what you did out there. You say it was reflex, but I don't care. It took a lot of guts."

Stiles shrugged. "I can't have one of my clients killed. Bad for business. Besides, I knew you wouldn't be able to get yourself out of the way in time."

"Why?"

Stiles grinned. "You white guys are too slow."

"Hey, any time you want to race, you let me know, pal," Gillette retorted, chuckling as he turned toward his office.

"What happened to you?" Debbie asked as Gillette approached.

"What do you mean?"

She was staring at him intently. "You look like somebody just tried to run you down."

"Is Tom in my office?"

"Don't avoid my question."

"*Deb.*"

She stuck her tongue out. "Yeah, and he's irritated about something."

"What?"

She shrugged "How would I know?"

"That's helpful," Gillette muttered, reaching for the doorknob.

"Sorreeee," she shot back. "Hey, what is *wrong* with you?"

He grimaced. "Nothing. Sorry." He motioned toward the office. "No calls while I'm with Tom. Okay?"

"Okay."

As Gillette opened the door, he glanced over his shoulder. Stiles was speaking to the man posted at the lobby doorway. "Except Quentin," he called to Debbie. "If he needs me, interrupt immediately."

"All right."

"Hello, Tom." Gillette held out his hand as he walked toward the other man.

McGuire was relaxing in one of the chairs in the corner. He stood up as Gillette made it to where he was sitting. "Hello, Christian."

They shook hands and sat down across from each other, the coffee table between them. Gillette saw instantly what Debbie meant. There was something eating at McGuire. "What's the problem, Tom?"

McGuire's eyes shot to Gillette's "What do you mean?"

"You're pissed off at something. I can tell. Usually it's like you're in the middle of a poker game. I wouldn't be able to read your expression if my life depended on it."

"You'd be pissed, too," McGuire snapped.

"Why?"

"I had to give up my gun to that prick by the lobby doorway," McGuire fumed, his face turning red. "What the hell's going on around here?"

The new policy Stiles had referred to. It had to be. Everyone would be searched at the Everest door from now on. No exceptions. "I've put Quentin Stiles in charge of my personal security. What he says goes." Gillette had never even known McGuire carried a gun. "It has to be this way." Stiles had probably implemented the policy just for McGuire. Just to piss him off. But so be it.

"And you took my people off the assignment. From what I understand, Stiles is totally in charge of your security now."

Stiles had made that request yesterday, and Gillette had agreed. "Yeah, that's right."

"I don't understand," McGuire complained. "What's the problem? Don't you trust me?"

"Calm down, Tom."

"*Calm down?* I've got a lot of satisfied customers who'll tell you we've done a tremendous job protecting them. But the guy who owns my business fires me. Now, *you* tell *me*. Should I feel good about that?"

"Tom, I—"

"How much diligence did you do on Stiles before you hired him?" McGuire pushed. "How do you know if he's any good?"

"Oh, he's good."

"How do you know?"

"I was attacked again a few minutes ago, and he saved my life."

McGuire turned his head to the side, as if he'd been struck by something. "*What?*"

"Yeah, right out on Park Avenue."

"What happened?"

"A guy ran his car into mine, then jumped out and tried to shoot me. But one of Stiles's men nailed the guy. They had it covered."

"Jesus," McGuire said softly. "Well, I'm glad you're all right. But I still don't understand why my people were taken off the job." His voice had gotten strong again.

"Too many fingers in the pie, Tom. Simple as that. Stiles wanted his guys on it and nobody else's. I don't know much about personal security, but it made sense to me from an organizational standpoint. Consolidation of leadership and all that. I okayed it."

"What happened to the guy who tried to shoot you?"

"He's dead."

"Good. Whoever's behind all this needs to understand that you're protected by people who know what the hell they're doing." McGuire looked down. "I'm glad Stiles's people are doing a good job."

"Thanks." Gillette stood up and moved to his desk. "You're here today to talk about buying the company." He clicked the computer mouse several times as he moved it around on the pad. "Right?"

"Yes, I—"

"Give me one second, Tom." Gillette punched in the Dominion Savings & Loan ticker and recoiled at what he saw. Dominion's stock price was off six dollars in overnight trading. Off almost 15 percent from yesterday's close. "Christ," he whispered.

"Something wrong?"

"No, nothing." Gillette moved back to the chair and sat down, wondering what was going on with Dominion. Focus, he told himself. On the task at hand. "So let's talk. Earlier this week you offered me 300 million for McGuire & Company."

"Which, according to my backer, is a fair price."

"Of course he'd say that," Gillette replied calmly. "He's on the buy side."

"Whatever. Look, he's pretty connected to Wall Street, and he tells me there've been investment bankers sniffing around Everest offering to take McGuire & Company public. Tells me you guys are close to signing an agreement with one of the Wall Street firms. He says if you do that, I won't have a chance to buy the company."

Gillette shook his head, irritated that the news had gotten out. Probably some young punk associate who couldn't keep his mouth shut had leaked it. "That's right," he admitted.

"What are they telling you they can get for it?"

"Five hundred million." Typically, Gillette would have kept his cards close to his chest, but McGuire needed to understand how big the difference in offers was. "Two hundred million more than you'll pay. That's a huge gap. One I can't ignore. I have a responsibility to my limited partners to listen to these guys. I'd have a lot of unhappy investors if they found out I had passed on $200 million."

"You're telling me the investors wouldn't be happy if you doubled their money? Which is what $300 million does."

"Not if I left two hundred on the table."

"They wouldn't have to know."

"Somebody would find out, Tom. Somebody would have a contact at one of the investment banks we're talking to. Just like your backer does. Then all of our partners would know, and I'd be out of a job."

"Yeah, well, your investors can kiss my ass," McGuire snapped. "They don't see how hard it is to run this company. They don't see the crap Vince and I deal with. The tough decisions we make on a daily basis. The risks we take. They don't see any of that. They don't deal with the stress."

"And they're happy not to," Gillette replied. "They just want to make as much money as they can, and they don't give a damn about your stress. That's why they have us hire you. To deal with all that."

McGuire took a deep breath, trying to keep his cool. "I don't know a lot about IPOs, but doesn't the process take a while? Isn't there a lot of back and forth with the SEC?"

"Usually," Gillette agreed.

"And isn't that market unpredictable? One day, IPOs are everywhere. The next, the door shuts and nothing goes public for a year."

"That can happen."

"Well, the deal I'm offering you will be quick, clean, and ironclad. We could have it done in thirty days. And you won't have people trying to find out if you wear boxers or briefs. We already know everything."

Now that Stiles had taken over his personal security, there was no reason to bargain. "Tom, you should think about how the sweat equity shares we gave you when we bought the company would be worth tens of millions in an IPO," Gillette advised strongly. "And I'll make sure the investment bankers don't lock up your shares. I'll make sure you get cash."

"But our backer is willing to give Vince and me *half* the company if you agree to sell it to him," McGuire countered. "For no money."

McGuire had mentioned that in the limousine, but Gillette wasn't buying it. Giving managers half the company for no money down was outrageous. Ten to 15 percent allocated over three to four years was normal—what Everest usually did. And he'd heard of very experienced executives getting as much as 25 percent, if performance warranted it. But never fifty. That kind of allocation made it nearly impossible for the investors to earn an acceptable return. So, if it was true, there was something strange going on. "Would you get any cash in his deal?"

"Some."

"But not much, right?"

"Enough. Plus, he's willing to double our salaries," McGuire continued quickly. "And, if we keep growing the company, our shares could be worth hundreds of millions a few years down the road."

"How much is enough, Tom?" As Gillette said the words, he realized how ironic they sounded coming from him. He was worth seventy million and he was working eighty-hour weeks—and dealing with assassins. But he needed to put McGuire in a box, so he pressed. "Isn't ten million guaranteed today pretty damn good?"

"No, it isn't. After taxes it would be under five, and that wouldn't be enough for a life's work. Stupid as it sounds, five million doesn't go very far these days. I want more. This is my best shot at *really* cashing in. There won't be another opportunity like this." McGuire spoke faster the more animated he became. "I'm going to turn it back on you. Isn't $300 million enough? Why do you have to be a pig and go for five?"

"It's my duty to my limited partners."

"Well, I have the same duty to myself."

"I can't accept a $200 million discount, Tom. It's that simple."

"After all Vince and I have done," McGuire muttered. "After the way we've slaved over the last three years for you and the rest of your damn partners here at Everest. That's how your going to treat us?"

"It all comes down to the best deal. You know that."

McGuire rose from his chair, glaring down at Gillette. "Screw you and your best deal, Christian," he hissed, turning and stalking from the office.

Gillette watched him go. Happy he'd hired Quentin Stiles.

. . .

"I heard about what happened this morning on Park Avenue," Cohen said, sitting down in front of Gillette's desk. "You all right?"

"Fine," Gillette answered. "Thanks to Stiles." He checked Dominion's stock price quickly. It had dropped another two dollars in early trading. He clicked on the "Company News" option, but there were no stories explaining the price drop. "His guys saved my ass."

"Really?"

"They're very good."

"I'm glad. Obviously."

"Yeah, McGuire was pissed that I called his guys off the job, but it was the right move."

"I saw Tom walking out a few minutes ago. He didn't look very happy."

"He wasn't. But when you saw him, I don't think he was ticked about Stiles taking over."

"What was it then?" Cohen asked curiously.

"Tom and Vince want to buy McGuire & Company back from us."

Cohen straightened up in his chair. "Wow. That's interesting. Did he mention price?"

"Yeah."

"How much?"

"Three hundred million."

"But the investment bankers are talking five hundred." Cohen had been in on the IPO discussions with the investment bankers. "And we're close to signing the deal."

"Which is why Tom's so pissed. He thinks I ought to ignore the I-bankers and take his $300 million offer."

"We couldn't do that. The limited partners would crucify us."

"Which is exactly what I told him. But, of course, he wouldn't listen." Gillette smiled thinly. "He got pretty angry about the whole thing at the end of our meeting."

Cohen took a deep breath. "Maybe it's a good thing you did take his guys off your security detail."

Gillette glanced up from the computer screen. "Ben Cohen," he said quietly. It was the first time he could ever remember Cohen saying something like that. Implying that someone's intent might be evil. "I'm proud of you."

A self-conscious smile played across Cohen's face. "Why?"

"Maybe someday you could take over one of our companies after all. You're finally starting to analyze motivation, not just numbers."

"What do you mean?"

"You think McGuire might be lax with my security because he's bitter that I won't sell him the company, right?"

"Yeah." Cohen hesitated. "You know, I've never really had faith in Tom and Vince."

"Why not?"

Cohen pushed out his lower lip. "I can't put my finger on it. Maybe it's because the whole time we've been involved with them, I've thought they were angling toward this goal. You know, buying the company back from us on the cheap. For a while I was worried they might hold down profits so they could buy it more cheaply, but I don't think they've done that. Not that I can tell, anyway. Probably because you've ridden their asses about performance from the day we acquired the company." Cohen gave Gillette a respectful nod. "I don't think Donovan ever fully appreciated what a great job you've done with that company."

Gillette stared at Cohen for a moment. "Thanks."

"I know Tom respects the hell out of you, Christian," Cohen continued. "He doesn't like you, but he respects you. I overheard him say that to Donovan once."

Starting with the day he'd graduated from Princeton, Gillette's father had urged him over and over never to completely trust anyone in business, but maybe Cohen had just earned it. Maybe he was the exception. They'd known each other for ten years, and Cohen had always been loyal, even after being passed over for chairman. He'd been deeply disappointed, but he'd been able to control his emotions and still be supportive and helpful. Unlike Faraday and Mason, who'd been openly resentful.

"You said you had some information for me," Gillette reminded Cohen.

Cohen cleared his throat. "We heard back from the engineering firm about the seismic shoot in Canada."

"And?"

"It's not good," Cohen said glumly.

"Why?"

"There's oil on the option properties, but not much. Nothing to get excited about, nothing that would really turn the dial in terms of Laurel Energy's value. I spoke to a couple of analysts at the firm earlier this morning. After they gave me the bad news, they said most people are starting to think that there really aren't a lot of big undiscovered fields left up in Canada. That the exploration guys are looking more to fields offshore from Africa and South America. Canada's played, I guess."

"That wasn't what they were telling us a few years ago when we got into this thing."

"Things change. Unfortunately," Cohen continued, "I've got more bad news. Lefors got a call last night from the corporate development people at U.S. Petroleum. They're out. They've terminated the offer to purchase Laurel Energy. U.S. Petroleum's been paralyzed by Harris's death. Nobody can do anything until a new CEO is named and that could take a couple of months."

Gillette rubbed his eyes. A hell of a day this was turning out to be.

"Sorry, Christian," Cohen said gently. "I know you wanted an early win. Selling Laurel to USP at the price they were offering would have been nice."

"What about the $5 million no-go fee?"

"Lefors mentioned that to the USP guys on the call. And they—"

"And they told him to pound sand," Gillette interrupted, anticipating what Cohen was going to say. "They probably told him to litigate."

"Not quite. They told him they'd pay us $500 thousand," Cohen explained. "What do you want me to do?"

"Have you looked at that letter of intent Lefors had USP sign?"

"I scanned it earlier this morning."

"How do you feel about the no-go fee language? Is it tight? Would we win in court?"

"It's pretty tight, but there's one clause in the paragraph that might give them some wiggle room. I'd say the odds would be sixty-forty us if we sued."

Sixty-forty. Not enough to justify several hundred grand in attorney fees. "Tell them we want a million bucks."

"Okay."

"Settle at seven hundred fifty. That's how it'll go down."

"Christian, there is one piece of good news," Cohen spoke up.

"What?"

"Yesterday afternoon a group named Coyote Oil contacted Lefors and started asking questions about Laurel."

"Coyote Oil?" Gillette had never heard of them.

"I've never heard of them either," Cohen acknowledged, reading Gillette's expression. "I'm having Lefors check them out. So far, about all he's been able to find out is that they're based in Casper, Wyoming. They're privately held, so there isn't much information available. Lefors asked them for some general stuff so we could qualify them. They're e-mailing that to us this morning."

"Have Lefors forward a copy of the info to Debbie so she can print it out for me," Gillette instructed.

"Okay."

"It'll be tough to get what USP was offering with the bad news on the option properties. We probably shouldn't even bother with them."

Cohen held up his hand. "Lefors said they were aggressive on the phone. Said they were trying to establish a base up in Canada quickly."

"You just told me Canada was played."

"Maybe they have information we don't. Fortunes are made faster with inside information than through slow and steady. We both know that. They claim they have a big backer, too," Cohen continued when Gillette didn't say anything. "Someone with very deep pockets."

"Everybody has a backer with deep pockets," Gillette said, exasperated, thinking about Tom McGuire. "Who is it?"

"They wouldn't say."

"Of course not." Gillette banged the desk with his fist. "They don't have anyone. They're on a fishing expedition. They aren't real."

"My gut says we give them a chance, Christian. You told me to always have a recommendation for you when I brought up something. Well, here it is: Give this a shot. Let it play out."

Another new wrinkle to Cohen's personality. Normally Cohen never paid attention to his gut—only hard data. Suddenly things were different. "What do you—"

"Like I said, Lefors mentioned to me that they were aggressive on the initial call," Cohen interrupted. "We should at least give them a chance."

"But they aren't going to pay what we want, especially if they're small. Even with a big backer they aren't going to have the strategic in-terest that big boys like U.S. Petroleum have."

Cohen shrugged. "I still think we should follow up."

Gillette studied the other man for a few moments. It seemed strange for Cohen to recommend going forward with a group he'd never heard of. He liked dealing with well-known players. But maybe this was a chance to test his instincts without risking anything but time. "Okay. Knock yourself out."

"Great," Cohen said approvingly, standing up.

"Don't go anywhere. We're not finished."

"What's up?" Cohen sank slowly back into his seat.

Gillette was hesitant to tell Cohen, but he wanted someone else's opinion. He wanted to make certain he wasn't being completely para-noid. And, of everyone he'd thought of going to, Cohen seemed like the best choice. Gillette took a deep breath. He was starting to trust the man. "Yesterday, Senator Stockman met with Paul Strazzi."

Cohen had been checking his notepad. "So?" he asked, glancing up. "He's probably just trying to shake Strazzi down for votes. The same way he tried to with you."

"They met in a Bronx warehouse. If the senator was looking for votes, he'd meet Strazzi at Apex."

"A Bronx warehouse?" Cohen asked curiously. "Really?"

"Yes."

"That is strange. How'd you find out?"

"I had Stiles put one of his people on Strazzi," Gillette explained.

"What do you figure is going on?"

Gillette hesitated, thinking about the best way to explain. "I had lunch earlier this week with Stockman."

"At the Racquet Club. I remember. And?"

"We hadn't even ordered and Stockman was turning up the heat on me about backing his campaign. Said he wanted me to tell our portfolio company employees to vote for him. Said he wanted to use our facilities for speeches and photo ops, and use our TV and radio network to support him."

"Incredible."

"Yeah, but I didn't bite. I said I wouldn't do it. I'm sure it was all he could do not to throw his gin and tonic against the wall."

"He told you how you'd have an enemy in Washington, I bet."

"Exactly," Gillette confirmed. "But there was something else."

"What?"

"He started talking about Dominion."

"Dominion Savings & Loan?"

"Yeah."

"What did he say?"

"He made it sound like he had information proving that we with-held data from the SEC during the IPO process, that the loan portfolio was in much worse shape than we reported. Basically, he said we de-frauded the public investors."

"That's ridiculous."

Gillette glanced out the window. It was a clear, beautiful day. The temperature had finally risen above freezing again. "Is it?"

"What do you mean?"

"Donovan and Marcie did that thing on their own. We never talked about it much at weekly meetings."

Cohen put a finger to his lips and thought for a moment. "That's true."

"So, how would we know what went on there?"

"The accountants were all over Dominion from the day we bought it," Cohen pointed out. "They would have found something."

"They didn't at Enron or Worldcom. Or any of the other big-company accounting scams. And Bill was very tight with the senior part-ner at the accounting firm on the audit."

"But banks and savings and loans are different. There's federal and state examiners, too. There's so much scrutiny someone would have fig-ured out what was going on."

"Not necessarily. As long as people keep putting money in, you can keep playing the shell game. You know, credit one person's loan payment with someone else's deposit."

"Yeah, but—"

"Stockman also claimed there were payments sent out to insiders *after* the IPO. Payments that shouldn't have been made."

"Fraudulent payments?"

"Yes."

Cohen spread his arms wide. "How in the world would Stockman know about all this?"

"From someone inside Dominion," Gillette answered. "Or someone inside Everest."

"No way," Cohen argued.

"Ben, don't go naïve on me again."

"Who then?" Cohen demanded. "Who's the rat?"

"Obviously, it wouldn't have been Donovan," Gillette answered.

"Obviously." Cohen stared at Gillette for a few moments, then his eyes grew wide. *"Marcie?"*

"I didn't say that."

"You implied it."

Gillette pursed his lips. "Yes, I did," he agreed quietly.

"But she'd be crazy to leak information like that," Cohen protested. "If Stockman used what she told him, she'd face criminal charges. Why would she implicate herself?"

"Why would she necessarily implicate herself?"

"Because . . ." Cohen's voice trailed off as he put the pieces together.

"Right," said Gillette, seeing that Cohen understood. "Donovan's dead. All the blame can be shoveled into his grave. They can say he was the one responsible for working with the auditors and someone at the company to hide what was going on. It's perfect."

"If what you're saying is true, then Donovan was murdered," Cohen whispered. "Whoever was responsible would need him out of the picture."

"Agreed."

"But why? What's the endgame?"

Gillette leaned back and ran his hands through his hair. "Who's our biggest rival?"

"Apex," Cohen answered right away.

"Right. Paul Strazzi. He doesn't want us to raise this next fund. He wants me to fail in the worst way. And he hated Bill. He'd want nothing more than to destroy Bill's legacy."

"But enough to have him killed?"

"Miles Whitman warned me that Strazzi would do anything to screw us. *Anything.* I think he was right. I think Strazzi was willing to do anything. And he did it."

A troubled expression clouded Cohen's face. "I still don't see the endgame. So we get some bad press on Dominion for a while if what Stockman told you turns out to be true. So what? Raising the new fund goes on hold for a while until we sell a few more portfolio companies at good prices and we continue to show the investment community how we kick ass in private equity. I still don't think Strazzi would kill someone to *maybe* put our next fund on hold temporarily."

"Exactly," Gillette agreed, leaning forward over the desk.

"Exactly *what?*"

"None of it would make sense if Strazzi thought he'd only be able to put us on hold temporarily. But it might if he thought he could take us out of the game permanently. Or take us over."

"Take us over?"

Cohen's reaction to this was going to be interesting. "Donovan's widow dropped by to see me."

"What did she want?"

"To let me know that her most important asset in the world was her stake in Everest. And to let me know she was worried about it."

"Why?"

"Someone warned her there were problems with our portfolio companies. With the liquid stuff, too."

"You mean our leftover IPO shares."

Gillette nodded.

"Like Dominion."

"Yes." Gillette checked Dominion's stock price again—off another dollar. "Then I have lunch with Stockman. When I wouldn't let him use Everest as his personal campaign platform, he goes off into the Dominion thing."

"You think Stockman is the one who spoke to the widow."

"Or one of his aides."

"Did you ask the widow who approached her?"

"She wouldn't say."

Cohen put his head back against the chair. "Are you worried the widow might sell her Everest stake? I mean, whoever buys it could call a vote, then use the 25 percent voting share that goes with the stake to elect their own chairman."

"The thought had crossed my mind."

"But, like I said before, so what? What if there's some bad stuff going on at Dominion? I don't think that alone would cause the widow to sell her stake. Dominion having problems wouldn't decrease the value of her investment that much."

"What if we had to reverse the entire transaction and pay a couple of billion bucks back to the public investors?"

Cohen cringed.

"And pay a huge fine on top of the two billion if the SEC proved that we conspired to conceal information from the auditors," Gillette continued. "On top of all those headlines the widow is reading in the newspapers, what if she thought there were problems with some of the Everest portfolio companies, too."

Cohen squinted. "Problems? Like what?"

Cohen had always been focused internally. On administration. On human resources, accounting issues, and the limited partners. Making certain they were kept constantly updated on events at the portfolio companies.

Every ninety days Cohen was responsible for compiling reports on each of Everest's companies and sending them out to the limiteds. Reports that included summary financial statements for the first three quarters of the year, and full-blown audited numbers for year-end. The reports described important events that had occurred at the companies during the previous ninety days—an acquisition, a major new product rollout, a strategic partnership. All things that would make the limited partners feel good about the portfolio companies—and, therefore, their investment.

One thing the quarterly reports rarely contained was bad news. Only when bad news was about to be reported by the press was it relayed to the investors.

Cohen had no way of knowing about dirty little secrets at the portfolio companies because dirty little secrets weren't discussed at the weekly managing partner meeting with Donovan. Donovan didn't want Cohen or Faraday knowing about them. He thought that the fewer people who knew about the bad stuff, the better. He felt Cohen was too much of a straight arrow and might insist that some of the dirty laundry be communicated to the limited partners, that Cohen might argue it was their fiduciary duty to disclose it. And Donovan knew about Faraday's drinking. He was worried Faraday might say something to someone who mattered after one too many scotches.

Donovan was keenly aware that much of business was psychological, that markets were fickle and could sway drastically on rumor and conjecture. These days so many conclusions were drawn based on snippets of information, companies could easily be convicted in the court of public opinion without having done anything wrong.

So Donovan had controlled bad information. Portfolio company problems were discussed in separate, off-site meetings. Only Donovan, Gillette, and Mason participated in those meetings because they were the only ones who held chair positions at Everest's portfolio companies.

Gillette gazed at Cohen, weighing the risk of telling him these things. The guy might have a panic attack and send out letters on his own to the limited partners, alerting them to the issues. Without approval. Which would create massive problems. Cohen might not understand that portfolio companies *always* had problems, some of which could look insurmountable or even sinister to the outside world. But they usually went away as long as everyone kept their cool.

"I'll give you a for instance," Gillette finally said. "Right now our waste management company has an environmental problem at one of its landfills."

Cohen squinted and swallowed hard. "Which one?"

"Easy, Ben."

"Which one?" Cohen pressed.

"It doesn't matter." The company operated more than thirty landfills, so there'd be no way Cohen could pin the site down. No one at the landfill was going to admit anything if he called around. The few people at the site who knew were under strict orders to say nothing. "I'll tell you that it's one of the rural facilities. It's way away from any major metropolitan area."

Cohen let out a frustrated breath.

"Ben, I'm the chairman of this company. My job is to determine when we can take care of a problem in-house and when a problem gets to the stage that the outside world has to know. Right now, in my judgment, it isn't at that stage."

"But how do you know?"

"You never know for sure."

"You aren't an environmental expert."

"But I'm working with someone who is. That's all I can do."

"What's the environmental problem?" Cohen asked. "Will you tell me that?"

"I will. But you have to keep it quiet. Can you do that?"

Cohen hesitated. "It's a slippery slope, Christian," he said, his voice wavering.

"Ben, at the most senior levels, that's what business comes down to every day. Negotiating slippery slopes. You haven't had any experience doing that. You've lived a protected life at Everest handling administration and looking after the limited partners. Donovan, Mason, and I have dealt with the tough stuff."

"Tell me what's going on."

Gillette eased back in the chair and put his feet up on the desk. "A few weeks ago we found out that a large pond on the property is contaminated. There are very high levels of mercury in the water. Everything in it basically floated to the top, belly up. Apparently, the people who operated the landfill before we bought the company were burying toxic drums in a field beside the pond and they've leaked into the groundwater. We found the drums last week, and we think we can contain the spill. I don't think we'll have to go to the EPA."

"Christian, that's ridiculous. You *have* to tell the EPA."

"Do you know how much money it would cost us if we did?"

"There must be insurance," Cohen argued.

"There's *supposed* to be, but there isn't. And what the EPA would make us go through would probably bankrupt the company. The CFO has already done that analysis."

"*Jesus.*"

"Yeah, Jesus. Now you start to understand what Bill, Troy, and I have had to deal with."

"What else is hiding out there in our portfolio companies?" Cohen asked quietly.

"That I know about?"

"Don't be funny, Christian."

"I'm not being funny; I'm being dead serious. What you have to understand, Ben, is that there are *always* problems at every portfolio company. You just have to learn how to deal with them. And the keys to doing that are figuring out how quickly can you get your hands around the problem, what can you do about it, and, most important, not letting it get to you. Ever. That's mostly what being chairman of a company is all about. Staying calm no matter what."

"What else is out there?" Cohen repeated tersely, uninterested in the lesson.

Gillette stared at Cohen for a moment. This was so risky. "We've got an issue at the records management company in California. One of our employees sold personal information to a direct marketing company."

"You got to be shitting me."

"Nope."

"What kind of information?"

"Drivers licenses, credit card numbers, home addresses."

Cohen's eyes widened. "My God. What steps have we taken?"

"The employee who sold the information was fired, and we're trying to assess what liability the company has. We've also alerted senior executives at the company that bought the information about what happened, that one of their midlevel managers was buying the information. They are cooperating with us fully. They fired their guy as well."

"Have you notified the individuals whose information was sold without their permission?"

"No."

"Why not?" Cohen demanded.

"It involved over twenty thousand people."

"So?"

"I can't have the California consumer advocacy people in there at this point. They're worse than the Gestapo. I haven't told you this, Ben, but we're no more than six months away from taking this company public, too. At the price the I-bankers are talking, it would be a ten times return for us. It would be one of the best investments we've ever made. If this thing leaks, the IPO could be delayed indefinitely."

"But these individuals have had their private information sold. Who knows what the people at the direct marketing company have done with the stuff."

"We're trying to figure that out. Trying to contain the spill. Just like at the landfill. So far there's no indication anything bad has happened. No indication that there have been illegal charges made on credit cards or anything like that. We think the guy bought the stuff just so he could target a set of consumers for a new product introduction."

Cohen looked out the window at something in the distance.

Gillette raised one eyebrow. "So, you still want to be chairman of one of our companies, Ben?"

"My God, it can't be like that at all of them."

"It isn't," Gillette agreed. "And the company I give you might be clean when you take over. The thing is, two weeks after you become chairman, you might get hit between the eyes with something out of left field." He hesitated, thinking through a scenario. "Let's say I make you chairman of our grocery store chain. At first, everything's great. Then one of our tractor trailers plows into a father and his three kids at an intersection. The father and two of the kids are killed instantly. The third one lives, but he's paralyzed for life. The cops find out that the truck driver was blind drunk and had cocaine in his system, too. They dig further and find out we aren't administering the required drug tests to our drivers. The mother of the three kids files a $500 million lawsuit, and the insurance company tells you they won't cover it because a clause in the policy says they aren't responsible for claims if we aren't administering drug tests. A $500 million settlement will bankrupt the company. You think the amount is absurd, but your lawyer isn't so sure. All the jury would hear about at the trial is that Everest Capital manages $20 billion. The woman might actually have a chance of getting her $500 million." Gillette crossed his arms over his chest. "What do you do, Mr. Chairman?"

Cohen hesitated, struggling for an answer. "I . . . I don't know."

"'I don't know' doesn't cut it, Ben."

"Well, I—"

"Let me throw you another curve. The state's attorney general's office decides the company has been negligent in the whole thing. They decide to press criminal charges against the senior executives. Which, by the way, is very possible. Guess what? You're the most senior executive of all. They show up at Everest and take you away. The news cameras are set up and rolling when you come out of the building and your girls see you in shackles, trying to hide your face."

Cohen shook his head. "All right, what would you do in that situation?"

Gillette smoothed his tie. "You wouldn't want to know, Ben," he finally answered, his tone guarded.

Cohen glanced at Gillette uncertainly, wanting to press but afraid, too. "How would Stockman be able to find out about these problems?" he asked.

"Simple. Troy Mason."

"Oh, shit. That's right."

"Troy knows all the stuff I just told you about," Gillette continued.

"See, there was this other weekly meeting you didn't know about, Ben. An off-site meeting, usually at a condo Bill rented on the Upper East Side. Bill, Troy, and I discussed all the major problems at all the portfolio companies at it so Troy was in on everything. He could give Strazzi a lot of information. Strazzi would then pass it on to Stockman. In fact, it wouldn't surprise me if Troy made copies of a few files in the days after Donovan died as an insurance policy. So he'd be sure to remember it all and be able to back up what he was saying with proof. In case he didn't get the nod to be chairman of Everest."

"Strazzi would have the money to buy the widow's stake in Everest," Cohen pointed out.

"One of the few people who would," Gillette agreed. "And, knowing Strazzi, he'd probably get it at a discounted value."

"We could make her an offer, too," Cohen suggested.

Gillette shook his head. "Nah. The only way we'd be able to come up with that kind of cash would be to use her stake as collateral. Bankers wouldn't lend us any money against it if they thought there were problems with our portfolio. And, believe me, Strazzi would make certain every banker in New York thought there was."

Cohen's face went pale. "You know what this means? It means Strazzi's the one trying to kill you."

Gillette stared at Cohen for a few moments. "I thought of that, too, but it doesn't make much sense. I can see why Strazzi would want Donovan gone, but not me."

"Why not?"

"He'd need Donovan dead so he could put the blame for Dominion on him. But he can get me out of the way by getting the widow's stake. Why risk being linked to another murder if there's another, less risky way to get what you want? Strazzi's ruthless but not stupid."

"I don't know," Cohen said, pulling a piece of paper from his pad and placing it on Gillette's desk. "If he's willing to commit one murder, why not another? I think we should go to the cops."

"With what?"

"With what we just talked about."

"We've got no proof."

Cohen bit down on his lower lip. "We should at least give the cops a heads-up."

"What's this?" Gillette asked, glancing at the paper Cohen had put down on his desk.

"Your consent to my becoming Everest's chief operating officer. You need to sign it."

Gillette leaned back. "This seems kind of formal."

Cohen shrugged but said nothing.

"Is it really necessary?"

"I told you," Cohen said, his tone turning serious, "I want people to know I have complete authority from you to do what I need to do. When you send out the e-mail, I want you to tell everyone about this," he said, nodding at the paper.

"All right," Gillette agreed, picking up a pen. He scribbled his signature at the bottom. "Here you go." His expression brightened as he handed the consent document to Cohen. "You know what just occurred to me, Ben?"

"What?"

"You haven't used Latin the entire time you've been in here."

Cohen nodded. "Hey, I'm trying to listen to the boss."

17

Conspiracy. *Two or more individuals working together in the shadows to carry out evil—assassination, overthrow, fraud.*

The strength of a conspiracy is measured by the commitment, planning, and ability of the conspirators to maintain secrecy.

But the success of a conspiracy is ultimately determined by the ability of the conspirators to make all traces of their bond evaporate after the crime is committed. Like specters fading into the mist, their relationships vanish, trails grow cold, and there is nothing and no one to connect.

Then no person of authority will question what has been achieved. Or, if they do, nothing can be proven or altered. And those who have been targeted—dead or alive after the crime—never get the justice they deserve.

TOM MCGUIRE CROSSED WILLOW STREET, striding deliberately, and moved down the sidewalk toward the Brooklyn Heights promenade—a wide walkway overlooking New York Harbor. From here, he had a panoramic view of Lower Manhattan.

McGuire ambled up to the black, wrought-iron fence at the edge of the promenade. Below him, cars and trucks roared up and down the Brooklyn-Queens Expressway. He leaned both arms on the top of the fence and checked his watch. Three minutes in front of noon. Three minutes early. He was always on time and despised people who were routinely late. People like Christian Gillette. Of course, he despised Gillette for more important reasons now.

"Hi, Tom."

McGuire turned toward the voice. His brother, Vince, moved up to the fence beside him. Three years younger, Vince was short and dark. A fireplug who wore his black hair slicked back and sported a gold bracelet and a pinkie ring. It was hard for Tom to believe they'd come from the same parents. About the only things they had in common were being at the FBI before founding McGuire & Company, punctuality, and poker faces.

"So?" Vince began in his gravelly voice. He'd smoked a pack of ciga-rettes a day until five years ago, when a doctor thought he'd detected a spot on Vince's lung. It had turned out to be a false alarm, but it had been enough to scare Vince away from tobacco for good. His voice still bore the scars of the habit. "What's the deal?"

"I met with Gillette this morning and he wouldn't budge. He's not interested in $300 million."

"Our guy won't go any higher?"

Tom shook his head. "No. Says if he pays more than three hundred his people will question him too hard, and he *definitely* doesn't want that. Neither do we. So we stick to the original plan."

Vince spat over the fence at a truck whizzing past beneath them. "What the hell happened on Park Avenue this morning?"

"Stiles's men were too quick. They've turned out to be very good, and our guy fucked up."

"Gillette's a tough target."

Tom ground his teeth. "Yeah, but remember we're using people we don't know well because we don't want any connection to us when this is over. Unfortunately, the people we've hired have turned out to be idi-ots. Look, we're gonna have to go to somebody we trust."

"But if they're caught—"

"I know, I know," Tom cut in, scratching his head.

Vince spat again. "Fuck Gillette. If he knew what was really going on, he'd sell us the thing for $300 million in a heartbeat. Then we don't get in any deeper."

"But then our guy doesn't get what he *really* wants."

"Fuck him, too," Vince shot back over his shoulder. "You know what? I think we just keep delaying our side of the deal until we buy the company. What's he going to do at that point? Go to the authorities? No way. He's in as deep as we are."

"Not quite."

"Deep enough," Vince said loudly.

"Look, he's smarter than that. He'd figure out what we were up to when thirty days from now Gillette's still alive. He'd make the closing, and his money, contingent on us doing what we promised to do—kill Gillette." Tom saw that his brother was getting uncomfortable. "Vince, we've got to stick with the original plan," he urged. "And, the next time we go, we've got to *make sure* we get Gillette."

Vince gazed out over the harbor, a pained expression on his face. "I don't know," he muttered. "This thing's getting too close. I mean, Donovan was easy. No way to link us to that." He took a deep breath. "But Gillette's becoming a problem."

"There's another problem." Tom hadn't told Vince everything. Hadn't wanted to upset him. "And it's a big one."

Vince glanced up. "What is it?"

"Gillette's close to signing an IPO deal with a Wall Street firm."

"To IPO *McGuire & Company?*" Vince asked incredulously.

"Yeah."

"You gotta be kidding. That prick. When did he tell you?"

"He didn't," Tom answered. "Our guy found out through a contact of his."

"What a shit Gillette is. He was gonna sell our company right out from under us."

"That's why I had to go to him last week and put the $300 million offer on the table. Our guy told me Gillette was going to sign with the investment bank in the next day or two. If he did that, we'd have no chance of buying the company. So I figured I could buy us some time with the offer. I figured Gillette would think twice about signing up to sell the company if we were pissed off. Then he went and hired Quentin Stiles."

"So we've got no choice," Vince said in a resigned voice. "We have to get Gillette."

"Yep. And fast."

Vince let out a long, exasperated breath. "All right," he said quietly.

"It's just a damn good thing that bomb in the limo went off thirty seconds early," Tom spoke up. The bomb had been set to detonate at a certain time. It wasn't controlled by a remote device, as McGuire had told Gillette. "It would have been a fiasco if it had gone off on time and Gillette had been killed then."

"Hey," Vince piped up angrily, "I thought I had a green light. The guy says he wants Gillette dead. I'm just trying to do my job. I didn't know it was premature."

"Easy, brother," Tom said gently. Vince's fuse was short. "I told you before it was my fault. I didn't know there was another agenda, that things had to happen in a certain order, that they had to get Mason out of the way before we could go after Gillette. I thought we had a green light, too."

"Was he pissed?"

"Oh, yeah."

"Well, everything turned out okay. So he shouldn't be—"

"Look, he's still backing us isn't he? He's over it."

Vince grunted. "Shit, the way things are going, that might have been our best shot to get Gillette."

"He's like a damn cat," Tom agreed. "It's like he's got nine lives or something."

"Yeah, and we've only taken a few shots at him so he's got a lot more left." Vince turned to look at his brother. "The guy Stiles's people killed today on Park Avenue—any way at all he can be linked to us?"

"No," Tom said firmly. "It was all in cash between us, and there were no relationships between him and anyone at our firm. I checked before I hired him." He chuckled. "Besides, the cops aren't buying Stiles's explanation that it was a hit gone bad. They think it was a case of road rage. Some woman at the scene told the cops she saw the whole thing. That the guy driving Gillette's car cut our guy off. That the guy jumped out of the car screaming and yelling with a gun right after he got cut off." Tom laughed harder. "Sometimes it's better to be lucky than good. I can guarantee you our guy wasn't screaming and yelling."

"Why would the woman lie like that?"

"Who the hell knows? Maybe she liked the attention she was getting from the cops."

"What about cell phone calls?" Vince asked.

"What do you mean?"

"Did he ever call you on his cell?"

"Never. Always used a pay phone and a prepaid calling card."

"You can't be sure of that."

"I'm sure, Vince. When he called, the area codes that came up on my caller ID were always from the cities he was in. And, even if on the off chance he did call me on a cell phone once or twice, so what? What does that prove?"

"Did he talk to you right before he tried to kill Gillette?"

"No. It was the day before."

Vince took a deep breath. "Good."

Tom scanned the area. There was a woman with a baby carriage sitting on a bench fifty feet away. She was definitely out of earshot as long as he kept his voice down. "Look, we've got to get Gillette, and we've to do it fast. You agree?"

Vince nodded.

"And at this point I'd feel better if I called in someone I had complete faith in. I know it's risky. I know it could link us, but we don't have any choice."

"Who are you thinking about?" Vince asked.

"Dominick," Tom answered immediately. "He's the best."

Vince looked out over the harbor for a few moments, then finally nodded. "Yeah, call him."

Cohen emerged from the Clark Street subway station into bright sunlight and glanced at his watch. One fifteen. He was early, but he wasn't familiar with Brooklyn Heights so being early was good. He had no idea how far the walk was.

"Excuse me," he called to a woman passing by.

"What?" she snapped.

"Which way is the promenade?"

She pointed. "That way. Just keep walking. You can't miss it."

Mason sat down in front of Strazzi's desk. As usual, Strazzi was smoking a big fat cigar. Mason hated smoke, especially cigar smoke. "Hello, Paul."

"Mr. Strazzi."

Mason's eyes flashed to Strazzi's. Yesterday, Strazzi hadn't wanted that. "Huh?"

"Call me 'Mr. Strazzi' today."

"Why?"

"Because I feel like it."

Strazzi was certifiable. Mason already sensed that others at Apex thought the same thing but weren't willing to say so because they were afraid they were being listened to. Mason had heard rumors about the office being bugged. But Strazzi was paying him $3 million in salary. Guaranteed for one year, thanks to the employment contract he had signed yesterday. If Strazzi wanted to be called 'Buddha,' so be it. "Um, okay, Mr. Strazzi."

Strazzi took a long drag off the cigar. "It's time for you to earn that big salary I'm paying you, Troy."

"I thought I already was."

"Do you enjoy Vicky, boy?"

Mason glanced up, his head suddenly pounding. He and Vicky had gone to the Parker Meridian Hotel three times this week: two lunches and once after work. "What do you mean?" he asked innocently.

"You know exactly what I mean. You and Vicky are screwing like rabbits." Strazzi was smiling broadly behind his cigar. "I bet your wife would go ballistic if she found out you were banging a secretary." Strazzi laughed harshly. "After less than a week here, too. Nice, Troy."

So pissed off she'd leave him immediately, Mason knew. Melissa had already told him if there was one more incident, she was gone. And that she'd pry as much out of him as the flamethrower lawyer she hired could pry. Running up big legal bills in the process. "Mr. Strazzi, I don't—"

"Don't waste my time, Troy." Strazzi tapped the cigar on the round ashtray. An inch-long ash tumbled to the glass. "I know what's going on, but your secret's safe with me. I just want information."

"Information?"

"Yeah."

"What kind of information?"

"About the Everest portfolio companies."

Mason tugged at his collar. "What about them?"

"I need to know where the problems are."

"Problems?"

"The dirty laundry, boy," Strazzi said, exasperated. "Every private equity firm has problems in the portfolio. I want to know about Everest's."

Mason gazed over the desk at Strazzi. He should have guessed. This was the real reason he'd been hired. "Why?"

Strazzi shook his head. "That's a need-to-know issue, and you don't *need* to know."

Strazzi was trying to cripple Gillette's attempt to raise a new fund. That had to be the objective, Mason thought to himself. He took a deep breath. What the hell. He didn't have any loyalty to Everest. Donovan was gone, and he hated Gillette. The prick had tried to ruin him. "I might be able to tell you a few things."

"I need more than that, Troy. I need hard data. I need proof. I need files."

"I can't get into Everest." Mason sensed an opportunity here. He'd made copies of several files the day after the chairman vote had taken place. "I've been barred from the place permanently. I can't get to the files."

"Use your imagination."

"Why don't you use your rat at Everest?" Mason suggested, certain Strazzi had already tried that. But those files were locked up tight. The Everest chairman and the other person on the board were the only ones with access. Which was why they were having this conversation. "Wouldn't that be easy?"

Strazzi's eyes narrowed. "You know damn well my *rat* can't get to all the files."

All the files. Strazzi had said *all* the files. Which meant his rat could get to *some* of the files. Which also meant his rat was at least a managing director, not some low-level associate. Only managing directors and above sat on boards.

"I might be able to help you out," Mason said, thinking about the file copies locked up in the wall safe in his apartment. "But I want a million bucks."

"Why should I do that?"

"Gillette gave me a million to leave Everest, but I had to sign a separation agreement to get it. One of the terms of the agreement was confidentiality. According to the agreement, I can't convey anything to anyone about the Everest portfolio unless a court makes me do so. I'd be taking a big risk telling you these things."

"You and I both know it would be almost impossible for Gillette to prove anything in court."

"Still."

"I could tell your wife about Vicky if you don't help me."

"What good would that do? Then I definitely won't get you anything." Mason paused. "A million dollars, Mr. Strazzi. It's pocket change for you."

Strazzi said nothing for a few moments, then nodded. "Okay." He eased back in his chair. "Now give me a taste."

"What do you mean?"

"Give me an idea of what kind of problems Gillette has on his hands."

A little preview wouldn't hurt. And he wasn't going to give Strazzi enough to figure anything out on his own. "Everest owns a waste management company."

"Regent Waste. I know that."

Strazzi had done his homework. Of course, you didn't get to be worth $5 billion being unprepared. "One of their landfills has bad contamination problems. The EPA doesn't know."

"Which landfill is it?"

Mason shook his head. "You can read that in the file. After I get my million."

"Half a million now," Strazzi said, "half a million when I have the files."

Mason thought about it for a moment. "All right."

Strazzi took another long puff from the cigar. "What else is there?"

"We—" Mason interrupted himself. "I mean, *Everest* owns a records management company in California. Drivers licenses, credit histories, employments records. There's an issue there, too. Again, government agencies haven't been informed."

"Good." Strazzi smiled. "Half a million will be in your account by close of business today. And I want the files on my desk by seven tomorrow morning. Understand?"

"Yes."

"Say, 'Yes, sir' to me, Troy."

Mason swallowed hard. "Yes, sir."

Strazzi pointed at Mason with the cigar. "If you try to run with my money, my people will find you. And it won't be pretty when they do."

Cohen sat on one end of the bench looking out over New York Harbor at Lower Manhattan. "Hello, Tom."

McGuire sat at the other end of the bench, ten feet away. "Hello, Ben." He didn't look in Cohen's direction either.

"I understand your meeting with Gillette didn't go well," Cohen began.

"Nope. He wouldn't budge. Wouldn't even consider 300 million for McGuire & Company."

"It's because we've got investment bankers telling us they can get five hundred."

"I know."

Cohen continued looking straight ahead. "And Christian was smart enough to hire Stiles. He didn't like you being in charge of his personal security while you were trying to buy the company back. He figured that if he pissed you off, you might tell your boys not to be as diligent as they otherwise would be."

"Did he actually say that to you?" McGuire wanted to know.

"In so many words."

"Fucker."

"Smart fucker." Cohen chuckled. "I told him I'd never really trusted you or Vince."

"Thanks a lot."

"Hey, you're the one who said there couldn't be any proof of connections when this was done. I thought it was a nice touch."

"I did say that. And it *was* a nice touch," McGuire added. "Look, you've got to make sure Gillette doesn't sign a deal with the investment bankers before we can get this in motion."

"All you have to do is execute on your end and there won't be a problem, but you're starting to make me think Christian is untouchable. Our guy is getting very frustrated. When we first decided to start this, I told him you were the best. I sold him hard on you. Now he's wondering. First, you guys blow up that limousine in front of the church, and, second—"

"Hey," McGuire broke in angrily, "you told me I had a green light."

"I also told you I wanted to know before you made any attempts on Christian's life. *Christ,* I would have been killed in that explosion, too."

"How was I supposed to know you were going to be riding with him?" McGuire snapped.

"All I'm saying is that our backer's getting angry. I told him you guys were the best. Don't embarrass me. *Get this thing done.*"

"Gillette's a dead man," McGuire said quietly. "Count on it. We're bringing in the best." He winced. "The problem is that this guy's worked for us before, so there's a connection issue. But he'll get it done," McGuire said confidently. "Despite Quentin Stiles."

"Good." Cohen looked out across the water. "There's something else we have to talk about," he said. "Something that could derail everything."

McGuire glanced over. "Oh?"

"Yeah, and it's going to mean another job."

"Christian."

Gillette looked up from a financial statement he was reviewing. Stiles stood at the office door. "Yes?"

"I have information for you."

"What?"

"That e-mail you got the other night in New Jersey. Right before you were attacked?"

Gillette sat up in the chair. "Did you find out where it came from?"

Stiles nodded. "From a store location in Los Angeles. Beverly Hills, specifically."

Gillette put down his pen slowly. Faith Cassidy had stayed at the Beverly Hills Willshire Hotel. She'd told him that when she called earlier.

The phone rang and Gillette recognized the number on his caller ID. "I have to take this, Quentin."

"Sure." Stiles backed out, closing the door.

Gillette picked up the receiver after the third ring. As agreed. "Hello."

"Falcon?"

"Yes. What do you know?" he asked impatiently.

"Give me the response first."

Gillette nodded, pleased that the informant was sticking to the procedure. "Five." This was the fifth time they had spoken.

"And."

"The season is winter. Now, what do you have?"

"The adversary moved. The subject has been played and will deliver in the morning."

"Thank you," Gillette said quietly. "Call me right away with anything else. Got it?"

"Yes."

Gillette hung up the phone, then opened the top left drawer of his desk. The number was scrawled on a piece of scratch paper hidden below two manila envelopes. He gazed at it for a few moments, then dialed.

"Hello."

Gillette recognized Jose Medilla's voice right away. There was no need to bother with coded confirmations. "Jose, it's Christian." He hesitated. This was a moment he hadn't been looking forward to. One Jose probably hadn't been looking forward to, either.

18

Quid pro quo. *Literally, this for that.*

There's always a quid pro quo. Nothing comes for free.

GILLETTE MOVED INTO THE LOBBY of the Waldorf-Astoria Hotel and headed up the plushly carpeted stairs toward the main lobby. He was surrounded by a security detail—five of Stiles's men. Stiles was already inside securing the lobby and dining room.

Earlier in the afternoon, Gillette had increased Stiles's fee to ten thousand dollars a day—over Cohen's protest. Stiles was dedicating so much of his time and so many resources to the job, Gillette felt it was necessary. And this wasn't going to last much longer. One way or the other, it was going to be over soon.

As he reached the top of the stairs, Gillette spotted Stiles standing beside a huge vase of fresh flowers on a table in the middle of the lobby. A wire ran from one ear down into Stiles's turtleneck, and a thin silver microphone curled around his cheek to his lips.

"I don't like this, Christian," Stiles said, as the men formed a barrier around them. "I don't like having you out in the open like this. Not after what happened this morning."

Gillette moved closer to Stiles and glanced around the lobby. "It'll be fine, Quentin."

Stiles's expression turned grim. "Don't tell me how to do my business, Christian. And I won't tell you how to do yours."

"Like I said, it'll be fine."

"Why don't we set up in a private room upstairs?" Stiles suggested. "That would be more intimate anyway."

Gillette shook his head. "It's our first date and I tell her we're eating in a private room because my head of security is worried someone might try to kill me if we eat in the dining room. That doesn't seem like a plan to me. Not if I want her to stick around through dessert."

"Still, I—"

Stiles stopped speaking as Isabelle moved toward them. She was wearing a black, strapless dress with her dark hair up off her dainty shoulders. For jewelry, she had on diamond earrings, a sapphire necklace, and a gold bracelet on her left wrist. Black suede heels finished her outfit. There was a hint of red on her full lips, and her fingernails were the same color.

Gillette gazed at her face as she neared him. Always mystery in those brown eyes—and it seemed more pronounced tonight. Like she was scared of something—or someone.

"Hello there," Gillette said quietly as she moved inside the security detail.

"Hi." She clasped her hands and looked down.

It was an uncomfortable moment for her, he knew. So he leaned down and gave her a gentle kiss on one cheek. The scent of a pleasing perfume came to his nostrils as his lips touched her soft skin.

"It's good to see you, Christian," she murmured.

Gillette slipped an arm around her, his hand coming to rest on the small of her back. He gave her a gentle hug. "It's good to see you, too." He nodded to Stiles over her shoulder, thankful Stiles hadn't searched her. "Did you enjoy yourself today?" He'd arranged for a woman from the Waldorf to spend the day with Isabelle. To take her to Fifth Avenue to buy a dress for tonight, to take her to have her hair done, and to help her pick out jewelry.

She looked up into his eyes. "I've never had a better day in my life. Thank you. How can I ever repay you?"

"Have dinner with me."

She smiled. "Love to."

"Let's sit down," he suggested, gesturing toward the dining room.

Stiles had made arrangements for them to sit at a quiet table in a back corner of the room. When they reached the table, Stiles held out a chair for her.

"Thank you." Isabelle smiled up at Stiles as she sat down.

He nodded back politely, and, when she was seated, moved away and stood against the wall.

"Aren't you going to get *my* chair?" Gillette called.

"Double my fee and I'll consider it."

"I just did, remember? Jesus, for twenty grand a day you ought to drive the limo, cook dinner, and play the piano," Gillette kidded, sitting down across from Isabelle. "Everything okay?"

"Perfect."

"What would you like to drink?"

"What are you having?"

"Water."

"No wine?" she asked, disappointed.

"No, but don't let that keep you from having some."

"Will you order for me?"

"Sure. Red or white?"

"Red, please."

When Gillette had ordered and the waiter was gone, Isabelle leaned across the table. "Does it bother you to have him watch you eat?" she whispered, motioning toward Stiles.

"No, I'm used to it."

"Why does he have to be around all the time? Those other guys, too?"

Gillette hadn't wanted to get into this so soon, but it was stupid to think she wouldn't ask about it. Anyone would. "Isabelle, in my position I have enemies. Quentin is in charge of protecting me from them. But it's just a precaution," he assured her.

"Is that why the men held me last night when they found the knife in my coat? Why they made me stay here in the hotel? Because they thought I was your enemy."

"They thought you might be working for someone."

"I hope you know how silly that sounds. How could I possibly be working for anyone? Right?"

"Right."

A faint alarm went off in Gillette's head. It would have been easy for someone to find out about his connection to Jose and Selma. He'd been to their house in New Jersey at least six or seven times since moving them down there. He'd met Selma at a charity dinner in the early summer where she'd been the waitress for the table, and when the dinner was over, he'd asked about her family. Ironically, it turned out Jose had been laid off in a downsizing at Blalock, the power-tool manufacturer Everest owned. He'd been working at the Newark, New Jersey, plant—commuting from the Bronx—and lost his job when the factory installed robots. Before leaving, he'd asked Selma if he could meet Jose.

They'd met a week later, and he'd turned out to be perfect. Exactly what Gillette was looking for. A man who would be unfailingly loyal to a person who made his family's life better. So Gillette had moved them to central New Jersey and gotten Jose another job.

"I mean, the *idea* that I would come to New York City with a knife to kill you is crazy," she continued, her voice low. "It's incredible that the men who work for you could even come up with that. The whole thing is ridiculous."

Isabelle had shown up out of nowhere. Neither Jose nor Selma had ever mentioned anything about Isabelle until the night last week when he and Jose had come in off the deck and she'd suddenly appeared. Which meant, if there was something going on, Jose or Selma—or both—might be cooperating with someone. Which also meant that his order might not be carried out tonight. But then he'd know what the deal was.

Gillette stared at her hard. "Sure. Ridiculous."

Killing someone was the easy part. Everyone was vulnerable. Presidents, kings. It didn't matter. Regardless of how much security there was. History had proven that anyone could be assassinated with enough planning and bribing. The hard part was leaving no traces or trail. Nothing authorities could later use to track down the assassin, then link him or her to others.

To leave no traces, the hit had to occur at a time and place of the killer's choosing. In the middle of a remote forest next to a stream, for example. Not in a crowded dining room where waiters and busboys could easily be members of a security force.

For now, it had to be just about surveillance. Just gathering information.

Unless, out of the blue, an opportunity presented itself.

. . .

"Fourteen."

Gillette took a sip of water. *"Fourteen?"* he repeated, astonished.

Isabelle nodded. "Yes. Nine sisters and five brothers."

"Where are you in all of that?"

"I don't understand," she said, her thin dark brows knitting together.

Gillette picked up the bottle of Merlot sitting on the table and poured Isabelle a second glass. "Which *number* are you?" he tried again, glancing over at her as he finished pouring. Her diamond earrings sparkled in the dim light. Suddenly he was tempted to have a glass. "Are you the youngest? The oldest?"

"Oh, oh," she said, finally understanding. "I am third from youngest."

He thought about it again: the taste of a nice Merlot would be so satisfying. Especially with Isabelle sitting across from him. He'd only had that one sip of gin at lunch with Stockman, but it had been delicious. Before that sip, he hadn't had a drop of alcohol since the night of his high school senior prom when he'd lost control of his father's Ferrari on a tight turn on Ocean Highway north of Carmel. The night he'd almost died.

"Did you leave a boyfriend back in Puerto Rico?" he asked.

She giggled, embarrassed by the question.

"Should I not have asked?"

"No, it's okay. I did have a boyfriend. I asked him to come here with me, but he wouldn't."

"I'm sure that's been hard."

Isabelle shrugged. "There was really no choice, you know? There aren't many good jobs in Puerto Rico. No way to really get ahead. You have to come here. But my boyfriend didn't want to leave his friends." Her expression turned sad. "What could I do?"

"When did you decide to come here?"

She looked up at him curiously. "Why do you ask?"

"Just wondered," he answered, taking a bite of his food. Trying to sound as if it had been just an innocent question anyone might ask.

"About a month ago. My boyfriend and I had a fight, and I was talking to Selma on the phone about it."

"Is she the one who invited you to come and stay with them?"

Isabelle nodded. "Yes. Of course. She said not to worry about my boyfriend. That I would meet someone nice here." She gazed at Gillette for a moment, then looked away again.

Gillette watched her look away, then down into her lap. Suddenly he wanted to reach out and touch her soft skin. Wanted to inhale her beauty. "Isabelle, I—"

She looked up and broke into a grin.

As if he'd done something amusing. "What is it?" he asked.

She leaned over the table and lightly wiped one corner of his mouth with her finger. Then held it up so he could see. "Mashed potatoes."

Gillette smiled slightly. "I forgot to tell you about my eating disorder."

"Oh?"

"I don't always get everything into my mouth."

She laughed, wiping off her finger with her napkin. "Why aren't you drinking a glass of wine with me?" she asked. "Is it because you have to work tomorrow? Or do you *never* drink?"

"I don't drink," Gillette answered. Now he was committed to not having any. Disappointing, but best. "I know a lot of people enjoy it, and I have no problem with that. But for me, it's just not—" He interrupted himself, spotting a familiar figure moving through the tables. For several moments he watched her approach over Isabelle's shoulder. As she neared them, he stood up. Dropping his napkin on the table.

Before Gillette could step into the aisle, Stiles whisked past him and moved toward the woman. At the same time a busboy put down his tray and fell in behind her.

"Can I help you?" Stiles asked smoothly, folding his arms across his broad chest. Putting himself directly between Gillette and the woman.

"Do you know who I am?" the woman snapped.

Stiles took a hard look at her, his expression morphing into one of recognition. "Sure. You're Faith Cassidy."

"That's right. Now, let me past so I can speak with Christian."

Stiles shook his head. "Can't do it."

"Christian and I know each other. Let me past," she insisted.

"Sorry."

Gillette tapped Stiles on the shoulder. "It's all right, Quentin. You can let her past."

"No, I can't. Not until we check her out and make sure she isn't carrying anything," Stiles said firmly. He nodded at the busboy, who was standing behind her. Obviously, he was one of Stiles's men.

"She's clean," the man confirmed after he'd patted her down.

Faith rolled her eyes, indignant at having to undergo the search. "What's going on, Christian?" she demanded.

Stiles moved aside so Gillette could pass.

"There've been a few incidents," Gillette explained. "We had to tighten security."

"I'm sorry to hear that, but you could have told him I'm no threat."

"I could have," he agreed.

"But?"

"But he's in charge. What he says goes."

"Oh, God," she groaned, looking past him at Isabelle, an annoyed expression contorting her face. "You certainly get around."

"She's a friend," he said, glancing back over his shoulder.

"Sure she is," Faith said sarcastically. "I thought we were going out when I got back from L.A. Or was our night no big deal? I thought it meant something to you. It did to me."

"I thought you were going to call," he said, avoiding her question.

Faith hesitated. "Yeah, well."

Gillette noticed people at the tables around them staring at her, whispering to one another and pointing. There was no privacy for a celebrity like Faith. "How did you know I was here?"

"What do you mean?"

"I don't think you landed at LaGuardia, hopped off the plane, and just happened to decide on the Jetway to come straight to the back of the Waldorf dining room. How did you know I was here?" he repeated.

"I called your office and your assistant told me," Faith murmured.

"My assistant went home before I left. You hadn't called at that point. Besides, I didn't tell her I was coming here."

"All right," Faith said, groaning. "I don't know who she was. I don't remember her name."

"Was it Marcie Reed?"

"Where were you tonight, Troy?" Melissa asked angrily, hands on her hips. "It's eleven o'clock."

Mason closed the door of their penthouse apartment, removed his coat, and dropped it deliberately on a chair. Buying time. Trying to think. He'd been with Vicky for the last few hours, over at the Sheraton on Seventh Avenue, and he was exhausted. He should have used the time in the taxi on the way home to come up with an alibi, but he'd passed out as soon as he'd eased onto the backseat of the cab. The driver had been forced to shake him awake after pulling up in front of the apartment building.

"Tell me, Troy!"

Mason grimaced. "Shhhh. You'll wake up the baby, honey," he said, moving toward her.

"I called Apex three times," Melissa said, ignoring him. "Everyone I talked to said you'd left a long time ago."

He tried to slip his arms around her, but she stepped back and turned away. Facing the sliding doors to the spacious balcony that overlooked Manhattan from forty-two stories up. "I had a business dinner."

"I bet. Who'd you eat?"

He shook his head and let out a long, frustrated breath. Why was he so driven to have sex with other women? Melissa was beautiful. She had a lovely face and, even at thirty-seven, an incredible body. And she was completely uninhibited. She craved sex and gave him anything he wanted. So why look elsewhere? He'd never be able to answer that question. He'd been asking himself the same thing over and over again for years, and he was no closer to an answer today than he had been the first time he'd asked himself.

He slipped his arms around her. This time she didn't move away. Just let her head fall back against his shoulder.

"Why am I not enough?" she whispered.

"You are, baby. I told you. I had dinner tonight."

"Don't lie to me, Troy," Melissa pleaded, turning to face him.

"I was at Carmine's with the CEO of this company I might buy."

"So, I'd see that receipt on the next Visa statement."

"I put it on the Apex corporate card I just got today."

Melissa shook her head. "You told me the other morning they weren't going to give you a corporate card. Remember? You were irritated because you were going to have to fill out all this paperwork to get reimbursed."

"I told Strazzi I didn't have time for that bullshit, so he finally gave me one."

Melissa rolled her eyes. "Sure he did."

"Honey, I—"

Someone rang the doorbell.

Strange, Mason thought. The doorman should have buzzed to let them know someone was coming up. "Yes?" he called.

"Pizza delivery."

Mason looked down at Melissa. "Did you order a pizza?"

"No."

"What's the name on the delivery?"

"What?" came the muffled reply.

"The name," Mason repeated.

"I don't hear you."

Mason cursed under his breath and moved quickly to the door, yanking it open in frustration. "What's the damn name on the—" He stopped short, swallowing his words as he gazed at the revolver, then at the two Hispanic men in the hallway.

"Back up," hissed the one pointing the gun at him.

Mason obeyed, putting his hands in the air without being told.

"Troy, what's going—" Melissa saw the men, shrieked, turned, and raced toward the baby's room.

The second man darted past Mason and caught her before she got far. Dragging her to the floor, pulling rope from his jacket, and binding her wrists tightly behind her back.

Instinctively, Mason made a move toward her.

"Take another step and I keel you, fucker," the man with the gun warned. He quickly closed the hallway door. "Then I keel her. And I keel her real slow. Lots of pain."

Mason froze, heart pumping madly. There was nothing he could do.

The man on top of Melissa stuffed a rag in her mouth, then pulled her roughly to her feet and pushed her onto the couch and down on her stomach. Then he bound her ankles, and, with another length of rope, pulled her ankles and wrists tightly together. "She's going nowhere now," the man said fiercely.

"Now him," the one holding the gun ordered.

The second man moved behind Mason and bound his wrists tightly behind his back.

"What do you want?" Mason asked, glancing at Melissa's terrified eyes. Flickering all around above the gag. "Money? Jewelry?"

"Shut up. Sit down there," the man holding the gun ordered, point-ing at a chair beside the couch.

Mason obeyed. "Tell me what you want," he pleaded.

"Information."

It was déjà vu. *"What?"*

"Information about companies at Everest Capital."

A chill raced up Mason's spine. "What companies?"

The man holding the gun pressed the barrel against Mason's cheek. "You tell me."

"I don't know what you're talking about."

"*Sí?* You don't know anything?"

"No."

"Okay. Sure you don't."

The man moved to where Melissa lay on the couch, not taking his eyes from Mason's. He smiled, pointing the barrel at her head. "What about her? You think she knows about these companies?"

"She knows nothing!" Mason shouted, standing up.

The second man moved quickly to Mason and slammed him in the stomach. He sank to his knees, wrists straining at the rope, gasping for breath.

Jose bent down very close to Melissa's ear and pulled the gag from her mouth. "Where does he keep his files?"

"I don't know," she whimpered. "I swear I don't."

"Why did you send me that e-mail from Los Angeles?" Gillette de-manded.

Faith looked at him strangely, putting a hand on her chest. "What e-mail? What are you talking about?"

They were standing in the middle of an upstairs room at the Waldorf that Stiles had hastily arranged. "The one from the coffee shop. What did you mean I needed to be careful? And who are 'they'?"

"I don't know what you're talking about."

"I know you sent that e-mail, Faith. We have a record of you doing it."

"You couldn't possibly have a record of it," she retorted. "They don't—"

"Don't what?" Gillette asked when she stopped short.

She said nothing.

"Faith, you have to tell me—"

"Why did you lie to me?" she demanded.

"Lie?"

"About your mother's death."

It was Gillette's turn to go silent.

"Did you think I wouldn't find out?"

"I figured you would sooner or later," he admitted. "I'm sure it wasn't hard."

"Why did you tell me she died that day?"

"She did for me. Maybe not physically, but in every other way. I'd had enough."

"You pulled her out of the pool, didn't you? You found her and you saved her life?"

Gillette stared back at Faith. "Yes."

"And you didn't tell me about your brother and sister, either. Why did you tell me you were an only child?"

"How did you—"

"I saw them mentioned in an article about your father's plane crash. Your mother was mentioned, too."

Faith glared at him for several moments, then her expression softened. Finally she smiled sadly, moved close to him, and slid her arms around his neck. "Thank you for helping me," she said softly, hugging him. "The label called this morning to tell me they were doubling my ad budget."

Gillette had called the music company's CEO yesterday and ordered the increase. "I told you I would."

"A lot of people tell me they'll help me but they don't." She gazed up at him. "Remember what you said to me at dinner? About trusting no one?"

He nodded.

"I trust you," she whispered, pulling his mouth to hers.

For a moment Gillette hesitated, then he pressed his lips against hers and kissed her deeply.

Jimmy Holt stumbled through the parking lot toward his car, drunk. It had been all he could do not to tell the other energy analysts from the office about the huge new oil and gas field in Canada, all he could do, as he stood at the bar and listened to them talk sports and women, not to cut in and describe the data he'd lifted from the tapes. Increasingly difficult with each beer.

So he'd left. Afraid that a seventh beer would make him spill his guts. Despite his boss's warning.

Holt fumbled through his pockets for his keys, his head spinning. Finally locating them. Pointing the car key at the door and pressing the button. Vaguely aware of the car's parking lights flashing and of reaching for the door. Knowing that he shouldn't be getting behind the wheel. But he wasn't going to leave his car here and have to come get it in the morning.

Suddenly he felt himself pitching forward. Forced to trot, then run, to keep from falling face-first. So drunk he was unaware it wasn't the alcohol causing him to stagger ahead. Unaware that he'd been violently pushed.

Holt's forehead slammed into the curb as he finally tumbled forward, the cement opening a gaping wound above his left eye. As blood poured onto the cement, Holt vaguely felt the barrel of the gun pressed to his temple. Then there was a flash and everything went dark.

Mason closed his eyes tightly, his heart in his throat. He was dangling over the railing of the balcony by his wrists, forty-two stories up. He tried to yell for help, but the heavy gag muffled his cries.

Then he felt himself dropping. He fell maybe only five feet and it lasted less than half a second, but now he was screaming like a baby as they hauled him back over the railing.

"Where are your files?" the Hispanic man hissed into Mason's ear, pulling the gag down around his neck. "Don't tell us and we'll drop your wife over."

"Wall safe in the bedroom," Mason gasped. "Let me go in there. I'll open it."

Kathy Hays sat on the porch of the cabin, listening to the sounds of the night. She pulled her sweater tightly around herself and shivered. It wasn't cold here in Mississippi, but it was eerie. She peered into the dark-

ness, certain she'd seen something move among the Spanish moss drap-
ing the trees. She held her breath and looked harder. Nothing. Just a
small tree moving in the breeze.

She let out a long breath. The time was going slowly.

"I'm sorry about what happened tonight," Gillette said quietly to Isabelle
as he held her.

"Don't worry about it," she whispered. "It's incredible to me that
you'd choose to be with me. I mean, Faith Cassidy is a superstar."

"Well, I—"

His cell phone rang and he pulled it hastily from his jacket pocket.
"Yes," he answered, turning away from her and pressing the tiny phone
tightly to his ear so she wouldn't hear.

"Christian, it's Jose."

"Yes?"

"You were right. He was keeping files on companies at Everest. We
got them. All the ones in his safe at his apartment."

"Perfect. I'll see you tomorrow." Gillette closed the phone, and gazed
at Isabelle. It was crazy to think she could be working with anyone who
would want to kill him. Wasn't it?

Stiles smiled as he snapped pictures of Stockman coming out of the
apartment building with Rita Jones on his arm at dawn. Gillette would
be happy. Which made Stiles happy. He liked Gillette. Hadn't thought
he would at first, but Gillette had proven to be a man of courage and
compassion. A man he respected.

Stiles chuckled as he snapped a picture of Stockman and Rita Jones
kissing on the street corner. People were so stupid sometimes. So in-
credibly stupid.

19

Choices. *Sometimes there are no good ones. Sometimes, because of our own actions, we create situations where any choice is awful. Then it comes down to making the one that's simply the least bad.*

MASON SAT IN HIS SPACIOUS office at Apex, dreading the inter-office call from Vicky that would let him know Strazzi was ready to talk. He glanced nervously at his watch: 6:58. They were supposed to meet at seven, but Strazzi was usually five to ten minutes early. Maybe, by some incredible stroke of luck, Strazzi had been delayed—or wasn't coming in. Maybe he'd been—

Mason's phone rang. He glanced at the screen. Vicky. He picked up the receiver slowly. "Yes?"

"Paul's ready to meet. He wants you in his office right away."

Mason swallowed hard. These were the bad times.

Three minutes later he was in Strazzi's office.

"Sit down."

"Yes, Mr. Strazzi."

"It's Paul today."

Mason sat down in the chair in front of Strazzi's desk. "Okay . . . Paul." Strazzi was one weird fuck. Maybe getting out of Apex was the best thing, which was surely how this was going to end up anyway. *Thrown out* was more accurate. Or worse.

"Do you have what I want?" Strazzi asked, his gaze intense.

Mason swallowed hard, felt his breath shorten. Strazzi versus the two men from last night. Neither option was much of a bargain.

But he'd lived through what the two men from last night would do—hung from his balcony forty-two stories above the street. Just before they'd left last night with his files, they'd told him if he gave Strazzi any information—even verbally—they'd kill him. Told him they'd know right away if he did because they had an inside contact, and somehow he believed them. He'd looked long and hard into the eyes of the one with the gun—dead, black, shark eyes—and seen a man who wouldn't hesitate to kill.

On the other hand, Strazzi was an unknown. His threats might be empty. There was that chance. And Strazzi's people couldn't be any worse than the two men who'd terrorized him and Melissa last night.

"Troy!"

"I don't have the files," Mason muttered, eyes down.

Strazzi banged the desk. *"What!"*

"I don't have the files," Mason repeated. The half million had hit his account late yesterday afternoon, as promised. "I'll give the money back right—"

"I don't give a damn about the money." Strazzi was seething. "Where are the files?"

"I don't have them anymore."

Veins in Strazzi's forehead bulged. "Did Gillette get to you?"

As Mason was removing the files from the wall safe in the bedroom last night, listening to Melissa's muffled sobs as she lay on the couch bound and gagged, he'd realized that only one person in the world could have been responsible for what was happening, only one person had the motive, the knowledge, and the courage. Christian Gillette.

There was no way to prove Gillette's involvement. The only way to prove it would be to locate one of the men and get him to talk, which wasn't going to happen. There were fifteen million people in the New York metropolitan area. It would be a complete waste of time to attempt to find the men. Besides, even if he could find them, they'd probably never admit to being involved with Gillette.

"No," Mason answered, glancing around the office, wondering if Gillette had bugged Strazzi's office. "He didn't." Wondering if that's what the two men meant when they'd warned him not to say anything to

Strazzi about what had happened. It wouldn't surprise him if there was a bug in here. Gillette would stop at nothing. He was that driven, Mason knew. "It wasn't Gillette."

"Then what happened?" Strazzi roared.

"I destroyed the files."

"You *what?*"

"Last night I reread the confidentiality agreement I signed as part of the separation agreement from Everest. It's a bear, Paul. Very tight. But what the hell was I supposed to do? I need that million bucks." He glanced up at Strazzi. "I spoke to my lawyer. He warned me I might do jail time if I gave you those files."

"That's ridiculous. This is civil, not criminal. You would—" Strazzi interrupted himself as he stood up, towering over Mason. "Where are the files, Troy?"

"I told you. I don't have them. I destroyed them."

Gillette greeted the three Coyote Oil executives, taking their business cards without looking at them or giving them his. Cohen and Kyle Lefors had already been in here with them for fifteen minutes.

"This is Don Hansen," Cohen said as Gillette shook hands with the third man. "Don's the CEO of Coyote."

"Hi." Gillette gave Hansen a quick nod, then sat down at the head of the table. He motioned for the others to sit, too, glancing first at Cohen, then at Lefors, who had already taken extensive notes, which were now spread out on the table in front of him. "So, you have an interest in Laurel Energy?" he asked before Hansen was seated.

Hansen pulled his chair up and folded his hands together on the table. "I heard you were a damn direct son-of-a-bitch," he said in a heavy Texas accent.

Hansen looked uncomfortable to Gillette, as if his suit was a size too small. As if he couldn't wait to get back to Coyote headquarters in Wyoming to put on his plaid flannel shirt, boots, Stetson, and jeans with a big silver belt buckle. "How'd you hear I was so direct, Don?"

"Your damn partners," Hansen answered, pointing at Cohen and Lefors with a wry grin. "They've been singing your praises. Said I better hold on to my damn wallet while I'm in here. Apparently, if I'm not careful, you'll get it from me and I won't even know you took it. They say you're one of the best damn negotiators around."

Hansen tossed 'damn' around as much as Faraday dropped the f-bomb, Gillette noticed. Everybody had to have their handle. "They did, huh?"

"Yup."

"Well, Don, time is money. As a CEO, I'm sure you appreciate that."

"Of course."

"So, what's your interest?" Gillette asked again.

Hansen sat up straight in his chair and forced a serious expression onto his face. "We're prepared to offer you what U.S. Petroleum did. A billion in cash for your stock, and we take over the Citibank debt."

"How exactly do you know what U.S. Petroleum offered?" Gillette asked, his eyes flashing to Cohen, who glanced guiltily away.

Hansen didn't answer for a moment. "Well, I, uh, uh . . ." he stammered.

"I told him, Christian," Cohen admitted. "I thought it would be more efficient that way. Everybody puts their cards on the table and we see what's what. No screwing around."

Gillette gritted his teeth. The first rule of negotiation was *never* to open the bidding as a seller. Cohen was terrible at this. "Why are you willing to pay us what U.S. Petroleum offered? Is it because of the option properties?"

Hansen shook his head. "No. Mr. Cohen told us the seismic tests you did showed there wasn't much to those properties. Some reserves, but no mother lode."

"Why a billion then?" No sense beating around the bush when both sides had perfect information. Thanks to Cohen singing like a canary, everybody knew everything. "The level of reserves at Laurel may not justify that kind of price."

Hansen smiled widely at Cohen and Lefors. "Damn. For a savvy negotiator that's one hell of a strategy your partner has. Negotiating against himself when I—"

"All the same," Gillette cut in. "Why?"

"Okay, okay," Hansen said, his head bobbing. Appreciating where Gillette was coming from. "Let me explain something. We're backed by a group who's trying to buy up reserves very quickly, specifically those in Canada."

"I know I'm repeating myself, Don, but *why?*"

Hansen's eyes flashed around the room and his head settled down into his shoulders, as if he wasn't sure he wanted to talk. "The confidentiality agreement we signed goes both ways, right?"

Before agreeing to meet with the Coyote executives, Gillette had instructed Lefors to make them sign a nondisclosure agreement that made Coyote liable for monetary damages if they disclosed any confidential information about Laurel Energy to the outside world.

"Yes," Gillette agreed. "Under the terms of the agreement Kyle had you sign, we have to stay quiet about anything you tell us concerning Coyote Oil."

"All right," Hansen said, his voice dropping. "Based on good inside information, we think there are still some huge undiscovered fields up in Canada. So, we need a base of operations there. We need critical mass."

The explanation seemed thin to Gillette. "Our information is that the experts think Canada is played."

Hansen began rocking slowly back and forth in his chair. "Mr. Gillette, I've been in this business forty years. Started out at seventeen on a rig in the Gulf of Mexico as a grease monkey. Now I'm a CEO. Been just about everything in this industry you can be and been almost every place in the world where there's reserves. You know what I've learned?"

Gillette knew what was coming. Guys like Hansen in every industry said it: When everybody else is getting out, you should be getting in. The contrarian play. Gillette could have given the speech word for word himself, he'd heard it so many times. But, in the unlikely event Hanson was serious about doing a deal, he wasn't going to steal the man's thunder in front of two subordinates and piss him off. "What's that, Don?"

"When everybody goes left, you go right, and when everybody goes right, you go left. If you do the opposite of what others are doing, as long as you have good information and conviction, *then* you make *big* money." He stopped rocking. "Unfortunately, your option properties are pretty dry. But, like I said, we think there are still some huge undiscovered fields in Canada. In the same general area as your properties. My experience is you don't find those gems unless you got feet on the ground so you can hear things you wouldn't from a thousand miles away. Laurel's an excellent company. We think a lot of the senior executives and believe they can help us make progress quickly. A couple of our guys know a couple of your guys from way back, so we're willing to pay a little more to get access and experience."

A decent speech, Gillette thought to himself. Probably practiced a dozen times on the flight from Casper to New York to make it sound natural, but there was still something forced about it. "Who's your backer, Don?"

"A European group."

"You've got to be more specific. If we're going to start negotiating, I have to understand that you have money, that you can come up with a billion dollars and convince Citibank to stay with Laurel after you take control. I'm sure you understand."

"Of course, of course," Hansen replied quickly. "How about if I get a name to Mr. Cohen and you two call them together. Or go visit with them if you feel like it. They're based in Switzerland."

Criminal liability. That was bullshit and Mason knew it. "Damn it!" Strazzi cursed loudly. Stockman was right. Without Mason's files, Donovan's widow might not agree to sell her stake in Everest. He'd told her he had proof. Not being able to produce the files might blow the whole thing.

Strazzi picked up the TV remote and turned the set on. He was scheduled to meet with her later, after the announcement had been made. He checked his watch: 12:55. He'd only have to wait another five minutes.

20

The Attack. *Most times you can't predict exactly where or when it will come. All you can do is prepare and try to anticipate what the enemy will do, then counter with everything you have when the guns go off.*

"THANKS FOR YOUR TIME TODAY." Hansen pumped Gillette's hand energetically. "I really hope we can get a deal done. This thing makes a lot of sense for everybody."

During the rest of the meeting, Gillette had quizzed Hansen hard about his experience in the energy industry, trying to make certain he was who he said he was. Toward the end of the meeting, Stiles had come into the conference room and placed a full background report on Hansen down in front of Gillette, which Gillette had read right in front of Hansen as Hansen described how he'd made a lot of other people a lot of money for a lot of years. How it was his turn to get rich. Admitting his Swiss backers had cut him a very good deal, but only because he deserved it.

"We'll get back to you next week," said Gillette. He and Hansen stood facing each other at the entrance to the Everest lobby. The other two Coyote executives were already headed toward the elevators. "Cohen and Lefors will follow up with your people by phone tomorrow morning. I doubt we'll actually go to Switzerland, but I appreciate your making that option available to us."

"Sure, sure. Anything to help move the deal forward quickly." Hansen paused and looked around the ornate setting.

Gillette noticed something wistful in Hansen's expression, which made him certain the Coyote Oil headquarters were barren compared to this.

"I look forward to hearing from you," Hansen finally said.

When Gillette turned back toward his office, he spotted Cohen walking quickly toward him. Cohen's face was pale. "What's the matter, Ben?"

"Come with me," Cohen urged, his voice low. "Right now."

When they were inside Gillette's office with the door closed, Cohen turned on the television and flipped the channel to CNN. "I just got word," Cohen said breathlessly. "From one of our contacts down in D.C."

"Word about *what?*"

Cohen pointed at the screen as the picture switched from a pretty blond anchorwoman to a wooden lectern. "This is it."

An alarm went off inside Gillette's head as he gazed at the screen. He moved quickly to his desk and clicked into Bloomberg, glancing back and forth between the television screen and the computer monitor. He'd checked the Dominion S&L stock price several hours ago, a few minutes after the 9:30 open. It had drifted down twenty-five cents in the first few minutes of trading, but there had been no major move at that point.

Gillette clicked the mouse one last time and the price flashed onto the screen. Off *fifteen dollars* to ten dollars a share. Dominion's stock had dropped 60 percent in the last three hours. Three billion dollars of shareholder value gone in less time than it took to play a pro football game. Three hundred million of that was Everest's. Fifty million the widow's.

Gillette glanced back to the television screen, his head pounding. Cameras were clicking madly.

Congressman Peter Allen moved behind the lectern and acknowledged the press corps assembled in front of him, smiling confidently at no one in particular. He was a tall man with gray hair and stark features who had a reputation in Washington for straight talk.

An aide nodded.

Allen took the cue. Buttoning his chalk-stripe suit jacket and putting on a dour expression, then turning his head slightly to one side for effect. "Thank you for coming today," he began in a low voice. "As most of you know, I'm Peter Allen, congressman from Idaho and vice chairman of the House Select Committee on Corporate Abuse. I'm here today to talk about another example of insatiable greed in the corporate boardroom, of insiders preying on unsuspecting small public investors, on individuals, to make themselves rich. In the terrible tradition of Enron, Worldcom, and Tyco." Allen paused to check his notes. "This time the guilty party is a well-known investment firm in New York." He looked up. "Everest Capital."

Allen took a moment to stare out at America without speaking, allowing the cameras to document his stern expression.

"The partners at Everest Capital recently sold one of their companies to the public," Allen continued. "A savings and loan business called Dominion. Many of us here in the Washington, D.C., area are familiar with Dominion," he added. "It has branches all around the District and across the Potomac River in Virginia.

"With a fast-growing loan portfolio, Dominion had been a highflier for Everest, so Everest decided to do an IPO. They decided to sell most of their ownership in Dominion to people like you and me. To dump it on us while it looked like Dominion was doing well. Trying to make us believe Dominion would do even better in the future." Allen paused. "Unfortunately, Dominion wasn't doing as well as the partners at Everest Capital led us to believe. The loan portfolio, mostly residential mortgages, was actually in terrible shape. Dominion bought a significant number of large, prepackaged portfolios from mortgage bankers, and, apparently, didn't do its diligence. Didn't review those portfolios as well as it should have before buying them." He took a deep breath to let everyone know this was a crucial point in the press conference. "I have information indicating that billions of dollars of those loans will never be repaid, that many of the loans are already nonperforming. In other words, the people who owe money on the loans haven't sent in their monthly mortgage checks in a long, long time.

"The Dominion executives, their outside auditors, and probably the senior partners at Everest have committed fraud. They should have told us that the loans were bad, that the people who owed Dominion money weren't paying. But they didn't. In fact, they provided false documents that tried to show that everything was fine, that people *were* repaying the loans." Allen held up a manila folder for effect. "That's how Everest did the IPO. With smoke and mirrors. Sound familiar?" he asked rhetorically.

"The bitterest pill to swallow here is that Everest made billions of dollars," Allen said tersely. "They still own a small piece of Dominion, which I suspect will lose a significant amount of its value today because of my announcement. But that loss will be tiny compared to the huge amount of money Everest got in the IPO: about $2 billion.

"So who really loses?" Allen asked the television cameras. "Not the partners at Everest Capital. Not the investment bankers who took Dominion public. Not the lawyers who made millions in fees documenting the IPO. None of them lose a dime. The people who lose are the ones who bought the shares from Everest Capital. The little guys. The IPO price was forty dollars a share, but, as we speak, Dominion shares are trading at," Allen hesitated, glancing at his aide off camera for the sign, "*three dollars* a share. That's almost $4 billion of shareholder value erased.

"This afternoon, I'll officially inform the Securities and Exchange Commission that I want them to begin a full investigation of the Dominion Savings & Loan IPO. Banking regulators will also be moving on Dominion headquarters to determine the extent of the fraud. In addition, I'll be contacting the chairman of Everest Capital, a man named Christian Gillette, to demand that he and his partners refund all the money they made in the IPO. I'll also be seeking a very large fine. It's clear to me that Everest insiders knew what was going on behind the scenes at Dominion. An Everest partner was chairman of the board before Dominion went public, and Everest owned a hundred percent of the firm before the IPO. Make no mistake: Everest knew what was going on.

"Finally, I'll be demanding that regulators initiate a full-scale investigation into Everest Capital on behalf of my committee. Everest owns a hundred percent of nearly thirty companies around this country. Big ones, too. We need to know what's going on at Everest so we can avoid situations like Dominion in the future, so we don't have innocent people being bilked out of billions."

Allen looked around, satisfied with his delivery. "Any questions?"

. . .

Strazzi slammed his hand down on the desk, then picked up the remote and muted the television as Peter Allen answered the first question from the press. Allen had mentioned Everest Capital several times. Mentioned Christian Gillette by name. Even described how he was going to have regulators open an investigation into Everest. Just as Stockman had promised. But Allen hadn't mentioned the specific portfolio companies Strazzi had told Stockman to give to Allen. Clearly because there hadn't been any documentation. Because Troy Mason hadn't forked over the files.

"Damn it!" Stockman might be right, Strazzi realized. Without those specific names mentioned during the press conference, the widow might not sell him her stake in Everest, might not be convinced that she should let go of that stake for the 50 percent haircut he was going to offer her.

"Paul." Vicky's voice blared through the intercom.

"What?"

"Senator Stockman is on 122."

Strazzi picked up the receiver and punched the extension. "What the hell happened, George?" he growled.

"Without the files, Peter wouldn't go along," Stockman explained, his voice barely audible.

"Why are you talking so low?"

"I'm about to make my own announcement. There's a lot of people around. Aides, reporters."

"I'm pissed, George," Strazzi hissed. "You told me this yokel from Idaho would play ball."

"And you told me you'd have the proof."

"If the widow backs off because of this, you can kiss my support good-bye," Strazzi warned.

"*What?* That's ridiculous. I've done everything I told you I'd do."

"Get Allen to call another press conference later this afternoon," Strazzi snapped. "Before four thirty. I'm meeting with the widow at five to close the deal. Just get Allen to say he'll be focusing on those companies when he investigates Everest. That's all you have to do. Just get him to mention the names. Nothing specific about why he'll be targeting those companies. I'll do the rest."

"I don't know if Allen will play ball."

"*Make* him!" Strazzi yelled, slamming the phone down.

. . .

"Jesus Christ," Faraday whispered as Allen's press conference ended. He had joined Gillette and Cohen in Gillette's office. "Is it possible what Allen said about Dominion is true?"

"Anything's possible, Nigel," Gillette answered calmly.

"Could they really make us give back the fucking money? All two billion?"

"Not before the investigation is finished. That'll take a while."

"But it could happen?"

"Sure. And we might be liable for that big fine Allen mentioned, too."

"Would we have to give what *we* got back, too?" Faraday asked anxiously. "Personally."

"Of course."

"Fuck me. All two million?"

"Yes."

"I paid taxes on that. I only netted a little over one."

"The SEC won't care. They'll want two. They'll tell *you* to deal with the IRS."

"Shit!" Faraday eyed Gillette. "How can you be so fucking calm?"

"Having a heart attack won't do any good," Gillette snapped, checking the Dominion ticker. The price had sunk to just more than a dollar.

Faraday snorted. "Two million might not be much to you, Christian. Thanks to Mommy and Daddy." Like many people, Faraday thought Gillette had a large personal net worth because of his family. "But for Cohen and me, it's huge. Our piece of Everest might be worth sixty million, but it isn't liquid. It's tied up in our portfolio companies. I can't use it to pay my debts."

"I understand."

"Well, what the fuck are you going to do about it, Mr. Chairman?"

Gillette glanced over at Cohen. He was typing out an e-mail on his Blackberry. His face was pale. "Ben."

"Yes, Christian?"

"I want you to call Walter Price immediately." Price was CEO of Dominion. "Tell him I'll be in his Washington office at ten o'clock tomorrow morning. Tell him I'll want a full report."

"Tomorrow's Saturday."

Gillette hesitated. He'd forgotten. He rarely paid attention to what day of the week it was anymore. "I don't care. Call him and tell him I'll be there at ten. Tell him to be ready."

"Okay."

"And tell Marcie Reed I want to see her at three o'clock here in my office."

Cohen stood up and nodded. "Starting your own investigation?"

"Yes," Gillette answered sharply, reading the words rolling across the bottom of the television screen. Smiling slightly to himself, despite everything that had just happened.

Stockman moved behind the lectern. It had been set up in a room in the bowels of the Senate side of the Capitol, an American flag on either side. His staff was lined up behind him.

"Thank you for coming today," he began. He was extremely satisfied with the turnout. Every major newspaper and television network was here. They'd all been briefed about the press conference this morning, and it made him proud to see that everyone had shown up. Obviously, they believed he was a serious contender. He cleared his throat. "I'll make this short and sweet. I'm here this afternoon to announce that I'm running for the Oval Office. I'm offering my leadership to the entire country now, not just to the great state of New York. And, as I've done in New York, I'll stand up for regular people. The man on the assembly line. Single moms trying to make it." He paused, making eye contact with several reporters. "Make no mistake, I *will be* the next president of the United States." He stared straight into the television camera, a steely expression on his face. "Questions?"

Several reporters thrust their arms in the air and shouted.

Stockman pointed at a young woman from CBS. "Yes?"

"Can you give us a specific example of how you'll stand up for regular people?"

Stockman thought for a second, then nodded. "Certainly. A little while ago, my colleague from the House, Peter Allen, laid out another example of corporate boardroom abuse. Everest Capital, an investment firm, defrauded thousands of public investors when it took one of its portfolio companies public. It's a savings and loan called Dominion, and, in a very short time, as a result of the fraud, the stock has cratered from a price in the forties to a dollar a share. Lots of regular people have lost money and probably will lose their jobs. It's a damn mess, but it didn't have to happen. I'll make investment companies like Everest Capital accountable. I'll make certain men like Christian Gillette aren't around to crush regular people again."

Gillette watched Stockman's press conference, his eyes narrowing as Stockman mentioned Everest and him by name. Thanks to Quentin Stiles, the campaign wasn't going to last very long. Unless Stockman cooperated.

"Christian."

Gillette looked up from the television. Marcie Reed stood at his office door. "Come in." He gestured toward one of the chairs as he turned off the television. "Have a seat."

"I'm busy, Christian," she said, sitting down across from him, her short skirt riding up her thighs. "Let's make this quick."

"We'll take as long as we need to," he said flatly.

Her eyes flashed to his, picking up on his tone. "What's going on?" she asked, her voice softening.

"Did you hear about Congressman Allen's news conference?"

She nodded deliberately. "Yes."

"And?"

"And what?"

"Marcie, Allen accused us of fraud in the Dominion IPO. You and Donovan ran that process for us. Bill's dead. That leaves you."

"Allen's wrong," she answered matter-of-factly. "As far as I know, there were no problems at Dominion when it went public. The auditors were all over it. I don't know where the congressman could be getting that kind of information. We'll be cleared."

She was good, Gillette thought. He'd seen her in action before, convincing a CEO she had sensitive information about his company when she didn't. Enabling her to manipulate him even though she was bluffing. "I'm going to ask you straight up, Marcie. Are you working for Paul Strazzi?"

"What!"

"Are you working for Paul Strazzi?" Gillette repeated.

"No. How could you possibly think that?"

"Like I said, you and Donovan did the IPO. The rest of us didn't hear much about it."

"What does that have to do with Paul Strazzi?"

"I think he's trying to take over Everest. I also think he's working with someone inside this firm."

"That's ridiculous," she said, shaking her head.

"Is it?"

"Yes."

"You and Bill didn't tell us much about what was going on with Dominion. Why was everything so hush-hush?"

"This is ridiculous," she said, standing up and heading for the door. "I'm not going to sit here and take it."

"Senator Stockman is about to get some bad news," Gillette called as she reached the door. "Information that would probably end his run for president if it were released to the public."

Marcie slowly turned back around.

"Information I will release." Gillette studied Marcie's expression, certain he saw fear, an emotion that he'd never seen her show before. "Unless he works with me. Unless he tells me what's really going on with Congressman Allen and who his contact is inside Everest."

"Why would Stockman know anything?"

"He's working with Strazzi."

"How do you know that?"

"I just do." He pointed at her. "Now, do you want to tell me anything, Marcie? Believe me, it'll go a lot better for you later if you cooperate with me now."

She stared at him for a few moments. "There's nothing to tell," she finally said.

Gillette saw indecision. "Why did you tell Lefors that Troy Mason was in the basement with a woman at Donovan's funeral reception?" he asked, hitting her with everything. "Why didn't you just come to me?"

Marcie shook her head. "That's absurd," she said, turning to go. "Absolutely absurd. I never told anyone that. I didn't know Troy was down there with a woman."

Gillette gazed at the empty doorway when she was gone. He'd detected hesitation in her reaction to questions about Dominion but not to the question about Mason.

21

A Price. *Everyone has one; you just have to find it. Then be willing to pay it.*

STRAZZI USHERED THE WIDOW INTO his office, holding the chair for her as she sat down. "Would you care for something to drink, Ann?" he asked politely, moving behind his desk. It made him want to puke to be so pleasant, but he had no choice. He needed her to relax, needed her to feel comfortable while they discussed her selling her Everest stake, so he made the effort, made those insincere gestures he hadn't made in so long, the kind of gestures others made toward him. "Water? Coffee?" he asked, sitting down, too.

"Hot tea," she answered.

Almost defiantly, Strazzi noticed. She was tense; the stress was obvious in her voice. And she was clutching that black purse in her lap with both hands like there was a million bucks inside and someone was eyeing it. Still, she seemed calm. "Of course, Ann." He picked up the telephone slowly, like he had all the time in the world. "Vicky."

"Yes?"

"Could you bring Mrs. Donovan some hot tea?"

"Right away, sir."

"Thank you." He smiled as he put down the receiver. "Vicky's wonderful," he murmured, trying to act as if this was just another day. "Always a joy to be around, always a smile on her face."

The widow didn't respond.

"Well, how are you, Ann?" Strazzi asked, forcing sadness into his tone and concern into his expression. "I'm sure this has been a difficult time."

"Don't put the act on for me, Paul. I know what you want. Let's not waste time."

Strazzi's expression hardened. "All right," he agreed, leaning forward.

"Do you have something you want me to consider?" she wanted to know.

"Yes."

"What?"

"Did you see Congressman Allen's press conference earlier this afternoon?" Strazzi asked, trying to dial up the heat before he got into the details of his offer.

"I did." The widow sniffed. As if she found the fact that he'd ignored her question annoying. "One of Stockman's aides called me beforehand so I was sure to see it."

"Then you understand how difficult the Dominion situation is. That savings and loan is going down. You might as well use your shares to start your fire on Christmas morning." Strazzi stared at the widow. "How much have you lost?"

"Fifty million," she answered indifferently. As if it had been fifty cents.

Strazzi leaned back in his chair, trying to figure out if she really didn't care, or if she was that good a poker player. "Dominion's the tip of the iceberg, Ann. You heard Congressman Allen. He's going to send in the storm troopers to do a full-blown investigation at Everest. If they find anything, Christian Gillette and his people will have a hell of a mess on their hands." Strazzi hesitated. "And, like I told you before, my information is that they *will* find things. Bad things." He paused again. "And they're going to have to pay a big fine related to Dominion. That alone could take them down."

"You told me you had proof there were problems with the portfolio companies," she reminded him.

"Uh-huh."

"Well, let me see it."

There was a light tap on the door and Vicky came into the office, buying Strazzi time.

"Here you are, Mrs. Donovan," she said, placing a cup of hot water, a bowl of tea bags, a spoon, and a small pitcher of cream down on a table beside the older woman's chair.

"Thank you."

Vicky smiled. "Do you need anything, Mr. Strazzi?"

"No."

Vicky turned and moved quickly out of the office.

"I don't have that documentation yet," Strazzi said frankly when Vicky was gone. And Allen hadn't called another press conference to mention the company names at Everest.

"Why not?" she demanded.

"I just don't," he said deliberately, trying not to let his irritation filter into his tone. Letting her see it would probably scare her. Maybe make her back off completely.

The widow slipped a tea bag into the hot water and began to stir. The spoon clinked off the sides of the cup. "I didn't hear anything specific in terms of portfolio company names from Congressman Allen during the press conference, either. I thought you said he was going to mention the Everest companies that were in trouble, not just Dominion."

Strazzi shrugged. "He didn't get around to it." This wasn't going well, he thought to himself. Not well at all. In fact, he half expected her to stand up and leave. Troy Mason was going to pay dearly.

They were both silent for a few moments.

"So, what's your offer, Paul?"

Strazzi's eyes flashed to the widow's. He'd been picking at a scab on the back of his hand, thinking about what he was going to do to Mason. He studied the widow's expression. She had tried hard to seem unconcerned about Allen's press conference, and nonchalant about her $50 million loss on Dominion. But now he saw how brittle her defiance was. She wasn't that good a poker player after all. There was panic seeping into the crow's feet at the corners of her eyes. He'd been around a long time and he could spot panic the moment it appeared. In addition, she was holding on to her purse so tightly now that her fingers were ghost white.

"Two billion," he answered quietly, thanking lady luck she hadn't brought a lawyer or an investment banker with her to negotiate. Probably because she didn't want to pay the multimillion-dollar fee. He'd heard she was cheap.

"In cash?"

"A billion in cash and another billion in a five-year note," Strazzi went on. "I'll pay the note off at the rate of two hundred million a year. Plus, I'll pay you 5 percent interest."

"That doesn't seem like a great deal."

"It's what I'm willing to pay," he answered firmly.

"A few months ago my husband told me the Everest stake was worth at least four billion," the widow countered.

"Maybe when the sharks weren't circling the ship and the ship didn't have a leak. But Everest is going down, Ann. At least, without me."

"What do you mean by that?" She perked up, listening intently. "What can you do?"

"I have connections. I can take the heat off Everest. I can get Allen to call off the dogs if I agree to get involved. If I tell them I'll clean up the mess. My people have already had preliminary talks with officials in Washington." Strazzi wagged a finger at her. "But, Ann, if I'm not involved, Allen will go after Everest with the big guns, make no mistake about it. I mean, look at it from his perspective. It's a great opportunity. It'll make him look like he's doing something to protect the public from Wall Street, which is always popular. Your stake won't be worth four billion in that scenario. In fact, it could be worth less than two. Much less. Maybe nothing."

"You just want to toss out Christian Gillette so you can get control of Everest," the widow snapped.

"A man doesn't offer $2 billion for something because he's feeling generous. Not if he's in his right mind. Sure, I want control of Everest," Strazzi continued, not giving her a chance to speak. "And, yes, I'd kick Gillette out. As fast as I could. So what? What do you care? As long as you get your two billion." The widow was gazing at him with a faraway look. He could see her indecision. She didn't know what to do. It was time to turn the screws—hard. "Hey, if you want to take a chance and try to ride out the storm with Gillette, have at it. I admire your loyalty. But remember this: Gillette doesn't have anywhere near the investment in Everest you do. He might take more chances because he has so much less to lose."

The widow stuck out her tiny chin. "I want two and a *half* billion, and I want it all in cash."

Strazzi felt his pulse jump. She was in. She was going to sell. She'd made the psychological leap. Now it was just a question of structure because they were close on price. "I won't go higher than two billion, but I'll increase the cash portion to a billion five. And, Ann, I can close this thing quickly. I already have a team of lawyers waiting at the first tee. I can have the cash to you by Monday afternoon."

"Two and a quarter. All cash."

Strazzi hesitated. He hated giving in—even a little. Especially to a woman. But he wanted this more than anything in the world. "Two billion in cash and $250 million in notes. Take it or leave it, Ann. That's my final offer, and it won't be on the table for long." He stood up and moved toward the door. "I'm going to get some coffee. When I get back, there's a fifty-fifty chance I'll still be offering you the deal. If I'm not, I'll offer you nothing."

As Strazzi reached for the knob the widow spoke up. "Can you really have the cash to me Monday afternoon?"

He smiled for a moment as he stood with his back to her. "Absolutely," he confirmed, turning around to face her. "No later than two o'clock."

She stood up and moved to the door beside him, staring at him intently as she opened it for herself. "All right, I accept your offer. I'm using the same lawyers Bill used for our personal affairs. Porter and Hughes over on Park."

"I know them."

"The partner I work with there is John Meyers. He's expecting your call."

"I'll get in touch with him right away."

"Good. I'll see myself out."

"I have several calls into Donovan's widow." Miles Whitman was sitting in one of the chairs in the corner of Gillette's office. "I don't call her much, but when I do, she usually calls me back quickly." He hesitated. "Not this time, though. I'm sorry, Christian," he said quietly. "I don't know what to tell you."

"She's meeting with Strazzi right now," said Gillette, sitting across the coffee table from Whitman.

"How do you know?"

"I'm having Strazzi followed. The widow showed up at his office about an hour ago."

"Are your McGuire guys tailing him?"

Gillette shook his head. "No, I—"

"Christian hired an outside firm," Cohen interrupted. He was sitting in the chair beside Gillette's.

"Why?"

"We don't trust Tom McGuire," Cohen said bluntly.

"Oh?"

"We may be taking McGuire & Company public soon," Cohen continued. "Earlier this week, Tom asked Christian about buying the company back. But at a much lower price than what the investment bankers are talking about in the IPO. Tom wasn't very happy when he found out we were thinking about taking the company public."

"I'm sure he wasn't." Whitman moved to a small refrigerator near Gillette's desk and pulled out a Coke. "You guys want anything?"

Both of them shook their heads.

"So you hired another security company to follow Strazzi just because of that?" Whitman asked, popping open the can as he sat back down. "Because you thought McGuire would be pissed off about not getting the company, and he might not tell you who Strazzi was meeting with? Or maybe tell Strazzi he'd been hired to tail him? Was that it?"

"It's more than that," Gillette answered. "You remember my limousine exploding at Donovan's funeral?"

"Of course."

"Well, there've been two more attempts on my life this week."

Whitman straightened up in the chair. "My God. What the hell's going on?"

"I don't know. But when Tom approached me about buying the company and I realized he had a conflict, I hired another firm. Partly because of that conversation you and I had at your place earlier this week. Remember? You asked if I could really trust him."

"Sure I remember."

"I'm glad I decided to do that," Gillette said. "The man I hired has turned out to be very good."

"Thorough, too," Whitman agreed. "I was basically strip-searched before I could come in here."

"Sorry about that, Miles, but, given the circumstances, I've got to listen to what my guy's telling me."

"When it's the kind of money that's involved here, I couldn't agree more." Whitman took a deep breath. "It's just a damn shame."

Gillette looked over at Whitman. "What is?"

"Everything. Dominion. Congressman Allen's press conference today. Strazzi going after the widow's stake." Whitman grimaced. "Unfortunately, I think it's going to put an end to your fund-raising. At least for a while."

Gillette ran his fingers through his hair. "If Strazzi gets the widow's stake, I don't think I'll be worrying too much about fund-raising. I'll be looking for another job."

Whitman nodded deliberately. "You're right. He'll install himself as the—"

Gillette's cell phone rang, interrupting Whitman.

Gillette picked it up off the coffee table and checked the display. It was Vicky. "Hello." As he listened to what she was saying, his expression turned grim. "Thanks."

"Who was that?" Cohen asked.

"An acquaintance."

"What's wrong?" Whitman asked.

Gillette took a deep breath. "The widow just agreed to sell her Everest stake to Strazzi for $2.25 billion." Gillette had gotten Mason's files, but it hadn't stopped Strazzi from getting what he wanted. Strazzi and Stockman had been able to scare the widow into selling her stake using Dominion's crash as the stick. "The transaction is closing Monday."

At least Stockman was going to get his for being involved, Gillette thought to himself. That was about the only thing he could take solace in at this point.

"So, Ben, are you now officially the chief operating officer of Everest Capital?" Whitman asked.

Cohen's eyes flashed to Gillette's. "Um, I, uh . . ." Cohen's voice trailed off. "Christian, I didn't tell anyone anything about this. I swear to you."

Gillette nodded at Whitman. "Yeah, I told Miles the other day." Cohen had that deer-in-the-headlights look. But why? "Well, actually, Miles asked if there had been any organizational changes and I told him I was promoting you."

"Oh," Cohen said quietly.

Suddenly Cohen seemed very uncomfortable, Gillette realized.

"I just don't want you to think I've been blabbing this all around," Cohen added.

"I'm sure you haven't," Gillette agreed. "Besides, it's no big deal if you have."

"So, is Ben officially chief operating officer?" Whitman asked again.

Gillette turned to Whitman. "Yes, he is."

Stiles pressed his arm against the pocket of his jacket, making certain the envelope was there. Then he moved out of the dark Manhattan doorway and fell in behind a man in a long winter coat who'd just passed by.

At the corner the man stopped, waiting for the traffic light to change. Rubbing his hands together to try to keep them warm as traffic roared by in front of him on Fifth Avenue.

"Chilly out tonight," Stiles said cheerfully as he ambled up beside the man.

The man gave Stiles a quick up and down. "Yeah, chilly," he agreed indifferently.

Stiles pointed at him. "Hey, I recognize you."

The man stopped rubbing his hands together, a curious expression coming to his face. "Oh?"

"Yeah," Stiles continued, "I saw you on television today when Senator Stockman made his announcement about running for president. You were behind him along with some other people. Right?"

"You've got quite a memory for faces."

"Always have." Stiles hesitated. "You are?"

"Frank Galway, the senator's assistant chief of staff," he replied, holding out his hand.

Trained to constantly chum for votes, Stiles thought to himself. "You must be pretty excited," he said, reaching into his jacket pocket.

"Yep," Galway agreed. "The senator is clearly the man to beat. He's got the experience and the track record. We think he'll be ahead when the new polls come out next week. Now *that* will be exciting."

"Well, I know he'll be excited about these, too," Stiles spoke up, pressing the envelope to Galway's chest.

"What the hell—"

"Photographs," Stiles said, his voice turning harsh.

Galway's fingers closed around the envelope.

"A few pictures of the good senator and a woman named Rita Jones coming out of their love nest in Queens," Stiles continued. "You're familiar with the place. You pay the rent."

"Oh, Christ," Galway whispered.

"Don't look so worried. As long as the senator cooperates, these pictures won't see the light of day."

"What do you mean, 'cooperates'?"

"I'll let you know when I contact you next." Stiles turned around and headed off abruptly.

Leaving Galway confused, concerned, and alone.

The apartment was in Greenwich Village. It was a quiet one-bedroom place on Houston Street in the West Village that Stiles used as a safe house.

Stiles's men had gone to great lengths to get Faith to it secretly. They'd smuggled her out a back entrance to the Waldorf after she and Gillette had said good-bye, then taken her up to Connecticut, changed cars in a dark parking lot, driven her to New Jersey and changed cars again, before finally bringing her back to the city. She'd been here since, protected by three of Stiles's men who were getting her what she needed so she didn't have to leave the apartment.

Gillette took off his coat and laid it over a chair by the door. He'd spent the last several hours enduring the same routine Faith had, and he was irritated. Stiles hadn't allowed him any contact with the outside world during the trip around the metro area. No cell phones, no Blackberry, no nothing. Gillette hated wasting time like that, but it had to be this way. They couldn't risk anyone finding out where Faith was. Or, worse, that they were the ones protecting her.

"Hi." Faith rose from the couch as Gillette came through the apartment door, putting down the crossword puzzle she'd been working on.

"Hello."

She went to put her arms around him, then hesitated, pulling back at the last minute. "How have you been?"

"Fine."

"Thanks again for your help with my contract," she said, hands clasped behind her. "With the ad budget, I mean. It's already been increased. There was a big spread in *USA Today*, and I've already heard a bunch of stuff on the radio."

Gillette smiled briefly. "No problem." He pointed toward the couch. "Let's sit down."

"Do you want something to drink?"

"No."

When they were seated, Gillette turned to her, putting one arm up on the back of the couch behind her. "Who are you working for?" he asked bluntly.

"Tom McGuire," she answered right away. "He approached me two months ago. I was supposed to keep track of you when he gave me the order, supposed to get close to you."

Gillette shook his head. "But why?"

She glanced down. "You know why," she said softly. "So McGuire could set you up."

"No, no. Why would you *do it*? You've got a great career going, you're immensely popular. Why would you agree to help Tom McGuire?"

"Careers in my business come and go very fast, especially when the music label isn't supporting you. I knew the record label was going to screw me on this album because Donovan told them to. It would have destroyed my career. McGuire promised me that whoever ultimately replaced Donovan at Everest would make sure my career was taken care of." She put her hand on his. "He told me you wouldn't help me, but you did. When I heard what they were going to do to you, I called right away. When McGuire approached me, he told me you had agreed with Donovan about pulling back support for me. He also told me that they were going to destroy you, not kill you. I'm no murderer, Christian. I had no idea they were going to do what they did to Donovan, either. If I'd had *any* idea what they were really doing, I would never have gotten involved."

Gillette nodded. "It's a good thing you contacted me when you did," he said softly. "I would have been dead. Literally." He paused. "Who's McGuire working with at Everest?"

She shrugged. "I don't know who. But I know it's someone high up."

22

Routines. Most of us are creatures of habit, more comfortable with order than anarchy. By maintaining a routine, we avoid original thought. We make it easier on ourselves.

But routines can also create opportunity for the enemy.

STRAZZI PUT ONE FOOT UP on the bench and tightened the laces of his running shoe, his breath rising in front of him as he leaned over. It was a crisp, clear Saturday morning in Central Park. The temperature was hovering around freezing and the sun was only halfway above the horizon.

He jogged several mornings a week in the park, usually doing around three miles. From Monday to Friday, the days he jogged would vary, depending on his hectic schedule. But, on weekends when he was in the city, he *always* ran on Saturday and Sunday mornings. And always at the same time.

Finished with the laces, Strazzi put his feet together and bent over, trying to touch his toes. For a man in his late fifties he was still in good shape. He straightened up, stretched his upper body, took a few quick breaths, then headed off at a slow but steady trot. Moving north along the eastern edge of the park. Tasting last night's cigar as he jogged.

Near Harlem, he cut left, toward the running trails he liked.

Ten minutes later he was moving along a narrow path through dense woods, thinking about how very soon he would control 25 percent of the Everest vote. How, once he controlled the widow's stake, he'd immediately call a meeting of the investors to vote on removing Gillette. Win the vote easily and install himself as chairman after convincing the rest of the investors that he was the best, really the only, alternative. That, without him, the government was going to descend on Everest like the Allies on Normandy.

He smiled to himself as the path turned steep. As chairman of Everest, he would control the two largest private equity firms in the world—and more than $40 billion. He wouldn't just be *a* god of private equity, he'd be *the* god.

Halfway up the hill, Strazzi thought he heard someone behind him. Despite his own loud, labored breathing, he was almost certain he heard footsteps. Twenty to thirty feet back, pacing him. He tried glancing over his shoulder, but tripped on a rock jutting out from the rutted path before he could spot anyone. He stumbled forward several steps, barely regaining his balance, sweat coursing down his face.

Forty billion dollars. Enough to make a man paranoid. Enough to make him a target.

The footsteps were still there. He was sure of it. Closing in on him as he headed through the most remote section of the trail, deserted this early in the morning.

Finally, he reached the top of the hill. Here the path was level and smoother. He could look back without having to worry about losing his balance.

When he did, he saw a man who was his size but much younger. The man wore running shorts, a Windbreaker, a baseball cap, and dark glasses despite the low light.

Strazzi put his head down and ran as fast as he could. His legs churned, and he gasped for air as lactic acid quickly built up in his muscles.

But the man behind him continued to gain ground. Strazzi could hear the footsteps pounding on the path. His pursuer was only a few paces back and there was still a long way to go before he'd break out of the woods. He tried to go faster. Tried to keep his legs under him as his lungs seared two baseball-sized holes in his chest. But his legs finally gave way, and he tumbled to the ground.

He felt the man's hand on his arm and tried to scramble away, but it was no use. "Help!" he yelled. "Help!"

"What's wrong, pal? Hey, you all right?"

Strazzi brought his hands slowly down from his face and gazed up into the dark glasses beneath the brim of the baseball cap. "Huh?"

"You all right?" the man repeated.

Strazzi bobbed his head, confused, then struggled to his knees as the man helped him up. "Yeah, yeah," he panted. "I'm fine," he said, suddenly embarrassed.

"Sit here," the man instructed, gently helping Strazzi sit on a large rock beside the path. "You need liquids. That's your problem." He pulled a small bottle of water from a pack around his waist, twisted the cap off, and handed the bottle to Strazzi. "Here."

Strazzi grabbed it and guzzled, hand shaking as he brought it to his lips. Wiping his mouth with the back of his hand when he was done. "Thanks," he gasped, handing the bottle back to the man.

"Sit here for a few minutes and catch your breath," the man advised. "Then walk out. Don't try to run anymore."

"I won't," Strazzi agreed. He watched the man jog off. He'd been certain his number was up.

Gillette gazed down at Washington, D.C., from the cabin of the private jet headed toward Reagan National Airport, cruising above the Potomac River through the clear, early morning. The city was off to the northwest. He could see the Capitol, the Washington Monument, and the White House, forming a neat triangle just to the south of downtown.

"A couple of minutes and we'll be on the ground," Stiles informed Gillette, slipping into the seat beside him. He'd just checked with the pilots. "We're cleared to land. No delays."

"Thanks," he said, still looking down on the city. "I like D.C.," he murmured, more to himself than Stiles.

"Not me," Stiles replied.

"Why not?" Gillette asked, turning away from the window.

"You ever try to get around in this city?"

"What do you mean?"

"The streets are screwed up, man. You think you're going east and you end up going west. Or you're almost where you need to be, then suddenly they throw a park in front of you. I mean, the road ends just like that." He snapped his fingers. "It's so damn frustrating. You can see the other side of the park where the road starts up again. A hundred yards away through the woods. But you sure as hell can't get there because the park goes left and right as far as you can see. So you ask somebody how to get over there," Stiles said, pointing toward the front of the plane as if he was pointing toward the other side of an imaginary park. "They laugh and tell you that you have to go to the other side of Maryland to get there."

"I'm gonna guess you were late for something once," Gillette said, grinning. "Probably a woman."

"Maybe." Stiles grinned back. "Anyway, that's why I like New York City. Streets go east and west and avenues go north and south. Except for some issues in Greenwich Village, it's pretty easy. This place is a nightmare." Stiles looked out the window past Gillette. "So, why do you like Washington?"

Gillette had come to Washington for an early spring weekend during his junior year at Princeton with several members of Tiger, his Eating Club. They'd gone out to dinner in Georgetown, and he'd met a girl at a bar. A dark-haired girl from American University. He'd spent the rest of the weekend with her. And the next, and the next, and the next. She traveled to Princeton on the train, or he went to D.C. They were inseparable from the beginning, and he hadn't cared about the crap he'd taken from his friends for being so suddenly devoted. It had been his first real love affair, and he'd been certain they would marry. But in May, two months after they'd met, she'd been diagnosed with an inoperable brain tumor. She'd died in August.

"Christian." Stiles nudged Gillette's elbow as they touched down. "Hey, so why do you like Washington?"

Gillette looked over at Stiles. "The architecture," he said, thinking about Isabelle, then Faith. "You gave the pictures to Stockman's aide last night?"

Stiles nodded. "Yeah. You should have seen the guy's face."

"Good. We'll call the senator when we're done here. Go see him in person and drop the bomb." Gillette unhooked his seat belt as the jet slowed down and eased off the runway. "You know what?"

"What?

"We should go out sometime, to dinner or something. We'll bring dates." Gillette picked up several folders from the seat pocket in front of him. "I assume there is someone."

"Yes, there is. I'd like that. Thanks." Stiles stood up as the plane neared the general aviation terminal. "Now, listen, we've got to be careful getting you off the plane. In fact, we've got to be careful the whole time we're here."

"Yeah?"

Stiles pulled his shoulder holster down from the overhead compartment and slipped into it. "I'm sure a lot of people know about you coming down here today. It would be logical for someone to try something. They'd have plenty of time to prepare, and they'd be able to pick their spot." He reached up into the overhead compartment again. "Put this on," he ordered.

"What is it?"

"A bulletproof vest."

"Quentin, I—"

"Put it on."

Gillette shook his head, taking the vest from Stiles. "Why do I feel like I'm not sure who's working for who at this point?"

"Senator Stockman."

Stockman looked up from his desk. He'd been drafting a speech. "What is it, Frank?" he snapped. He hadn't slept well last night, and he was in a foul mood.

Galway grimaced. "I have to talk to you about something, sir."

"Is it important?"

"Very."

Stockman let out a heavy sigh. "Sit," he said, pointing at a chair in front of the desk. "What is it?"

"I was approached on the street last night."

Stockman put down his pen. "Oh?" He'd heard an ominous tone in Galway's voice.

"I thought at first this guy was just being nice. Said he'd seen me on TV while you were delivering your announcement about running."

Stockman spotted an envelope in Galway's trembling hand. "But he wasn't."

A confused look came to Galway's face. "Sir?"

"He wasn't being nice."

Galway swallowed hard. "No, he wasn't."

"What did he want?"

"He wanted to give me these," Galway explained, reaching forward and handing the envelope to Stockman.

Stockman took the envelope, placed it on his desk, and removed the stack of photos. Carefully examining each one before finally looking up at Galway. "We have a problem," he said calmly.

"I thought you might see it that way, too, sir."

"Have you shown these to anyone else?"

Galway shook his head.

"Did the person who gave you these say what he wanted?" Stockman asked.

"No, sir."

"Did he give you a way to contact him?"

"No."

"Did he say when he would contact you again?"

"Sometime this weekend. Nothing specific."

Stockman ran his hands through his silver hair and shut his eyes tightly. Christian Gillette. It had to be.

Strazzi had been sitting on the rock for five minutes, letting his heart settle down. "All right," he muttered to himself, "time to get home." As soon as he got back to the penthouse, he was going to hire a full-time bodyguard. Like Gillette had done. "Come on, get up," he urged himself, groaning.

As Strazzi made it to his feet, he noticed the man. He was standing twenty feet away in the middle of the trail. The same man who'd helped him a few minutes ago.

Strazzi smiled and waved. "Thanks again for the water. It hit the spot."

The man said nothing.

"Hey, did you hear me?"

The man began walking toward Strazzi. When he was ten feet away, he reached behind his back and pulled a pistol from a holster. Aiming it directly at Strazzi's chest and squeezing the trigger.

Strazzi scrambled off the rock the second he saw the gun, but the bullet still struck him. It caught him in the shoulder and put him down as it tore out his back. Strazzi groaned and grabbed at the wound, but still was able to pull himself to his feet and stumble into the woods, ducking around trees as he ran. He hurled headlong into a sapling when he looked back to try to see if the shooter was there, tumbling to the ground as it snapped under his weight. But he was up again instantly, moving deeper into the thick cover.

The second bullet got him in the back of the thigh, tearing his hamstring. He pitched forward, landing heavily in the thick cover of leaves, grabbed his leg and screamed in pain.

The assassin moved deliberately toward where Strazzi lay. He always enjoyed these last few seconds—when the victim knew it was over. He wondered how it felt to know the number of breaths remaining could be counted on the fingers of one hand. He'd killed a lot of people in his life, but the question always came to him at this moment. Had from the very first time. How did it feel to know death was close and there was nothing that could be done?

He stood over Strazzi for several seconds, gazing into his eyes. Trying to comprehend the terror Strazzi was enduring. Strazzi wasn't yelling anymore, just whimpering pitifully, overcome by the inevitability of his death.

The assassin leaned down, pressed the barrel to Strazzi's temple, and pulled the trigger. Blood, bone, and brain blew out the other side of Strazzi's head, onto the leaves. After a violent tremor, his body went still.

Walter Price was the chief executive officer of Dominion Savings & Loan. Three years ago, Donovan had recruited Price out of Citibank, where he'd headed their huge retail operation. He had given Price ten million a year plus bonus plus stock options to make Dominion a player. To grow it fast. Which Price had done, increasing Dominion's asset base from three billion to forty. A huge increase that Gillette now feared might have been accomplished mostly by sleight of hand.

"It just isn't true," Price said evenly. "We have less than two hundred million in nonperforming loans. That's about half of 1 percent of our total asset base. That's nothing. It's right in line with industry averages. A little better, actually."

"Then why does Congressman Allen hold up a folder in front of the television cameras and say he has proof that you have billions in non-performing loans? How do you explain that?"

"I can't," Price replied simply.

"You gotta do better than that, Walter. I told you to have a report ready for me. You haven't prepared anything."

"There's nothing to prepare. We're fine."

"Walter, I—"

"Look, Christian, we have state and federal examiners around all the time. It's ridiculous how much time they spend in our offices. And we have our own internal people constantly spot-checking. If there was anything to find, someone would have."

"You're telling me I have nothing to worry about."

"I'm telling you to go out and buy as many shares of our stock as you can. By this time next week our share price is going to be back up where it was before all this bullshit. Maybe higher."

Gillette sat back in the leather chair and thought for a second. Assume what Price was saying was true. Assume there wasn't anything wrong. Assume all of this had been neatly choreographed. But if you assumed that, you also had to accept what Price was saying would happen, that when no one could find anything wrong with Dominion, its stock would go shooting back up. There'd be some pissed-off investors who'd dumped at the bottom because they believed they might as well get something before the shares were delisted. But there would also be some extremely happy people who'd speculated and bought when the price was a buck and change because the downside was so small. So what was the point?

Then it hit him. Of course. This was Strazzi's way of manipulating the widow, of scaring the hell out of her so she'd sell her stake in Everest. Strazzi had tried to get information on the portfolio companies from Mason to cement his case, but he'd been beaten to the punch. However, it hadn't mattered. All he'd ultimately needed was Dominion's implosion. And, after Monday, it wouldn't matter if the stock came roaring back. Strazzi would own the piece of Everest he wanted. The widow might cry foul, but he'd just tell her to go screw herself.

Gillette nodded to himself. There was a way to check it all out.

"I appreciate you meeting with me, Walter," he said, standing up and shaking the other man's hand. He needed to get going right away.

Because the answer wasn't in Washington. It was back in New York.

23

The Showdown. *Someone must lose.*

"THEY HAVE TO GO," GILLETTE said firmly, pointing at Galway and another aide as he and Stiles entered Stockman's office.

"All right," Stockman muttered, motioning for them to leave.

"But *my* man stays." Gillette gestured toward Stiles as the two aides disappeared through the doorway.

Stockman nodded.

Gillette sat in front of Stockman's desk while Stiles moved to the window, checking on the two men he'd left on the street with Gillette's driver.

"It's two o'clock Saturday afternoon," the senator spoke up. "What in the hell's so damn important that you had to see me right away?" the senator asked angrily.

"I think you know."

"What's that supposed to mean?"

"Quentin gave your aide the photographs last night," Gillette answered. There was no need to be evasive. It was time to hit Stockman between the eyes. "I'm sure you've seen them by now." He watched Stockman clench his teeth, then take a deep breath. Trying to stay in control. The senator had a nasty temper, and Gillette could tell he was close to erupting. "Right?"

"Yes," Stockman admitted curtly.

"You've been seeing the Jones woman for a while, haven't you? In fact, you've brought her to Washington a few times."

"Well, haven't we been busy?" Stockman asked.

"All things done in the dark eventually come to light."

"Your father should have listened to that advice, son," Stockman said, and sneered. "If he had, he might still be alive. Or maybe you don't know why your mother drank so much."

Gillette's eyes flashed to Stockman's. It wasn't the first time someone had implied that his father's plane might have been sabotaged, and, for a moment, it threw him. Which he knew was exactly what Stockman wanted. To distract him. Maybe tempt him to trade pictures for information about the crash instead of the conspiracy.

"You should be glad I'm a rational man, Senator," Gillette finally said, his voice devoid of emotion, forcing himself to focus. "Glad this is only about you and me reaching an understanding that benefits me in business. Glad I don't have time for revenge."

"If all you wanted was to destroy my chance of being president, these damn things would already be at *The New York Times*," Stockman said, reaching into a drawer and dropping the envelope full of photographs on the desktop. "I know that." He hesitated. "So, what *do* you want?"

"Answers."

"Answers to what?"

"Are you and Paul Strazzi working together to force me out of Everest Capital?"

Stockman hesitated.

"If you answer my questions," Gillette continued forcefully, "I burn the duplicate set of those photographs. If you don't, *The Times* will have them within the hour."

"Yes," Stockman answered quietly. "We've been working together."

"Why?"

"I want votes and Strazzi wants Everest. It's as simple as that. Plus, Paul hated Donovan," Stockman added. "There was that, too."

"What about Dominion Savings & Loan?"

"What about it?" Stockman hissed.

"There aren't really billions of bad loans at Dominion, are there?"

"It's your investment," Stockman retorted snidely. "You tell me."

"Goddamn it, answer me."

Stockman clenched his teeth again.

"*Senator.*"

"No, there aren't. No more than there are at any other savings and loan that size."

"Why does Congressman Allen think there are?"

"What do you mean?" Stockman asked, grimacing as he glanced at one of the photographs.

"I saw the press conference yesterday afternoon. Allen claimed he had evidence that there were billions."

"Allen owes me."

"Still, I don't think a prominent congressman calls a press conference and accuses the partners at Everest Capital of fraud without documentation—no matter how much he owes you. He could be writing his own ticket out of Washington."

Stockman mulled over the question. "Okay, we had help."

"Where?"

"Inside Dominion."

"What kind of help?"

"Earlier this week, somebody ran a few official-looking reports indicating that the loan portfolio was in terrible shape. Grossly inflating bad loans. I gave Allen that report."

"Who was the person inside Dominion who ran the false reports?"

"I don't know," Stockman snapped. "I wasn't involved in that. That was Strazzi's responsibility."

"Who's Strazzi using inside Everest?" Gillette demanded.

Stockman's eyes flashed to Gillette's.

"Come on, Senator. You must have someone inside Everest, too. That's the only way Strazzi would have been able to convince a senior person inside Dominion to cooperate, to run those reports for Allen."

Stockman looked around the office like a caged animal. "Marcie Reed."

Gillette made certain not to react, despite being elated to have nailed the rat. He'd deal with her later. "A few more—" His cell phone rang and he pulled it out quickly. Isabelle. He'd bought her a cell phone yesterday and, like a child, she couldn't stop using it. He shut off the ring and shoved the phone back in his pocket. He was going to see her in a few hours anyway. "Is this Dominion scam something Strazzi's been planning for a long time?" he asked.

Stockman drew a measured breath. "No. Strazzi was just being opportunistic," he answered deliberately. "I know he's been trying to figure out a way to take Bill Donovan down for a long time. But, like I said, in terms of Dominion, he just took advantage of the situation."

"You mean you don't think he had Donovan killed," Gillette said bluntly.

"That thought never crossed my mind."

"Bullshit, Senator. That's exactly what you were thinking. Because it makes so much sense. Without Donovan around, Marcie Reed can pin the bad loans on him, claim he was the one who knew and didn't tell anyone. Am I right?"

Stockman stared at Gillette, a blank expression on his face.

"You really only have to convince one person there are problems at Dominion," Gillette pointed out. "And that's Ann Donovan. So she'll sell her Everest stake to Strazzi for a rock-bottom price. Then he can throw me out with that huge voting bloc of hers. Right?" he asked again, boring in on the truth. "Once Strazzi has her stake, you don't care if the world finds out that the story about the bad loans isn't true. It doesn't matter then. I mean, Allen will be hot as hell, but what do you care? You've probably got something on him that's ten times worse than the fraudulent report you provided him. So, what's he going to say? Nothing," Gillette answered his own question. "I would have come after him with everything I had for screwing our reputation. But if the plan had worked, I wouldn't have been around to do that. Strazzi would have been chairman. After Strazzi takes over, you tell Allen he has nothing to worry about, that you'll protect him. He's pissed, and he loses a little credibility, but the public has a short memory." Gillette stared hard at Stockman. "That's how it was supposed to go down, right?"

"Yes," Stockman agreed.

"You provided access to Allen. In return, you got Strazzi's support, including his multibillion-dollar money bag, I'm assuming. That's why you weren't concerned about being able to raise campaign money when we had lunch. You knew you had whatever you needed."

"Nice work, Detective."

"How long has Marcie Reed been working with Strazzi?" Gillette asked.

The senator shrugged.

"Come on."

"Six months."

"How long have *you* been working with him?"

"Longer than Marcie Reed."

"Did Donovan know about you and Strazzi working together to take him down?" Gillette asked, thinking about what McGuire had told him, how Donovan had found out something nasty about Stockman.

"Yeah," Stockman admitted. "He found out about it three months ago. He had someone on the payroll in my office here in New York who reported back to him. I fired the fucker when I found out what was going on."

"So why did you approach me at the funeral reception about supporting you?"

"I don't understand."

"You already had Strazzi with you," Gillette pointed out. "If I'd agreed to help you, I'm assuming you wouldn't have given Allen the fraudulent Dominion loan reports. But then you would have lost Strazzi and all his money."

"I wasn't convinced Strazzi's plan to fleece the widow was going to work," Stockman answered. "Besides, what I wanted *most* was your TV and radio networks. I can always raise money when the media endorses me."

Gillette stood up. Marcie and Kyle were meeting him at Everest, and there was something he needed to do before they arrived. "I'll be in touch," he said, reaching the door.

"Well?" Stockman asked, standing up, too.

"Well, what?"

"I answered your questions. Give me the other set of photos."

Gillette stopped and turned around. "Let me ask you one more time. Did Strazzi have Bill Donovan killed?"

Stockman shook his head. "No," he said firmly. "Paul's a tough son-of-a-bitch, but he wouldn't take it that far."

Gillette gazed at Stockman for a few moments, then motioned to Stiles. "Let's go."

"Hey!" Stockman roared. "What about the photographs?"

Gillette glanced back again. "Senator, I'm not sure I'm done with you yet."

.   .   .

As they waited for the elevator in the hallway outside Stockman's office, Gillette and Stiles were silent. But after they'd gotten into the car and the door had closed, Gillette spoke up. "Send the photographs to *The Daily News* Monday afternoon. We'll claim we don't know anyone at *The News*, and we have no idea how they got them. Okay?"

"Yup."

Gillette checked his watch as he sat in front of Marcie's computer: 3:30. Marcie and Kyle were supposed to be here at 4:00 so he could go over the companies each of them would be taking charge of as chairperson. They'd grumbled about it being short notice—and Saturday—but both had agreed to come.

He flipped on the computer, drumming his fingers on her desk as the CPU hummed to life. While the virus program scanned the hard drive, he picked up her phone and dialed the lobby.

"Yes?" Stiles was sitting at the front desk.

"Quentin, don't let *anyone* past you until I say so."

"You don't have to tell me twice."

"I'm in Marcie Reed's office."

"I know."

Gillette was about to hang up, then brought the phone back to his ear. "You know, if this security thing doesn't work out, you always have a job as the Everest receptionist."

"You're a helluva guy, Christian."

Gillette grinned as he hung up and inputted Marcie's password. He kept everyone's password in a file on his computer, which updated automatically if anyone changed theirs. Early last week, he'd brought in a technology specialist from the outside to set up the program. The guy had promised him that the internal technology people at Everest would never detect what he'd done.

Gillette hit the Enter key, then went quickly to Marcie's e-mail, searching her messages for any correspondence related to Dominion. He wanted to have something other than Stockman's claim that she was Strazzi's rat, some tangible piece of evidence, because Marcie was tough. He assumed she wouldn't roll over at just an accusation.

Of course, she was probably going to join Apex as soon as Strazzi bought the widow's stake. She'd certainly inked that deal before agreeing to help Strazzi, so it wasn't as if threatening to fire her was going to get him anything. But if he had evidence that she'd helped Strazzi manipulate Dominion's share price, she'd have to answer to the SEC for securities fraud. The public had lost billions, and she'd be facing a long prison sentence. Under those circumstances, she'd talk.

He searched her incoming messages first, then the deleted ones. There were hundreds, and it would take time to do this thoroughly. He checked his watch again: 3:45. If he couldn't find anything now, he'd come in tomorrow and go through the files with a fine-tooth comb. He'd have plenty of privacy then.

Finally, Gillette searched the sent items folder, reading certain ones based on the subject line. Scanning quickly. As he scrolled down, one message caught his eye. He raced back up to it, having flashed past it in his haste. The subject was "Payments" and it had been sent to a KHays@MPBrands.com. MP Brands was one of Everest's portfolio companies, the one Kathy Hays worked for. His eyes narrowed. KHays had to stand for Kathy Hays—the woman he'd caught Mason with in the basement of Donovan's mansion, the woman Lefors had told him about as he'd come out of Donovan's study.

Gillette clicked on the message.

"Christian." Stiles's voice blared through the intercom.

"What?"

"Marcie Reed just got off the elevator."

"Stall her," Gillette urged, his eyes flashing over the e-mail. It said:

You'll be paid $250,000 when it happens, and $25,000 a month for six months after that. At the end of six months, you'll be on your own. You'll resign from MP Brands as soon as it happens.

Gillette checked the date and time of the e-mail—two weeks ago yesterday, at 1:45 in the afternoon. He glanced down and reread it.

So Strazzi had made certain Mason would be fired from Everest. He'd paid off Kathy Hays to set Mason up. Then Marcie had told Lefors at the reception that Kathy Hays was down in the basement with Mason, knowing Lefors would run to Gillette with the information, knowing Lefors would instantly see an opportunity to have Mason fired and be promoted to managing partner.

Strazzi wanted Mason because he knew all about Everest, and he wanted Mason bitter so he'd give up that information readily. It had all worked perfectly until Jose had shown up at Mason's apartment and gotten the files. But, in the end, the widow had still agreed to sell out just because of Dominion.

Hopefully, there was still time to stop the transaction between Strazzi and the widow. Gillette was confident that if the widow understood what was really going on, she wouldn't sell—if for no other reason than because she'd realize her stake was worth much more than what Strazzi was offering, and that, when the real story came out, Dominion's stock price would climb back to where it had been before and the feds wouldn't go after Everest.

As Gillette quickly printed out a copy of the e-mail, he heard a commotion outside, growing louder and louder from down the corridor. He recognized Marcie's voice. She was yelling at someone.

He snatched the copy of the e-mail from the printer and headed through the doorway, remembering as he moved past the executive assistant's desk outside Marcie's office that he'd left her computer on. As he turned around to shut it off, she and Stiles appeared around the corner. Stiles was trying to restrain her gently, but it wasn't working.

"*Get your hands off of me,*" Marcie demanded. "I mean it."

"Ma'am, I—"

"I'm going to my office!" she yelled at him. "I'm a goddamn managing partner here and you better not try to—" She stopped short when she saw Gillette by her executive assistant's desk. "Hello, Christian."

"Hello, Marcie," he said calmly, folding the e-mail copy and sliding it into his pocket. "What's the problem?"

"Your personal goon tried to keep me from coming in even after he searched me. He put his damn hands all over me."

Gillette motioned for Stiles to move off. "When Lefors gets here, let him come in," he called.

"Right."

"Quentin was following my orders, Marcie," Gillette explained when Stiles was gone. "He wasn't doing anything wrong."

"What's going on around here?" she demanded, pushing her hair back over one ear. "Why all the CIA-headquarters-level security?"

Gillette hesitated. "There've been two more attempts on my life since the limousine explosion," he answered.

Her eyes widened and she brought her hands to her mouth. "Oh, my God. What's going on?"

She could have won an Oscar for the performance, but he wasn't buying it. It was looking more and more like Cohen had been right. Strazzi was behind everything: the murder of Bill Donovan and the limousine explosion. Probably the other two attempts to kill him as well. And Marcie was working with Strazzi. As far as he was concerned, she was guilty by association. "I think someone's trying to take over Everest."

"Who?"

"I—"

"Hi, Christian," Lefors called, appearing around the corner. He was holding a half-eaten Three Musketeers bar. "Hi, Marcie."

Gillette nodded. Marcie looked away.

"Let's go to the small conference room outside my office," Gillette suggested, trying to understand what was going on between them. Was it petty rivalry—or something deeper? "We'll talk there."

"I'll be down in a minute," Marcie said, heading toward her office. "I've got to get something."

Gillette watched her disappear through the doorway, wondering how he was going to explain her computer being on. He gestured to Lefors and they moved down the corridor to the conference room. "How do you feel about Coyote Oil?"

"Good," Lefors answered. "I went through the information they sent and they look real."

Gillette hadn't had a chance to scan what Coyote had sent over. "Are you and Cohen going to call Switzerland?" he asked as they moved into the conference room.

"Yeah. Late tomorrow night, I think."

"Ask the tough questions, Kyle."

"I will."

Marcie entered the conference room a few moments later. Gillette saw she was upset right away. Her cheeks were flushed and her lips were drawn tightly together. As she sat down, she crossed her arms over her chest. She'd seen the e-mail to Kathy Hays on the screen and knew someone had been spying on her. "What's wrong?" he asked.

"Nothing," she snapped, staring at the tabletop.

"Come on," Gillette urged. This wasn't going to end well for her, so they might as well get on with it. "Tell me."

"I think you know."

Gillette glanced at Lefors, who was studying Marcie intently. "Know what?"

"You turned on my computer and went through my e-mails. Or *he* did," she hissed, jabbing an outstretched finger at Lefors.

Lefors held up his hands. "*Moi?*"

"Yeah, *you.*"

"I don't know what you're talking about."

"Sure you don't."

"Why would I do something like that?" Lefors asked innocently.

"Because you don't want me to get promoted. You're trying to find something to hurt me with, something bad to show Christian so that he won't make me a managing partner, too."

"That's ridiculous. I think every private equity firm should have a token female partner."

"You asshole!" she yelled, springing up from her chair.

"Enough," Gillette ordered, silencing both of them. "I need a few minutes alone with Marcie," he said to Lefors. "Wait for me in your office."

"Okay," Lefors replied, standing up and moving to the door, giving her a triumphant look as he headed out.

When Lefors was gone, Gillette motioned for Marcie to sit back down. "Is there anything you want to tell me?" he asked. She was twirling her hair.

Her eyes moved slowly to his. "That sounds ominous."

"Take it however you want. Just answer me."

She shook her head. "I've got nothing to say."

Just like her, Gillette thought to himself. Deny, deny, deny. He was going to have to drag it out of her. "Have you been working with Paul Strazzi?"

"Paul Strazzi?" she asked, putting a hand on her chest. "Of course not. Why would I do that?"

"That's a good question."

"Then why would you think I was?"

"Because Senator Stockman says you have."

"*What?*"

"Yeah. I was in Stockman's office two hours ago, and he told me you were Strazzi's hookup on this Dominion thing, the one here at Everest who directed someone at Dominion to cook the books and make it appear that there were billions in bad loans. So the stock price would tank when Congressman Allen made his announcement yesterday. Which it did."

Marcie's eyes widened and she stopped twirling her hair.

"Strazzi's trying to take over Everest," Gillette continued. "He's convinced Ann Donovan to sell her stake in Everest to him. That stake has a 25 percent voting bloc that goes along with it, which would give him enough votes to kick me out and get himself elected chairman." Gillette paused. "But I'm sure you already knew all that."

Marcie shook her head. "No, I didn't—"

"Marcie, don't insult me."

She gazed at him for a long time, then her shoulders sagged slightly.

"Tell me the truth," Gillette pushed.

Still she didn't answer. "If you were involved, you've got big problems with the feds," he pointed out. "Criminal problems. If you come clean with me, I'll do what I can to protect you."

Her eyes darted to his.

"Who's the person at Dominion you worked with?" he asked.

She hesitated.

"Don't aggravate me, Marcie. I can—"

"Okay, okay. It's a guy named Marty Reisner. He's the chief information officer at Dominion. He knows everything about Dominion's software systems. He's a magician with data."

Gillette nodded. "Why'd you do it, Marcie? Why'd you help Strazzi?"

"Come on, Christian. Donovan was never going to promote me, and Strazzi offered me a lot to join Apex. It wasn't much of a decision."

"But the bad loan reports were run *after* Donovan was killed. You must have known that I'd promote you, or at least thought I might. Why risk getting caught up in a scandal without finding out what I was offering?"

"Strazzi's giving me a much better deal than you ever would. A lot of independence, too. I invest in whatever I want, and I get a huge chunk of the ups. That's the bottom line. And I'm not worried about the feds. They won't be able to link me to any of this Dominion stuff. In the end, it's Reisner's word against mine."

"*And* Stockman and Strazzi's word," Gillette reminded her. "No, you've got a big problem. Did you know Strazzi was going to kill Bill Donovan," he asked bluntly.

"*What? No.* Bill drowned."

"He was murdered, and Strazzi was behind it. You must have known what was going on."

"I didn't know anything."

"Sure you did. It fits perfectly. Donovan had to be out of the way for Strazzi to be able to buy the widow's stake. And the whole thing would have worked if Stockman had shown just a little restraint. I never would have been able to figure out what was going on if he wasn't having an affair with the Jones woman. I never could have gotten him to talk."

"Affair?" Marcie asked hesitantly.

"Yeah. And I have photographs."

"Jesus," she whispered. "Look, Christian, I didn't know anything about Donovan being murdered. I swear. Strazzi approached me a few months ago and offered me a deal. Help him find a way to take Donovan down, and I get to run all that money myself. As far as I know, Strazzi was just being opportunistic with this Dominion thing. He just wanted the widow's stake so he could kick you out. I don't believe he had anything to do with Donovan's death."

Gillette leaned back. No way to know yet if she was lying. "I was the one who turned on your computer this afternoon, Marcie," he said. "Not Kyle. I went through your e-mails looking for things about Dominion." He watched her closely, but she didn't react. Just started twirling her hair again. "I didn't find anything. Which didn't surprise me. I was sure you wouldn't send anything incriminating by e-mail. There would always be a record on the server."

"Right," she said quietly. "I'm not stupid."

"But I did find this," he said, pulling the Kathy Hays e-mail from his pocket and sliding it across the table toward her. "This came from your sent items folder. What it shows is that Strazzi set Troy Mason up with this woman, Kathy Hays. Through you," he added.

Her hand moved slowly across the polished tabletop to the paper. She opened it and gazed at the words. "I didn't write this."

"Come on, Marcie," Gillette pushed angrily. "Tell me the truth."

"I mean it. I didn't write it." She checked the top of the e-mail to make certain it was from her computer. "Someone got on my computer while I was out."

"Marcie, you're in a lot of trouble with this Dominion thing. You must know that. Like I said, if you work with me, I'll do everything I can to help you. I know people down at 26 Federal Plaza. I can't promise anything, but I'll do my best."

"No one can prove anything," she said defiantly.

"Admit that Strazzi set Mason up," Gillette demanded.

"Maybe he did, but I didn't know about it. I did not write that e-mail," she repeated firmly.

"Kyle said he knew the woman was in the basement with Mason at the funeral reception because you told him."

"He's lying," she said tersely.

"But what about this e-mail?"

"*I didn't write it!*"

Gillette held up his hands. "Okay, fine." This was going nowhere. "I want you out of here right now," he said calmly. "I'll call you tomorrow to tell you where we go from here."

"Does this mean I'm fired?" she asked, rising from her chair.

"Yeah. You're done."

"Fine," she said, stalking toward the door. "Don't bother calling me."

Gillette watched her disappear, then picked up the phone quickly and dialed the lobby. "Quentin."

"Yeah?"

"Find Marcie and get her out of here right now. Don't let her take anything. Tell her we'll box up her personal crap and send it to her. Got it?"

"Yup."

Gillette put the phone down and headed to Lefors office.

He was reading a newspaper, feet up on the desk, a bag of Fritos in his lap.

"Hey." Lefors tossed the paper on the desk when he saw Gillette and dropped his feet to the floor. "What the hell's going on with Marcie?"

Gillette shook his head. "Nothing." He wasn't going to tell Lefors anything at this point. Something told him Lefors knew a lot more about what had happened over the last week than he was letting on.

"Did you want to talk about the companies I'll be taking over?" Lefors asked expectantly.

"We'll do that later. Right now I need you to answer one question."

"Okay, what?"

"How did you know Kathy Hays was in the basement with Troy Mason at the funeral reception?"

Lefors gave Gillette a strange look. "You already asked me that."

"I'm asking again."

"Marcie told me."

"You sure you want to stick to that story?"

"Yes," he answered after a few seconds.

Gillette stood in the doorway for several moments, staring at Lefors. Then he turned away and headed toward his office.

"It's true. I agreed to sell my Everest stake to Paul Strazzi," Ann Donovan confirmed. "I'm sorry, Christian. Both of us know what that means. Paul intends to remove you as chairman. You're a nice young man and I'm sure that it's a terrible disappointment but I had no choice. You'll find something else."

"Could I just say—"

"I had to do what I had to do," she interrupted. "I had to protect myself. This Dominion thing was very scary to me. I lost something like $50 million. I don't come from a wealthy family. I still worry about money. Paul's paying me over $2 billion and most of it's in cash. Given everything that was going on, I had to take his offer."

"Besides Dominion, what else do you think is going on at Everest, Mrs. Donovan?" Gillette asked.

She glanced past him, admiring a painting of the estate hanging over the fireplace. "I understand that there are other problems with the Everest portfolio companies."

"Did Paul Strazzi tell you that?"

"He and one other person."

"Was it Senator Stockman?" The widow's eyes raced back to Gillette's, and he had his answer. "Did Strazzi actually show you any evidence of problems with our portfolio companies? Did he give you any specifics?"

The widow hesitated. "No."

"Mrs. Donovan, what I'm about to tell you will come as a shock, but you have to hear it."

"It doesn't matter what you tell me, Christian. I'm not going to change my mind."

"Strazzi manipulated the Dominion stock crash," Gillette kept going. "With Stockman's help. It was all done so you'd sell your stake at a discount. Even Strazzi couldn't pay you what your stake is really worth, which is over four billion, according to Ben Cohen. Even Paul Strazzi doesn't have that kind of money for one investment. He had to figure out a way to drive the price down."

"I don't believe you."

"One of the people who reports to me at Everest was in on it, Mrs. Donovan. I confirmed that this afternoon."

"No—"

"You've got to listen to me," he said firmly. "You're making a huge mistake. As soon as the market figures out what these guys did, Dominion's stock price is going to come screaming back. You'll regret this."

She closed her eyes. Her head was shaking badly. "I don't know anything about problems with loan portfolios, and, to tell you the truth, I don't care. All I know is that the value of my Dominion investment is worth almost nothing." She put a hand on her frail chest. "I spoke to my lawyer a little while ago, and he says there shouldn't be any problems. Everything is on track. Monday afternoon I'll have $2 billion in my account. Real dollars, Christian. Not a piece of paper that says I own a fund I don't understand."

Gillette sat in his office, just the banker's lamp on. It was nine o'clock. He was supposed to be meeting Isabelle for a late dinner at his apartment at ten. He should have been looking forward to it, but he was distracted. He'd been so certain he could change the widow's mind.

"Sounds like the widow is pretty set on what she's going to do," Cohen said.

"Yeah," Gillette agreed softly.

"That's too bad."

"Yeah."

"Well, just so you know, I checked out these guys at Coyote Oil," Cohen said. "I talked to their backers in Switzerland."

Gillette looked up. "That fast? Lefors told me you were calling them tomorrow night. Their Monday morning."

"Um, I didn't want to wait."

"So they were in the office on a weekend?"

Cohen shook his head. "No. Hansen gave me their cell phone numbers. I talked to the lead guy in Europe. We had a conference call with him and some of his subordinates a few hours ago."

Gillette checked his watch. "Jesus Christ, what time was it over there?"

"Midnight."

"They must really want to do this deal."

"They do," Cohen agreed. "Turns out they've got some big insurance companies from Norway and Sweden in on the deal, people who understand the oil and gas business very well."

"Which ones?"

"I've got the names in my office. I'll get them to you Monday."

"So you're satisfied this all checks out?" Gillette asked.

"Yeah, yeah," Cohen said enthusiastically. "We talked to senior people in the investment arms of each of the big insurance companies, too. They're ready to pay us what we want. The deal can be done in thirty days."

"Lefors was on the calls, too?"

"What?"

"You said, 'We talked to the senior people.'"

"I did?"

"Yeah."

"No, Lefors wasn't on the calls. It was just me."

"Oh." Gillette glanced around the office and shook his head. "It doesn't add up, Ben. Why would Coyote overpay like that? Especially with such sophisticated backers."

"Who cares, Christian? Let's just get it done."

The phone rang, distracting Gillette from a nagging thought, one that had been running through his mind ever since the Coyote Oil executives had visited. He picked up the receiver, not recognizing the number on the screen. "Hello."

"Christian."

"Yes?"

"It's Miles."

"Hi, how are you?"

"Fine. But Paul Strazzi isn't."

"What do you mean?"

"He was found dead an hour ago in a remote section of Central Park. He was murdered."

"*Murdered?*" Gillette asked. Cohen was studying him intently.

"Yes. Shot to death."

"Jesus. Do the police know who did it?"

"No. They aren't even saying if it was a robbery or some kind of hit."

"What the hell was Strazzi doing in a remote section of Central Park?" Gillette asked.

"Jogging, probably. He was religious about it. He and I talked about it at lunch last week."

"Well, then it can't be a random robbery. I doubt anyone would think he was carrying much cash if he was jogging. It must have been a hit."

"I wouldn't rush to that conclusion," Whitman cautioned. "Hell, it could have been a gang. Sometimes they kill people indiscriminately. What's it called, 'Wilding'?"

"What time was Strazzi killed?" Gillette asked.

"I don't know." Whitman was silent for a few moments. "So, Christian, how are you going to celebrate?"

Celebrating another man's death. A strange thought. "I'm not going to celebrate, Miles." Not even if he was trying to have me killed, Gillette thought to himself.

"You know what I mean," Whitman said softly.

"I'm having a late dinner with a friend tonight."

"Really? Where are you going?"

"I haven't decided yet."

"You know there's this new place down in SoHo called Nom de Plume. It's a writer and actor hangout. You're bound to see celebrities. I know the guy who owns it. It's next to impossible to get in there, especially on a Saturday night, but I can call him and get you a table."

"Thank, Miles, but I—" Another line on Gillette's phone rang. "I've got to take this," he said recognizing the number.

"Let me know if you want me to get you in there."

"Thanks." Gillette picked up the other line. "Hello."

"Christian."

The voice was almost inaudible. "Yes."

"It's Ann Donovan."

She must have heard the news about Strazzi, too. "Hello, Mrs. Donovan," he said calmly.

"Did you hear?" she asked meekly.

"About?"

"Paul Strazzi."

"Yes, I did."

"My lawyers just called because Strazzi's lawyers called them. The deal with me is off," she said, her voice shaking. "I hope I didn't offend you in any way when you were here this evening."

Now wasn't the time to gloat. "Of course not." Now was the time to build a bridge. "I heard what you were saying, Mrs. Donovan. You aren't comfortable having so much of your net worth tied up in Everest. You want to diversify, which is smart. And I think I can help if you want me to."

"Thank you, Christian," she said, her voice growing stronger.

"But you have to work with me."

"Yes, yes, of course," she agreed, relief obvious in her tone. "Of course."

"No negotiating behind my back."

"No, no. From now on I'll call you right away if *anyone* approaches me. Okay?"

"Yes, that's exactly what I want." He paused. "Good night, Mrs. Donovan. I'll be in touch with you soon."

"Good night, Christian. Thank you for your understanding. And, again, I hope you weren't upset with me today."

"Not at all. I understood." Gillette hung up the phone and glanced over the desk at Cohen, who was looking back like an expectant father.

"Well," Cohen demanded, "what happened?"

"Paul Strazzi was murdered in Central Park."

"*What?*"

"That was the widow. The deal's off to sell her stake."

Cohen relaxed into his chair and let out a long breath. "Congratulations, pal."

"Thanks."

A sly grin came to Cohen's face as he lounged in the chair. "So, how did you do it?"

"Do what?"

"Kill Strazzi."

Gillette leaned forward and began searching the Web for stories on Strazzi's death. "Go get Stiles," he ordered, ignoring Cohen. "Tell him I want to see him right away."

"I feel so much for you," Isabelle whispered, pulling back from the kiss for a moment. "It's all happened so fast."

"I know," Gillette agreed.

"It scares me," she said.

"It shouldn't."

"Why not?"

Gillette hesitated, gazing at her long, black hair cascading down one side of her neck. "It just shouldn't." The phone on the end table beside the couch rang. He was tempted to ignore it, but then he saw who it was. "Yes, Miles."

"Are you going down to SoHo?" Whitman asked. "You need to tell me now if you are. I'm going to bed."

Gillette smiled over at Isabelle. "No, I'm staying right here. But thanks."

"Okay. Hey, why don't you come out here to Connecticut tomorrow for lunch? I've got some ideas I want to talk to you about. Ideas about the new fund. You've never been out here, have you?"

"No, I haven't."

"Well, call me in the morning. We'll set it up."

"Yeah, sure." Gillette hung up, hesitating a second before turning back to face Isabelle. "Where were we?"

"Right here," she murmured, slipping her arms around his neck and kissing him deeply.

Stiles pressed the two buttons on either side of the Glock's barrel, releasing the top half from the bottom so he could clean the gun. He was sitting in Gillette's study on the first floor of the apartment, cleaning apparatus spread out in front of him on old newspapers covering the desktop.

Gillette was upstairs with Isabelle. Alone with her. And that made him extremely uncomfortable. Gillette hadn't convinced him yet that she could be trusted.

24

"QUENTIN, I WANT YOUR ASSESSMENT of the last twenty-four hours."

Stiles stretched and groaned. He'd fallen asleep in Gillette's study chair a few hours ago, cleaning his gun, and his neck was sore from sleeping in an awkward position. "I'm not sure there's much to assess."

"Strazzi's dead," Gillette reminded Stiles, checking his watch. It was almost nine o'clock.

"Big deal," Stiles muttered, getting up from the chair and sprawling onto the study's long leather couch. "You make it sound like he was the Wicked Witch, we're the Munchkins, and, now that he's dead, we can all come out and play."

Gillette took a bite of an apple he'd gotten in the kitchen on his way downstairs from the bedroom. "I think Strazzi was the one trying to kill me. I didn't for a while, but now I think he was. I think he was responsible for Donovan's murder, too. Donovan had to be out of the way before he could put the Dominion thing in motion, then go to Ann about her Everest stake."

"Wouldn't just the Dominion scandal have accomplished the same thing?" Stiles asked sleepily. "Wouldn't Donovan have come under the hot lights the same way you are now?"

"But that wasn't real and, if he were alive, Donovan would have been able to prove it right away," Gillette argued. "Even if the feds had somehow been able to force him to sell the stake because, by some huge coincidence, there actually was something bad going on that Strazzi didn't know about, Donovan would have sold it to someone else. Never to Strazzi."

Stiles thought about it for a few moments, then nodded. "Yeah, I guess you're right."

Gillette took another bite of the apple. "Did you get anything from your friends at the NYPD on Strazzi's murder?"

"Yeah, he was definitely hit. Whoever pulled the trigger knew what they were doing, too."

"But who would want Strazzi dead?" Gillette asked, more of himself than Stiles.

"That's the million-dollar question."

"I can think of a lot of people who'd *want* him dead," Gillette said, "but nobody who'd actually pull the trigger."

"Or *arrange* for the trigger to be pulled?"

"Not if it really came down to it."

They were silent for a few minutes.

"Isabelle still upstairs?" Stiles asked.

"Yeah." Gillette looked up. "By the way, did your guy get to Canada yet?"

"I'm expecting his call soon." Stiles said, checking his watch. "So, how was your night?"

Gillette smiled. "Excellent. A lot of fun, and no sharp blades in the back. Imagine that."

Stiles put his hands underneath his head and shut his eyes as Gillette walked out. "Yeah, imagine that."

Pepper Billups had been working with Stiles and QS Security for three years.

Like Stiles, Billups had been Secret Service but was now enjoying the private sector. The money was better—if you were willing to work the hours—and there was more satisfaction. Even on days like this, when he'd just finished flying eight hours straight. First from New York to Calgary on a Gulfstream V, then from Calgary to Amachuck on a little King Air through some rough turbulence.

The trick to days like this was being able to sleep on any kind of equipment in any kind of weather. Before joining the Secret Service, Billups had been an Air Force pilot flying the big cargo planes—C-5s and C-130s. He'd been through his share of bad storms, especially during long flights like the ones from Delaware to Guam. During those flights, the crew would take turns at the controls, catching a few hours sleep strapped to a cot in the back with the cargo. If your turn to sleep came while you were flying through the massive thunderclouds that built up over the Pacific in the summer months, so be it. It was sleep or exhaustion, so he'd figured out how to sleep. Compared to some of those flights, a King Air and turbulence over Canada was a day in the park.

Billups descended the steps of the small prop plane in the darkness of the early morning, bundled up in his parka against the freezing cold. As he reached the snowy, windblown tarmac, he was approached by a short, wiry man sporting a ski hat and a full beard.

"Ernie Grant?" Billups asked.

"That'd be me. You must be Pepper Billups."

A grin spread across Billups's wide face. "How could you *possibly* tell?"

"When my contact said you were black, I told him I didn't need any further description. We don't get many of you guys up here. No offense," he added.

"None taken," Billups assured the other man, who seemed friendly enough.

"Follow me," Grant called loudly over the wind, turning and heading for a Jeep that was barely visible, twenty yards away, in the gray light.

Billups followed Grant to the idling Jeep, slamming the door shut after he'd hopped inside. Shivering. Glad it was warm inside. "Christ," he said, rubbing his nose. "What the hell's going on?" It felt like someone had sprayed Novocain in his nostrils.

"The inside of your nose is frozen," Grant explained. "Couple of seconds and it'll thaw out. From now on, if you have to run while you're outside, cover your nose with your arm."

"Right." Come to think of it, he'd seen Grant do that as he sprinted for the Jeep. "So, let me get this straight, you're a big-game guide?"

"Yeah."

"What kind of big game do you have up here?"

Grant gunned the Jeep's engine and peeled out toward a gap in the chain-link fence surrounding the tiny airport. "My specialty is reindeer. Guys come from everywhere for 'em." He smirked. "I guess there's something about blowing away Rudolph. I don't get it, but these guys love it."

Billups grunted. He didn't get it, either. "You were with the Mounties, right?"

"Yeah, until about five years ago when I got into the guiding thing. There's a lot more money in that."

"But you trained with Quentin Stiles at some point, right?" The Jeep's engine was loud, so they had to yell to hear each other. "At Glynco or something." Stiles always seemed to know someone from somewhere. The guy was amazing.

"Yup."

"Well, I appreciate you helping us out."

"Glad to do it. First we'll stop at the garage and look at the truck, then we'll go over to the police station and you can see the body. Okay?"

"Sounds good."

Ten minutes later, Grant pulled up in front of what looked like an abandoned building. It was next to a church that wasn't in great shape either. "This it?" Billups asked skeptically.

"Yeah. Come on," Grant called, climbing out of the Jeep and heading across the snow toward the building.

Billups covered his mouth and nose with his arm and followed. A door in front opened as they neared the building, and he hurried inside after Grant, stamping on the cement floor to get the snow off his boots. To his surprise, the inside of the garage, though messy, was warm and modernly outfitted.

"Which way, Marcel?" Grant asked a small man in greasy overalls.

Marcel gave Billups the once-over, then waved for both of them to follow him. He led them to the back of the shop and a Ford Explorer. "Some guys coming down from the oil fields found it abandoned out near Lake McKenzie. We towed it back in."

"Where's Lake McKenzie?" Billups asked Grant.

"About fifty miles north of town. What was wrong with it, Marcel?" Grant asked, turning toward the little man and pointing at the SUV.

Marcel shrugged. "Don't know. The guys who found it said the battery was dead, but I haven't looked at it yet." He hopped in behind the steering wheel and turned the key. Nothing happened.

"Yep," Grant said. "Battery."

"Or the starter's gone," Billups observed.

Marcel lifted the hood and climbed up on the bumper to get a better look. "But why would the battery die out by Lake McKenzie when the guy was coming down from the oil fields? Why would he turn off the engine, then try to restart it? Even if he was refueling, he wouldn't have turned the engine off for that long, certainly not long enough for the battery to die." Marcel leaned under the hood, scanning the engine with a flashlight. "Hold this," he said, handing Billups the light. "Right here." He pulled Billups's hand. "That's it. Keep it right there."

Billups watched the little man lean farther over the engine.

"That's strange," Marcel said, scratching his head with his dirty fingernails.

"What is?" Grant asked.

"Give me the flashlight." Marcel snapped his fingers as he reached back.

Billups handed it to him.

A few moments later Marcel jumped down from the bumper.

"What was it?" Grant asked.

"Alternator plug was out."

"So what?"

"So the truck was running off the battery the whole time," Billups answered for Marcel. "It would have kept going for a while, but, when the juice was drained from the battery, the engine died."

"The guy driving this thing didn't know much about engines," Marcel spoke up. "It's not like it would have shut down right away. It would have been a gradual thing. The lights would have flickered before going out. It was snowing that night, so the windshield wipers would have gone slower. The engine would have had power surges. Anyone who knows even a little bit about engines would have stopped and seen that the plug had been pulled out."

"*Pulled?*" Billups asked.

Marcel nodded. "I'm pretty sure."

"How can you tell? Maybe it just fell out."

"I don't think so. I plugged it back in, then tried to pull it out. It's hard to pull out, and there were fingerprints in the grease down there."

"You think someone caused this guy's truck to break down?" Billups asked. "You think it was intentional?"

"Yeah, I do."

. . .

Gillette tossed the apple core in the kitchen trash can, then climbed the stairs to the second floor of the apartment and moved down the hallway toward the master bedroom. Strazzi had to be responsible for everything. It was the only explanation Gillette could come up with that fit. He scratched his head. It still felt like he was missing something.

So he went over it again.

Strazzi had killed Donovan. Actually, based on what Faith had told him, McGuire or one of his men had probably committed the murder—at Strazzi's direction—undoubtedly in return for Strazzi's willingness to buy McGuire & Company and give Tom and Vince half the company for free. Strazzi had to be Tom and Vince's backer. Then he'd put the Dominion scandal in motion to scare Ann Donovan.

Gillette reached the bedroom doorway. He hesitated, biting his lower lip. But if all that was true, why would Tom McGuire give away Stockman's affair with Rita Jones? That made absolutely no sense. Knowing about Stockman's affair was what had enabled Gillette to figure out Dominion, enabled him to force Stockman to tell him that Marcie was involved. And Marcie had told him what was really going on. Knowing what was really going on at Dominion might have enabled him to derail Strazzi's ultimate objective.

Most important, there was still Strazzi's murder to explain.

Then it hit Gillette. Why the Explorer had been found abandoned fifty miles from the nearest town, tapes still in the front seat. He pulled his cell phone from his pocket and dialed the home number of Heidi Franklin, a young Everest associate he hoped had no hidden allegiances.

A few minutes after leaving Marcel's garage, Billups and Grant pulled up in front of the town's tiny police station, which, on rare occasions, also served as the morgue.

"Hello, Bill," Grant called as he and Billups came through the front door.

Bill Harper was chief of police. He and a lone deputy comprised the entire force.

"Bill, this is Pepper Billups. He's here from New York to ask a few questions and to look at the body."

"Hello, Pepper," Harper said gruffly, sipping from his coffee mug as he rose and came out from behind the desk.

"Where is it?" Billups asked.

"Out back," Harper replied, jabbing a thumb over his shoulder.

"Let's go."

Harper glanced at Grant.

"He's all right," Grant said. "A friend of a good friend."

Harper grabbed his coat off a hook and led them to the back of the building, then out a creaky door into the cold. They trudged across a small field through the gloom and a foot of snow to a tiny shack. Harper pulled a set of keys from his pocket, fumbling through them for the right one as the wind whipped the snow up. Finally, Harper found the key, inserted it in the lock, and turned.

It was damn cold up here, Billups thought. And it wouldn't get much lighter than it already was because they were so far north. The world was a dull gray, as though a volcano had erupted nearby and ash was obscuring the sun. As he followed Grant and Harper into the shack, Billups wondered what in the world possessed people to live up here. They had to be crooks or loners, running from something. Or they were socially incapable. Of course, Ernie Grant seemed to be a good guy.

Harper flicked on a bare bulb hanging from the ceiling. "Right there," he said, pointing at the body. It was lying on a piece of plywood supported by two sawhorses, and had been draped with a grimy blanket.

Billups moved slowly across the room and pulled the blanket back, grimacing as the dead man's face came into view. The eyes and the mouth were wide open. Thanks to the cold there hadn't been much deterioration. He didn't like dead bodies. Not like some guys he knew, who were fascinated by them. "Where'd you find him?" Billups wanted to know.

"Local guy fished him out of Lake McKenzie not more than a quarter of a mile from where the SUV was found," Harper answered. "For this time of year, finding it was a million-to-one shot. The guy was doing some ice fishing and thought he'd hooked the biggest walleye of his life. Shook him up pretty bad when he saw an arm coming up through the hole instead of a fish."

"What are you going to do with him?" Billups asked.

"Hand him over to the family. They're coming up tomorrow."

"How'd you identify him so fast?"

"His wallet was still on him."

"And he was one of the guys shooting seismic up north?"

"Yep. In charge of it for Laurel Energy, according to his family."

"So that was definitely this man's SUV I just looked at over at Marcel's garage?" Billups asked, thinking about how Marcel believed that someone had tampered with the truck.

"Yeah."

"How do you think he got in the lake?" asked Billups.

"Put there."

"How do you know?"

"With the ice as thick as it is right now, someone would have had to cut a hole in it to get a body in there," Harper said confidently. "He wouldn't have just fallen in. Highly unlikely in this scenario."

"Aren't there places where streams or rivers come into or leave the lake? Don't those areas stay free of ice?"

"Yeah, at both ends of the lake. Unless it's *really* cold. But the north end is a few miles from where his Explorer was found, and it's through dense woods. I don't see this guy leaving his truck to traipse through the woods. He'd stay on the road."

"Is the south end closer?"

"Oh, yeah."

"How much?"

"Not far from where the truck was parked."

"So maybe he went in at the south end."

Harper shook his head. "I doubt it."

"Why?"

"The current flows north to south. I don't think his body would have drifted *upstream*."

"Uh-huh. Well, it's possible he could have gotten lost in the storm and gone up to the north end. It was snowing, wasn't it?"

"Yeah. Heavily."

"So it's possible?"

Harper moved up beside Billups. "It's possible, but I really don't think it happened that way. Like I said, I think somebody put him in the lake." Harper pulled the blanket up from the side. "Look at this," he said, pointing at the dead man's fingers.

Billups glanced down. They were smashed. "Ah, Jesus. What happened?"

"Experience is everything in my line of work," Harper said. "About four years ago, around this same time, a guy in town named Lennie Mitchell killed his wife. Tossed her in the lake through a hole he'd cut in the ice with a chain saw. Wanted it to look like she'd fallen in. Same way I think whoever killed this man did. Lennie's wife was a loner. Liked to ice fish by herself. Lennie claimed she went up to the lake by herself one afternoon. Which she did a lot. I knew that. Trouble was, this time she didn't come back." Harper paused. "We found her at the south end of the lake a few weeks later and her fingers looked just like this. See, Lennie'd stepped on them over and over as she tried to pull herself out of the hole. He broke every one of them. He admitted that to me back there in the office one Sunday morning. He couldn't lie to me anymore." The wind made an eerie sound as it whipped through the shack's eaves. It sounded like an animal in pain. "I bet if we were to go up to Lake McKenzie and look real hard, we'd find a depression in the ice. A place where some-body cut a hole in it to throw this guy in. It'll already be iced over, but the depression should still be there."

Billups stared at Harper. "Why would someone have killed him? You said his wallet was on him. Was there money in it?"

"Yeah. And credit cards. It wasn't a robbery."

"Then what was it?"

Harper shrugged. "To tell you the truth, Mr. Billups, I don't have a damn clue."

Gillette pushed open the bedroom door, expecting to see Isabelle's form beneath the covers of the king-sized bed. But she wasn't there. He glanced toward the bathroom. The door was closed. She had to be in there.

"Isabelle," he called.

No answer.

"*Isabelle.*"

Still no answer.

Gillette moved slowly into the room, listening for sounds from the bathroom—running water, footsteps—but heard nothing.

"What the hell?"

As he turned back toward the door, he saw her, knife clenched in both hands. He reeled backward, hands to his face, yelling as she came at him. *"Jesus Christ! What are you doing?"*

At that instant, Stiles burst into the room and grabbed Isabelle from behind just as she reached Gillette. They flew past him and tumbled to the floor. Seconds later, Stiles had the knife in one hand and Isabelle's wrists clasped tightly together behind her back in the other.

Gillette's cell phone rang. He glanced at Stiles, who was lounging on the couch, eyes closed. They'd moved back to the study after turning Isabelle over to the police. "Hello."

"Christian?"

"Yes."

"It's Tom McGuire."

"Hello, Tom."

"How are you, Christian? Everything okay?"

"Sure. Why wouldn't it be?"

"Just a question, Christian. That's all."

"Okay."

"Hey, have you signed the deal with the investment bankers to do the IPO yet?" McGuire wanted to know.

"No."

"Oh, great."

Gillette heard relief in McGuire's voice. "I'll probably do that next week."

"Let me talk to you one more time about buying the company before you do," McGuire pleaded. "I have some ideas."

What a traitor, Gillette thought to himself. He had no reason to doubt Faith. She'd saved his life. "I don't think it's worth either of our—"

"*Please*, Christian. Please. You owe me that much."

"We're too far apart in price."

"Maybe not as far as you think. I've spoken to my backer and I think I can get him to come up."

"To five hundred million?"

"I think so."

"So talk."

"No, not over the phone. I want to do it in person."

"Why?"

"I want this to be face-to-face, man-to-man."

"Where are you, Tom?"

"My house on Long Island. I hate to ask, but could you come out here? My wife's going somewhere with her sister today, and I have the kids."

"Tom, that's really—"

"Christian, I haven't asked for many favors over the last few years," McGuire interrupted. "Vince and I have kept our heads down and done what you've asked. We've done pretty well, too. We've always delivered good numbers. Please. I really need to talk to you," McGuire urged.

Stiles sat up slowly and stared at Gillette, able to hear McGuire pleading on the other end of the line.

"All right," Gillette agreed, staring back at Stiles. "What time?"

"Two o'clock," McGuire replied. "How about I e-mail you directions on how to get here?"

"Fine. How long's the drive?"

"About an hour."

Gillette hesitated. "Okay."

"Thanks, Christian," McGuire said graciously. "Really. Thank you very much."

"It's okay, Tom. I'll see you then."

"What did McGuire want?" Stiles asked when Gillette had hung up.

"To see me again about buying the company."

"When does he want to see you?"

"Today."

"What time?"

"Two o'clock. At his house."

Stiles shook his head. "Are you thinking what I'm thinking?"

Gillette nodded. "Yeah, I am." A setup all the way.

Stiles's cell phone rang. He snatched it off the coffee table, checked the number, and answered. "Hello? Hey, Pepper. What?" Stiles was silent for a few moments, listening to Billups relate what he'd found out. "Really? Yeah. Okay, call me if there's anything else."

"What is it?" Gillette asked when Stiles had hung up.

"That was Pepper Billups," Stiles replied. "The guy I sent to Canada to poke around, as you suggested."

"Did he find anything?"

"Yeah. Apparently the guy who was in charge of the seismic shoot up there for Laurel Energy was definitely murdered."

"Jesus."

"The truck he was driving was tampered with," Stiles continued, "and the cops are pretty certain he was thrown into some lake near where the truck was found." Stiles put the phone back down on the coffee table. "Wasn't that the guy who was bringing the seismic tapes back for analysis?"

Gillette nodded. "The tapes were recovered. There were some Laurel people a few hours behind the guy. They stopped when they saw his truck, got the tapes out of the front seat, looked around for him for a while, then reported him missing when they got to town." He glanced out the window. Everything was falling into place. All he needed was one more piece of the puzzle.

"What is it?" Stiles asked, reading Gillette's expression.

"It's—" Gillette's cell phone rang again. "Hello."

"Christian, it's Ben."

"Hello, Ben," Gillette said deliberately.

"Sorry to bother you on a Sunday, but these guys at Coyote Oil are really bugging me about moving forward."

"Oh?"

"Yeah, and I think we should. I mean, they've agreed to our price."

"Uh-huh."

"Well?"

"Well *what*?"

"Can I tell them we have a deal?"

"Yes," Gillette agreed after a few moments.

"Great, thanks."

"Sure."

"You okay, Christian?" Cohen asked.

"Why?"

"You seem distracted."

"I'm fine."

Cohen hesitated. "All right. Talk to you later."

"Yeah, later." Gillette ended the call, then dialed Heidi Franklin's number at Everest. "Heidi? Yes, hello. Look, I'm sorry to make you go into Everest on a weekend, but it was very important. Right." He hesitated, gazing intently at Stiles as the young woman told him it wasn't a problem because she only lived a few blocks from the offices. "Did you check it out, Heidi? Were you able to find it? Oh, that's great. And how long does he have?" Gillette nodded. "Thirty days." That would explain why they'd had to start the Coyote Oil process so soon.

. . .

At a few minutes before one o'clock, Gillette moved out of the elevator and headed through the lobby toward a limousine waiting on Fifth Avenue to take him to Tom McGuire's house on Long Island. Halfway across the lobby, one of Stiles's men fell in beside him. Stiles was taking absolutely no chances at this point.

After hanging up with Heidi Franklin, Gillette had told Stiles his theory about what had happened in Canada. That the tapes the Laurel Energy men had recovered from the front seat of the Explorer abandoned near Lake McKenzie on their way back from the oil fields weren't authentic, that they had been put there to be found by whomever had tampered with the Explorer and murdered the man found in Lake McKenzie by the fisherman. These tapes told a very different story from the ones the men who had murdered the Explorer's driver had stolen.

Gillette believed that Laurel Energy had stumbled onto a *huge* field with the option properties—and the executives at Coyote Oil knew it. That they were behind the incident at Lake McKenzie. They and their backers. Which was why they were so hot to get the transaction moving, why they were willing to pay what U.S. Petroleum was willing to pay despite the fact that the tapes left in the Explorer showed that there wasn't much of anything in the ground up there.

Gillette had also told Stiles he was convinced that Ben Cohen was involved. He'd told Stiles how Heidi Franklin had checked the Everest Capital operating agreement and confirmed that, upon the death of the chairman, the chief operating officer would assume control of Everest for a period of thirty days. The reason it hadn't happened after Donovan's death was because there *had been no chief operating officer* at that point. Donovan had never appointed one. Thus the need for a quick chairman vote three days after Donovan's death.

If Gillette was out of the way, Cohen would be in control for thirty days. But that might not be enough time to get the Laurel deal with Coyote done before his term was up and someone was elected chairman. Maybe not enough time to get all the necessary approvals. Which was why they'd started the process now, before Cohen's thirty days had begun to tick.

The burning question was, who were 'they'? Strazzi was dead. His wallet was gone but McGuire was still working. As was Isabelle. He could send Faith to McGuire to try to figure out who was pulling the strings, but that would put her in terrible danger. McGuire was sharp. He'd wonder why Faith had dropped out of sight for two days only to reappear asking lots of questions.

Before leaving his apartment to come downstairs, Gillette had called the senior partner at the engineering firm in Texas that had performed the original analysis of the tapes found in the Explorer. He'd directed the partner to have the seismic tests reshot, this time under intense security. To have armed guards present while it was being done, and to have the guards bring the tapes back to the engineering firm from Canada. To keep the tapes under lock and key, with one person guarding the lock and another guarding the key. To spare no expense to make certain the same thing didn't happen again. The partner promised to have the shoot redone within thirty days, and to make the circle of people involved much smaller this time.

"Good afternoon, sir."

"Thanks." Gillette nodded to the doorman as he headed out of the lobby. It had warmed up overnight. At one in the afternoon, there was bright sunshine and it was more than sixty degrees. Gillette took a deep breath of fresh air as he headed down the steps, then checked warily up and down Fifth Avenue. Stiles's man in the lobby was beside him and there were two more men by the waiting limousine.

Vince McGuire sat in the front seat of a sedan with one of his men, watching the entrance to Gillette's apartment building. They were both smoking, front windows rolled down in the warm weather.

"Hey, here he comes." Vince nudged the driver as Gillette came through the doorway and moved down the steps. "Don't lose his limo on the way out to Tom's house," he warned. "You hear me?"

"Yeah, I got it."

As Gillette reached the bottom step, one of the two men standing by the limousine suddenly pulled a pistol from his shoulder holster, aimed it at the other guard's chest, and squeezed the trigger. Then, before the man next to Gillette could react, the shooter turned the gun on him and fired, putting him down with one shot, too.

Gillette spun and raced up the steps back toward the front door, but the assassin was too quick, squeezing off another round almost instantly, sending Gillette to the steps.

The assassin raced up the stairs to get to Gillette, hurdling the moaning guard. He pointed the gun directly at Gillette, who was still trying to crawl up the stairs, and fired again. "That's for Paul Strazzi!" he yelled, then sprinted back down the steps to a dark car that had screeched to a halt in front of the building and jumped into the backseat. Then the car squealed away.

"*Jesus Christ!*" Vince yelled, tossing his cigarette out the window. "*Did you see that shit?*"

"*Yeah! What the fuck's going on?*"

"Did you hear what the guy yelled after he shot Gillette the second time?" Vince asked excitedly.

"Yeah," the driver answered. "'That's for Paul Strazzi.' That's fucked up."

Vince started to open his door to check out the scene, then heard the sound of sirens and stayed in the sedan.

Moments later, several ambulances pulled up and the EMTs raced to the fallen men. Within five minutes all three were inside the ambulances and headed to hospital.

Vince shook his head. "I can't believe this," he said, pulling out his cell phone and dialing Tom. "I mean, there's no way Gillette's alive. The guy hit him square in the back of the head with that second bullet."

Tom answered on the second ring. "Hello."

"Tom, it's me," Vince said excitedly.

"What is it?"

"You're not going to believe this. Somebody just shot Christian Gillette."

"*What?*"

"Yeah. It just happened. Right in front of his building. A couple of Stiles's men were shot, too. Must have been an inside job because it looked like the shooter was the third guy on Gillette's security detail."

"Makes sense," Tom muttered. "Stiles had him wrapped up tighter than a ball of barbed wire."

"Get this, Tom," Vince continued. "The guy put a second bullet into Gillette as he was lying on the steps, then shouts, 'That's for Paul Strazzi.'"

"*For Strazzi? What?*"

"I'm telling you, Tom, that's what the guy yelled."

Tom glanced out the window of his home. "But why . . ."

"They must have figured Gillette learned Strazzi was behind the Dominon thing and took matters into his own hands. That Gillette had Strazzi killed."

Tom nodded to himself. "Yeah. I guess that's right." He chuckled. "The only thing that really matters is he's dead. We're off the hook, Vince."

25

PITTSBURGH WAS A SEVEN-HOUR drive from New York City. They'd taken one of the standard sedans Stiles's men used on assignment—not Gillette's Porsche nor Stiles's BMW. They did the speed limit. They used the blinkers. They did their best to be anonymous as they headed west on the Pennsylvania Turnpike.

They'd taken turns driving and, fortunately, it had been an uneventful trip. But, by the time they'd checked into a Motel 7 on the outskirts of the city at nine last night, it had been too late to accomplish anything but have dinner.

They'd divided the night into two four-hour shifts and took turns staying awake watching television—and the door. Gillette had taken the first shift. From eleven—when Stiles had begun snoring—to three. Every so often picking up Stiles's .40-caliber pistol that lay on the table beside his chair. Trying to get used to the feel of it in his hand.

Stiles had taken the three to seven shift—when he'd awakened Gillette. They'd left the motel at 7:30 and gotten breakfast at a Denny's up the street. Now they were sitting in a grocery store parking lot, waiting.

"You think McGuire bought the scene in front of the apartment building?" Gillette asked, sitting in the passenger seat.

"Who knows?" Stiles answered. "But we had the hospital in on it. You were DOA," he said, smiling. "And there were two phone calls checking up on your status. We got the numbers, but they turned out to be pay phones in Manhattan." Stiles glanced over at Gillette. "You haven't called or e-mailed anyone, have you?" he asked. "I know how itchy your fingers get to contact people."

"No one," Gillette said firmly. He let out a long breath. "Hey, she's been in there a while."

They'd watched a middle-aged woman park the car and go into the store thirty minutes ago. She still hadn't come out. Quentin had decided to wait until she came back out, figuring she'd be less likely to take off without what she bought.

"Think somebody got to her in the store?" Gillette asked.

"Wouldn't surprise me," Stiles answered. "We know they're keeping an eye on the house off and on. If this thing's as big as you think, nothing would—"

"There she is," Gillette interrupted, pointing at the woman coming out of the store. She was pushing a full cart toward a dark blue Chevy Caprice. "Let's go."

They got out of the car, checking for anyone suspicious as they headed toward the woman. As they'd planned, Stiles hung back when they neared her, watching the area while Gillette closed in.

"Good morning, ma'am," Gillette said pleasantly. "How are you today?"

"Fine," she answered, stopping beside her car and giving him a curious look.

"Sure is nice out today."

"Yes, it is."

She was being nice enough, but she was suspicious. Her hands were clasping the handle of the shopping cart tightly and her eyes were darting around. "Do you mind if we talk?" he asked.

"Talk?"

"Yes. It's very important."

She stared at him intently. "What is?"

Gillette picked up one of the grocery bags from the cart, one that looked heavy. He nodded toward the backseat. "Let me help you with these."

"Oh, thank you." She unlocked the car and opened the back door.

Gillette put the bag on the seat, then picked up another one from the cart and put it in the car. "I need to talk to you about your daughter," he said, looking her straight in the eye, trying to convey the gravity of the situation.

"My daughter?" she asked, putting a hand to her chest.

"Yes. Your daughter Kathy."

The woman brought her hands to her mouth at the sound of her daughter's name. "Is she all right?" the woman asked, her voice beginning to shake.

"She's fine," Gillette assured her.

"Then what is it?"

Gillette glanced at Stiles, who nodded subtly. The parking lot was still clear. "I need to know where she is."

She shook her head. "I have no idea," she said quickly.

Too quickly. Jackpot. "Mrs. Hays, I run an investment firm in New York. We own and run companies. Up until about a week ago, Kathy worked for one of those companies. It's called HP Brands. Does that sound familiar?"

She stared back at him blankly.

"Mrs. Hays. Please help me."

"Yes," she whispered. "That's the company."

"Your daughter resigned very suddenly last week." He hesitated. "There was a problem."

"A problem?"

"Turns out she was having an affair with one of my partners. He's a bad guy, and I fired him for it, but I'm worried that he's looking for her. There's no telling what he'll do when he finds her. From what we can tell, he's obsessed with her."

The woman looked up at Gillette for a long time, a gentle breeze blowing a few strands of her long gray hair across her face. "Kathy told me not to say anything," she murmured.

"You have to tell me, Mrs. Hays. I'm a friend. I really am."

Vince McGuire walked quickly down Eighth Avenue toward McGuire & Company headquarters, located in a high-rise on Fifty-seventh Street. It was nearly 10:30. He almost always got to the office late, but usually stayed until eight or nine at night. Tom was the one who got in early and left early because he lived all the way out on the island.

Vince was about to reach into his overcoat for his cell phone when he felt a pair of strong hands grab his shoulders from behind. Then a hood came down over his head, obscuring the world. Before he could react, his hands were bound tightly behind his back, and he was being hustled across the sidewalk and into a car.

The last thing Vince heard before the door slammed shut was the sound of his cell phone clattering to the sidewalk as it fell from his pocket. Then he felt the car leap ahead.

Gillette's cell phone rang, and he pulled it from his pocket. "Hello." They were already a hundred miles southwest of Pittsburgh on I-79. A thousand miles to go.

"Christian, this is Jose."

"Yes?"

"We have the package."

"Good. I'll be in touch." Gillette hung up abruptly, not wanting to stay on the cell phone long. "They got Vince McGuire," he said to Stiles, who was driving.

Stiles rolled his eyes. "You're taking a big chance, Christian. Kidnapping is a serious crime."

"You don't think Vince McGuire is involved?"

"It doesn't matter what I think. It's what I can prove. And right now I can't prove anything. Besides, even if he is involved, you still kidnapped him."

Gillette glanced out the passenger window at the rolling countryside. "Call me Chris," he said quietly.

"Huh?"

"Call me Chris," Gillette repeated, louder this time.

"But I thought—"

"My friends call me Chris."

Stiles was silent for a minute. "What made that woman—"

"You and I could be friends, Quentin," Gillette interrupted. "And I really need someone with your talents," he added quickly, self-conscious about what he'd said. "I need personal security all the time."

"Just keep QS on the payroll."

Gillette shook his head. "No, I want *you* on the payroll."

"I have a business to run, Christian. Uh, Chris. People who depend on me."

"What do you take out of the business a year?"

Stiles shifted uncomfortably behind the wheel. "None of your business."

"Come on."

"No."

"What's the big secret?" Gillette was accustomed to being direct—and having people answer his questions. Nothing important could be accomplished without straight talk. "Do you take a million out a year?"

"No."

"Half a million?"

"Look," Stiles said, exasperated, "I've mostly been putting money *into* the business. It's growing, so it needs cash."

"Now we're getting somewhere," Gillette said, satisfied. "How about this? We hire someone to take over for you at the company. Everest invests a little bit so you don't have to put any more cash in, and you come to be my head of security. You still own, let's say, 80 percent of the stock. So you control it. But somebody else deals with all the headaches."

"That's great, but—"

"And I'll pay you a million a year to be head of Everest security."

"Jesus," Stiles whispered.

"Now, aren't you glad you kept listening?"

Stiles glanced at the interstate stretching out in front of them. "So, what made that woman tell you where her daughter was?"

Gillette smiled over at Stiles. "My eyes," he said, pointing at his face. "Women just can't resist them."

Stiles laughed loudly. "You're delusional, you know that?"

Gillette's smile grew wider. It was the first time he'd ever heard Stiles really laugh.

The phone rang once more, then finally the voice mail message kicked in. Again. No one had seen Vince at the office all day. He hadn't come in and he hadn't called.

Tom McGuire checked his watch. Five o'clock. Vince did this sometimes when he was stressed. Just went away without telling anyone.

He let out a long, frustrated breath. Something told him this wasn't one of those times.

He picked up his cell phone and tried to call Faith. But it was just like with Vince. Voice mail.

"Damn it!"

"This is it." Stiles pointed to the left at a dented metal mailbox illuminated by the car's high beams. It was affixed to the top of a peeling white post at the end of the first driveway they'd seen in half a mile.

"Forty-seven, Route 12," Stiles continued. That was the address the woman gave you, right?" he asked, pointing at the black numbers on the box.

"Yup."

It was almost one in the morning. They'd driven straight through from Pittsburgh, stopping only twice for gas and food.

Gillette swung the car onto the dirt driveway and cut the lights, his heart beginning to race. "What's the plan?" he asked, making sure his voice didn't give away his uneasiness.

"First," Stiles answered, reaching beneath his seat, "you need to take this." He pulled out another Glock 40, the same type of pistol he carried. "Here," he said, handing the weapon to Gillette. "Do you know how to use it?"

Gillette took the gun, suddenly feeling more secure. "I thought with Glocks you basically pointed and pulled," he said.

"You've got to chamber the first round," Stiles said, reaching for the gun.

"I know." Gillette slid the top half the gun back, then let it go. Metal on metal made a grinding noise as it snapped back into place. "Bullet chambered."

Stiles handed him an extra fifteen-round clip. "Be careful. Will you?"

"Sure, sure." Gillette took the extra clip and shoved it in his pocket, then looked out the window into the dark woods. This was the very southwestern corner of Mississippi. Between two tiny towns called Centreville and Gloster. Just across the border from Louisiana. "Pretty grim around here, huh?"

Stiles grinned. "You telling *me* that, white boy?"

Gillette opened the car door and climbed out, slipping the barrel of the pistol between his jeans and his belt at the small of his back. Then he closed the door softly behind him and jogged back toward the mailbox.

"Hey, where are you going?" Stiles hissed, getting out of the car, too.

Gillette heard him call but didn't answer. He reached the mailbox in seconds, pulled it open, and reached inside. Not expecting to find anything. But there was junk mail—a few flyers and envelopes. He pulled out two pieces and headed back to the car.

"What you got?"

"Hopefully a name," Gillette muttered, opening the door and holding one of the envelopes down into the car so he could see it in the light. It was exactly as he'd expected. Marcie hadn't been lying. At least, not about being the one who'd known Troy Mason was in the basement with Kathy Hays at the funeral reception. It was clear to Gillette now that she really hadn't known anything about that.

"What's the name?" Stiles asked.

Gillette shut the car door, dousing the interior light. "Michael Lefors."

Stiles moved around the front of the car to where Gillette was standing. "*Lefors?*"

Gillette looked up. "Yeah. Michael Lefors. As in Kyle's father."

"You gotta to be kidding. I thought they lived in a Louisiana trailer park."

"They did. They must have moved here. Maybe Kyle helped them after he made some bucks in New York. Anyway, it's only about forty miles from here to where they used to live in Louisiana."

"So Kyle's involved."

"Obviously," Gillette agreed. Marcie hadn't sent the e-mail to Kathy Hays. It had been Lefors. He'd snuck into her office to send it from her computer to frame her. "Lefors made this place available to Kathy Hays after she set up Troy Mason. So no one would find her."

"So no one could figure out who's really pulling the strings," Stiles added. "I mean, whoever that is must have paid her, right? Why else would she do it? Why would she set up somebody, then quit her job?"

"Maybe they had something on her," Gillette speculated, replaying Stiles's words in his head. *Who's really pulling the strings.* Whoever was backing McGuire, that was who.

"I think she did it for money," Stiles said firmly, shaking his head. "Still, the whole thing is kind of confusing."

"Why?"

"I thought you told me that Troy Mason went to work for Paul Strazzi at Apex after you fired him."

"Yeah, so?"

"Then *Strazzi* must have paid Kathy Hays off. He wanted Mason out of Everest so he could get information on the portfolio companies, so he could scare the widow. A woman he made a widow with Tom McGuire's help. So, like you said before, Strazzi had to be McGuire's backer." Stiles paused. "But Strazzi's dead and McGuire still called you to talk about buying the company. Makes no sense."

"Ben Cohen knows," Gillette said quietly. The little bastard. Cohen never could have been chairman—even for thirty days—without an angel. So he'd sold himself out. Playing the part of the puppet in exchange for a chance to run Everest. In exchange for selling Laurel Energy for billions less than what it was really worth. The fraudulent tapes had indicated that there was no oil in the option fields when there really was. Gillette was certain now that the new seismic tests would show vast reserves beneath the surface of the properties.

McGuire was the muscle, Cohen the brains. But who was the dark angel? Maybe it was someone else at Apex. Maybe Strazzi had been double-crossed by Stockman, and Stockman was working with someone else there. Or maybe it was Cohen *and* Faraday working with another group. Faraday had uncountable connections to the insurance companies and the pension funds. Maybe he and Cohen were working together and had agreed to sell Laurel to someone for a rock-bottom price in exchange for having their own fund. Gillette glanced ahead into the gloom. The answer had to be at the other end of this driveway.

He motioned to Stiles. "Let's go," he urged, opening the car door.

Stiles shook his head and closed the door again. "We go on foot," he said quietly. "We don't want anyone up at the house to see us coming."

As they moved cautiously up the driveway a light rain began to fall, rustling the leaves. The thick clouds made the night very dark, and they were forced to move slowly, picking their way carefully along the rutted dirt road as they headed toward the house.

"I hope there aren't any damn snakes lying on the road," Stiles muttered. "You know, they come out at night."

Gillette stopped abruptly and pulled the pistol from his belt. "What kind of snakes do they have down here?" he asked, pointing the gun down and ahead.

"All kinds."

"The *poisonous* ones, Quentin," Gillette said, starting to move forward again slowly. "What kind of poisonous snakes do they have down here?"

"Copperheads and some rattlers. But the ones you have to worry about are the cottonmouths. I've got buddies from down here who tell me stories about cottonmouths actually coming into boats after people."

"Great."

A quarter of a mile farther on they reached the house—a quaint cabin set in the middle of a clearing. Tall trees soared a hundred feet above it. The cabin was completely dark except for a porch light. There was a compact car parked in the circle in front of the raised porch.

"Now what?" Gillette asked.

"We go in."

"What if the door's locked?"

"I can take care of that," Stiles said, patting his shirt pocket. "I brought a set of picks. I can get into anything."

"That's breaking and entering."

"This from a kidnapper?"

Gillette wiped moisture from his forehead. The rain was coming down harder. "Are we going right through the front door?" For all they knew, there were people in the cabin guarding Kathy Hays. People who probably had guns, too.

"Not if we can avoid it. Let's check around back and see if there's another door. I don't like how open that porch is. We'd be sitting ducks up there, especially with the light on." Stiles waved. "Follow me."

Gillette trailed Stiles as he moved across the lawn and around the back, shading his eyes from the chilling rain. "This thing still work if it gets wet?" he asked warily as they pulled up by a large oak tree.

"The gun?"

"Yeah."

"It'll work. Don't worry. By the way, if you aim at somebody, aim to kill, not to wound. Do you understand?"

"Absolutely." He'd be more than happy to put whoever he was shooting at down for good.

Stiles pointed at the cabin through the dim light. "There's the back door. Probably leads into a mud room or the kitchen or something. I say we try to get into the house that way."

Gillette nodded. "Let's do it." He sprinted to the door, following Stiles across the lawn. They leaned their backs against the house when they reached it. Stiles tried the door—it was locked—then pulled a small case from his shirt pocket, opened it, selected a pick, and went to work.

"Bingo," Stiles whispered, stowing the case back in his pocket when the lock popped. "Ready?"

Gillette clasped the gun tightly. Beads of perspiration were seeping into his eyes, stinging like hell. "Yeah."

"If an alarm goes off, we're out of here," Stiles said. "Back into the woods that way." He pointed. "Then we wait and see what happens. Got it?"

"Yup."

Stiles reached for the knob and turned it slowly.

Gillette braced for the scream of an alarm, but it never came. There was a gentle click and the door swung open.

Stiles glanced over his shoulder. "Come on," he whispered.

The inside of the cabin was dominated by a musty smell and it was pitch-black. He could barely make out Stiles's shape only a few feet ahead.

They stole through the kitchen into a large living room, then down a hallway, checking the bedrooms as they went. All empty—until they came to the last one at the end of the corridor. Stiles put a finger to his lips and pointed, then nodded, indicating that there was someone in the bed.

The two men moved stealthily through the cabin's back door—the one Gillette and Stiles had just entered—guns drawn.

Stiles slipped into the bedroom, leaned over the bed, and pressed his huge palm to Kathy Hays's mouth.

Her eyes flew open instantly and she tried to scream, but Stiles's hand stifled the sound. She grabbed his wrist with both hands, trying to pry it from her face, but it was no use. He was much too powerful. She made a move to strike his face, but he pointed the gun straight down at her.

"I'm your friend," he hissed. "Stop."

When she saw the gun, she went still and tears welled in her eyes.

"I'm going to take my hand away, Kathy," Stiles said softly. "We're not going to hurt you," he assured her as Gillette sat down on the other side of the bed. "We just need to ask you a few questions. Do you understand?"

She nodded, her eyes wide open.

"You aren't going to scream, are you?"

She shook her head.

"Good. Here we go." Slowly Stiles slid his hand from her mouth.

She gasped and pulled the covers to her neck. "What do you want?" she asked, her voice shaking. "Please don't kill me," she pleaded.

"We're not going to hurt you," Gillette said quietly. "Like Quentin said, I just need to ask you a few questions. Okay?"

"Okay," she answered hesitantly.

"Do you recognize me?" Gillette asked, leaning down close so that she could see his face in the faint light.

"No."

"I'm the one who came into the room in the basement at Bill Donovan's funeral reception. When you were in bed with Troy Mason."

"Oh, Jesus," she said, bringing her hands to her face. "You're Christian Gillette."

"That's right."

She tried to struggle away, but Stiles held her down.

"*Stop it,*" he demanded. "Don't move until I tell you to."

"It's all right," Gillette said soothingly, trying to calm her down. "As soon as you've answered my questions, we'll leave."

"What do you want to know?" she asked, her voice shaking even more violently. A tear slid down one side of her face.

"Were you paid to set up Troy so I'd fire him?"

She swallowed hard and nodded. "Yes."

Of course, Gillette thought to himself. It was an easy way for whoever was behind all this to get Troy out of Everest without having to resort to murder. Whoever was behind it wanted Cohen to be chair-

man so they could get the Laurel deal done with Coyote. They'd probably realized that the investors would never elect Faraday, so it came
down to Mason and him. Mason could be eliminated using Kathy Hays.
Then there would only have to be one murder. His. It was all becoming
clear.

Now it was time for the money question. The whole reason he and
Stiles had made this trip. And the key to everything. Gillette could feel
his palms sweating. "Who approached you to set Mason up?"

Kathy gazed up at Gillette for several moments without answering.
The sound of her breathing filled the room.

"Tell me," Gillette demanded *"Now."*

Kathy swallowed again. "A man named Miles Whitman," she whispered.

Everything stopped and the world disappeared for a moment. *Miles
Whitman.* Miles Whitman was the one behind the murder attempts, the
one behind the McGuire brothers' bid to buy the company, the one who
was trying to buy Laurel Energy so cheaply. Gillette fought to breathe.
Miles Whitman was the dark angel.

Gillette's mind reeled back to the day last week he'd met with Whitman and Cohen in his office. The day he'd found out that the widow was
going to sell her stake in Everest to Strazzi. When Whitman had pushed
to learn whether or not Cohen was officially the chief operating officer
yet. How Cohen had reacted so oddly. The reason was apparent now.
Cohen had been swimming in paranoia, worried that Gillette would
somehow figure out that Whitman was the puppet master—and Cohen
the puppet.

But what was Whitman's motivation in all of this? He was already
one of the most powerful people in the financial world.

Another thought struck Gillette like a hammer. Whitman had said
on the phone that he and Strazzi had talked about how Strazzi loved to jog
in Central Park in the mornings. Whitman would have known Strazzi's
schedule. Whitman had had Strazzi hit because if Strazzi got the widow's
stake in Everest, Whitman wouldn't have been able to buy Laurel.

The bullet slammed into Stiles's side, below his left arm, sending
him flying onto the bed beside Kathy as the report of the pistol exploded
in their ears. She screamed a bloodcurdling scream as she tore the covers
back and rolled toward Gillette.

Gillette dropped to one knee and began firing at the bedroom door-way over Stiles's prone body. Stiles was grabbing at the wound. There was a groan and a heavy thud as someone tumbled to the floor in the hallway outside the bedroom, then there was more gunfire. But the shooter's aim was high, and both Stiles and Gillette emptied their clips at the door.

As he fired the last bullet and the sound of the explosion faded, Gillette heard footsteps moving swiftly away down the hall. "Stiles!" he yelled, reaching into his pocket for the second clip. Popping the empty one and inserting the new one holding fifteen precious rounds. "You all right?"

Stiles groaned, dropping down to the floor and crawling toward the door. "Never . . . taken one in the lung," he said.

Gillette heard someone moaning outside the bedroom door, then the sound of voices outside the house. Three, maybe four men yelling to one another. He crawled over the bed, moved to the door, and peered into the hallway.

A man lay on his side, clutching his stomach, a pistol on the floor by his head barely visible in the darkness. Gillette burst into the hallway and grabbed the gun, then hurried back into the bedroom and knelt beside Stiles. The big man had dropped his gun and was sitting back against the wall, blood pumping from the wound in his chest, the blood making an ever-widening circle on his shirt.

"Jesus, Quentin."

"It's bad," Stiles gasped. "I know . . . Chris."

"I'm gonna get you out of here, brother. I promise." Gillette glanced at Kathy. She was sitting on the floor in a far corner of the room, sob-bing. Holding her knees tightly to her chin and rocking. He pulled out his cell phone and pushed a button at random, lighting the screen. No signal way out here in rural Mississippi. It had been that way in the drive-way, too, but he'd hoped he'd get something here. "Shit." He glanced at Stiles, then at Kathy. "Stay here. Don't move."

There had to be a phone in the house somewhere. He'd noticed the lines overhead as he and Stiles were coming up the driveway. The best bet was the living room, he figured. He looked down the hallway and saw that someone had turned on a light in the living room. He moved that way, holding the gun in front of him, swinging the barrel from side to side, trying to anticipate where the one who'd run away was hiding, trying to anticipate which door he'd come out from behind.

He spotted the phone on a table by the fireplace and raced toward it. As his fingers closed around the receiver, he heard glass smashing and bullets whining angrily past.

Gillette dropped to his stomach as the huge front windows disintegrated under the hail of bullets. He aimed at the lamp and pulled the trigger, shattering it with one shot, and the room plunged into darkness. But the steady stream of bullets didn't stop.

Gillette grabbed the phone again and dialed the number he'd memorized. Tom McGuire's cell phone number. He could barely hear it ringing over the barrage. "Pick up!" he shouted. "Pick up!"

Suddenly, there was the sound of hurried footsteps on the porch and the front door flew open. Gillette fired blindly at the door as the phone continued to ring in his ear. Someone went down heavily outside, but then a torch skittered across the living-room floor. It came to rest against a couch and the upholstery caught instantly.

"Hello."

Finally an answer.

"Tom!" Gillette shouted above the noise of the flames, which were suddenly as loud as a freight train. "It's Christian Gillette."

"*What the fuck?* How are you—"

"Yeah, I'm not dead." There was nothing but silence. "Tom!" Obviously he was stunned. "Tom!"

"What the hell do you want?"

"I know you're outside the cabin, Tom. If you ever want to see your brother alive, call off the dogs! I've got Vince back in New York! If the people who have him don't hear from me by six this morning, he's a dead man."

Tom McGuire let the cell phone fall away from his ear. He had fifteen of his men around the cabin, and the flames in the living room were growing brighter and brighter. Soon, the flames and the smoke would become too much, and everyone trapped inside would have to run. Then they'd be caught. Then they'd be dealt with. It was a perfect plan.

Perfect.

Except that Gillette was still alive. And he'd gotten Vince.

.   .   .

Gillette watched as the flames climbed higher and higher—until they were licking the ceiling. They'd have to run for it, he knew. They only had a few more seconds.

Then the bullets stopped.

26

THE UNOPENED BOTTLE OF SCOTCH sat squarely in the middle of the desk. Gillette, seated in his leather chair, stared at it through the gloom of the late evening, then at the computer screen—the only source of light in the office. Dominion's stock price stared back at him: forty-seven dollars a share. In the first few trading days of the week the price had regained everything it had lost—and then some.

There was a gentle tap on the office door. "Christian."

It was Faraday. "What?"

"Can I come in?"

Gillette hesitated. He wanted to be alone, but Faraday had been trying to see him and he had been putting him off for a while. "Yes."

Faraday moved into the office and sat down in front of Gillette's desk. "How you doing?"

"Fine."

"I'm sorry about Stiles," he said quietly.

"It isn't over yet. He could still pull through."

Faraday cleared his throat. "I also wanted to say how sorry I am about the way I've treated you since Bill's death."

Gillette glanced up. The apology seemed sincere. He'd heard honesty and contrition in Faraday's tone. "Thanks, Nigel."

Faraday settled into the chair. "Now, will you please tell me what the fuck happened over the last couple of weeks?"

Gillette rubbed his eyes. This would take some time and he was tired. But Faraday was the only other managing partner left, and he needed to know what had happened so he could explain it to the outside world. "Over the last couple of years, Miles Whitman made some terrible investments. He took a bath on a bunch of technology stocks, then put a pile of money into some very speculative energy projects in South America that went bust, too."

"How much did he lose?"

"Over five billion."

Faraday whistled. "Jesus H. Christ."

"He was hiding it all from the CEO of North America Guaranty and from NAG's board of directors. Not only because of the size of the losses, but because he was outside his charter, too. He wasn't supposed to be investing in those kinds of things."

"He might have a criminal problem."

"I think he definitely has a criminal problem. In more ways than one."

"But what does all of that have to do with us and Laurel?" Faraday asked.

"Whitman found out that our option property in Canada contained the mother lode. Huge oil and natural gas reserves. So he came up with a plan to have a shell company called Coyote Oil, that NAG ultimately owned, buy Laurel cheap. Ultimately, he was going to turn around and sell Laurel a few months after he got it to one of the big oil companies. He knew he'd rake in more than enough to cover his losses on the tech stocks and South American power investments. Then he was going to allocate the gain from Laurel internally to the bad investments to make it look like he hadn't done anything wrong. He was senior enough at NAG to manipulate information like that without anyone knowing."

"How did he find out that our property had those huge reserves?"

"He secretly shot seismic up there about six months ago," Gillette answered.

"Didn't we just do that?"

"Yes."

"So then we should have known about the reserves."

Gillette pulled a glass from the lower left-hand drawer of the desk and placed it beside the scotch bottle. "People who were working for Whitman switched the tapes we had taken with tapes that showed the reserves were small."

"How'd they do that?"

"The guy in charge of the shoot was bringing the tapes back one night alone. Whitman's people had tampered with the truck, and it stalled out on the guy in the middle of nowhere near Lake McKenzie. At that point they jumped him. They cut a hole in the ice and made him take a swim. Needless to say, he didn't last very long. An ice fisherman dragged him out a few days later, dead. The guy thought he'd caught the fish of a lifetime. He was a little surprised when he saw an arm coming up at him through the hole and not a fish."

"Holy shit."

"In water that cold you don't last long." Gillette glanced at the scotch bottle again. He couldn't stop thinking about Stiles. The guy had saved his life twice. Now he was fighting for his own life. "Anyway, that's when they switched the tapes. The tapes we analyzed showed that there was a minimal amount of reserves on the property. The authentic tapes reconfirmed the shoot Whitman had done six months ago on the property."

"But how did Whitman know you'd sell Laurel to him?" Faraday asked. "I mean, maybe you just would have held on to it if the price wasn't right."

"That's why he sent the McGuires after me. In return, he was going to give them half their company back. He was going to have NAG buy McGuire & Company, then give them half the stock for no money down."

"But the limited partners might have brought in someone that would have held on to Laurel, too."

"Not for at least thirty days," Gillette said.

"Why not?"

"Once I was gone, Cohen would have automatically become chairman of Everest Capital for a minimum of thirty days."

Cohen had been arrested as an accessory to Bill Donovan's murder.

A confused expression came to Faraday's face. "Why?"

"It's in our operating document. Upon the death of the chairman, the chief operating officer automatically becomes chairman for a period of not less than thirty days."

"Really? I had no idea."

"Neither did I," Gillette replied grimly. "I guess I should have thought something was up when he pushed so hard for me to give him the title."

"So, let me get this straight," Faraday continued. "Whitman has Donovan murdered and sets up Troy Mason with this woman Kathy Hays."

"That's right."

"But he backed you in the partner meeting where you were elected chairman."

"He knew Troy or I would win the vote at that meeting, and he wanted both of us out of the way so he could get Cohen into the chair position. In exchange for Whitman getting him the chairman position, Cohen was going to sell Laurel to Coyote Oil for basically nothing."

"But why did Whitman back you so hard?"

"Because he knew he could take Troy down without having to kill him. He knew Troy's weakness. He had Lefors tell me that Troy and Kathy Hays were in the basement at the funeral reception. He knew me well enough to know I'd fire Troy on the spot. He also knew that if Troy was elected chairman, any sexual harassment suit would go bye-bye. The chairman isn't going to fire himself."

"Oh, okay. Now I get it." Faraday glanced longingly at the bottle of scotch. "Did I hear that the cops nabbed Lefors?"

"Yeah. This afternoon in New Orleans."

"What was he doing there?"

Gillette shrugged. "I don't know."

"What about Whitman?"

Gillette shook his head. "He's gone. Into the mist. Just like Tom and Vince McGuire. Whitman probably stashed money in banks around the world in case something like this happened. Probably did it for the McGuires, too."

"Do you think Whitman was behind Strazzi's death, as well?" Faraday wanted to know.

"Yup. Strazzi was about to ruin everything with the Dominion thing. If he'd gotten control of Everest, he would have installed himself as chairman. Cohen wouldn't have had a chance."

"Do you think Whitman would have let Cohen stay on as chairman after the thirty days?"

Gillette shrugged.

They were silent for several moments.

"So what are your plans, Christian?" Faraday finally asked.

Gillette glanced up. "We're going to raise the next fund. All fifteen billion of it." He grinned. "And we're going to buy Apex."

Faraday's eyes bugged out. *"What?"*

Gillette reached for the bottle. "I'm going to buy it from Strazzi's estate. Nigel, in a very short time we're going to be the most powerful private equity firm in the world." He leaned forward and put the bottle down in front of Faraday. "Here, a small gift for your loyalty. Now, go figure out how to raise $15 billion in six months. And I'll figure out how we're going to make Apex ours."

Faraday grabbed the bottle and stood up. "Yes, sir," he said, moving to the door. When he reached it, he stopped and turned around. "Thanks for keeping me around, Christian. Seriously. If I'd been you, I'd have probably fired me."

Gillette smiled and nodded. He almost had.

When Faraday was gone, Gillette reached for his Blackberry and scrolled through the Outlook, looking for a number, thinking about Isabelle. How she'd turned on him. How she'd admitted that McGuire had gotten to her. How he'd been obsessed with covering as many angles as he could. How he'd threatened to kill Jose and Selma if she didn't help. How he'd threatened to kill her. Gillette shook his head. A shame, but she was going to spend a long time in jail.

When Gillette found the number, he punched it into his desk phone quickly, then listened to the ring, hoping the person would answer.

"Hello?"

He took a deep breath and relaxed into his chair. "Hi, Faith. How are you?"